PRAISE FOR T SOUND BITES

"Tom Wilmeth has been reviewing and writing about lots of music, for decades. His jazz knowledge is encyclopedic, but he also branches into other realms besides jazz. He has a knack for finding significant episodes in musicians' careers and captures these historic events in print. Insightful and gets at the heart of what is happening."

— Gary Burton

"Wilmeth's writing touches a nerve. When I heard Bob Dylan singing 'Like A Rollin' Stone'—that was me. I got hooked on Wilmeth's book more with his pieces on Louis Armstrong. When I heard him blow that horn and the croak in his voice come in, stand back Loretta."

—Hal Holbrook – Mark Twain Tonight!

"Tom Wilmeth sent over a big fat sampler of his new anthology—ruminations, observations, book and record reviews, obituaries, and conversations with an impressive variety of artists, from Captain Beefheart to Neil Young to—Jack Benny! Motorhead, the Dark Star Orchestra, James Brown, Bobby Blue Bland, Prince, Miles Davis, Jean-Luc Ponty, Weather Report, Bing Crosby, Montana Slim, Merle Haggard. Bob Dylan, the Beatles, and Springsteen, natch. There's a piece about an obscure but important record label. A paean to 8-track tapes. An entirely invented conversation with Barry Manilow. And writings about quite a few midwestern artists I never heard of. The man has immense ears and an articulate tongue. I'm learning a lot."

— David Gans
Musician / Author / Radio Producer

"Wilmeth's music writing is filled with all the passion of a lifelong connoisseur, aficionado, enthusiast, evangelist. If he could take you to a concert or sit you down in front of a record player to help you understand, he would. This book is your invitation to the moment when the lights go down or the needle hits the wax."

— Cheryl Pawelski - Producer/Co-Founder,
Omnivore Recordings

SOUND BITES: A LIFETIME OF LISTENING

SOUND BITES:
A Lifetime of Listening

Writings on Music

by

Tom Wilmeth

SOUND BITES: A LIFETIME OF LISTENING
Muleshoe Press

Copyright © 2016 by Thomas Wilmeth
www.muleshoepress.com

Author services by Pedernales Publishing, LLC.
www.pedernalespublishing.com

Cover design: Barbara Rainess and Jose Ramirez

Library of Congress Control Number: 2016904963

ISBN 978-0-9974091-7-8 Paperback Edition
ISBN 978-0-9974091-8-5 Hardcover Edition
ISBN 978-0-9974091-9-2 Digital Edition

Printed in the United States of America

For Tony Davidson

Special Thanks to Richard Western, an editor and friend in the truest and best sense.

This collection is also dedicated to some remarkably supportive and patient readers:

Ellie Wilmeth, Cindy Wilmeth, Dylan Wilmeth, Orlo Wilmeth, Keith Little, Mike Toft, Pete Onsgard, Al Koch…

…and, of course, _____.
(your name here)

TABLE OF CONTENTS

Introduction   "The Green Door".....*xix*

Preface   Why Write Here? Why Right Now?.....*xxi*

Part One—Popular (and unpopular) Music: Pop and Rock

Concert Commentary   Grand Funk Railroad.....*3*

Concert Commentary   The Association.....*5*

Bonus Track   The Monterey Pop Festival.....*6*

Concert Commentary   The Baja Marimba Band.....*7*

Concert Commentary   Chuck Berry.....*8*

Concert Commentary   Poco and Eagles.....*10*

Concert Commentary   The Sons of Champlin.....*12*

Concert Commentary   The Allman Brothers Band with
                      Big Brother and the Holding Company.....*13*

Bonus Track   The Guitars of *Layla*.....*14*

Book Review   *Midnight Riders:*
                      The Story of the Allman Brothers Band.....*14*

Concert Commentary   Elton John.....*15*

Hangin' with the Stars #1   Elton John.....*18*

Concert Commentary   Frank Zappa.....*19*

Letter to a Friend   Frank Zappa: Where to Begin?.....*20*

Bonus Track   Rock Journalism.....*22*

Remembrance   Captain Beefheart.....*23*

Artist Commentary   "I Knew Tom Waits Back When"..…....*25*

Bonus Track   The Making of *Small Change*.....*28*

CD Review   Tom Waits: *Mule Variations*.....*29*

CD Review   Tom Waits: *Alice*.....*31*

Bonus Track   Artist-Sanctioned Bootlegs.....*31*

Concert Commentary   Jackson Browne.....*32*

Concert Commentary	The Doobie Brothers.....*34*	
Bonus Track	One Name—Many Bands.....*35*	
Hangin' with the Stars #2	Michael McDonald *35*	
Second Hand News	The Guess Who Play for "Friends of Theirs"!.....*36*	
Bonus Track	Bachman & Turner and "American Woman".....*40*	
Commentary	Mixin' it Up!.....*40*	
Bonus Track	American Beatles.....*42*	
Bonus Track	"You Can't Do That".....*42*	
Remembrance	Richie Havens.....*42*	
Remembrance	Joe Cocker.....*45*	
Concert Commentary	Joan Baez.....*47*	
Hangin' with the Stars #3	Joan Baez.....*48*	
Concert Commentary	James Taylor.....*49*	
Hangin' with the Stars #4	Carole King.....*51*	
Concert Commentary	Arlo Guthrie.....*53*	
Concert Commentary	Steve Goodman.....*54*	
Book Review	*Steve Goodman: Facing the Music*.....*55*	
CD Review and Commentary	Crosby, Stills, Nash & Young: *CSNY 1974*.....*55*	
Hangin' with the Stars #5	David Crosby.....*56*	
Second Hand News	Neil Young.....*57*	
CD Review	Neil Young & The International Harvesters: *57*	
One Question with	Neil Young!.....*60*	
Second Hand News	Buffalo Springfield.....*61*	
CD Review and Commentary	The Who: *Live at Leeds*.....*62*	
Bonus Track	Pete Townshend on The Beatles.....*63*	
Concert Commentary	The Rolling Stones with The Stray Cats.....*64*	
Bonus Track	"The Price You Pay".....*65*	
One Question with	Keith Richards!.....*66*	
Commentary	Paul Simon Pledge Drive: Phone Lines are Open!.....*66*	

Concert Commentary	The Beach Boys.....67
Concert Commentary	The Kinks with Cheap Trick.....69
Book Review	*Here Comes the Night: The Dark Soul of Bert Berns and the Dirty Business of Rhythm & Blues.....71*
One Question with	Neil Diamond!.....73
Book Review	R&B (Rhythm & Business): *The Political Economy of Black Music.....73*
Concert Commentary	Jack Benny with The Des Moines Symphony Orchestra.....74
Concert Commentary	Corky Siegel with The Kettle Moraine Symphony 75
Concert Commentary	Yes..........77
Bonus Track	The Art of Osibisa.....79
Concert Commentary	Yes 79
Concert Commentary	Heart with The Little River Band.....83
Concert Commentary	Squeeze with A Flock of Seagulls, and The Pretenders.....84
Concert Commentary	Eric Clapton and Cream..........86
CD Review	Eric Clapton: Back Home.....92
Bonus Track	"Eric Clapton—phone call, please.".....92
Remembrance	Jack Bruce.....93
Concert Commentary	Todd Clouser's A Love Electric.....94
Concert Commentary	Aaron Williams & The Hoodoo.....96
Concert Commentary	Lil' Ed & The Blues Imperials.....97
Concert Commentary	Rahn Lawrence.....99
Book Review	Janis Ian: *Society's Child—My Autobiography.....102*
Book Review	*Kaleidoscope Eyes: Psychedelic Rock from the '60s to the '90s.....102*
Book Review	*The Encyclopedia of Dead Rock Stars: Heroin, Handguns, and Ham Sandwiches.....103*
Book Review	*Killer Show—The Station Nightclub Fire: America's Deadliest Rock Concert.....103*
CD Review	Elvis Costello: *The Juliet Letters.....104*
Remembrance	Lou Reed.....105

Concert Commentary	Bruce Cockburn.....*107*	
CD Review	Bruce Cockburn: *Small Source of Comfort*.....*109*	
Concert Commentary	The Dark Star Orchestra.....*110*	
Concert Commentary	Motorhead with Clutch and Valient Thorr.....*114*	
Bonus Track	The Clash.....*124*	
Concert Commentary	Anthrax with Death Angel and Testament.....*125*	
Bonus Track	"I Can See for Miles".....*131*	
Remembrance	Bobby "Blue" Bland.....*132*	
CD Review	James Hunter: *People Gonna Talk*.....*134*	
Bonus Track	Gil Scott-Heron.....*134*	
CD Review and Book Review	*James Brown Jazz* and *The One: The Life and Music of James Brown*.....*135*	
Bonus Track	A Heavily Sampled Artist.....*137*	
Book Review	*Prince: Chaos, Disorder, and Revolution*.....*138*	
Concert Commentary	Stevie Wonder.....*139*	
Book Review	*Paramount's Rise and Fall: A History of the Wisconsin Chair Company and its Recording Activities*.....*153*	
Book Review	*Do Not Sell at Any Price: The Wild, Obsessive Hunt for the World's Rarest 78 rpm Records*.....*154*	
Bonus Track	Peter Buck and R.E.M......*155*	
CD Review	Girls: *Broken Dreams Club*.....*155*	
Remembrance	Trish Keenan, vocalist for the band Broadcast.....*156*	

Part Two—Jazz

Book Review	*What a Wonderful World: The Magic Of Louis Armstrong's Later Years*.....*163*	
Book Review	*Louis Armstrong's New Orleans*.....*165*	
Book Review	*Louis Armstrong: Master of Modernism*.....*168*	
Bonus Track	Louis Armstrong and Jimmie Rodgers *168*	

Book Review   *Bing Crosby: A Pocketful of Dreams, The Early Years: 1903-1940*.....*169*

Remembrance   Mitch Miller Memories.....*171*

Remembrance   Leigh Kamman: Portrait of a Jazz Broadcaster.....*174*

Commentary   Stubborn Isolationist: Jazz on the Radio.....*179*

Commentary   Rough Times for Smooth Jazz: Ed Roth and the Radio.....*181*

Concert Commentary   The Don Ellis Orchestra.....*182*

Concert Commentary   The Stan Kenton Orchestra.....*184*

Bonus Track   Stan Kenton and Tex Ritter.....*186*

Interview   Eddie Harris.....*186*

Concert Commentary   Toshiko Akioshi/Lew Tabakin Big Band.....*194*

Concert Commentary   Stanley Clarke.....*194*

Commentary   "All About the Bass".....*196*

CD Review   Christian McBride: *Live at Tonic*.....*196*

Concert Commentary   Ron Carter Quartet.....*197*

LP Review   *Best of Dexter Gordon*.....*200*

Hangin' with the Stars #6   Two Views: Dexter Gordon and Woody Shaw.....*201*

LP Review   John Coltrane: *The European Tour*.....*202*

Concert Commentary   Sonny Rollins.....*204*

LP Review   Stanley Turrentine: *Inflation*.....*205*

Remembrance   Gerry Niewood.....*206*

Concert Commentary   Ella Fitzgerald and Cleo Laine.....*207*

Concert Commentary   Grace Kelly.....*210*

CD Review   Grace Kelly: *Live at Scullers*.....*212*

Concert Commentary   The Manhattan Transfer.....*213*

Concert Commentary   Stan Getz.....*214*

Interview   Gary Burton.....*215*

Bonus Track   Ralph Towner and Tim Hardin.....*222*

Commentary   *The Tennessee Firebird:* Gary Burton in Nashville.....*223*

Concert Commentary   Chick Corea and Béla Fleck.....*231*

Concert Commentary   Pat Metheny.....*233*

Concert Commentary Herb Ellis.....*235*

Concert Commentary Jim Hall.....*236*

Concert Commentary Howard Roberts.....*237*

Bonus Track Sight-Reading and Trend Setting in the Studio.....*238*

Concert Commentary Anthony Cox and Mark Waggoner.....*238*

Concert Commentary Alex de Grassi.....*240*

LP Review Kenny Burrell: *Live at The Village Vanguard* and The Heath Brothers: *Live at the Public Theater.....241*

Concert Commentary Kenny Burrell Trio.....*243*

Bonus Track Andy Williams.....*246*

LP Review Jean-Luc Ponty: *A Taste for Passion.....247*

Concert Commentary Eberhard Weber and Jean-Luc Ponty.....*248*

Concert Commentary Daryl Stuermer.....*249*

Interview Bobby Lyle.....*251*

Concert Commentary Bobby Lyle.....*257*

Interview Leroy Jenkins.....*258*

Concert Commentary Leroy Jenkins.....*264*

Interview Oscar Peterson.....*266*

LP Review Keith Jarrett: *Nude Ants.....272*

Artist Commentary Keith Jarrett.....*273*

Bonus Track Elton John and Keith Jarrett.....*276*

Concert Commentary Miles Davis.....*277*

Bonus Track If Miles Likes You........*278*

Commentary Huge Hunk of Herbie: Hancock on Your Radio.....*278*

LP Review Jeff Lorber Fusion: *Wizard Island.....281*

Concert Commentary Weather Report.....*282*

Remembrance Four Nights with Jaco Pastorius.....*285*

CD Review Wynton Marsalis: *Live at the House of Tribes.....291*

Concert Commentary Jazz at Lincoln Center Orchestra with Wynton Marsalis.....*292*

Concert Commentary The Dan Nimmer Trio.....*294*

Concert Commentary   The Mike Kubicki Trio.....*296*

CD Review   Charlie Haden and Hank Jones:
Come Sunday.....*298*

LP Review   Bill Evans: *We Will Meet Again*.....*299*

CD Review   The Dave Brubeck Quartet:
Their Last Time Out.....*300*

Remembrance   Dave Brubeck.....*302*

Interview   Dave Brubeck.....*304*

Part Three—Country

CD Review   Eddy Arnold:
The Tennessee Plowboy and His Guitar.....*323*

CD Review   Wilf Carter (Montana Slim):
Cowboy Songs.....*324*

Book Review   *Ernest Tubb: The Texas Troubadour*.....*325*

Book Review   *The Handbook of Texas Music*.....*326*

Book Review   *Lefty Frizzell: The Honky Tonk Life of Country Music's Greatest Singer*.....*328*

Book Review   *Merle Haggard: My House of Memories*.....*329*

Commentary   *American Masters: Merle Haggard*.....*330*

Book Review   *Willie Nelson: An Epic Life*.....*331*

Book Review   *George Jones: I Lived to Tell It All*.....*332*

Book Review   *Patsy*.....*333*

Book Review   *Finding Her Voice: The Illustrated History of Women in Country Music*.....*335*

Book Review   *All Over the Map:
True Heroes of Texas Music*.....*336*

Commentary   *Livin', Lovin', Losin':
Songs of The Louvin Brothers*.....*338*

Remembrance   Charlie Louvin.....*340*

Remembrance   Phil Everly.....*342*

Concert Commentary   The Everly Brothers.....*345*

Concert Commentary   Dwight Yoakam.....*347*

Concert Commentary   Joe Ely.....*348*

Concert Commentary   The Clark Family Experience.....*349*

Artist Commentary   Cowboy Junkies.....*350*

Bonus Track   Vanilla Fudge.....*351*

CD Review   Junior Brown: *The Austin Experience*.....*352*

CD Review   Béla Fleck: *The Bluegrass Sessions—*
Tales From the Acoustic Planet, Volume 2.....*353*

Hangin' with the Stars #7 Bill Monroe.....*353*

Bonus Track   Hank Williams III.....*355*

Concert Commentary   Chasin' Mason.....*355*

CD Review   Texas '55: *Extreme Hillbilly*.....*356*

Concert Commentary   Glen Campbell.....*357*

Concert Commentary   John Hartford.....*360*

Commentary   Webb Pierce:
The Ty Cobb of Country Music.....*361*

CD Review   Hank Williams:
The Unreleased Recordings.....*366*

CD Review   Hank Williams: *Revealed:*
The Unreleased Recordings.....*367*

Commentary   Art at 78 rpm:
A History of Hank Williams' Releases.....*368*

Bonus Track   Hank and Elvis.....*391*

Part Four—Beatles, Bob, Bruce, and Barry!

Commentary   In Praise of 8-track Tapes.....*395*

Bonus Track   The Wisdom of Harry Nilsson.....*398*

One Question with   Barry Manilow!.....*399*

Concert Commentary   Bob Dylan with The Band (1974).....*403*

Book Review   *Bob Dylan: The Recording Sessions,*
1960-1994.....*408*

Bonus Track   Mark Twain and Bob Dylan.....*410*

Book Review   *Just Like Bob Zimmerman's Blues:*
Dylan in Minnesota.....*410*

Commentary   Jazz in the Key of Bob.....*412*

Bonus Track   "I Want You".....*416*

Bonus Track   Johnny Cash, Flatt & Scruggs,
and Chet Atkins.....*417*

Commentary	Last Thoughts on Bob Dylan's "Last Thoughts".....*418*	
Bonus Track	"The Lonesome Death of Hattie Carroll".....*421*	
CD Review	Bob Dylan: *The Bootleg Series, Volume 6— Concert at Philharmonic Hall*.....*421*	
CD Review	Bob Dylan: *The Bootleg Series, Volume 10— Another Self Portrait*.....*425*	
Bonus Track	How many CDs = a box set?.....*430*	
Commentary	By the Time We Got to Mole Lake........*430*	
Commentary	Bob Dylan's Sacred Song.....*437*	
Bonus Track	Religion Tours and Comedy Records.....*440*	
Book Review	*Bob Dylan—A Life in Stolen Moments; Day by Day: 1941-1995*.....*441*	
Indirect Questions	Mick Ronson.....*442*	
Concert Commentary	Bob Dylan (2012).....*443*	
Concert Commentary	Bob Dylan (2015).....*447*	
Artist Commentary	Bruce Springsteen.....*449*	
Book Review	*A Day in the Life: The Music and Artistry of The Beatles*.....*453*	
Book Review	*Memories of John Lennon*.....*454*	
Book Review	*McCartney*.....*455*	
Concert Commentary	Paul McCartney.....*455*	
One Question with	Paul McCartney.....*459*	
Bonus Track	John and Paul.....*460*	
Remembrance	George Harrison.....*460*	
Commentary	What I Learned from Elvis Presley.....*463*	

Appendix A	**Recommended Recordings**.....*469*	
Appendix B	**Collated Transcriptions of various versions of Bob Dylan's spoken introduction to "Last Thoughts on Woody Guthrie"** *481*	
Appendix C	**Works Cited and Sources Consulted**.....*483*	

A Word about the Author.....*494*

A Word about the Writings.....*495*

Index.....*497*

INTRODUCTION

"The Green Door"

When I was about 3 or 4 years old, my mother would take me with her when she went out for coffee. For me, the best place to go was to the Masons' house. I would be sent to their son's room to play while my mother and Florence chatted. His bedroom contained a variety of boyish possessions such as model cars and baseball pennants. But all I ever saw was his small record player. Every time we would visit, I sat in front of the little turntable and played the same record. Over and over. And still again. It was a 45 rpm single called "The Green Door," a #1 hit in 1956 for Jim Lowe.

My mother would later verify this. "Oh yes. We would go to the Masons, and I would send you off to listen to 'The Green Door.' It kept you happy." The record had been severely cracked, but would play fine if I was careful to align the broken plastic. The flip side was an amusing novelty tune—but the A-side, "The Green Door"—that song was dark magic. I can hear it right now.

The impact of "The Green Door" on me was profound. The sound of temple block percussion and an insistent piano; lyrics about a mysterious party held behind an ominous green door; the singer experiencing another sleepless night, wondering what the group finds so funny. He wants to join them.

When trying to peek past the door, he sees an eyeball clouded in thick smoke, staring back. He tries to bluff his way in, saying that a friend sent him; he is laughed at. Smoke, noise, derisive laughter, and especially the music created a vaguely dangerous yet oddly appealing atmosphere—both to the singer and to me.

Even at my very young age, I related to this troubled soul. What lay behind that green door? I had to find out.

PREFACE

Why Write Here? Why Right Now?

During a conversation on Bob Edwards' radio show some years back, longtime ´CBS News correspondent Mike Wallace indicated that he had forgotten most of the thousands of interviews he ever conducted. Several years before his death, Pete Seeger said that he could remember only a few dozen songs, if that, when he once knew hundreds. Ramblin' Jack Elliot appeared on TV the other night and told the host, "You know why I'm sure I played the Newport Folk Festival? 'Cause somebody just told me I was there." Funny, and yet…

So before allowing my own memories to evaporate into the nether world of Proust's lost time, I wanted to commit some recollections to print while I still clearly remember them.

The formats are varied. Included are reviews of concerts and recordings. There are book reviews and my interviews with musicians, as well as general essays on music.

I sometimes offer less traditional entries, such as my remarks about concert performances that I did not personally attend. A few encounters are labeled, "Hangin' with the Stars." These are exchanges with famed musicians that actually occurred. Also included are a handful of brief conversations that did *not* occur. I call these my "One Question With" interviews, where I ponder what question I would ask a performer, had I the opportunity. In these, I create a response for the artist.

The book is arranged by genre, so chronology takes a back seat to subject matter. The first section is *Popular (and unpopular) Music*, where I mainly discuss rock, pop, and blues music. The other sections are *Jazz, Country Music,* and a final section reserved for specific performers, called *Beatles, Bob, Bruce, and Barry!*

POPULAR (AND UNPOPULAR) MUSIC:

POP AND ROCK

"People will pay to watch people make sounds."

—David Byrne

Concert Commentary

Grand Funk Railroad
Veterans Memorial Auditorium
Des Moines, Iowa
December 31, 1970

ONE OF THE FIRST real rock concerts I attended was Grand Funk Railroad, held in Des Moines' Veterans Auditorium on New Year's Eve, 1970. A high school friend of mine and I had somehow traded for front row seats. I think whoever originally bought these tickets must have realized how loud the band was going to be. Not the loudest concert I ever attended, but Grand Funk was very very loud. At the end of the show, my friend's voice sounded oddly distorted, as if he had been inhaling helium. Even the next day at school, the sound of things was not yet back to normal. That's not good.

Grand Funk, as expected, delivered crunchy thud rock. That's why we were there. Even so, I remember liking the set most when they cut back on the bombast and calmed down a bit. This was especially true when Mark Farner played electric piano on "Mean Mistreater." That the band's guitarist switched to piano for one tune meant they had no full-time keyboard player. This was the original trio.

The *Closer to Home* album was their latest release, and the group had seen an edited version of "I'm Your Captain" get some radio play. It was their first substantial hit single. Still, I was disappointed when they played the tune that night, as they omitted one of the song's verses, shortening it to the single version. Why? I wondered if this were a mistake or a one-time thing in Des Moines. Years later I picked up a live CD of this tour, recorded just weeks after the Iowa show, where they also played the shortened version of "I'm Your Captain." So, I learned, it wasn't just truncated for the Midwest crowd. A burning question finally resolved!

I clearly remember that Farner was able to get all sorts of wah-wah effects out of his very beat-up Fender guitar, without using a foot pedal. It seemed odd that just by turning the guitar sideways he could get these effects. When I discussed the show the next day with others at school, an influential teacher insisted that Farner was sort of lip-synching his guitar parts to a prerecorded tape. It seemed far-fetched, but this would explain things. I was hanging on the front of the stage at that concert, so I saw it up close—there was no equipment present on the stage to produce those effects. Or so my memory tells me. To this day, I wonder if that guitar was prerecorded or, if not, how did he manage those effects without a foot pedal?

A story concerning that Grand Funk concert would later come from Jerry Silver, the owner of a Des Moines record and "head" shop. I interviewed Silver about something unconnected to the concert for my high school newspaper, but he was eager to tell me about Grand Funk. Describing the events of the evening rekindled his anger, more than a year after the fact.

Silver was the promoter for the band's appearance in Des Moines, meaning he put up financing for the show. Silver told me that before the concert began he went backstage and met the band, shaking their hands, exchanging obligatory "right-ons" and the like. It was 1970, remember. They were "cool," he said, and seemed "very nice." But then in walked the band's manager, who grabbed Silver by the collar, threw him against the wall and screamed, "NOBODY talks to Grand Funk!" Silver said that he was so mad that if the hall hadn't already been filled with seated concertgoers, he would have pulled out of financing the show. Easy to say, but I thought he meant it; he was still fuming.

Things which gave this story some added credence are revelations that would surface much later about Grand Funk's business dealings. Their manager, Terry Knight, was apparently ripping off money from the band in a big way. It was likely Knight who grabbed Silver backstage in Des Moines, not wanting any sort of discussions about money to take place between promoter (who would know what he was paying to get the band) and the musicians (who may have been given different numbers). Speculation on my part, to be sure.

A Midwestern group by the name of White Lightning opened this New Year's Eve show. As I look back, these guys were probably better musicians than the headliners—very tight. They were quite well received and ended their set with a smokin' version of "The William Tell Overture" (4th movement only). True. And hot.

Grand Funk Railroad would become increasingly popular during the mid-1970s, but not with my crowd. Most of us soon felt that we outgrew them, but maybe we were just being cool. I thought it was sort of odd when the band released a cover of Little Eva's "The Locomotion," but admitted that their single "We're an American Band" rocked hard. Both of these hit records were produced by Todd Rundgren. Frank Zappa produced the band's final studio album, so somebody still liked them!

It's interesting now to read comments of band members, some included on their reissued recordings. Guitarist and lead singer Mark Farner defends the group mightily. Bassist Mel Schacher is very matter-of-fact about their legacy and the uneven quality of their performances at the time of their success. I enjoy the live CD from their 1971 tour I mentioned, and I occasionally pull out my 8-track tape of Grand Funk's later live album, from 1975, called *Caught in the Act*. Nothing wrong with either set. Makes me wish I had not been such an elitist; makes me wonder if I still am.

Concert Commentary

The Association
Veterans Memorial Auditorium
Des Moines, Iowa
August 15, 1970

FAR FROM THE REALM of Grand Funk, The Association were ballad specialists. The group scored just a handful of hits, but they were very big hits. Their vocalists could really sing, and the band could rock out pretty well on its own terms. The opening of their set is where they probably rocked hardest, with a fiery version of Bob Dylan's "One Too Many Mornings" followed immediately by their first hit, "Along Comes Mary."

This was one of those shows that should have been in a smaller venue. It was a good performance, but the hall's acoustics were terrible. Lots of echo in a basketball arena. In fact, a comedy team opened the show and it was hard to understand a word they said. The comedians themselves even commented that the hall's echo was killing their timing.

I owned The Association's live LP, and was disappointed that the Des Moines concert was shorter than the set performed on the album. I also thought it odd that they did not play their song "Dubuque Blues." I mean, how many songs are there about Iowa towns? Not many. And how many times is a big name band in Iowa to play a gig? Probably more than they would like.

The show ended with the megahits "Cherish" and "Windy," and we went home satisfied. But even at this early point I was realizing the difference between a good performance and a good venue. The Association played well, but it was largely lost in that huge room. Like the comedians who opened for them, the band seemed very aware of the acoustical battle they were waging (and losing) all evening.

Many years later, I learned that The Association decided not to record Jimmy Webb's strange and lengthy song about a rain-soaked cake, "MacArthur Park." Bad move; that unique epic might have really rejuvenated their career in the late 1960s, and I think the group could have done a fine job with it. But to be fair, everybody passed on that odd song. Why do you think it was finally recorded by Richard Harris?

Bonus Track

The Association had a fast and furious arc of success. They were invited to open The Monterey Pop Festival in the summer of 1967. Their set was warmly received by the audience and by fellow musicians, including Steve Miller. Just two years later, The Association's music would have been quite out of place at the Woodstock festival. This speaks more to the rapid changes in the music scene during these years than to the quality of this group. The 1970 live recording I mention above clearly documents that The Association was fine in concert.

Concert Commentary

The Baja Marimba Band
KRNT Theater
Des Moines, Iowa
January 10, 1969

MY FRIEND WAS OBSESSED with Herb Alpert and The Tijuana Brass. But that group was so big that they were not going to be coming to Des Moines any time soon. So instead, he settled for seeing The Baja Marimba Band. I went along. And while I didn't find much of the music very memorable, certain parts of that evening stayed with me a long time.

The concert was not well attended. The Baja Marimba Band's front man first acknowledged the size of the audience in a positive way by saying that "we would have our own little party" that night. But before long his tone changed. He was openly complaining about how the band had left 80 degree weather in Los Angeles that morning to play a poorly attended January gig in Iowa. Sorry.

At one point, two members of the band did a comedy routine that involved one marimba player following an oblivious trumpet player around the stage. The humor centered on the musician's misunderstanding of what "follow" means in music terminology. I didn't think much about it until I happened to see this group again at the Iowa State Fair (opening for Bob Hope), where they did the exact same comedy bit. It dawned on me that this segment was simply a planned part of the act every night. Choreographed show biz. That's fine, but it wasn't very funny the first time. Even to a junior high student.

Opening for The Baja Marimba Band was the group Friend & Lover. Their online biography describes them as having been a "folk singing duo," but this was no folk duo; it was a rock band! Their music was quite a contrast to the headliners, as group leader Jim Post even acknowledged. He sullenly apologized once or twice for their high decibel volume level. "But that's the way it's gotta be," he said. They did one tune about a circus, and closed with their hit single, "Reach Out of the Darkness." Sounded just like the record. But they were loud, especially for older people coming to hear marimbas.

Late in their set, Post acknowledged the group's musicians. He paused as he was about to introduce the keyboard player, finally going over to ask his name. It struck me odd that he would not know the name of his own band member, but it was probably a local guy they hired for this one show. Post tried to cover, saying, "This is what your high school dropout is doing, ladies and gentlemen! He's a professional rock musician!"

Canned comedy segments, band members who weren't really band members, surly group leaders who apologized for their volume but wouldn't turn down. It all struck me very odd. This was a different sort of entertainment than the variety shows on TV. I didn't care much for the music that night, but I began to understand the unique allure of going to concerts.

Concert Commentary

Chuck Berry
Des Moines Ice Arena
Des Moines, Iowa
Fall 1972

NOBODY COULD HAVE PREDICTED it, but in the summer of 1972 Chuck Berry had his first Top 10 chart entry in over eight years. It came in the form of a live recording called "My Ding-A-Ling." The song went to #1. Even more amazing—this was Chuck Berry's first #1 hit ever! Although it was a lightweight novelty number, Berry performed the song with conviction. That fall, the veteran performer had booked himself into a tour schedule that was heavier than usual, capitalizing on his renewed fame.

I wanted to see Chuck Berry, but not because of "My Ding-A-Ling." Our local Top 40 radio station played two oldies each hour. It was there that I heard Berry's biggest hits and made the connection between these songs and some of my early Beatles records, including "Roll Over Beethoven" and "Rock & Roll Music." But I also liked the hits that I knew as distinctly Berry's, such as "No Particular Place to Go" and "Sweet Little Sixteen."

Because the performer did not appear on television during this era, and me being a child of radio, I admit that I did not know Chuck

Berry was a black man until he stepped onto that Des Moines stage. I have been told that this was often true with some members of his audience during his first wave of popularity in the 1950s. So I guess I fit in well with his original fan base.

And speaking of original fans, I think I spotted some that night. While the area in front of the stage was filled with white teens, seated in the bleachers of this hockey arena I saw a few older African American couples patiently waiting. And wait we did. After the two local bands had each played their sets, it was whispered that the star had not yet arrived. One of the bands volunteered to play some more. But the audience was restless, and the group's initial set had not been well received. Finally, someone announced that Berry's flight had landed and that he was getting a police escort to the hall.

Chuck Berry was very professional. He acknowledged that this would be a late show. The audience cheered; we felt special. At one point he tried to get a little musical response going between his guitar work and the drummer. But, as usual, Berry had hired a local, unrehearsed band for his backing group, and the nervous drummer was confused about what was being asked of him.

Chuck played the hits I knew, and he played some of his songs that I would later discover. I recall that he often looked at his watch during the performance, but he was friendly toward the audience. When Berry was certain he had performed long enough to satisfy the contract, his fingers burned up the neck of his guitar into the opening lines of "Johnny B. Goode." Then he abruptly stopped. "I forgot! Wait!" He signaled the surprised band to quit playing. This was not a prearranged act; he had truly forgotten to sing his recent hit. Berry then performed an unhurried, crowd pleasing version of "My Ding-A-Ling." *Then* he hit the opening of "Johnny B. Goode" again, and the audience danced off into the night.

Concert Commentary

Poco—   and   **Eagles—**
"Coulda Been a   "The Winner"
Contender"   University of
with Shawn Phillips   Northern Iowa
KRNT Theater   Cedar Falls, Iowa
Des Moines, Iowa   April 28, 1974
May 22, 1971

I CAN DATE MY NIGHT with Poco to 1971, as I went with my then girlfriend Diane. The show was held at the KRNT Theater, a huge auditorium built by the Shriners in 1925. Foundations of both this theater and the dating relationship would soon crumble. Shawn Phillips opened. Not a lot to say about Phillips except that he was a very enthusiastic performer. He presented a long set while switching between many acoustic guitars. Phillips seemed in a rush to get as many tunes across as possible.

Although his waist-length blonde hair gave him a lot of 'hip' status, I thought Phillips played too long. I would later get his album *Second Contribution*, which was great. I am guessing that he was doing some of those tunes, but I didn't know his music that night. Late in the 1970s he tried different things, including an instrumental LP (with short hair). He sort of faded away with no real hits or lasting success, but I sure liked that one album.

Phillips played a 12-string guitar during his set, which was new to me that night. Also new was the pedal steel guitar, an instrument used in Poco's lineup. I had never seen a steel before and was intrigued by the way it was played. The steel guitar would soon become an important part of my country music education, but on this night it was foreign to me. I bought the live Poco album *Deliverin'* after that concert and have always liked it. That music still holds up.

Poco was a band that should have been bigger. There were others trying this style of country rock who labored in greater obscurity, certainly, such as the groups Cowboy and Mason Profit. The Eagles would become huge a few years later, essentially performing the style of country rock that Poco was playing that night. Kenny Loggins and former

Poco member Jim Messina forged a successful career and produced a couple of big hits that had even more of a Poco-esque good time appeal than the Eagles. Messina had left Poco a few months before the Des Moines show, but he is still with them on the live *Deliverin'* record.

I always felt that Poco got cherry picked. Messina left, and Poco's front man Timothy B. Schmidt would join a later version of the Eagles to play bass and sing harmony vocals. Schmidt joining Poco's thunder-stealing nemesis, the Eagles, was sort of like Bill Champlin joining Chicago: going over to the other side.

To my mind, the lineup with Schmidt and Joe Walsh was never really the Eagles. The hits kept coming and band members became major rock stars, but I felt that the group had become less interesting. This occurred around the time Randy Meisner and Bernie Leadon left. Not that these two guys were the dominant front men or the main writers, but the Eagles seemed a more holistic group at the beginning.

I saw the Eagles before they became rock gods. It was at SUNI-Daze, held at the University of Northern Iowa in late spring 1974—our version of a rock festival. I went over to the football field to see Steely Dan play, but they refused to go on because it looked like it might rain. Too bad; I would have liked to see them at that time. I was at a second show later that same year, at the Iowa State Fair, where "the Dan" were supposed to perform, but they again cancelled—this time because some of their equipment was malfunctioning. Many unhappy people at that concert who had also been in Cedar Falls for the group's previous no show. You'd a thought George Jones was fronting the band.

The reason this vignette comes to mind is that the Eagles were performing their Cedar Falls set just before Steely Dan was supposed to play. After Steely Dan abruptly cancelled, the Eagles agreed to return for another six songs or so to appease the disappointed crowd. They were a struggling band then—or at least there were no big hits yet. That's another show I wish I could watch now. The Eagles would have been working hard, no doubt, and playing some tunes during that added section that were probably not in their normal set list.

Concert Commentary

The Sons of Champlin
Ingersoll Theater
Des Moines, Iowa
ca. 1972

SPEAKING OF BILL CHAMPLIN, my friends and I were all very much into the first couple of albums by his eponymous San Francisco horn band The Sons of Champlin, for which he played keyboards, doubled on guitar, and sang lead. The first release, *Loosen Up Naturally*, was especially strong. It had politics covered with the side-long song "Freedom," and the band members' heads were shown to be in the right place with "Get High." But in addition to both of these "right on" anthems, all of the other songs on this double LP were good.

So we were excited to learn that the band was booked for a small Des Moines hall, a former movie theater. The Sons (as they called themselves at this point) had an instrumental makeup very much like Chicago and Blood, Sweat & Tears. Unlike either of these groups, however, The Sons never had a song on Top 40 radio. Too bad. They were a fine group.

The concert was good, but the band had clearly grown weary of their early catalog. When people yelled for the song "Get High," guitarist Terry Haggerty would lean into the microphone and say, "We are." Clever, but we wanted to hear what passed for an underground hit. Our hip FM station played this song quite a lot, so most of the audience was familiar with it, whether they owned the album or not.

I knew very few of the tunes played at the show and was disappointed that they didn't touch their first album. It was an unusual concert for me; I had never seen a rock guitarist sit down to perform, but Haggerty remained seated all evening while playing some fine lead lines. What saved the band's choice of material was the encore—an expanded version of Ricky Nelson's 1963 hit "Fools Rush In."

The Sons would continue to tour and record, still searching for a hit or at least a larger audience. Capitol Records dropped them and they began their descent onto smaller, less well distributed labels—all the while producing good music. I have read in various places that The Sons of Champlin did not court success. I doubt that. In fact, I recall reading an interview with Bill Champlin in the 1970s where he said he would do anything to have the new LP be a hit. Sounds pretty normal to me. Tom Waits once told me to watch out for the ones who say they don't care about the charts. They are probably watching them closer than anybody.

After The Sons split in the early 1980s, I was surprised to learn that Bill Champlin had joined the group Chicago. With guitarist Terry Kath dead and bassist Peter Cetera gone, this band was a shell of its glory years. Chicago had traded guitar-driven songs for ballads. More than this, I thought that for Bill Champlin to join Chicago was like… like a member of Poco joining the Eagles.

Concert Commentary

The Allman Brothers Band
with Big Brother and the Holding Company
University of Iowa Fieldhouse
Iowa City, Iowa
February 19, 1972

I SAW THE ALLMAN BROTHERS in 1972, a unique year for the group. Duane was gone but bassist Berry Oakley was still alive. This one year window of touring saw the band trying to cope simultaneously with huge loss and exploding popularity. The great album achievement of *Live at Fillmore East* was behind them, and *Eat a Peach* had been released just the week before this show. With their next album, *Brothers and Sisters*, they would reach new and unexpectedly large audiences through their one huge radio hit, "Ramblin' Man." But the concert on this winter night attracted the band's original, album-oriented fan base.

Dickey Betts carried the guitar load all night, and the group was very good. Still, an air of sadness hung over the Iowa City Fieldhouse that evening. Opening the concert was Big Brother and the Holding Company. This San Francisco band had once included Janis Joplin, but was now disintegrating and in its final days.

Big Brother without Janis, and the Allmans without Duane. It was becoming increasingly clear to this still young audience that time would not forever be our friend.

Bonus Track

> *Interviewer to Duane Allman, concerning the Layla album:*
> *"How are we supposed to know which guitar is you and which is Eric Clapton?"*
> *Duane: "I'm playing the Gibson; Eric's on the Fender."*
> Oh...Thanks?

Book Review

Midnight Riders: The Story of the Allman Brothers Band
By Scott Freeman
Little, Brown, and Co., 1995

Like the Allman Brothers Band itself, *Midnight Riders* is best when Duane is present. As soon as the band became big, the major players died. Or such was the oft-heard lament. Unfortunately, this assessment rings sadly accurate throughout this new biography. Scott Freeman's account is balanced, with his focus generally remaining on the music itself. Although the band members' involvement with drugs and groupies is not ignored, the author wisely truncates these accounts, so the book rarely reaches the level of sensationalism. And with the Allman Brothers, describing the excesses of rock stardom could easily dominate the account.

Freeman portrays the unlikely rise of a southern garage band. He points to the Allmans' various obstacles, including their geographic location. Ultimately, the group trailblazed a music path from Macon, Georgia, that would be followed by many others. As the author correctly insists, the Allman Brothers were an innovative band. Freeman steps over the line a few times in his attempt to make his subjects appear a bit more than they were, such as when he credits the group with introducing drum solos to rock music. However, he does an especially good job of showing the band's blues roots, as well as their unconventional forays into sustained instrumental passages.

Midnight Riders reminds the reader that this was a band that, in its prime, could present complex musical interplay and keep things interesting—even on lengthy numbers. And here is where the sadness lies: the Allman Brothers had such a brief time to really shine, with Duane Allman at the helm. Freeman should be credited for portraying Allman as a human being, possessing both pleasant and ugly traits. Concerning Duane's guitar skills, the biographer sometimes leans toward a true fan's unsupportable rhetoric, as when Freeman puts Allman toe to toe with Jimi Hendrix as an innovator on the instrument.

Sloppiness occasionally creeps into the book in both writing and research. Freeman tends to repeat himself at times, not for emphasis but for a lack of editing. He fails to differentiate the dates of various 1971 Fillmore East shows, leading the reader to believe that all the material on *Live* and *Eat a Peach* is culled from a single weekend stand. Also, he omits a solo LP or two from his generally thorough discography.

In spite of some correctable flaws, *Midnight Riders* does justice to the Allman Brothers Band, and it avoids what could have easily become tabloid journalism. The work is intelligent, insightful, and written with a discerning ear. Freeman can't help it that as his book continues, it must describe the unravelling of a once great band.

Concert Commentary

Elton John
Hilton Coliseum
Ames, Iowa
October 14, 1972

I WAS FIRST MADE AWARE of a wild piano player named Elton John by my friend Jim, so it was only appropriate that he and I should see Elton together. The concert was at the field house in Ames, about 30 miles from Des Moines. I had to play sousaphone in my high school marching band that night, so Jim was waiting in the parking lot with his car. When I was freed from the half-time performance we high-tailed it to the concert, knowing that we would be a bit late. I recall changing out of my cumbersome band uniform in the car as Jim sped northward.

We arrived at intermission. A group by the name of Family had played first. From what I later heard, we missed little. However, I have always been grateful that they opened that night, since it allowed me to see the entire set by Elton John, which was perfect from first note to last.

Elton came out to center stage alone, thanked the audience for attending, sat down at the grand piano and played "Tiny Dancer." This was no stripped-down version; he gave it a full length treatment, which would be true of each song he played that night. And as others have noted, few of Elton's John's songs were short. Years later, during my college days in Cedar Falls, a local band began to assemble a medley of some of his numerous hits. It became way too long to be a reasonable part of a set, so the idea for a medley was abandoned, and each song was played as an individual piece. Better that way, anyhow, I thought.

After the impressive solo performance of "Tiny Dancer," bassist Dee Murray joined John for "Your Song." Drummer Nigel Olson entered for the third tune, and they played as a trio for a few more upbeat numbers. Then Elton introduced the guitarist, Davey Johnstone, who had just been added to the band. Johnstone's slide technique was useful in replicating the sound of their new single "Rocket Man," and he was also great throughout the rest of the concert. *Honky Chateau* was Elton John's current LP. I thought it was OK, but I really liked the previous release, *Madman Across the Water*, far better. *Madman* was more maudlin; less pop.

Elton's set was close to three hours in length with no break—unusually generous for the era. He did a great expanded version of "Levon" and of "Madman." He later pulled out the minor yet brilliant "Mona Lisas and Mad Hatters," a high point of *Honky Chateau*. Late in the concert, I was thinking that he had pretty much played everything I came to hear. Then he went into "Country Comforts"—a jewel I had forgotten about. Loved it, and surprised by it.

After the final numbers of the lengthy main set, the band returned for an encore. Elton said he knew of Americans' reluctance to hear unfamiliar songs at concerts, but he would like to close with two new numbers that would appear on his next album. He then sang "Daniel" and "Crocodile Rock." Wow. Those songs were great, even on first hearing. But I look back on them now as somewhat bittersweet, for to me they would come to represent a major turning point in Elton John's career. And not for the better.

Elton would hit superstar status with his next few albums. He was at his commercial peak during my college years, but I had pretty much stopped paying attention to him after *Honky Chateau*. John would eventually fall from favor with audiences and critics a few years after this and then fight his way back. He was big when I saw him in 1972, no doubt about it—he filled the Hilton Coliseum, after all—but soon he would become well known for his flamboyant extravagance rather than for his music.

I would meet a lot of people in college who attended that memorable concert in Ames and would attest to its power. Two friends had odd reactions: One always complained that Elton didn't play "Burn Down the Mission." I guess I was fortunate not to expect it. I had the live album entitled *11/17/70*, on which "Burn Down the Mission" is an 18-minute set closer. Even at this stage of my musical growth, I knew that when a performer features one tune as such a huge signature piece during a tour, the song is often removed entirely from the following tour.

Witness Jimi Hendrix's career-making version of "Wild Thing" at Monterey Pop. After a while he dropped the tune completely and replaced it with other concert closing rave-ups—at Woodstock, for example. When Elton's concert included extended versions of both "Levon" and the slower "Madman Across the Water," I assumed (even as he played them) that these were the replacements for his "Burn Down the Mission" feature. That was understandable, and fine with me. But my friend could never talk about that night without faulting Elton for not playing "Burn Down the Mission."

Another friend who had also been there was worse. He had seen some brief footage of an Elton John concert on TV about two weeks before the Ames show, and said there had been a dozen women dancers who came on stage at the end. He said in Ames we got four women. I don't disagree with his count, but I didn't care about the number of dancers at the close. It did not matter in the least to me, but this was a real sore point with my friend. Sorry. What I do remember is having the foresight to take along a pair of binoculars. Helped a lot, as we were pretty far back. The binoculars also allowed me to see that during the last number, lyricist Bernie Taupin was on stage dancing around. Only one Bernie Taupin though.

Post Script

Memory is a funny thing; it's odd what resides in the backwaters of our minds. I recall clearly how much I had liked the downsized four-piece concert arrangements of several songs that had originally appeared on his studio LPs as lush orchestral works. Elton's decision to recast these songs for his small group meant that the sound would often have a much harder edge. This was always a sticking point with some Texas friends who went to see Elton in New York City shortly after the first album came out. They wanted the chamber pop string sound of The Left Banke, but instead got a hard rockin' piano trio on the lines of Jerry Lee Lewis. They complained endlessly about that.

Thirty-four years after that concert I bought the two-CD Elton John set called *Rare Masters*. It includes tracks like B-sides of singles and alternate takes. Worth having. One of the studio outtakes is of the song "Madman Across the Water." The minute I heard it, I thought, "THAT is the way he did it when I saw him." The recording is edgier than the official release, with Mick Ronson on a more prominently mixed guitar. Taken at the same dirgeful tempo as its counterpart, this longer, alternate version served as the template for John's concert arrangement. I remember that guitar part clearly; I rarely remember my passwords.

Hangin' with the Stars #1

Over the years, I have had a few encounters with some famous musicians. The "Hangin' With the Stars" entries in this book are not interviews, but brief and unplanned exchanges. I find them worth recounting, as they often illuminate unguarded personality traits of the performer. Here is my first entry.

A few years after that Elton John concert in Ames, I had a brief interaction with the man himself. I was selling admission tickets at the main gate of The Iowa State Fair. Elton John was scheduled to play the grandstand. That afternoon, an unusually nice limousine arrived at the fairground gates. I had the feeling that Elton John might be in the back seat. I was somewhat surprised that the limo driver stopped for a ticket, but he did. And I was correct; in the back seat was the evening's star. I leaned past the driver and said something to Elton about loving his Ames concert a couple of years before. He graciously responded, "Oh yeah. Thanks very much. That was a really good night, wasn't it?"

The limo drove on. I was amazed; Elton actually remembered that Iowa show? Don't all those tour dates run together for a performer? Then I started thinking that the answer he gave me would have served well for any show that somebody complimented him on. Smart guy. He wasn't bullshitting me; he was being pleasant to a fan. And whether he recalled the Ames show or not, he was right—it had been a really good night.

Concert Commentary

Frank Zappa   and   **Frank Zappa**
Auditorium Theater   University of Iowa
Chicago, Illinois   Fieldhouse
May 16, 1973   Iowa City, Iowa
                            September 24, 1977

I ATTENDED TWO CONCERTS by Frank Zappa, one in 1973 and another in 1977. Poor seats and bad sound for both shows left few positive impressions. Even so, I do recall that the Chicago concert included a lengthy and unflattering musical narrative by Zappa concerning England's royal family. The band's encore was "King Kong," one of the very few songs I knew that night. It was an unusual encore, though. Zappa said that they didn't feel like leaving the stage and coming back, pretending to be awed and honored by the applause. So he just announced that their last tune would serve as the encore. Zappa was not following traditional show business custom, but he was humorous about it.

At one point between songs, somebody in the audience asked Frank why they could not smoke in this Chicago theater. Zappa, a lifelong advocate of cigarettes ("tobacco is my favorite vegetable"), announced to the audience: "Why can't you smoke in here? Because some guy in a small office downtown is worried about losing *his job*!" The crowd cheered as Frank stuck it to "the man," and the band went into the next number.

This 1973 ensemble had some well-known performers. George Duke was on keyboards, and Ian & Ruth Underwood were still with Zappa at this time. Jean-Luc Ponty was playing violin with the ensemble, but not for much longer.

That Zappa concert is one of the many shows I wish I could go back and sit through again. Maybe in a better seat.

Letter to a Friend

Frank Zappa: Where to Begin?

Frank Zappa was an articulate spokesman for the topics he cared about. From artistic censorship to concert hall fidelity, he was able to cogently present his point of view in a lucid manner. So it sometimes disappointed me when Zappa seemed to aim so low with many of his lyrics. Admonishing listeners not to eat yellow snow seemed puerile. But I must simultaneously admit that some of his shocking crudities on the early albums were what originally caught my attention and made me investigate this performer.

Zappa sometimes complained in interviews (or he at least acknowledged) that many of his fans knew only his first three LPs. I myself was among those who liked these early albums best, but I did stay with Zappa for some of his later work. A good friend wrote to me not long ago, saying that his daughter wondered where she should begin if she were planning to dive into the vast musical world of Frank Zappa. Here is my response, indicating some albums to search out in the man's library of recordings.

Dear Al,

Your daughter asked where to start with the music of Frank Zappa. My knowledge of Frank is a bit spotty, but here goes:

The first three LPs are seen by many as Zappa's Golden Era. They are very funny and musically interesting, even now. A bit crude at times, but these included songs that were unusual in that they made fun of the hippy movement even as it was in full bloom.

These three albums are *Freak Out* (1966, among rock music's first double LPs); *Absolutely Free* (1967); and *We're Only in it for the Money* (1968, this album's graphics feature an elaborate parody of The Beatles' *Sgt. Pepper* album cover). Zappa later followed this trilogy with the double LP *Uncle Meat* (1969), which is uneven but includes some great sections.

Zappa hit his second major stride with the largely instrumental album *Hot Rats* (1969), which remains remarkable. Many other jazzy instrumental albums followed, most notably *Waka Jawaka/Hot Rats* (a 1972 sequel of sorts, as you might guess), and *The Grand Wazoo* (1972), a big band jazz group. These were a far cry from the humor and garage band material found on the first three albums and, as such, Zappa lost a lot of his old audience while gaining a new set of fans.

In 1972 Zappa released a high-water mark live LP called *Just Another Band from L.A.* This was a super tight group, featuring the two vocalists from The Turtles, Flo & Eddy (Mark Volman and Howard Kaylan), and the Turtles' drummer Ansley Dunbar. Really great music; really crude humor. Side two was a four-song set, ending with a stunningly hot "Dog Breath." (Strangely enough, the 1971 concert recording with the same band, *Live at the Fillmore East*, blows hard. Avoid it.)

Zappa had a commercial breakthrough in 1973 with the album *Overnight Sensation*. On it, he retreated from instrumentals in favor of actual songs, including one about a dental floss ranch in Montana. He also retained his penchant for very unorthodox humor, such as on a number about a sexual wager made with Dinah Moe Humm. This LP was followed in 1974 by a similar outing called *Apostrophe*. Big hits for Frank, but neither album did a lot for me.

I sort of got off the Zappa boat after that. He did a live album in 1975 with Captain Beefheart called *Bongo Fury* that you can ignore for now. I started to get interested again in 1976, with a double LP called *Zappa in New York*, but didn't follow him all that closely.

There are many albums after that, but I can't speak specifically about them except for the double CD, *The Best Band You Never Saw in Your Life* (1991), which is a good summation of the later touring band at its peak. Zappa released a collection of his guitar solos excerpted from concert recordings, called *Shut Up 'n Play Yer Guitar*, volumes 1-3. For guitarists, great; for the rest of us, a bit indulgent.

Frank got involved in classical music, in political material, and music censorship. Then he got cancer and died. Too soon. His son Dweezil Zappa tours as *Zappa Plays Zappa*. I recently saw a DVD of that band and they were great. Dweezil is a hot guitarist. They were performing songs from the later days of his father that I did not know well. Even so, I thought that the group was well rehearsed on these complex numbers and the material very engaging. I later saw Dweezil on a package show called *Experience Hendrix*, but the younger Zappa was not given the chance to shine much that night. In sum, here are my suggestions for your daughter:

Early Pick – *We're Only in It for the Money*
Breakthrough Instrumental – *Hot Rats*
An Overlooked Peak – *Just Another Band from L.A.*
Later Touring Days – *The Best Band You Never Saw in Your Life*

Still glad you asked?

Best wishes,

Tom Wilmeth
Grafton, Wisconsin

Bonus Track

Frank Zappa reminds us that "most rock journalism is written by people who can't write, interviewing people who can't talk, for people who can't read."

Remembrance

Captain Beefheart
"Something about the Fidelity"
December 19, 2010

Sorry to hear that 2010 must end with the death of Captain Beefheart (Don Van Vliet). Beefheart was the type of artist who had removed himself from the public eye so thoroughly that most people who even recognized the name would need to check their computer to see if he were still living. When somebody has already been gone from the scene for such a long time, it's hard to say that he will be missed. Those who were influenced by his music have already been missing him for over 20 years. What is incontrovertible is that he will be remembered.

I think that, like many people, I first became aware of Captain Beefheart though the *Zapped* sampler album of early 1970. *Zapped* was one in a series of inexpensive albums that featured songs from recent Warner Brothers/Reprise releases. It was one of the still healthy record industry's better promotional ideas. *Zapped* was more focused than most of these collections since the record company wasn't using it to promote everything from James Taylor to The Fugs on one anthology. The *Zapped* compilation included recordings taken only from the Bizarre and Straight labels, both under the absolute control of Frank Zappa, and distributed by Warner Brothers.

Following the brief instrumental "Overture" by Alice Cooper (still a *group*—not one person), Beefheart arrives, grabbing attention with an urgent narrative about some sort of impending doom involving a blimp. But it is the Captain's track from side two—I still hesitate to call it a song—"Old Fart at Play," which made me wonder if something new was afoot. At first, this just seemed to be a Kerouac-flavored bathroom humor recitation over disjointed Ornette Coleman riffs and insistently driven rhythms—radical at the time because of the outrageous subject matter. But...just what *was* the subject matter?

After this, I did buy the record from which these Beefheart tracks were culled, *Trout Mask Replica*. It was an expensive double album but worth having on several levels. First, the cover (described precisely by the record's title) was unlike all others; second, by playing any part of the album one could immediately clear a crowded room (at that time in Des Moines, Iowa, anyway). More than merely strange, though—it was unique, haunting, and unforgettable. Much of side one remained my favorite material, but that may be the result of not hearing the other three sides nearly as much. I'm not sure if it was endurance or tolerance, but *Trout Mask Replica* did require a period of adjustment for the listener, especially for one still in junior high. I always felt that "Old Fart at Play" was a well-chosen selection for the *Zapped* sampler, as it was an accurate representation of this unique Beefheart album.

I stayed with Beefheart's career more than some of my friends and less than others. His vocals were featured on Zappa's "Willie the Pimp," from the previously mentioned *Hot Rats* album of 1969 (a track also included on *Zapped*). I was somewhat cold on Zappa when *Bongo Fury* was released in 1975, so the fact that Beefheart sang with Zappa's band on this record didn't matter much to me. I lost track of the Captain until 1978 when *Shiny Beast (Bat Chain Puller)* got a big push from Warner Brothers, and rightly so. I searched out his first album, *Safe as Milk*, but never really considered myself a fan or true aficionado. Even so, I was sorry to learn of his death earlier today.

That's the personal background part of the obituary. What follows is the brief section that might actually add to the conversation: I was a huge Tom Waits devotee in his early years. I still am a fan, but I was really taken with his first records and truly got on board with the release of *Nighthawks at the Diner* in 1975. Even living in the great Midwest, I was able to see Waits several times—on tours promoting his *Small Change*, *Foreign Affairs*, *Blue Valentine*, and *Heartattack and Vine* albums.

During one post-gig encounter, I expressed dismay to Waits that he had not been given an equal share of time on *Soundstage*, a concert program that aired on Public Television in 1975. For this broadcast, Tom Waits shared the hour with Mose Allison in separate sets. "The original guy for the other half of that *Soundstage* show was Captain Beefheart," Waits told me. "We got into rehearsals and the Captain was unhappy. He picked up this real *Leave It to Beaver* type of director by his lapels and [shifting to a carefully articulated guttural] said 'something about the fidelity.' Everybody on the set got real nervous after that, and the next thing I knew, the Captain was off the show."

Not long ago, I read that Captain Beefheart and his Magic Band were scheduled to perform at the 1967 Monterey Pop Festival. However, guitarist Ry Cooder either left the group right before this famous festival, or he didn't think the band was ready to perform. (I have heard both accounts.) In any event, Beefheart's Magic Band had to cancel. Would exposure from The Monterey Pop Festival have helped Beefheart? Who knows. Would his band have made it into the movie? Also unknowable. But for now I'll leave you with that—the only Captain Beefheart-related story in my arsenal that might come close to being useful.

Post Script

Beefheart's occasional collaborator, Frank Zappa, was also invited to play The Monterey Pop Festival in 1967, but Zappa also opted not to perform. However, Zappa refused the invitation because he did not want to share a bill with a collection of bands he regarded as inferior musicians.

Artist Commentary
"I Knew Tom Waits Back When..."

Speaking of Tom Waits, I must confess that, like many, my entry point to his music was the Eagles' recording of his song "Ol' 55." I was in the radio station record library one Saturday morning in 1975, getting ready to do a long afternoon music show. I saw Tom Waits' *Closing Time* album shelved with the folk LPs. No big shock to find it there, in retrospect, as Waits was one of many acoustic singer/songwriters to emerge in the early 1970s. I wondered how the man performed his own version of this song, so I put on side one of the album and was immediately hooked.

The Eagles' pretty harmonies were replaced by one voice and a small combo featuring Waits at the piano. Now the song made more sense, with its hopeful longing expressed in the singer's not yet gravelly voice. Waits himself would soon back away from this record, performing virtually none of it at his live shows. I listened to both sides of the record repeatedly after first discovering it. *Closing Time* was great late-night music for me, and I often played it after returning from the radio station about 3:30 in the morning, when the rest of Cedar Falls had long been in bed.

I didn't play his second album very often, *The Heart of a Saturday Night*, but I am familiar with most of the individual tunes. I liked the live *Nighthawks at the Diner* set once I got used to the style. Very different—rhythmic hipster stuff, yet…melodic. Many current fans are critical of these early records, through *Heartattack and Vine*: "The drunken hobo image," they dismissively say. But within this early era of 1973 to 1980 lies some of Waits' best material.

One day I was in the local record store and was surprised to see a new release called *Small Change*. I immediately bought the album and took it home. When I put on the first side, I truly thought my turntable had broken and was not playing the record at the correct speed. Waits' voice sounded lethargic and coarse. As he sang the opening of "Tom Traubert's Blues," I wasn't sure what to think, but I could not remove the needle from this seven-minute epic.

Next came "Step Right Up," a fast-paced narrative placed within a sparse musical backing. This number can now be viewed as the culmination of Waits' hipster persona. The entire *Small Change* album is strong and is the high point of this era for him. It features numerous beautiful ballads, including "I Wish I Was in New Orleans," and some remarkably clever material, such as "The Piano Has Been Drinking (Not Me)".

I saw Waits perform several times, starting with an Iowa City show in 1976 on the *Small Change* tour. Afterwards, the manager of Hancher Auditorium told me that they had never had as many people walk out of a concert as had left early that night. Ry Cooder was supposed to headline the show, but his backing group didn't arrive, so Cooder played an opening solo set. Waits closed the show. Most of the audience was there to hear the far better known Cooder, and some left when Waits wasn't to their liking.

I saw him again in 1977 just as the *Foreign Affairs* LP was released. In addition to performing most of this new record, Waits played all but one of the songs from *Small Change*. He seemed aware that this was his strongest material. We spoke after the concert—a conversation during which he was kind to a fan and candid in his assessments. Waits was dismissive of other artists' versions of his songs, openly regretting that he had granted permission to a couple of artists. (This was long before Bruce Springsteen recorded his "Jersey Girl.") He didn't single out the Eagles' recording of "Ol' 55" by name, but I did. Waits said it was OK, "if you like that sort of thing." He was quite unhappy about a recent cover version of his song "(Looking for) The Heart of a Saturday Night."

Waits praised the vocal work of Lambert, Hendricks & Ross, but had absolutely no time for the harmonies of Crosby, Stills, Nash & Young. I told him that I held his writing in high esteem and mentioned a few contemporary singer/songwriters who I felt were his peers, but he did not seem complimented by these comparisons. I got the distinct feeling that Waits wanted to be thought of as existing in an earlier era, and to be viewed as older than he really was. He seemed eager to inhabit a world that had already vanished.

This time shift can be seen in the cultural references within his song lyrics, including "I Wish I Was in New Orleans." Waits told me, "People get on me and say, 'You're too young to have been at Ebbets Field.' They don't get the fact that a song can be written from *any* person's point of view. *I* didn't go to Ebbets Field. The *guy in the song* did!"

In a 1979 Australian television interview, host Don Lane repeatedly indicates to the audience that Waits' age is 28, but that this performer is intentionally playing a much older role. It is clear that Waits was not pleased by this public outing of his age. This entire interview is somewhat contentious, with Waits openly marveling (in mocking tones) that the American Lane has become a popular Australian television host.

One thing that struck me was how much Waits enjoyed playing with language, even during our casual conversation. But he also lamented that his audience often expected him to create new lyrics every night, especially on "Step Right Up," which he viewed as a series of specific and polished lines. Members of his backing group drifted in and out of the green room, grabbing food from a Spartanly furnished hospitality table. More than once, he told a band mate: "Don't let the bus take off without me." He turned to me and said, "I've seen that happen."

Waits was clearly proud of his new song, "Burma Shave," and he told me how it related to his cousin back in California who would take him driving at crazy fast speeds. I assumed that one of the new album's major pieces, "Potter's Field," was sung at every stop of the tour. It had been a highlight of that night's concert. But Waits told me he didn't perform that one very often—only if he thought the audience was "really listening."

He said the band always liked it when they got to the song "I Can't Wait to Get Off Work," because they knew that their evening was about over. After we talked a while, he jumped up as if he had forgotten something. We walked quickly to the stage area. "This is my favorite part of the night," he told me. "I love to watch them pack up." The roadies were just finishing loading the equipment. I knew this would be the end. I thanked him for being so generous with his time; he thanked me for knowing his career so well. We continued to talk, and Tom Waits even walked me partway to my car before someone shouted to him that the bus was leaving. I felt that Minneapolis had been a good night for him; it sure was for me.

Bonus Track

During a brief conversation in the fall of 1976, I told Tom Waits how much I was enjoying his newest album, Small Change. *Because I thought he might be interested, I also said that Asylum Records didn't seem to be manufacturing it very well, as each copy of it I had heard contained a lot of surface noise. He looked at me for a moment and said, "You do know...I'm not at the plant when those records are pressed." Sort of a put-down, true. But even while glibly answering this unexpected criticism, Waits was engaging and pleasant. And funny.*

CD Review

Tom Waits
Mule Variations
Epitaph Records, 1999

Mule Variations will prove the most appropriately titled CD of the summer. Tom Waits' first album of new material in over six years shows the artist stubbornly plowing his musical field exactly as he pleases and on his own timetable. *Variations* is also accurate, with Waits' new songs echoing his entire divergent career but avoiding any backward glancing.

The recording has a casual atmosphere, as one can hear creaking chairs and occasional background noises on a few of the numbers. Some of the solos are not particularly well miked, and most of the set has the aura of inspired if imperfect first takes. It is reminiscent of J. J. Cale's early LPs, sounding as if they were informally recorded on his front porch. But while Cale settles into a relaxed folksy groove, Waits has different motives. He seems intent on rubbing a little grit into the perfect audio of CD technology, a grit that parallels most of the songs' themes.

Mule Variations begins with a number that pounds its way into your brain—a struggling musician's lament that recounts all the things lacking in his life. For consolation, the singer defensively repeats the song's title—telling himself he's "Big in Japan"! This shouted self-justification seems funny at first, but on a deeper level it becomes sad and unsettling. With this vignette, as in all of his best work, the characters Waits portrays on these 16 tracks are varied and realistically vivid—from an individual verging on paranoia, wondering what his neighbor is building, to a man completely and unashamedly in love.

While masterfully portraying the situations of others, Waits himself may also be involved with some of the attitudes found on *Mule Variations*. "The Chocolate Jesus" initially appears to mock its subject, until one sees that the lyrics are critical of society's reduction of Christ to the level of a Star Wars action figure. The questions concerning religion become darker and less answerable during the next number, "Georgia Lee," where the singer wonders why God didn't intervene when the song's central character lay dying in a field.

In fact, one senses spiritual concerns at several points on this new set. This idea is strengthened when considering one of the few recording projects this artist has taken on in recent years. In a brief but noteworthy cameo, Waits' distinctive voice is heard repeatedly and sincerely articulating the title line at the conclusion of Gavin Bryars' moving soundscape, "Jesus' Blood Never Failed Me Yet."

The final track on *Mule Variations* is "Come On Up To The House." But instead of stepping into a house like the one Lyle Lovett recently constructed as a tribute to his fellow Texas songwriters, Waits invites us in for a more individualized tour. In this house we find extensions of the paradoxes expressed on this set's opening number—simultaneous acceptance and rejection. This final portrait is not offered with a defeatist attitude, but with one that reflects realism and recognition. It's the same clear eye for life that this unique artist has always possessed when portraying the scenes that surround him, from *Small Change* to *Rain Dogs*. But here Waits seems to turn his gaze inward as well as outward. Because we repeatedly see ourselves on both sides of the world he presents, the music withstands close and repeated scrutiny.

Much is being made of two things tangentially related to this new release—one is the length of time that Waits has been away, the second is disappointment over the man's current refusal to tour. The first shows a refreshing attitude—an artist who puts out new songs only when he feels that he and they are ready. Most of *Mule Variations* can certainly stand beside Waits' best work, which does make the second point frustrating. Seeing him perform this material in a small theater could be magical, since his concerts have often been atmospheric extensions of his songs' moods. But like his rejection of a rigid release schedule, Waits simply refuses to go back on the road right now. Must be that mule in him.

CD Review

Tom Waits

Alice

Epitaph/Anti Records, 2002

I just finished listening to Tom Waits' new CD, *Alice*. Surprisingly enough, I found it reminiscent of his first LP, *Closing Time*. The format echoes that 1973 album right down to the brief instrumental track at the end of the set. The further into the *Alice* CD I delved, the more the tunes seemed uncharacteristically melodic compared with much of this performer's recent work. Like my first encounter with Waits' *Nighthawks at the Diner*, in 1975, and *Small Change* the following year, *Alice* has again surprised me by its stylistic changes, demonstrating that Tom Waits is comfortable creating a wide variety of music forms.

Bonus Track

At one point of a backstage conversation, Waits told me that the only way he could get an album out exactly how he wanted it would be to release his own bootleg. Thinking that he might be searching for source material, I told him that his record label had sent our radio station some promotional concert tapes of him. He became agitated at this, saying, "That's what I mean! Asylum has stuff of mine that I have no idea about." I thought it best not to tell him that I had made a cassette recording of his concert that night from my seat in the audience.

Concert Commentary

Jackson Browne

University of Iowa Fieldhouse
Iowa City, Iowa
April 20, 1978

DURING THE ERA when I was singing the praises of Tom Waits' early albums, many of my college friends were entranced by the Southern California sound, and especially Jackson Browne. I had bought his first album, *Saturate Before Using*, and liked it well enough. It even had the hit "Doctor My Eyes," which I thought was a superior tune (and still do). But this gentle first album did not inspire me to follow up on Browne's next records. I am told that I missed his best work, found on *For Everyman* and *Late for the Sky*.

I briefly got on board with *The Pretender*, his fourth LP, which his true fans say is OK but not great. Then came *Running on Empty*, the commercial nature of which had the true Jackson Browne fans worried, even if they would admit this only to each other. The album was touted as the first record to present live versions of all-new music by an artist. The claim was crap, of course, for Quicksilver Messenger Service had done this years earlier with *Happy Trails*, and I think the Grateful Dead could probably also lay claim to it. I thought *Running on Empty* was quite good, even if it couldn't live up to the worshipful accolades of the press. So when a Jackson Browne concert was announced for Iowa City's field house in 1978, I gladly accompanied my friends to the show.

Karla Bonoff opened the concert, or was it Kim Carnes? Carlene Carter? Karla Bonoff, I'm pretty sure. It was one of the sensitive Southern California singers, I'm certain of that. After an emotive piano set, Jackson Browne came out. This was the type of show where I thought I would know a few of the big songs, and that would be about it. On the trip down I was telling my friend Jeff how much I was looking forward to hearing "Here Come Those Tears Again" and especially "Doctor My Eyes." "No way will he play either of those!" Jeff scorned. "Those are way too commercial, and he's past all that stuff now." My friend was clearly embarrassed by those numbers. He insisted that "Tears" was just used as filler on Browne's *Pretender* album. Maybe he felt they were too melodic. Or too concise.

So I was doubly pleased when Browne played complete versions of both songs at various points of the concert. And they were very well done. He walked to the front of the stage, had somebody hit a chord on the piano, and launched into a fine reading of "Here Come Those Tears Again." He allowed multistring man David Lindley quite a lot of room on "Doctor My Eyes."

Overall, though, the concert was too much for me. After a while, all of the tunes started to sound remarkably similar. This was especially true of the slower numbers, and there were a lot of slow tunes. True, I did not know his work very well, but I was not alone in finding the sameness a bit dulling. I'm glad I was there, although it is certainly not one of the great concerts I have attended. The high points were high, and Browne could pull off the *Running on Empty* stuff really well, which makes sense as it was live material to start with.

As the years went on, I must admit to taking a certain amount of satisfaction in seeing my friends fall away from their Jackson Browne discipleship. "Lawyers in Love" seemed to be a turning point for them. One former acolyte even admitted to having left a concert by Browne before it was over. It's hard to remain a brilliant young prodigy, no doubt about it. I leave Jackson Browne as I found him: "Doctor My Eyes" is great!

Post Script

Honorable mention must be given to Jackson Browne for providing encouragement to a despondent Stevie Ray Vaughn after being booed at a Montreux, Switzerland, gig in 1982. Browne praised the Texas guitarist, indicating that Vaughn was killing it with his music. Jackson Browne went so far as to offer Stevie Ray a place to record once they got back to the States. We thank him for that!

Concert Commentary

The Doobie Brothers
Civic Center
St. Paul, Minnesota
August 13, 1982

I wrote this concert review for a weekly arts paper in St. Paul. This was back when we believed that if a band announced a "Farewell Tour," it meant that they were actually retiring from the road. We learned.

NO NEED TO MENTION the tunes here. They played them *all*, from multiplatinum on down. Front man Patrick Simmons often reminded the packed house that this was the last time around for the Doobie Brothers, and thanks a lot. Repeated as it was throughout the night, this speech could have seemed phony and rehearsed were the entire ensemble less into the music, or if Simmons didn't come off as actually wanting you to hear the band play its song book one last time.

There were no surprises; none were necessary. With the amount of first-rate tunes the Doobies carry with them, all that was expected were hot renditions of well-known tracks from the band's 11-year, multi-membered career. They delivered these numbers with high energy and intense concern for the music. If this final tour is a product of band member infighting, it was not evident Friday night. Every song was treated with professional, if not loving care by the eight piece ensemble.

Other than the early radio hits, the group concentrated on their last three albums, alternating the lead vocals of Simmons and songwriting mother lode Michael McDonald. Two new songs were presented in the second set—one each from McDonald and Simmons. The solo material clearly demonstrated the divergent directions that each performer will take after this tour. Simmons will rock on, and McDonald plans to keep crooning.

As the band began its final run of multiple hits to close the concert, only once did a tune not come up to full smoke. On "What a Fool Believes" someone's harmonies were off. This was no major disaster and was quickly forgotten as the band continued to sail through its strongest material. "Sail through" may not be quite accurate, as they were never in a hurry to get through a tune. If anything, they took a lot of McDonald's songs downtempo, where they worked even better than at the pace of the records.

The Doobie Brothers were always like a favorite bar band whose set list you could recite with ease. Although you know exactly what you're in for before the music begins, you are not disappointed because of the freshness of the performance. The Doobs realize the game is up, and that it would be useless to try to recapture past glories or to continue as a nostalgia band. In spite of, or perhaps because of the demise of this group, the crowd and the band both seemed glad to be able to crank it up one last time.

Bonus Track

Like Fleetwood Mac, The Doobie Brothers existed as more than one band. That is, the long history of the group can be divided into the Tom Johnston era, with early hits including "Long Train Runnin'" and "China Grove," and the later Michael McDonald dominated era, with "What a Fool Believes" and "Minute by Minute." Either way, The Doobie Brothers traveled a long road from once being the house band for the Hells Angels of northern California.

Hangin' with the Stars #2

Some 20 years after the 1982 St. Paul concert, I saw Michael McDonald participate in a songwriters' night at The Bluebird Cafe in Nashville. McDonald was seated at a small electric keyboard, with the other three musicians playing acoustic guitars. They would go around the circle, each taking his turn at performing a solo number. The host seemed a little intimidated both by McDonald's presence and by his inclusion of unusual chords. He jokingly threatened to summon the Music Police to enforce the law of using only A, C, and G chords while playing within Nashville's city limits. McDonald performed some new material, a few of his Doobie Brothers songs, and one or two solo hits, including

"I Keep Forgetting." At the intermission, I went up to McDonald and told him that I had seen him before, but in a somewhat larger room. He laughed at this and seemed like a very approachable guy.

Second Hand News
The Guess Who Play for "Friends of Theirs"!
KRNT Theater
Des Moines, Iowa
November 4, 1971

This is the first of three essays about fondly remembered concerts that I did not attend. A word of explanation is in order. I often listen to the weekly radio show Randy Bachman's Vinyl Tap *on the CBC. Some years back, Randy's former broadcast partner Denise McCann was talking about her Canadian copies of Beatles singles. Knowing that the Canadian Capitol Records and American Capitol Records labels differed on certain releases, I thought I would write and ask her for confirmation about one of the records she mentioned owning. I could have checked the computer, but I prefer to bother people.*

Denise got back to me immediately to say that she may have mis-spoken about what was on the B-side of her Beatles record, but she wasn't sure. Then I recalled how she has talked on the radio show about how her family had moved from Iowa to San Francisco just in time for the true culture explosions of the 1960s. So I can cut her slack for having some San Francisco brain damage from this era. We all have similar damage, of course, but few of us have anything as cool as living in San Francisco in the 60s to blame it on. But I digress. I told Denise that I had a story about Randy's former band, The Guess Who, which they might both enjoy. She said she would like to hear it. And that story is what follows.

I was a big fan of The Guess Who. I got excited about this Canadian group at the same time most U.S. listeners really became aware of them—when they were signed by RCA Records and had Top 10 radio success with the beautiful ballad, "These Eyes." The two-sided hit "Laughing" and "Undone" would soon follow; great stuff. "No Time" was the next single. I immediately bought this, as I had the other two

45s. I couldn't afford LPs yet as cash flow from my paperboy gig was still a couple of years off.

My friend Don had The Guess Who's *Canned Wheat* album, which included the hit "No Time." And yet it didn't. This was the first time I had ever heard a band change a song's album arrangement for its radio version. The single release of "No Time" was not just a trimming of the LP version to make it more time-friendly for radio. It was a completely different recording of the song. The album includes a darker version of "No Time," taken at a slower tempo than the more upbeat and brighter sound of the radio hit.

I was intrigued. And since Don already owned *Canned Wheat*, when I did have some money I bought the band's earlier album *Wheatfield Soul*, their second to be released under the retooled group's leadership of Randy Bachman and Burton Cummings. This album sold well because it contained the hit "These Eyes." In addition to its solid pop and rock songs, *Wheatfield Soul* included an odd concluding number called "Friends of Mine." This was a 10-minute, largely spoken-word opus which was quite strange, but simultaneously intriguing. I was drawn to it for a while and then moved on.

Time passed. The Guess Who enjoyed continued success with the Bachman/Cummings lineup. One night in 1970 I heard "Friends of Mine" on our local radio station for Top 40, KIOA 940. I distinctly remember thinking at the time: It's odd that the station would be playing "Friends of Mine," as it was not a hit, was far too long for their format, and was not even a new release. In retrospect, I am guessing that the DJ that night needed a break of some sort and so played a lengthy track. Listening to "Friends of Mine" that night, I still found the song odd, but odder still was hearing it on our local pop music station. Others from my junior high school (and across Des Moines) must also have found it strangely compelling.

Multitudinous requests poured in to KIOA for "Friends of Mine." The station seemed to play it grudgingly for a night or two after the initial airing. Then they realized what they had, and the station began to build their entire broadcast evening around this unusual album track. The announcers promoted it heavily throughout the evening before finally airing it around 9:30 P.M., just prior to an imposed 10 P.M. bedtime for many of us. After a while, KIOA became so territorial about the song that they included their station ID logo at a key juncture of the piece—just to remind those at home who were recording the song where they got it, I suppose. And to assure those listeners just tuning in that this was indeed the area's Top 40 station, just on a 10-minute detour.

At the height of the wildly improbable regional success of "Friends of Mine," it was announced (by KIOA) that The Guess Who would be playing a concert in Des Moines. The group was now riding high on their biggest hit, "American Woman." I was into the background elements of music by then enough to know what would be expected of the band, and that they would likely not be prepared for it. I considered writing a letter to The Guess Who, offering a warning of what was in store for them. They would be playing to a crowd who had bought tickets to hear "Friends of Mine," which I was quite certain was no longer in their active repertoire.

I did not attend the concert, although I continued to buy the group's new singles. The next day, I was curious to know how the concert was received. But as it was not reviewed in *The Des Moines Register* and I didn't know anybody from school who had been there, I had no clue as to what had transpired.

The following summer I attended a Methodist Church Camp in backwoods, Iowa. One of the boys there with whom I struck up a friendship had been at that Guess Who concert. He was from a farming community and had travelled some distance to get to Des Moines for the show. "How was it?" I asked. Without further provocation he snapped, "Well, they didn't play 'Friends of Mine.'" The radio signal of KIOA had obviously reached him. Because I wanted *him* to tell the tale and not sound like I knew all about it, I expressed surprise, sympathy, and indignation.

What happened that night? He remembered it well: The group came out and did a few songs—a couple of the hits. Maybe four songs into the set, a lone voice from the audience cried out: "Friends of Mine!" The band laughed a bit, he said. They obviously knew the song title, but were probably surprised at the request. An anomaly, they likely thought. But following their next tune a volley of shouts from different parts of the auditorium came forth: "Friends of Mine! Friends of Mine!" The band seemed a bit stunned and definitely irritated. What the heck?! Was this a put-on?

The Guess Who continued to play its usual set. "Friends of Mine" not being a number for which you can just wing it, they had to ignore the requests—for the rest of the evening—playing their numerous hits and undoubtedly pushing new material. I'm sure it was a good concert. I asked my camp friend if the group acknowledged the repeated requests in any way. He said that "a couple of times they sort of mumbled, 'Yeah. They're friends of ours, too'. But that was it."

So what should have been a normal night for the group in the wilds of the Great Midwest became a most unusual gig. It was also not a normal night for the frustrated audience, who had been subjected to a bait and switch tactic. Still, the band could not be faulted for disappointing the crowd. This could be an example of serendipity working *against* two groups, both band and audience. Perhaps.

In retrospect, I would like to know if The Guess Who were booked for the Des Moines show *after* "Friends of Mine" became a surprisingly big if short-lived radio staple in Des Moines. If so, the guy who did the booking would be guilty of deliberate misrepresentation. Maybe. Or perhaps the booker innocently thought that all bands could play every one of their songs at any time without rehearsal. Some bands, undoubtedly, can do this—but not many. Maybe the booker was a disreputable guy looking for a filled hall, or maybe the gig had been booked long before the radio outburst of "Friends of Mine." I don't know, and it really doesn't matter now.

I think this must have been Randy Bachman's last tour with the group. He would soon depart from the still successful Guess Who largely due to health issues and some religious differences stemming from his conversion to Mormonism—or so I have read. He would have a good run with the band Bachman-Turner Overdrive, and later with the previously mentioned Canadian radio show. From Bachman's recent on-air remarks, it is clear that if there had been any animosity with former band mate Burton Cummings it has been put to rest. Forgiveness—what a concept! Randy Bachman always speaks with warmth, respect, and humor about Cummings and about his own experiences with The Guess Who.

As I said in the introduction to this essay, I told Denise McCann that I had a Guess Who story that she might like; and there it is. Denise did get back to me after receiving this concert description. She said that Randy did not recall this gig, but that he had most likely departed from the group by this point. She said it in a nice way.

Bonus Track

In 2012, my wife and I saw Bachman & Turner play a show at the Treasure Island Casino in Red Wing, Minnesota. They apparently use this name instead of the original, more recognizable Bachman-Turner Overdrive moniker because of some legal issues with former band members and business colleagues. (Ownership of band names is a book unto itself.)

The concert was a crowd pleasing, no nonsense set of traditional, guitar-driven rock. A couple of guys behind us had been big fans during the original BTO heyday. As the concert ended, they both commented on how the show was "better than they had expected." And true, it was a solid and enjoyable performance. Bachman led the quintet through their hits, "You Ain't Seen Nothin' Yet" and "Takin' Care of Business," and some album tracks, such as "Stayed Awake All Night" and "Hold Back the Water." Interestingly, the one song of the night that immediately drove the crowd to its feet came from Bachman's old band, The Guess Who. This is understandable, for the opening chords of "American Woman" are as recognizable as anything in 1970s rock.

Commentary
Mixin' it Up!

The Guess Who's two different recordings of "No Time" caught my attention. But the first time I saw such changes overtly discussed was on the back of an album by Harry Nilsson. Selections from two of Nilsson's early RCA albums had been altered by the artist and then repackaged. The original LPs were *Pandemonium Shadow Show*, from 1967, and the following year's *Aerial Ballet*. Nilsson had a big hit with "Everybody's Talkin'," which came as a breath of fresh air to Top 40 radio in the fall of 1969. Nilsson's recording of this Fred Neil song was used by the producers of the movie *Midnight Cowboy*, who found it on the *Aerial Ballet* album.

By the time Nilsson hit the Top 10 with "Everybody's Talkin'," both *Aerial Ballet* and *Pandemonium Shadow Show* were already out of print. The radio hit ignited interest in Nilsson and created demand for more material by him. However, instead of merely reissuing the two records, RCA allowed Nilsson to take songs from each album (including "Everybody's Talkin'," of course) and release a new disk. Nilsson must have been unhappy with some aspects of the original albums, or at least he thought he could improve on them, for instead of simply selecting tracks from each for this new collection, he decided to alter the sound of the songs he chose by remixing them.

The remixed album was entitled *Aerial Pandemonium Ballet*; and if the combined title was not enough of a clue that this was not a completely new release, small photos of the two original album covers adorned the front of this unusual re-release. The front cover is admirable for its truth in advertising, but it was the back of the album jacket that I found fascinating. Beneath every song title was a description of how the original recording had been altered. Each song was "remixed," but deeper specifics included: "new background vocals," "edited out bridge," "slowed down track," and "dumped second voice." It was like Nilsson thought enough of the musical intelligence of his audience to confide in them. Or so I took it.

Suddenly, the world of recordings became a far more complicated place for me. Remixes would become common, but before computers it was still not the norm. The disco era saw extended versions of dance records. Usually, though, once a song was released it was left unaltered.

People debate whether Nilsson's remixes improved the material from the two original albums. Regardless of this rancor among critics, Nilsson's brief descriptions of his remixed songs opened a sonic door for me that remains open to this day. This album also led to questions such as: Just what is the accepted, official version of a recording? And why? Is it always the first release? Is it the album recording or Top 40 radio's better-known single version? Is it the artist's decision? What if the artist changes his mind after the record is released? The list gets long, and these points are best left for another time. Harry Nilsson had subsequent hits and became notorious for his time spent in Los Angeles with John Lennon. For me, his lasting legacy comes from his earliest work and his decision to openly alter (and describe!) this already released music.

Bonus Track

There were many variations to the world of remixes. In college, we agonized over what seemed then like ancient texts—The Beatles' first recordings. We would compare our American releases of specific songs with their British counterparts. These U.K. records sounded a bit different from the parallel U.S. versions, but they were definitely the same take of each song. The British records sounded somehow cleaner and more crisp. We chalked it up to the superior English pressing of the album. It was only much later that I learned how a small amount of reverb had been added to the American releases. As such, the British records had less echo and a drier sound, which accounted for the aural differences.

Bonus Track

Lennon and McCartney's "You Can't Do That" is on Nilsson's Pandemonium Shadow Show, *but is not included on the reconfigured* Aerial Pandemonium Ballet LP. *This is odd, since Nilsson's inventive arrangement of "You Can't Do That" is such a standout track. In fact, the arrangement garnered positive responses from The Beatles themselves. I guess Nilsson was happy with the way it was presented on* Pandemonium Shadow Show *and left it alone. All three of those albums are worth hearing.*

Remembrance

Richie Havens: Music That Opened Woodstock ...and My Mind
April 24, 2013

My parents would not let me go to the *Woodstock* movie when it first played theaters in the spring of 1970. I would later sneak out and see it, of course. Many times. But I initially had to be content with the expansive soundtrack LP, which I secretly used my paperboy money to buy.

I listened to that record as if my life depended on it. And maybe it did. Richie Havens pulsated his way through my speakers halfway through side one. He was simultaneously singing and shouting something about "Freedom." I felt hip because even in ninth grade I recognized lines he had included from a much older song—plaintive cries about feeling like a motherless child.

I studied that entire triple album very closely, so it was with great interest when I finally attended the movie some months after its release. There was Havens in a free flowing outfit with sweat pouring off him. His teeth were distinctively uneven and he sang as if he were in pain, while his foot pounded heavily on the stage.

But the visual which struck me most unexpectedly was not the man's physical appearance; it was the way he played guitar. Havens used his huge thumb to produce bar chords up and down the guitar neck. No picking—pure rhythm. I didn't know about open tunings at the time and was surprised at the sounds he could create using this method. Sort of an anti-fingerstyle approach. But it worked!

I started to search out Havens' albums, early records on Verve-Forecast and his more recent releases on the poetically named Stormy Forest label. After the mystique of Woodstock faded for many—or rather—once record sales declined for the performers who had been unexpectedly thrust into the spotlight, Havens' albums were staples of cutout bins. It wasn't difficult to fill out my collection.

I liked the early studio records well enough—*Mixed Bag* and *Something Else Again*. But it was the live material from the early 1970s that spoke to me most clearly. The first side of *Richie Havens On Stage* featured solo recordings of "From the Prison," "Younger Men Get Older," "Old Friends," and "God Bless the Child." This was a perfect set that ran deep and stayed in my psyche much longer than its 20-minute playing time.

Over the years, I followed Havens' career sporadically but never completely lost interest. When the two highly produced studio LPs on A&M Records were released in the mid-70s, they were initially ignored and later used as examples of the artist's alleged sell out. But I thought that this pair—especially *The End of the Beginning*—was remarkable for

Havens' interpretations of "We Can't Hide It Anymore," "Dreaming As One," James Taylor's "You Can Close Your Eyes," and Havens' original "I Was Educated by Myself." Wonderful.

After a second LP for A&M produced no radio hits, the label dropped him. Less than a decade after Woodstock, his time was spent between the road and, later, recording some voice work for television. There would be an occasional new release or compilation in the ensuing years, but the brief glory days were over.

One of the most recent recordings I have by Havens is among my favorites. In 1987, a tribute concert was held for Harry Chapin at Carnegie Hall. Varied performers from Pete Seeger to The Hooters to The Smothers Brothers took part. I bought the CD of this concert because it included Bruce Springsteen singing Chapin's song "Remember When the Music." I was a Bruce completest at the time (and admittedly remain so) and acquired the disk specifically for this Springsteen track.

In listening to the tribute, I enjoyed performances by Graham Nash, Pat Benatar, and Bruce. But it was Richie Havens' arrangement of Harry Chapin's minor hit "W-O-L-D" that I found absolutely devastating. The song is written as a first-person account from an aging disc jockey, speaking on the phone to his ex-wife. Things are not going well for him. Havens' stark, solo acoustic guitar performance conveys the character's sorrow. In contrast, Chapin's own studio recording is overproduced; the song's pathos is lost in the jangle.

Havens sings "W-O-L-D" in a way that Harry Chapin would have applauded, and it remains the definitive version of one of the best songs ever written about radio. This performance represents Havens' great talent as an interpreter of songs, as his arrangements convey new yet appropriate elements of an already familiar work.

The current flurry of obituaries carry information about Richie Havens being the first performer at Woodstock, which is certainly where I learned of him. They also praise his ability to interpret songs of Bob Dylan and of The Beatles. All true. But it's the deep catalog material where the real jewels lie. Search them out.

Remembrance

Joe Cocker
December 22, 2014

A friend of mine tells the story about seeing the *Woodstock* movie with a group of acquaintances. During the car ride home, they discussed the film's performances in detail. At one point, a young woman earnestly, if politically incorrectly, remarked, "And wasn't it nice that they let that 'retarded man' sing a song."

The "retarded man" was, of course, Joe Cocker. With a stage presence like no one before or since, Cocker was distinctive in many ways. From his odd, off balance stance to the occasional air guitar to the arguably spastic movements, Cocker was visually arresting. Or unsettling, depending on your view. But unusual stage presence aside—that voice! Somebody once called Joe Cocker the only true disciple of Ray Charles' singing style. High praise, and perhaps true; I can think of no other.

Woodstock made Cocker a star, but he had been working hard for quite a while before this single-gig breakthrough. He released a well-received debut album in April 1969 that included guest heavyweights Stevie Winwood and Jimmy Page. The album showed Cocker as a great interpreter of song. Like Richie Havens, Cocker had the talent to bring new and interesting readings to both Bob Dylan and The Beatles. A string of impressive summer dates in the U.S. to promote the album landed Cocker on the cover of *Rolling Stone* in September 1969. Even so, except for those who saw him in concert, he was still largely unknown. This would change the day the *Woodstock* documentary was released, in March 1970.

Like other performers who gained fame through their *Woodstock* involvement, Cocker was initially pigeonholed into what the public allowed him to play. Fellow festival performer Alvin Lee and his band Ten Years After could never escape their new audience's single-minded memory of the movie's scorching footage of "I'm Going Home," even though the group considered itself more of a blues band than hard rockers.

Joe Cocker was able to eclipse his Woodstock reputation, but sometimes for the wrong reasons. His "Mad Dogs and Englishmen" tour in 1970 was a triumph of impromptu organization and uninhibited performing, thanks largely to musical director Leon Russell. The subsequent live album was a huge success and seemed to prove that the Woodstock Nation had not disbanded. However, Cocker would soon balance these remarkable performances with unsteady concerts. He also accrued a scrapbook worth of bad press for his offstage activities.

After a poorly received 1972 U.S tour, most fans lost interest. Substance abuse hounded Cocker, and various unsuccessful comeback attempts became too uncomfortable for fans to watch. Suddenly, John Belushi's spot-on imitation of Cocker's performance eccentricities no longer seemed all that funny.

Through it all, Cocker's studio work showed that he remained a superb interpreter of songs. What other rocker had the guts to sing "Bye Bye Blackbird" on a debut album, turning it into a deep soul number? Songs by Randy Newman, Jimmy Webb, Harry Nilsson, Alan Toussaint…even Prince. He could sing them all and sing them well, making each into a distinct Joe Cocker performance. And this was true even if you already knew the song, as with "A Little Help from My Friends."

There were islands of optimism and renewal for Cocker. In 1974 he released the album *I Can Stand a Little Rain*, which featured some remarkable ballads. It included his biggest hit to that time, the fragile "You Are So Beautiful." Almost eight years later, "Up Where We Belong" would be his last Top 10 hit. The song was a duet with Jennifer Warnes and seemed a perfect showcase for Cocker, vocally and stylistically. In the 32 years since this #1 song, Cocker again retreated to the shadows, occasionally releasing a fine collection of his unmistakable interpretations, as with the *Night Calls* CD from 1992. Even so, Cocker's story is weighted down with a sadness that comes from wondering what could have been.

After a career of stellar peaks and dark valleys, Joe Cocker returned an optimist. As he left the stage after his Woodstock 25 performance in 1994, Cocker yelled to the crowd, "See you at the 50th!" He can't make that gig, but he won't be forgotten.

Concert Commentary

Joan Baez
Northrop Auditorium
Minneapolis, Minnesota
February 21, 1982

BEWARE: THE LADY HAS A CAUSE. Before you buy a ticket to a Joan Baez concert you should know that there will be a lengthy spot somewhere in her set, an intermission of sorts, where the music will cease and the diatribes begin. The problem with Baez's Northrop concert was that her lecturing dominated the evening.

Before the house lights dimmed, a friend asked if I knew what Baez's latest fight was about. I said no, but I was sure Joan would let me know. While Baez spoke about injustices around the world, I remained uncertain as to what was making her angry enough to preach instead of play. She hit so many different topics with such regularity that it turned into a medley of *Life Is Heck*. From El Salvador to Reagan to Poland to whales to nukes to discrimination to pollution to communism to…well, name your favorite gripe and if Baez didn't give it three minutes of monologue, she at least had a verse dedicated to it in one of her new songs.

Early in the concert, Baez stated that she was there to have you listen to a lot of her new material; then she would play a little of what you came to hear. While honesty is to her credit, these introductory remarks proved all too accurate. The new songs were melodious, but the lyrics were probably inferior to the writings of many freshman English students in attendance. Throughout most of her recently written material Baez was without focus, drifting through several unrelated topics, or causes, per song.

Baez must be admired for attempting to perform tunes she is not positive she can completely remember. "Sweet Sir Galahad" of 14 years ago was requested and performed. Baez played a beautiful rendition of this piece after getting through some opening verse stumbling blocks, where she asked the crowd for assistance. After performing one song in Spanish, she agreed to sing another when several people requested it. The set included John Prine's "Hello in There," even though Baez afterwards said that the song's depiction of old people was insultingly inaccurate.

Complaints concerning flash bulbs and even the volume of her own instrument were scattered between tunes throughout the night. (She thought the guitar too loud.) When calls for Bob Dylan material went up, Baez declared the obvious—that his writing was without equal among her peers. She then played "A Hard Rain's A-Gonna Fall." This was the Baez concert we came for. The proper atmosphere was finally setting in when the concert came to an abrupt conclusion. The mood that took so long to establish was broken by a quick halt and a one-tune encore. Baez could still evoke the old magic at the drop of a song, but didn't seem very interested in doing so.

Hangin' with the Stars #3

It was during this Joan Baez concert that she and I had our most intimate moment, and I'm sure we both remember it fondly. I was always taken with her *In Concert, part 2* album from the early 1960s. This was definitely a folk music recording, featuring just Baez and her guitar. The program included "Jackaroe," a Spanish number, "'Nu bello cardillo," two Bob Dylan songs, plus the anthems "We Shall Overcome" and "The Battle Hymn of the Republic." A tragic and haunting lament called "Three Fishers" was my favorite selection on the record. At a lull in the 1982 Minneapolis concert, I shouted this title. Baez stopped tuning for a moment, looked up and said, "Wow, you've got a good memory." She did not sing the song.

At the risk of sounding like a concert heckler, I admit to a second call later in the program. At the conclusion of her unintentionally truncated rendition of "A Hard Rain's A-Gonna Fall," I shouted, "What did you hear?!" Miss Baez had neglected to include this verse in her performance of the song that night.

While Baez herself did not respond, I soon received a rebuttal from an unexpected source. I was discussing Baez's concert the next day with some people at the station where I worked—Minnesota Public Radio in St. Paul. I mentioned that Baez had dropped a verse from "A Hard Rain's A-Gonna Fall." Although I had not realized that he was uncharacteristically present in the radio station's break room with us, Garrison Keillor came forward to gently lecture me. "You have to remember, Tom, that people get nervous

> on stage, under all those lights. Sometimes they forget things." And with that, he drifted away.
>
> Nervous? Maybe. But Joan Baez struck me as being far too cavalier for this ailment.

Concert Commentary

James Taylor
BMO Harris Bradley Center
Milwaukee, Wisconsin
November 4, 2014

"THIS TUNE BEGINS with a walk down a dirt road and ends with me driving a tank." James Taylor made this remark about his song "Country Roads," but the comment could have applied to his entire Milwaukee concert. The unmistakable sound of Taylor's beautiful ballads was a constant throughout the evening, but so were some hard driving moments that added momentum to a distinctive night of music.

The first set featured a new song about "Today" and recognizable album tracks including "Lo and Behold" and "Copperline." Engaging from the start, Taylor opened with "Something in the Way She Moves," which was his 1968 audition piece for Paul McCartney and George Harrison. "Paul liked it enough to sign me to Apple Records," Taylor remembered, "and George liked it enough to go home and write it himself." Many have pointed to this bit of plagiarism by Harrison, but the original songwriter now only laughs about it.

Pleasant as these first songs were, it wasn't until the band hit a groove on Buddy Holly's "Everyday" that the evening really took off. The 10-piece ensemble then locked in on "Sweet Baby James," "Carolina on my Mind," and the first set's closer "Shower the People." Interspersed between the music was Taylor's narrative about the background of each selection. A seasoned stage professional, Taylor knew to keep the stories short and upbeat; his audience had come for the songs.

James Taylor is on a lengthy tour, but his voice is as clear and recognizable as if you were playing one of his early albums. He seemed genuinely pleased to be in Milwaukee, even taking time to set down his guitar and don a Brewers jersey. "They'll never forgive me at Fenway Park for this," he joked. The occasional declaration of love came from individual audience members. Taylor smoothly dealt with each impassioned pronouncement, humorously deflecting the amorous calls with self-deprecating quips.

When a flurry of specific song requests was shouted simultaneously, Taylor smiled and said, "It's odd. I feel like I am in some sort of a bidding war." After more shouts, he concluded: "I don't mind it, but it's odd." Not many of these requests went unfulfilled during the 2½ hour concert. As the second set progressed, "Handy Man," "Stretch of the Highway" and "Only One" were performed, as was the blues exercise "Steamroller," with Taylor strapping on an electric guitar and giving his band some room to solo.

The backing group featured Lou Marini on reeds and Steve Gadd on drums. The names may not be familiar, but you know their work. For Gadd, think of the opening drum pattern on Paul Simon's "50 Ways to Leave Your Lover" and the drum breaks on Steely Dan's song "Aja." For Marini, get out your live *Blues Brothers* album (or watch the movie again). Michael Landau played electric guitar in Taylor's backing ensemble; Jimmy Johnson served as the group's Music Director and played electric bass. Fiddler Andrea Zonn gave several tunes a folky and occasionally Celtic feel, while Walt Fowler's trumpet brought some brass to the mix and Luis Conte's percussion added texture.

Various keyboards were played by Larry Goldings, and an excellent vocal trio included Arnold McCuller, Kate Markowitz, and Zonn. This headliner can afford to take a quality band with him on the road, and the musicians served their leader well. Each song was perfectly orchestrated and executed. And fortunately, even in a structure designed for basketball, the sound of this concert was excellent; every musician could be heard.

James Taylor is now 66 years old. During his time in the music industry he has experienced unbelievable highs and unenviable lows. His songs were praised by The Beatles! Later, his work was briefly dismissed by both the rock press and a once adoring public. He has been inducted into the Rock and Roll Hall of Fame, appeared on the cover of *Time* magazine, and been institutionalized for mental health issues. He was every young woman's fantasy date, and a heroin addict.

But fans who attend the current tour care little about dark corners in this performer's past or for his bright Beatle accolades. They care about James Taylor, who they see as one of their own—a talented survivor of a turbulent era. This was profoundly evident when the songwriter unveiled his best-known composition. With no spoken introduction, he played an introspective guitar line from which the opening notes of "Fire and Rain" slowly emerged. After singing this song at virtually each of his concerts for the past 40 years, it seems remarkable that Taylor is able to keep it fresh. This great song evidently still speaks to its writer as well as to his audience.

As expected, the second set finished strong, with "Up on the Roof," "Mexico" and "Your Smiling Face." Some gems were saved for the encore which, interestingly, consisted entirely of songs not penned by Taylor. These included the Irish ballad "Wild Mountain Thyme," Marvin Gaye's "How Sweet It Is to Be Loved by You," and Carole King's "You've Got a Friend." But if James Taylor did not write these numbers, he certainly made them his own—just as he did with the Milwaukee audience last Tuesday night.

Post Script

This concert has sort of an odd postscript. Two nights later, during a show in Moline, Illinois, Taylor told his audience that they were superior to Milwaukee's crowd, who seemed to be "carved out of wood." Somebody caught this remark on a cell phone and posted it. Taylor apologized to Milwaukee, explaining that it was a "cheap shot," meant to "fire up" the Moline audience. Even caught in an embarrassing situation, the man has class.

Hangin' with the Stars #4

Carole King
Hilton Coliseum
Ames, Iowa
February 4, 1976

Tapestry was one of the most successful albums of the early 1970s. Even now, it holds remarkable statistics for sales and for its number of weeks on the *Billboard* album chart. More than this, the songs from this album still resonate.

Carole King did not often tour, so when the announcement came that she would be in Ames, Iowa, several of us scrambled for tickets. It was a good show, with a surprisingly guitar-heavy lineup and King at a grand piano. During the set she would occasionally talk about the environment and how much she was enjoying the Midwest (even in winter), but she mainly she stuck to the music.

King played almost all of *Tapestry*, of course. But I found one of the set's highlights to be the song "Music," a waltz on which she let her band trade solos. "Jazzman" was also good, but I missed David Sanborn's alto saxophone.

King was not always the most patient of performers. During the encore, as people were yelling final requests, she icily said, "Either you're going to shout or I'm going to sing; we won't have both." She then played "Natural Woman," so all was well.

Midway through this concert, between songs, King paused to take a brief drink of water. I took this opportunity to cup my hands and shout "Pleasant Valley Sunday" in clearly articulated tones. There was a slight ripple of laughter and comments by members of the audience. Most of them probably did not know that Carole King penned this song with her former husband Gerry Goffin. The Monkees had the big hit with it, of course, but she was the one who wrote it.

Carole King slowly put down her drink, leaned into the microphone, and said: "That song doesn't exist." As she was now a serious artist, King obviously did not want to be associated with either "Pleasant Valley Sunday" or The Monkees. Days of pounding out pop songs in New York City's Brill Building were far behind her. I wonder if her reaction would have been the same had I shouted "The Locomotion," "I'm Into Something Good" or "Porpoise Song."

Can't know these things for sure, but that night she was way too cool for "Pleasant Valley Sunday." That's her prerogative, of course; but I'll bet she still cashed the song's royalty checks.

Concert Commentary

Arlo Guthrie

Pitman Theater, Alverno College
Milwaukee, Wisconsin
April 21, 2006

ARLO GUTHRIE HAS BEEN forced to live his life in shadows. His famous father Woody Guthrie has been a touchstone for politicized folk music since the 1940s. Often best known for being the son of the man who wrote "This Land Is Your Land," Arlo has also lived in the intimidating shadow of the disease that killed his father, a hereditary neurological disorder with symptoms similar to Lou Gehrig's Disease.

In 1967 Arlo released his first album to enthusiasm that has been unmatched in his career. The record was called *Alice's Restaurant*, and it contained a lengthy narrative describing Guthrie's arrest for littering and its unexpected aftermath. The 18-minute work was not quite a talking blues and not quite a folk song. It made Arlo's name famous but proved to be a millstone on the order of a band with one huge hit. After a few years of fame that often centered on this song, Guthrie refused to play "Alice's Restaurant." To the dismay of some single-minded audience members, his moratorium on the piece lasted for decades.

Time changes all things, and Arlo Guthrie now embraces the once shunned epic, at least to a point. He has embarked on a 40th anniversary tour of "Alice's Restaurant," which he brought to Alverno College's Pitman Theater last Friday night. And while he did perform the song, his almost academic rendering of "Alice" was not the high point of his two lengthy sets. Instead, Guthrie offered songs of white-faced cattle and of various dreams, both darkly cryptic and patriotically inspirational. He performed a stirring rendition of "St. James Infirmary" as a tribute to New Orleans, and credited Bob Dylan's influence by playing "Mr. Tambourine Man." Between the songs, Guthrie was relaxed and engaging as he offered several warm accounts of his father, inviting the audience to see Woody Guthrie as a man rather than an icon.

The backing group included son Abe Guthrie on effectively subtle keyboards, and utility man Gordon Titcomb on steel guitar, mandolin, guitar, and banjo. Arlo himself played some fine lead lines on both

12- and 6-string guitars. He played piano for much of the second set, which included "City of New Orleans."

Credit must be given to a performer who can navigate the legacy of a famous father and the lingering shadow of his "Alice" fame. There is little the man can do about these parts of his past except to move beyond them. Last Friday, Guthrie emerged from all shadows, personal and professional, by addressing them directly with humor and style. It was clear that he is comfortable with his past and is willing to share its winding back roads with an appreciative audience.

Concert Commentary

Steve Goodman
University of Northern Iowa
UNI-Dome
Cedar Falls, Iowa
April 27, 1978

BECAUSE OF MY JOB with the University of Northern Iowa campus radio station in the mid-1970s, I would sometimes be able to get into concerts early. This was true when our school hosted a performance by Steve Martin. I went for the sound check, and while Martin was not present, opening act Steve Goodman was. Goodman played partial verses of several songs so the sound techies could get the audio levels set; he also walked around the stage for the benefit of the lighting crew.

After some tuning and consultations with roadies, Goodman launched into a complete, stellar version of "Your Cheatin' Heart." I was mesmerized. I had become a huge Hank Williams disciple in the preceding years, but this intense and heartfelt performance seemed like a personal validation of my interest.

I returned to my apartment that afternoon and immediately learned the song on my acoustic guitar, which was far more accustomed to Bob Dylan numbers. I had always loved Hank's version of the song, of course, but Goodman's sound check performance was revelatory, as I heard new things in the song. It was like listening to Chet Atkins' solo guitar arrangement of Williams' "I Can't Help It if I'm Still in Love with

You." There are different elements at play, with new light shed onto an already well-known canvas.

Based on the polished rendition he offered at the sound check, I was convinced that "Your Cheatin' Heart" would be part of Goodman's performance that night. But no; his brief set included no Hank Williams numbers. Goodman played the song that afternoon because he loved it and wanted to hear it. Me too.

Book Review

Steve Goodman: Facing the Music
By Clay Eals
ECW Press, 2007

Steve Goodman's legacy is sometimes thought to be based on one song, "The City of New Orleans." Clay Eals provides a welcome correction to this view. His biography spotlights a host of achievements in this Chicago native's life. It is a work based on extensive research; Eals conducted more than a thousand interviews with Goodman's friends and associates, ranging from Steve Martin to Hillary Clinton. The presentation of this research is complemented by an 18-track tribute CD and hundreds of photographs, including a title page shot taken at Goodman's 1976 Summerfest appearance in Milwaukee, Wisconsin. Goodman's fatal battle with leukemia is an undeniable part of the story, but Eals never loses sight of the reason he undertook this massive and successful project: to celebrate Goodman's music.

CD Review and Commentary

Crosby, Stills, Nash & Young
CSNY 1974
3 CDs / 1 DVD
Rhino Records, 2014

Crosby, Stills, Nash & Young were huge during my high school years. I was never able to attend a concert by this short-lived super group, but their specter loomed large for quite a while, even after the quartet split up. Here is an item related to this band, one that demonstrates why I largely write for myself instead of for on-demand publication.

I was hired to write a review of this 2014 release. The paper gave me 50 words to assess the four-disk set, one that came with a lot of backstory. 50 words—this is what I came up with:

"From Eagles to Fleet Foxes, the harmonies of CSNY have served as a template. What the band later called their Doom Tour of 1974 is documented here, thanks to the painstaking archival efforts of Graham Nash. Their acoustic set is the highlight, showing why these guys were so remarkably influential."

I felt that the paper had allowed me to write not a review, but rather a brief product teaser.

Hangin' with the Stars #5

It was 2005, and we were at Milwaukee's Summerfest to see David Crosby lead his own band. I had run to the bathroom before the show. On the way back to join my friends, I saw Crosby heading toward the stage. He was a little ways off, walking away from where I stood, so I shouted distinctively: "Hey David! How about singing 'Mind Gardens' tonight?" As if he were awaiting a cue, his arm immediately went up with middle finger extended. Crosby didn't turn; he didn't break stride. But his quick acknowledgement amused me greatly.

"Mind Gardens" is an odd tune that Crosby wrote when he was still a member of The Byrds. It clutters the second side of their 1967 album *Younger Than Yesterday*. From Crosby's reaction, I guessed he was not all that fond of it any longer. I didn't really want to hear the song; I just wanted to needle him.

His set opened with a hot version of "Wooden Ships," followed by a couple of tunes from his solo albums that I didn't know. Then my friend bloodied some guy's face for throwing beer on him, and we were escorted off the grounds by security. Just a normal evening at Summerfest. So I don't know what other tunes Crosby played that night, but I'm pretty sure "Mind Gardens" wasn't one of them.

Second Hand News
Neil Young
Veterans Auditorium
Des Moines, Iowa
February 27, 1973

Another fond remembrance of a concert that I did not attend.

Neil Young played Des Moines early in 1973 in support of his *Harvest* LP. This was a tour during which he seemed intent on alienating any newfound fans. It was also on this tour that the elusive *Comes a Time* LP was recorded. Many probably went to the concert expecting an evening of songs like "Heart of Gold." And the Des Moines show did open with a couple of acoustic numbers in this vein. Young then complained that the audience was too rowdy for his acoustic music, so he brought out the band. Neil closed the set with a cluster of his better-known numbers, including "Heart of Gold," but by that time the audience was no longer with him. I know of no concert attendee who praised that evening's performance.

I didn't see Neil that night in Des Moines, but I did see him at a Farm Aid concert in Milwaukee in 2010. As I had anticipated, the set was short on music and long on speeches about agriculture and politics. Still, it was good to finally hear him play a couple of tunes live.

CD Review

Neil Young & The International Harvesters
A Treasure
Reprise Records / Neil Young Archive Series #9
Recorded in concert, 1984 & 1985. Released 2011

This release is a bit difficult to assess because it's hard to separate the music from the events surrounding this artist's career in the mid-1980s. I mean, how many performers get sued by their own record company for not sounding enough like themselves? Few. But this is what Geffen Records did to Neil Young after he submitted a string of albums which were not in line with the expectations of both his label and his audience.

Evidence for the prosecution includes *Trans*, from 1982, an odd experiment in vocoders and electronics. This was followed in 1983 by *Everybody's Rockin'*, credited to The Shocking Pinks, on which Neil offers a short Rockabilly rave-up. These uncharacteristic styles incensed his new label because the records sold so poorly and confused his audience. Young apparently tried to appease Geffen in 1985 with his appropriately titled *Old Ways* album, but then immediately toured with a country band he christened The International Harvesters.

Young took this dip into country music seriously, hiring crack players and appearing on *Nashville Now with Ralph Emory*, who wasn't quite sure what to make of his rock star guest. In fact, the first track on this live CD comes from the *Nashville Now* cable show. Maybe Emory would have been less surprised if he had been aware of Neil's brilliant and respectful interpretation of Don Gibson's "Oh Lonesome Me" a full 15 years earlier. Still, if Ralph Emory was a dumbstruck observer, many of Neil's actual followers had gotten off the fan boat years before. Young followed the huge success of *Harvest* in 1972 with a tour of largely unrecognizable selections and dense electric sound, as documented on the live *Time Fades Away* LP. Neil's new fans also faded away when his subsequent studio albums bore little resemblance to *Harvest*.

So: battles with Geffen Records and the artist's indifference to frustrated fans aside—how is the music on *A Treasure*? It's good, and this is a most welcome set. Nearly half of the songs are previously unreleased in any form. And of the rest, only the true devotee attending these concerts would have recognized many of the tunes. *A Treasure* could be called a historical document, but that doesn't mean it's inferior. The band is tight and Young keeps the songs concise. No 16-minute guitar workouts here.

Young released his car-themed *Fork in the Road* CD in 2009, but it is clear that his mind has wrestled with the subject of efficient automobiles since at least the early 1980s. On "Motor City," first heard on *Reactor* (1981), Neil is angry over North America's automotive situation. Interestingly, the take included here comes from a 1984 Los Angeles show. I will leave it to the Neil obsessives to research whether the song was in his set list throughout the International Harvesters' tour or whether it was included on this night as a specific shot at the Los Angeles car culture.

If "Motor City" criticizes America's addiction to cars, "Southern

Pacific" offers an homage to railroads. "Amber Jean" contains more traditional love song elements, including references to the moon and to the girl's pretty eyes. "Let Your Fingers Do the Walking" is a humorous western lament about a woman who formerly gave "good phone" to the singer. But no more.

"Nothing Is Perfect" might first appear to be a criticism of God's plan for mankind, but it is ultimately a song of gratitude. Neil here sings of comparisons, urging the listener to look closely at the shadows of life. By viewing the dark side one will see that there is so much to be thankful for, including bountiful food and love, and a safe place to live. This unexpected song of appreciation perhaps speaks to the contented nature of the singer. Young praises an unnamed honest woman, who assists Neil on his journey as he strives to remain positive and be a useful member of society. Yet in the midst of this portrait of bliss comes one verse about soldiers burying their dead and firing guns indiscriminately. Another verse describes airport hostages and an abused workforce. A very odd lyrical juxtaposition, this, but Young makes his point: Doesn't an awareness of the bad make the good seem all the better?

One of the few nods to the past is among the highlights of the set. "Flying on the Ground Is Wrong" was first recorded in 1966 when Neil was a member of Buffalo Springfield. This is a fine arrangement of a number that shows the high quality of Young's songwriting abilities, even at the beginning of his career.

Maybe in an effort to stress the country aspect of the set, Neil uses "Are You Ready for the Country?" and "Get Back to the Country" as concert bookends to this CD. But without the brand of International Harvesters on the label, I doubt that all of these songs would be termed Country Music. Notwithstanding the presence of fiddle and steel guitar, some of these tracks would easily fit into live shows from Young's other eras. This is never more true than with one of the new offerings, "Grey Riders," which features thick electric guitars that would be at home on Young's fine *Le Noise* release from last year. Interestingly, it is "Grey Riders"—uncharacteristic of the collection—that has been released to radio as this set's first single.

I'm glad to have these beautifully recorded concert tapes released. Unknown material and surprising trunk songs placed within a well-paced live overview. In its own way, this CD *is* "a treasure," as it documents an unexpected and brief era of Young's performance history in a most engaging manner. When do we get a similar live document for Neil's short-lived Shocking Pinks endeavor?

One Question with Neil Young!

If I had the opportunity to ask one question of a specific individual, what would I ask? Here is the first entry.

Tom Wilmeth:—Hello Mr. Young! You were slow to release some of your mid-1970s albums onto CD. It is true that some of these albums were…uneven affairs, but this rarely stops an artist from rereleasing his own back catalog, thereby cashing in on the money that a new format guarantees. Now that all of your studio records—including the long delayed *American Stars 'n Bars* and *On the Beach*—are out there on nonbootleg, official CD releases, you still hold back the 1973 live album *Time Fades Away*, which *Uncut Magazine* just this month rated as the #1 oddity for major LP releases not currently available in any format. Man, you even trumped The Beatles, whose unavailable *Live at The Hollywood Bowl* LP is at #3 on the list! Concerning technology, you were way ahead of the curve with *Time Fades Away*, and evidently proud of it. On the record label itself you mention how the live recording is digitally mixed to 2-track. The problem with this early digital technology is its inherent murky sound and the fact that the master recording cannot be remixed, so the audio really can't be enhanced. You have been quoted as saying that *Time Fades Away* is your "worst album." And while that is really saying something, many would disagree. The *American Music Guide* calls it "the most gripping music of Young's career." So my question concerning *Time Fades Away*: do you refuse to re-release it because you dislike the songs, your performance of the songs, or the unchangeable audio mix?

Neil Young:—I get "cutting edge" technology credit for going straight to 2-track digital in 1973, but am reviled for my unprecedented electronic work on my 1982 *Trans* album.

TW:—Life is unfair, I know. Can you answer the question about *Time Fades Away*?

NY:—I'm not sure that the soundtrack to my movie *Journey Through the Past* is available on CD.

TW:—Good point; I'll look into it. Most people wouldn't admit to owning that one, though.

NY:—The tracks on *Time Fades Away* were recorded during a tour that was not a good experience for me. I'd rather just bury the whole project.

TW:—By holding it back, you call more attention to it and make it more desirable, regardless of its quality. Also, that wasn't a live hits collection; most of those songs are unique to that release.

NY:—Bob Dylan recently went out of his way to visit the house in Canada where I grew up. So bite me.

TW:—You win. But your *Archives* box set takes self-importance to a new level of grandiosity.

NY:—Hey. Get the Blu-ray! It's cleaner.

TW:—You buying?

Important *Nota Bene*: The above exchange is complete and total fiction.

Second Hand News
Buffalo Springfield
KRNT Theater
Des Moines, Iowa
May 6, 1967

Crosby, Stills, Nash & Young never came to Des Moines, but Buffalo Springfield had been in town in May 1967, playing the old KRNT Theater. I was not there. At 11 years old and concluding the sixth grade, I had not yet become aware of group.

But even if my friends and I had known about the band being in town, we might have missed them. The name Buffalo Springfield did not appear anywhere in the advertisements. The concert was billed as a "California Sound" package show, headlined by The Turtles. Also appearing unbilled was The Association. Probably a pretty good night! I later spoke with someone who attended. He told me that at one point of Buffalo Springfield's set, Neil Young announced: "We don't usually play Top 40 songs; but in this case…" And with that, the opening note of "For What It's Worth" rang through the hall. Loud.

I lamented not being there until I realized that this was a multi-band event, meaning that each group likely had about 25 minutes of performance time. But that's 25 minutes more of Buffalo Springfield than what I had seen. I still lament it.

Years later, stories surfaced about wild hotel parties associated with this Iowa stop. I can't attest to the parties, but I do know that, for one reason or another, the band became forgetful enough to leave a bass guitar at the concert hall. A classmate of mine was the daughter of the booker for the KRNT Theater. One day she mentioned that Buffalo Springfield had left one of their instruments at the venue. We didn't believe her, so she invited us to her father's office at the theater. He brought out a weathered guitar case and there it was—a road weary Fender bass, probably belonging to Bruce Palmer. We offered to buy it, but he smiled and pleasantly declined. "They might come back for it, you know."

CD Review and Concert Commentary

The Who
Live at Leeds
Deluxe, 2 CD edition
January 2002

I wrote this pithy little review in early 2002. Little did I know that my sarcasm concerning the inclusion of sound checks was about to be-come commonplace; they would soon be released as enticing additions to Expanded Editions of CDs. Elvis Costello was among the first to in-clude alluring, previously unreleased songs recorded at sound checks as incentives to fans to consider buying anew the albums that they already owned. Phish has made a series of entire CDs culled from their preconcert warmup sets. Fans want them; they sell. Here is the review:

Rejoice! For now we are able to purchase a CD copy of The Who's *Live at Leeds* for the third time (at least). The latest expanded version includes the complete performance of *Tommy* from that fabled night in early 1970. It's tempting, to be sure, but I myself will hold out for the next upgrade release of the *Leeds* CD, which is sure to also include the sound check.

Post Script

I saw The Who three times, and I enjoyed each concert. They played the hits and sections of their rock operas. Yet both shows seemed disjointed, as if they could never really find the groove. Admittedly, after the mystique of Woodstock and the dashed hope that they might perform all of *Tommy*, each show left me a bit disappointed.

The final time I saw The Who was in St. Paul, during what is now laughingly remembered as their "Farewell Tour" of the U.S. This was 1982. At the end of the concert, someone threw a watch onto the stage. Townshend appeared genuinely amazed. A watch. A retirement watch? Seemed appropriate. Some fans now think that those boys should have heeded the fan's gesture and hung it up after that tour.

Bonus Track

In January of 1966, on the British television program A Whole Scene Going, *Pete Townshend was asked to evaluate the musical quality of The Beatles. Initially acknowledging this as "a tough question," he then proclaimed: "When you hear the backing tracks of The Beatles without their voices, they're flippin' lousy." If you say so, Pete. Maybe we are thinking of two different groups named The Beatles.*

Concert Commentary

The Rolling Stones
with The Stray Cats
St. Paul Civic Center
St. Paul, Minnesota
November 21, 1981

THE ROLLING STONES are such an important band that it is easy to forget about them. Sounds crazy, but it's true. Their legacy fills books. Box sets are required to hold their hits. And yet, because they have been around for so long, they are often taken for granted.

I have seen The Rolling Stones only once. When I was preparing for this November 1981 concert, I was steeling myself for an aged, faded band. True, *Some Girls* had been a real return to form a couple of years before, but how powerful could they still rock in concert? Mightily, as it turned out. "When the Whip Comes Down" had a forceful and rolling feel to it, and "You Can't Always Get What You Want" came as a welcome surprise. They went on way too long on a couple of cover tunes—"Just My Imagination" was one—while Mick rode the cherry picker into the crowd.

This was the first concert I had ever seen with no visible amps on stage—a completely wireless situation, with NO audio dropouts. It was a white stage, and the lighting crew took full advantage of this blank pallet. I recall the band performing one unremarkable tune just to let the light crew show off—that is, it seemed to me that the band played a backing role to what lights were doing. And rightly so; very impressive. Most everybody at the radio station where I worked thought themselves too hip to catch this show, but they sure wanted a full report the next day on the technical aspects of the stage set up. I gladly complied.

I know the concert took place on a Saturday night because I went straight from working Garrison Keillor's *Prairie Home Companion* broadcast to my seat in the St. Paul Civic Center. I walked! It was great. I remember Keillor closing that show with an admonition to his theater audience to be careful as they left the World Theater since the downtown area would be alive with Stones fans.

Keillor needn't have worried. The element of danger was long gone from Stones' concerts by this point. Some still spoke of the violence that accompanied the 1969 and the '72 tours, but by 1981 there was nothing threatening about the band or its audience. This was a professionally staged show for an excited but well behaved crowd. And that was fine with me; I wasn't looking for an Altamont experience. Even Mick Jagger has acknowledged that the band became more of a good time rock and roll group as the 1970s wore on. But the most important thing—they were still great!

The opening act for the Stones that night was a new, unknown trio called The Stray Cats. They would become quite big for a while playing retro rockabilly. Their ascent to national fame began as openers on this tour. The Cats were a good time; the bass player stood on his upright bass. The group members were invested in the whole nine yards of showmanship, including Brian Setzer playing guitar behind his back. Lots of fun. But after about six tunes, it all started sounding pretty similar. I would hold to that assessment throughout the Cats' brief run. Still, it was cool to see these guys on their way up.

As for The Rolling Stones: were they still "The Greatest Rock & Roll Band in the World," as they had once been touted? Well hell, maybe they are. Or maybe they were that night in 1981. "Who wants to be a 40-year-old Rolling Stone?" Mick Jagger famously asked interviewer Tom Donahue in early 1971. He got over that sentiment, I guess. And I'm glad he did.

Bonus Track

I was working at a radio station in St. Paul when The Rolling Stones played there in 1981. Several people seriously considered notifying the police when learning of an unpopular colleague who was reselling his concert ticket for the outrageous sum of $50. Fifty dollars. Not complaining; just saying...

One Question with Keith Richards!

If I had the opportunity to ask one question of a specific individual, what would I ask? Here is the second entry.

Tom Wilmeth:—So Keith, I see you are advertising your own line of designer luggage. Want to tell us about it?
Keith Richards:—Get lost.
TW:—Explain why you would shill for a project like that.
KR:—Money.

Important *Nota Bene*: The above exchange is complete and total fiction.

Commentary
Paul Simon Pledge Drive: Phone Lines Are Open!
Spring 2014

Did Paul Simon have another Broadway bomb after *Capeman* that I didn't hear about? Did he invest heavily in Toyota last year? Maybe in BP? Perhaps he is the money man behind the *Spiderman* musical. For whatever reason, Mr. Simon seems to need cash. There is no shame in acquiring money, of course, but in the past he has seemed excessively smug about the whole advertising game and its use of popular songs in television commercials. Particularly *his* songs.

I love my Simon and Garfunkel albums and many of Simon's solo records. But I also love a tape of a Paul Simon concert that my friend Keith recorded on August 26, 1984, in Mesa, Arizona. It's a clear, audience recording of a fine performance featuring just Simon and his acoustic guitar. In the middle of this generous, 25-song set, the artist makes pointed comments about how he always refuses to license his songs for advertisements. He explains in mock seriousness, "Being fabulously wealthy, I don't need to sell my music that way." He was amused, however, when prior to this Arizona concert he was approached by the sales department of Midas Muffler. They had gone to the trouble of recording a demo tape of an ad featuring "The Sounds of Silence" that they hoped Simon would approve for use in their commercials.

Both Simon and the audience had a good laugh as he played the company's audition tape that equated "The Sound of Silence" with the quality of quiet provided by Midas Mufflers. Entertaining. Funny. But I couldn't help of think of this elevated attitude recently when I saw two different car ads featuring Paul Simon songs. And not just the songs; the ads use his original recordings! The first is pretty obvious, to the point of being silly. A winter scene, and a car is seen sliding on ice. No shock when "Slip Slidin' Away" is heard playing over the visual, except for the surprise that Simon has agreed to cash in on Madison Avenue. The other television ad uses the instrumental backing track from Simon and Garfunkel's haunting "So Long, Frank Lloyd Wright."

Many artists have gone down this road, of course. Michael Jackson aggressively sold Pepsi-Cola, and even Bob Dylan has not been beyond the reach of advertisers' lucrative offers, licensing his music to sell everything from lingerie to ice cream to cars. But I don't recall Jackson or Dylan getting sanctimonious during concerts about the use of their music. Perhaps his own silence would have served Simon better on this topic.

Concert Commentary

The Beach Boys
UNI-Dome
University of Northern Iowa
Cedar Falls, Iowa
May 14, 1978

IN THE UNITED STATES, even before there were Beatles there were Beach Boys. This is true for the American music scene as a whole and at my home in Des Moines. I'm not sure how or why, but my brother had four early Beach Boys albums and a few of their 45s. This was back when an album cost four dollars and a 45 rpm single was about 69 cents. I played those Beach Boys records a lot. Initially their odd songs, like "The Lonely Sea," appealed to me most. I thought that "No Go Show Boat" was a hoot. The group was musically exciting and lyrically interesting. They were singing about things for which I had absolutely no interest—cars and surfing—but I liked the music. I was especially drawn (as we all were) to the harmonies of the ballads.

But also, like most everyone else, I thought that The Beach Boys lost their luster in early February 1964. It happened all at once—on a Sunday night when a new British quartet appeared on *The Ed Sullivan Show*. We still respected The Beach Boys after this, but it was never the same. Even Brian Wilson would later lament that after The Beatles arrived in America, his band "looked more like golf caddies than rock and roll stars." He continued, "And 'I Want to Hold Your Hand' wasn't even that great of a record." Were these sour grapes, or a clear-eyed assessment from a fellow songwriter?

Years later, in the early 1980s when I worked at Minnesota Public Radio, I would have detailed discussions about music with a fellow board operator. We talked a lot about bootleg recordings of major bands. I once indicated that I knew of no Beach Boys concert bootlegs—something I found odd for a group with such a lengthy career. My radio colleague simplified it: "Those boots aren't out there because nobody wants them." Ouch. But probably right, at least at that time.

I saw The Beach Boys twice. My most vivid memories come from a show held at the UNI-Dome in Cedar Falls, Iowa, in the spring of 1978. It was an unusual tour for a couple of reasons. First, Brian Wilson was actually there with the group! This was a big deal since Brian had not toured with them in many years. As he had in his previous touring days, Brian played the bass guitar, or so it appeared. I'm not convinced his instrument was plugged in; I think they also had a second bassist named Ed Carter standing in the shadows at the rear of the stage, doubling Brian's bass guitar part.

Brian seemed completely uninvolved. Throughout the entire concert he made facial contortions like he was trying to remove a pesky fly from his nose. It was very odd, to the point of making me alternately uncomfortable and amused. Carl Wilson was clearly in charge of the onstage proceedings. Carl often had to give his older brother, Brian, a visual down stroke during the middle of a song to indicate where the downbeat was (in the 4/4 time structure). Sad is what it was.

As they ran through their well-known catalog, the group didn't seem to be working all that hard. However, to their credit, it was not strictly a greatest hits review; they also performed a few newer songs and off the beaten path tunes. These included "Lady Lynda," "It's OK," and "Everyone's in Love with You." I yelled for "Leaving This Town." Carl looked directly at me, standing by the lip of the stage, but they didn't play it.

The other notably strange thing about this concert was the presence of Charles Lloyd on saxophone. Lloyd opened the concert with a short solo set, then joined The Beach Boys as a member of their backing ensemble. This was unexpected because Lloyd was a well-respected tenor saxophonist in the 1960s world of hard core jazz. Once seen by some as the next John Coltrane, Lloyd never made it anywhere close to Coltrane's status. I've heard that Lloyd became associated with The Beach Boys because of their mutual inspiration from transcendental meditation.

When I lived on Olive Street in Cedar Falls, Iowa, I had a slightly older housemate named Rich, a complicated guy who played keyboards in area rock bands. When he became a Born Again Christian, Rich completely turned his back on secular music. Even so, he would occasionally reminisce to me about some of his favorite concerts. One was a Beach Boys show from what must have been the very early 1970s. According to Rich, the group was playing nothing but their new music—from the *Holland* and *Sunflower* albums, I am guessing. Rich told me that the band was working hard, were very professional, and that the only old songs of the night came during the encore, presented as a hits medley. As I have repeatedly asked: Where are bootleg tapes of *that* tour? *Those* are The Beach Boys concerts I'd like to hear!

Concert Commentary

The Kinks
with Cheap Trick
Hancher Auditorium
Iowa City, Iowa
April 11, 1977

THE KINKS WERE UNUSUAL for their staying power, even after their string of hits had dried up. They were a first-wave British Invasion band that was still together. However, nobody of my generation had ever seen them in concert. I later found out that The Kinks could not tour America for several years because of some tax problem or legal dispute which arose during an earlier American visit. Or so the story went; easy to believe, though. Leader Ray Davies even acknowledged from the stage that it was often hard to convince people that they were the real Kinks, having been gone for so long.

I liked their radio hits, but the only Kinks LP I owned was *Lola Versus Powerman and The Moneygoround*, which I had bought in high school. I enjoyed the whole album; "Apeman" was fun, while the title trilogy on the economics of rock music seemed uncomfortably realistic and, therefore, interesting. The songs of Ray Davies were reminiscent of Frank Zappa for the occasional reference to unfair business practices in the music industry. Also, the album included the title's huge hit, "Lola." On the album, the lyrics to the song mention "Coca-Cola," where on the radio single Davies sings about "cherry cola." This was important stuff!

I learned of several Kinks' album tracks thanks to Des Moines' FM radio station KFMG. The real Kinks fans knew the albums *Village Green Preservation Society*, *Arthur*, and *Muswell Hillbillies*, from which they played very little that night in Iowa City. In fact, Ray seemed a bit distracted early in the set and indicated that they were going to do a section from their album *Preservation Act II*. Some knowledgeable fans were excited by this announcement and cheered, but then Davies realized his error and corrected himself. He said they would be featuring the new *Sleepwalker* album. Too bad.

I don't recall a lot about what they played, probably because I did not know *Sleepwalker* that well. In fact, it might not have been released yet. I do recall some of the hits, "Lola," and a fine performance of "Celluloid Heroes" and "Waterloo Sunset." We wanted to hear "Alcohol" from *Everybody's in Show Biz*, but they didn't do it. I recall that Ray Davies had a surprisingly gentle and unassuming stage presence.

A band that would become very big opened the show—Cheap Trick. Their hard rock seemed crude to many of the people there to hear the clever lyrics of Ray Davies. Some in the balcony vigorously booed the group. But later, even some devoted Cheap Trick fans would quietly confide that the Iowa City gig was not a good one. Maybe it was just not their audience.

While Cheap Trick was emerging as a band to be watched, The Kinks would soon strike me as a group which had outlived its usefulness. I thought there was trouble when they began their series of concept projects. These thematic storytelling albums included *School-boys in Disgrace* and *Soap Opera* (1975-76). One problem with such song cycles, and rock operas in general, is that quality tunes often take a back seat to plot and situation. Always a bad choice. Even The Who's great *Tommy* falls prey to it at times, although I would defend the inclusion of each tune on it.

The Kinks had the distinction of being an established band who, when switching labels from RCA to Arista Records, had a specific contractual proviso that the group could release no concept records of any sort. Arista got what it wanted with a couple of albums of individual songs, and both The Kinks and their new record company did very well in the process. In retrospect, neither *Sleepwalker* nor the follow-up *Misfits* can compare with their earlier peaks, but the band was still at it—in the studio and on the road. And by 1977, this was more than almost any of their British Invasion counterparts could say.

Book Review

Here Comes the Night:
The Dark Soul of Bert Berns and The Dirty Business of
Rhythm & Blues
Counterpoint Press, 2014
By Joel Selvin

I like to think that I have at least a tentative grasp on recorded music of the 20th Century. Then I meet a person or read a book that makes me realize how very little I know. This is not self-deprecation; it's an acknowledgement of the vast stretches of the art form called Music. One area of this spectrum I know least well is the business realm.

Music publishing, copyright ownership, royalties, and composer credit—these are arguably peripheral to the creation of music, and yet each is absolutely inseparable from its presentation in any recorded form. It is not a widely discussed field. In 1964, John Lennon surprised many by announcing that The Beatles "made more money out of writing songs than we do out of appearing and running around waving." That is, from playing concerts and touring.

A book published earlier this year accentuates the multiple, interconnected layers of the music business. Joel Selvin's *Here Comes the Night: The Dark Soul of Bert Berns and The Dirty Business of Rhythm & Blues* fills a hole in the history of American music. What makes the book so remarkable is that very few music lovers realized that this specific subject was in need of illumination.

Selvin's scene is New York City just before and during the first years that The Beatles forever changed the music business. Songwriting is the key element, and this book regularly reminds the reader that without a good song, nobody is making any money. In fact, the song is far more important than the artist, as groundbreaking producer Phil Spector knew so well.

Spector makes important appearances in *Here Comes the Night*, as do other industry heavyweights such as Jerry Wexler, Ahmet Ertegun, Tom Dowd, Alan Freed, Dick Clark, Jeff Barry & Ellie Greenwich, Gerry Goffin & Carole King, Jerry Leiber & Mike Stoller, and Morris Levy. But the book belongs to Bert Berns. If his name rings no bells, you are in good company. This lack of recognition is the very reason that Selvin undertook the task of writing his biography.

Yet biography is too narrow a term for *Here Comes the Night*, for in it Selvin offers the complete context of Berns' world. This includes an insider's look at the American music industry during midcentury. Berns' interactions with the names listed above show that he was working with the newly elevated hierarchy of independent record labels—Atlantic, Stax, Roulette, Bang, and Scepter.

Among the performers passing through Berns' orbit are Neil Diamond, The Drifters, Van Morrison, Ray Charles, Bobby Darin, Ruth Brown, Solomon Burke, The Isley Brothers, Big Joe Turner, Aretha Franklin, and a very large cast of artists who really can't even be called one-hit wonders. But each did release a record that was in some way connected with Bert Berns, who served as songwriter, producer, session musician, or in a combination of these roles.

Neil Diamond plays a large part in the latter part of the book, as he becomes entangled in unsavory situations that he can't control. Diamond survives, but not unscathed. The serious nature of Diamond's plight is underscored when we see the singer approach Berns' widow at her husband's funeral in a desperate attempt to get out of a contract.

Here Comes the Night focuses on the overlooked figure of Bert Berns. By doing so, Joel Selvin explores a much larger and equally unknown world: what the author himself terms "the dirty business of rhythm & blues." This should be the next music book you read.

One Question with Neil Diamond!

If I had the opportunity to ask one question of a specific individual, what would I ask? Here is the third entry.

Tom Wilmeth:—Mr. Diamond, you recorded the song "Shilo" for the Bang label, with whom you had your first six Top 40 chart entries. You subsequently signed with Uni Records, where you had your second wave of great chart success. After scoring several Uni label hits, Bang Records issued your older recording of "Shilo" as a single, to which they still had the rights and which then, belatedly, became a radio hit. My question: Is the Bang Records single version of "Shilo" the same take that appears on your first album for the Uni label, *Velvet Gloves and Spit*?

Neil Diamond responds:—Security!!

TW:—Hey big shot, I have both versions. I just don't feel like hearing that song twice in a row to figure it out.

Important *Nota Bene:* The above exchange is complete and absolute fiction. Mr. Diamond has never had the pleasure of being hectored by me.

Book Review

R&B (Rhythm & Business):
The Political Economy of Black Music
By Norman Kelley
Akashic Books, 2006

Joel Selvin's book on Bert Berns focuses on a specific man in a specific time. Norman Kelley writes in broader terms, but his lessons are equally important. In fact, this book should be read by every musician who has ever played a gig for money. The title stresses the "black" thread that runs through the essays included here, but Kelley's updated collection of articles on the music industry could provide clear-eyed assistance to all performers trying to make a living in the business, regardless of color. Topics range from artists' rights and royalty payment theft to the problem that the jazz genre currently faces—competing with its own past. The record companies are usually the villains here, but Kelley rarely allows his useful book to become shrill or pointlessly bitter.

Concert Commentary

Jack Benny with The Des Moines Symphony Orchestra
KRNT Theater
Des Moines, Iowa
September 25, 1971

I'M NOT SURE NOW how I got there, or why, or who I was with. It must have been an evening school excursion. No matter. Jack Benny's performance with the Des Moines Symphony Orchestra rates as one of the best concerts I have ever attended. Period.

In 1971, Benny was travelling the country, performing fundraisers for and with local orchestras. His Des Moines stop came in the midst of my high school years. At this time I played tuba for the school band but had little interest in classical music. Emerson, Lake & Palmer's *Pictures at an Exhibition* was about as close as I came.

The Des Moines Symphony played the first half of the concert, with Jack Benny joining them after the intermission. He was gracious and funny and told a few stories between the brief classical numbers. I don't recall what he said so much as how he said it. His delivery was hilarious. I can understand why Johnny Carson wrote a college thesis on Jack Benny's comedic timing.

Benny played his theme, "Love in Bloom," on which he purposefully hit many sour notes. It was funny visually as well as musically, with Benny inducing sour, silent reactions from the conductor and members of the orchestra. Also performed that night was a serious number—the first movement of Mendelssohn's "Violin Concerto in E minor," on which Jack Benny was the soloist. At the end of this challenging piece, Benny breathlessly said, "That's the best I can play, folks, and I'm not kidding!" The house erupted in sustained applause.

When the concert ended, the performer returned to center stage to acknowledge the appreciative audience. Benny began, "Well, I was thinking of doing just a little more if you don't have anywhere else to..." He broke off abruptly. "Oh! *Of course* you don't have anywhere else to go. This is Des Moines!" The delighted crowd howled with laughter. He proceeded to imitate various famous violinists. I hadn't a clue about who he was parodying, but I found it very funny nonetheless.

As we left the building, I noticed something I had never seen before—a handful of patient fans waiting by the Stage Door for an autograph or a word with the star. More than simply their presence, I was struck by the fact that these were adults! And they seemed just as thrilled at the prospect of meeting Jack Benny as their kids would have been with talking to Mick Jagger. I remember wanting to join them. After that concert, Jack Benny had attained rock star status for me.

Concert Commentary

Corky Siegel with The Kettle Moraine Symphony
Ruth A. Knoll Theater
Hartford, Wisconsin
January 24, 2004

How FAR IS IT from Chicago to Hartford, Wisconsin? For harmonica virtuoso Corky Siegel the distance is not measured in mere miles, but in quantum leaps. Siegel has attempted to do for the harmonica what Béla Fleck has done for the banjo—unleash the stylistically fettered instrument onto brave new musical worlds and widening audiences.

Siegel is the namesake of the Siegel-Schwall Band, a seminal blues quartet from the Windy City that has been releasing albums since 1966. He began recording with conductor Seiji Ozawa and the San Francisco Symphony in 1973 for the prestigious classical music label Deutsche Grammophon. In recent years he has also led his genre-bending group Chamber Blues to critical success. Saturday, at Hartford's intimate Knoll Theater, Siegel joined The Kettle Moraine Symphony Orchestra as featured soloist for composer William Russo's "Street Music: A Blues Concerto."

"Street Music" is that rare mixture of a full symphony with a non-traditional featured instrument that actually succeeds on various musical levels. The composer does not use the orchestra merely as a backdrop for harmonica solos. Instead, under the baton of Albert Asch, different instruments took up themes that initiate conversations with Siegel's harmonica, beginning with a low brass trio and moving through sections of the orchestra.

Siegel was in good form throughout the half-hour piece, which offered enough breathing room for him to present formal classical interludes, as well as some less structured blues-flavored harmonica cadenzas. In addition to harmonica, Siegel happily demonstrated his Chicago based piano chops on the hall's Steinway grand, as the middle movements of "Street Music" call for various piano styles, including stride and 12-bar blues.

The featured soloist was clearly having fun winning over an audience largely unaware of their guest's lengthy and varied musical tenure. His body language often acted as joyful co-conductor, to the delight of both audience and orchestra members. In Siegel's hands the unexpected pairing of symphony with harmonica defied limits, conjuring musical portraits free of category.

No one would ever confuse Hartford, Wisconsin, with Chicago. But Corky Siegel's recent visit to The Kettle Moraine Symphony served as musical diplomacy. By bringing fine samples of blues and classical music to the area, he was able to make Chicago seem as if it were just down the road.

Concert Commentary

Blues harpist Corky Siegel performs with an orchestra. Such cross-pollinating genre experiments were not new. Duke Ellington used symphonic elements in his extended piece "Black, Brown, and Beige" decades earlier. In 1965, jazz pianist Bill Evans recorded an album incorporating arrangements of works composed by Bach and Chopin for his jazz trio with symphony orchestra. By the mid-1970s, these genre experiments had been encroaching into the rock world, with several bands striving to compose epic works that demanded to be taken seriously. Hit singles were no longer the goal for these artists, or so they would profess.

One of the bands that tried mightily to expand the horizons of progressive rock into a symphonic landscape was Yes. The results of their endeavors, like the reception by audiences and critics, were mixed. Depending on one's vantage point, Yes' double album from early 1974, Tales from Topographic Oceans, *is either the zenith or the nadir of these symphonic rock experimentations.*

Yes	and	**Yes**
Tales from Topographic		*Relayer* tour
Oceans tour		University of Iowa
Met Sports Arena		Fieldhouse
Bloomington, Minnesota		Iowa City, Iowa
March 5, 1974		December 7, 1974

IT WAS THE DAY of competing concept albums. These were usually expensive, double-album affairs. There were many. The Who set the template in 1969 with their rock opera *Tommy* and released the song cycle *Quadrophenia* in 1973. Now others decided that they too had goals loftier than placing pop songs onto the radio. Many even seemed discontent with rock star status. They wanted to be viewed as artists.

I had been a fan of Yes for several years and was excited to see their *Tales from Topographic Oceans* tour. They were clearly excellent musicians, and the interplay exhibited on their live *Yessongs* record was impressive. The musicians at my college, even the jazzers, agreed that these guys could play their instruments.

I was fortunate to get good seats for the show. We were close enough to read a small sign that Rick Wakeman had placed on top of his keyboard stack. It read: "No computer can take my job." Funny. We would soon learn that Wakeman was not thrilled about the *Topograpic Oceans* project; he left the band at the conclusion of this tour to continue a career of making his own thematic rock music albums.

The concert was great. The sound was excellent and the light show was impressive. No expense had been spared to make the stage resemble the artwork on the *Topographic* album cover, both designed by

Roger Dean. The band emerged from a tunnel leading onto the stage and proceeded to play the three songs from their *Close to the Edge* LP. This was the crowd-pleasing part of the show.

They then played their new album, or at least three of its four lengthy sides. Dense, complex, often interesting, sometimes meandering—this challenging music was well performed and it was impressive to see this level of musicianship in rock players. The band encored with "Roundabout," and the night was over. It would have been nice to hear a few of their older songs. But this was a remarkable evening of music, and I have always been happy to have seen the band on this particular tour.

Later that same year, Yes was again touring the states. They had released an album called *Relayer*. And while it contained three long songs, it was scaled back from the high-minded pretensions that accompanied their *Topographic Oceans* set. That concert was also good, with an even more impressive light show. Older songs were still completely eschewed in favor of new material except, again, for their one large radio hit, "Roundabout," used as the encore.

They did not exactly disown the previous tour's *Topographic* project, since they closed the main set with a brief medley of major themes taken from the first three sections and then burned through all of side four. (I know these four pieces have actual titles, but I always think of them as sides of the album.) Some say that the group quickly released *Relayer* and went back on tour because they knew that *Topographic Oceans* had cost them some fans. It had cost them their keyboard player, certainly. The group would continue to scale back their lengthy numbers, soon producing albums that contained almost normal length songs.

Whether *Tales from Topographic Oceans* is viewed as a peak or a valley for this band, I was glad to have been there to see Yes at the most experimental end of its spectrum.

Bonus Track

A radio colleague of mine in St. Paul had an interesting theory about the unintentional ramifications of Yes' distinctive album cover art. He told me: "Man, the only reason that Osibisa sells any records at all is because Yes fans get high and buy them, thinking they are getting Yes albums." Another riddle solved?

Concert Commentary

Yes
Summerfest
Milwaukee, Wisconsin
July 2, 2010

IT HAD BEEN 35 YEARS since I had seen the quintessential prog rockers Yes. For some reason, I had been on a bit of a Yes revival during the past few months—buying used CDs of *Close to the Edge, Yesshows,* and a copy of one of their myriad of compilations, *The Ultimate Yes,* a good but not perfect three-CD overview of the band. The strangest part of the renewed interest was my close re-examination of their epic work *Tales From Topographic Oceans.*

So when my son pointed out that Yes was going to be at the same large outdoor stage for Milwaukee's Summerfest where we had seen Elvis Costello the previous summer, I was interested. I was also surprised that these boys were playing one of the free side stages. However, Milwaukee's annual Summerfest is good about getting large if fading names for their entertainment. I was, to be honest, somewhat concerned about seeing the band live. I remember watching a concert video of the group that had been taped in the 1990s and was not especially impressed.

We arrived at the Summerfest grounds in early afternoon, about seven hours before Yes would play their 10 P.M. set. We enjoyed a fine time, seeing a marginal Steely Dan tribute band, followed by an excellent set by The Heavy. But we were getting pretty tired and the decision had to be made: boogie quick after The Heavy set to the far end of the grounds to try to get seats for Yes, or head for home. We were there; let's go see Yes. I rushed us through the increasing crowds and we were able to get some bench seats. Good. We were all weary, and I'm not sure I would have fired up to stand for 45 minutes waiting for the band to come on.

As I looked at the stage, I thought about how the mighty had fallen. This was a bare bones set up, with a single large projection screen behind it. Gone were the elaborate sets that I had seen years before. I guess that makes sense; there was no longer any point in putting together complicated and expensive stage props designed by their album cover artist, Roger Dean. Yes was on the road to make some money and to play for the faithful, who were at an age where the extraneous stage trappings mattered less than just having the band show up and rock the house. And this is exactly what happened.

The quintet took the stage right at 10 P.M., accompanied by the dramatic conclusion to Stravinsky's "Firebird Suite," a concert prelude they have used for decades. Pretentious? Arrogant? At this point it really doesn't matter; it's what they use for an entrance. Yes launched into the first song. It was one I barely remembered, "Machine Messiah," but I was impressed with the sound, the tightness of the band and the fact that their lead singer sounded a whole lot like Jon Anderson. A whole lot! The fact that Anderson is not with Yes for this lengthy tour is a bone of contention with some fans and with the singer himself. No matter. I wasn't expecting Anderson, and vocalist Benoit David had his part down!

During this first number we were able to move away from some talking drunks and into far better sightlines. I would say better seats, but this was a standing concert. Not just standing, but standing on the benches. Fine; my son didn't mind at all. We were both tired from a long day, but the music lifted us up.

After this first tune, drummer Alan White laid down a slow, steady beat. I was amazed, then, when the band hit the opening chords of "Yours Is No Disgrace," a very fast number in its recorded versions. I truly wondered, "Can this really be the tempo they mean to take it?" Clearly it was. They smoldered on this tune at less than half speed for probably 15 minutes. A full version, to be sure. Guitarist Steve Howe looked like an aging history professor, but played like he was on fire. I must have said aloud no less than four times: "Howe is really having a good night!" Unlike the sluggish renditions offered up by the Steely Dan tribute band from that afternoon, Yes *meant* to play "Yours Is No Disgrace" at this tempo. Very unexpected, very fresh, and very great!

We had talked earlier about watching part of the set and then heading out when Yes hit their material we didn't know. Never happened. At one point my son tapped me on the shoulder and said, "Is this their third tune?" "I think so," I replied. "They have been playing for 45 minutes!" It seemed to me like about 10. People around us also stared in disbelief when this time reference was given. I learned later that my son had been a bit uncertain about attending this concert. He likes Yes a great deal but was at Summerfest earlier in the week and saw The Moody Blues on this same stage. He departed after only a few songs. "No spark," he said. He would later indicate how glad he was that we opted to attend this Yes concert and stayed for their full set.

Speaking of which, as I gushed on the bus ride home, "This was a set list from heaven!" Following the opening pair of numbers, they performed excellent versions of "And You and I," and later "I've Seen All Good People." I kept expecting some material I didn't know, but the most recent tune they touched after the opening number was "Owner of a Lonely Heart," which was an actual #1 *Billboard Magazine* hit for them in 1984. A very impressive, brief number.

Another pleasant surprise came when the guitarist announced a change of pace. As the rest of the band left the stage, Steve Howe sat down to play a 10-minute set of acoustic guitar. Howe's playing often suggested themes rather than actual songs. And as he ripped through some country-flavored fingerstyle guitar licks, it became clear that Howe had listened to a lot of Chet Atkins. This acoustic respite was welcome too because the entire audience joined Howe in taking a seat for a few minutes. That helped.

Howe, a longtime guitar collector, showed class later in the evening by pointedly acknowledging Wisconsin as "the birth place of the great Les Paul" before the beginning of "Perpetual Change." This song was noteworthy as a real showcase for the interplay between Howe's electric and Chris Squire's famous Rickenbacker bass guitar. It also featured Benoit David's vocals on the beautiful lyrics and surprisingly gentle melody which make up the song.

Suddenly, or so it seemed, we heard the opening acoustic harmonics to "Roundabout." I knew this had to be a set closer, and it was.
Howe had his unique method of keeping the electric guitar strapped
on while reaching over it to play an acoustic guitar mounted on a
stand. Unusual but functional. He also played a bit of steel guitar in his
way of making it sound unlike any other steel player I've ever heard.
They departed the stage and then returned to encore with a very hot
rendition of "Starship Trooper."

We saw a good set on a good night. I went online later and discovered that, perhaps surprisingly, the boys did not perform "Owner of a
Lonely Heart" all that often these days. I was glad they did hit that one,
as it is one of my son's favorites and was the song that first grabbed his
attention toward Yes. Also, they had not played "Yours Is No Disgrace"
in months! I was really glad for that one as well, and in retrospect that
tune was my favorite of the evening. But they were all good!

Although I had seen the band twice before this night, the previous
shows were the specialty tours of *Tales from Topographic Oceans* and
the subsequent *Relayer* tour, when they were rarely touching their back
catalog. As such, the only tune Yes played at Summerfest which I had
previously heard them perform was "And You and I," and even that
was a very different arrangement. On Friday, they were far closer to
capturing the more subtle elements of the studio recording, as opposed
to the bombastic nature of the *Yessongs* version.

Another thing I learned after the concert was how deeply some
people feel that this is not really Yes. OK, but as I pointed out on the
bus trip to the festival site, the only original member of the band still
playing with them is Chris Squire. He acted as sort of de facto group
leader, while Benoit David served as the reserved front man, knowing
that he was fortunate to have made the leap from singing with a Yes
tribute band to singing with the real thing. It happens.

But make no mistake, this was Yes: Chris Squire, Steve Howe,
drummer Alan White (although I confess to preferring Bill Bruford).
The core of the popular lineup was solidly in place. Different vocalist,
true, but more than capable, and keyboards handled well by Oliver
Wakeman, the son of the band's most famous former member, Rick
Wakeman. This too happens.

Post Script

For subsequent tours, singer Benoit David left the band, as did Oliver Wakeman. In the summer of 2015, Yes bassist and cofounder Chris Squire died just as a tour with the band Toto was getting started. I see by the official Yes website that they will continue to play concerts; Billy Sherwood is the group's new bassist. With the passing of Chris Squire, Yes now includes none of its original members but somehow remains Yes. I plan to see them when they come around here again.

Concert Commentary

Heart
with The Little River Band
McElroy Auditorium
Waterloo, Iowa
June 29, 1977

IF YES WAS TRANSCENDENT Art Rock, Ann and Nancy Wilson's band Heart were bringing things back to earth with a more straight ahead brand of rock. The sisters came from Seattle. This was before Seattle became known as the grunge music center of the world. This sister act reminded people that power pop (and women) could rock hard.

I saw Heart in Waterloo, Iowa, on their second headlining tour. They had a couple of hits by his point, but for some reason I couldn't talk anybody into going to this show with me. When I saw them, they had scored with one Top 10 hit ("Magic Man") and one lesser ("Crazy on You," which peaked at a surprisingly low position of #35). The week following this concert, Heart released "Barracuda" as a single.

Bands fronted by women were a tough sell in the mid-1970s. The hard rock, all female band Vixen never crossed over to the mainstream. A Taste of Honey had one huge hit with "Boogie Oogie Oogie," and The Runaways were still a couple of years off. The jury was out whether the Wilson Sisters could make a career of music, having just released their second major label album, *Little Queen*.

Heart played a good set for the John Deere workers of Waterloo that night. I tried to get an interview with one of the sisters after the show, but they sent drummer Mike DeRosier out to talk instead. He was pleasant enough, very professional. But it was clear that he had already been through this routine too many times. I asked if Heart were worried about the jinx of the third album. He seemed surprised at this, and stressed that it was the second album that usually sunk a band. Heart had successfully sidestepped this scenario with radio hits off of *Little Queen*. I thanked him for his time and he pretended to destroy my cassette machine. But he did come out to talk!

Opening that night was The Little River Band, from Australia. This was just before they had their own headlining tours in the U.S. They had been on the circuit long enough to have smoothed out their show to the point of extreme professionalism. At this time The Little River Band had one moderate hit—"It's a Long Way There," which reached #28 on the *Billboard* singles chart. The bigger hit "Help Is On The Way" (#14) would be released that fall. They were touring the States like mad. It paid off a few years later. Here they were struggling to break through. It was interesting to see these finely honed veteran performers from Australia juxtaposed with an American group still rough around the edges—like a really good bar band that suddenly makes it big.

Concert Commentary

Squeeze   and   **The Pretenders**
with   Orpheum Theater
A Flock of Seagulls   Minneapolis,
Orpheum Theater   Minnesota
Minneapolis,   August 24, 1981
Minnesota
July 5, 1982

THIS SHOULD HAVE BEEN a great concert. In the summer of 1981, I was enthralled by Squeeze's *East Side Story* album. Every track on this long record was good, and it even included the radio-friendly song "Tempted." But somehow, the concert was not all that remarkable. Maybe group leaders Difford and Tilbrook were beginning to believe the rock press claims that they were the new Lennon and McCartney.

Squeeze was on tour to promote their new release, *Sweets from a Stranger*, a record that did not move me nearly to the degree that *East Side Story* had. It was a professional show, and they closed with their well-known early tune, "Pulling Muscles from the Shell," but did not do much from *East Side Story*. I was, in a word, disappointed. What made things doubly irritating was how a friend kept telling me that he had seen Squeeze play Minneapolis the previous year. In a bar! And they played all the songs from *East Side Story*. Irritating companion.

Opening for Squeeze was A Flock of Seagulls. Their sound level was way too loud for the theater, with the treble especially unbearable. In fact, several of us did the unthinkable—we walked out on live music to wait in the lobby. From this lobby gathering comes my most vivid memory of the evening, as we discussed the recent death of James Honeyman-Scott, guitarist for The Pretenders.

I saw The Pretenders when they were still the original quartet. The group was just beginning their tour for the much anticipated (and delayed) second album. That album was not on the same level as their first, and the concert could not meet our perhaps unreasonably high expectations. Even those who were deep into the band thought they were having an off night. I wonder now if we were witnessing the start of this band's collapse. For me, the most impressive tune of their set was "Private Lives," but my overall impression of the show was that the band was coasting.

Shortly after this Minneapolis concert, the tour had to go on hiatus because drummer Martin Chambers had severed arteries in his wrist by putting his fist through a pane of glass. Rock and roll! Not too much later came the dismissal of bassist Pete Farndon for incapacitating substance abuse, followed immediately by the death of Honeyman-Scott. Success can sometimes be a sad story.

The Pretenders and Squeeze—two bands with remarkable albums; two concerts that failed to impress me as much as I had hoped.

Concert Commentary

Eric Clapton & **Eric Clapton** & **Cream**
Mississippi   Dane County   Madison Square
Valley   Coliseum   Garden
Fairgrounds   Madison,   New York City,
Davenport,   Wisconsin   New York
Iowa   July 8, 1975   October 26, 2005
July 27, 1974

"CLAPTON IS GOD." It really was a catch phrase when I was in junior high school (1967-69). This proclamation was scrawled on many walls and blackboards. We would be delighted to find it often and unexpectedly, like "Kilroy Was Here" graffiti in an earlier generation. It was hype, of course, but as a radio mentor said of The Beatles' early days: "There was actually something there to hype!" Once in the late 1980s, my wife asked me if Clapton was really all that good. I was initially surprised by this, but I assured her that Eric was the real thing. Her question was not really unfair. Clapton had a rough go of it for a number of years, both personally and professionally. He had fallen off the musical radar of many formerly devoted fans. But in those early days: Wow!

Like most of us, I learned about Clapton through his work with Cream and especially the hit single "Sunshine of Your Love," which was pretty heavy stuff for the radio back then. That guitar riff was constantly flowing from my mouth—being sung so frequently that friends were threatening physical violence if I didn't stop. I would soon backtrack to Clapton's days with John Mayall and the one great LP he recorded with Mayall's band, the Bluesbreakers. I then went back farther, into The Yardbirds' albums, but was largely disappointed with Clapton's involvement, or the lack thereof. Having said this, I love and defend The Yardbirds, but it is really not the place to go for Clapton worship.

A 30-minute tape recently surfaced of Eric live with the Yardbirds at a club in England. It was released as *Live! Blueswailing, July 1964* on the somewhat questionable Castle label. Fearing it to be a well packaged bootleg that would quickly disappear, I grabbed it immediately. The recording is interesting for historical purposes, and of course I am glad to have it. But the tunes don't allow Clapton much solo space. The seven-song recording presents a previously unknown, unedited set from a young Eric Clapton. This is all a plus. It's just not that engaging of a listen.

One of the first non-Beatles albums I ever bought was *Best of Cream* (eggplant cover). Although my brother was encouraging me to expand my musical horizons, he couldn't relate to this music. But it grabbed me hard. From that point, I bought the rest of this short-lived band's records. *Goodbye Cream* had been released only recently, and I was surprised to find a copy in cutout bins. Well worth it for the two great cuts—a live version of "I'm So Glad" and a studio precise "Badge," with an uncredited George Harrison on the song's centerpiece guitar solo. It would still be years before we learned that it was Clapton on the second guitar part of The Beatles' "While My Guitar Gently Weeps," but many immediately discerned that it was George playing on "Badge." And that was another cool thing about Clapton—Eric had a Beatle connection.

I envisioned Clapton hanging out at George's house. Doing what, I didn't know. I would discover that he was over there becoming a heroin addict and stealing George's wife. Life of a rock star. At least Eric was able to turn his pain into the *Layla* album. No bad ones on that LP.

I was aware of *Blind Faith*, the fragmented ashes of Cream and the first use of the term "super group," as far as I knew. But I did not immediately get the record. Like many, I lost track of Eric after he briefly toured with Delaney & Bonnie and then put out his first solo record. Still, I was excited to go see Clapton in the summer of 1974 when he was to play at a race track in Dubuque, Iowa. These were the days of crowded "festival seating," with promoters striving mightily to profit from the mystique of Woodstock. Sell the dream! I was a willing customer.

I think back to those concerts now and wonder: How was that supposed to work? Thousands jammed into a race track infield dirt area (not the seats, mind you) to watch bands perform on an elevated flatbed truck. I'm not sure anybody else was on the bill. I do remember that we sat for a very long time in the hot sun waiting for Clapton to hit the stage. Somebody played current albums through the P.A. system all afternoon, but it was a pretty dire scene. Fans could buy nothing to drink, yet questionable pills were being sold in the open, as were unauthorized T-shirts. I was later mad at myself for not getting one. A

T-shirt, that is. Relationships were expiring all around us, imploding from excess heat and a lack of liquid. Would-be hippy society was breaking down.

About the time the sun was setting Clapton came on stage. Made sense; it was finally cooling off a bit. It's one of those shows that I clearly recall being there and was glad to attend, but it really was not a lot of fun and certainly not worth what you had to put up with. Clapton did play "Badge," but ignored the rest of the Cream catalog. He also played very little from *Layla*. I think he was pushing his first two solo LPs really hard. Remember, that was in the days (which are probably still with us) when the performer was not especially interested in playing what the ticket-buying public wanted to hear. The star was going to play what interested him at any given time. Great for the artist; often less great for the fan. But then, one could argue that the true fan is willing to let the artist be the artist—that is, perform whatever he or she chooses.

Most popular musicians ignore their own hits at their peril. Even Beatle Paul disappointed some fans with his first solo tour in 1976 by playing so few Beatles tunes. McCartney was stressing that he was now a solo act. I could accept that from Paul, but my interest in Clapton's solo career soon faded. I found myself instead returning with increasing frequency to my live Cream records, the *Layla* album, and later the double live Derek & the Dominoes album *In Concert*. True, this set did not have Duane Allman on second guitar. And, unfortunately, Clapton chose not to play some of the best songs from *Layla*, including "I Looked Away," "Bell Bottom Blues," "Keep On Growing," or even the title track. Still, it's a fine record that features many, many great Clapton guitar solos. Derek & the Dominoes *In Concert* may be the best live set of his career.

Following this outdoor Iowa gig, I would get the chance to see Clapton again, this time in Madison, Wisconsin. It was a fairly long drive from Cedar Falls, Iowa, but several of us made the trek. Santana opened. This is a good example of a show that sounds like it can't miss. And yet, we were all disappointed. Maybe we were tired; maybe it was our seats, far from the stage in a huge sports arena. But for whatever reason, the concert just wasn't making it for any of us. Santana had just returned to playing concerts comprised of the band's recognizable hits, and we were still mad at ourselves for not travelling to see this band's jazz-oriented *Lotus/Welcome* tour just two years earlier.

After Santana played, Clapton came out. But the performance never seemed to catch fire. A long drive home awaited us, so we left before the show was over. We walked out on Eric Clapton! That amazes some, but it's true. We weren't mad so much as bored. I learned that others shared our frustration that night. A radio colleague had also made the trip and returned with a similar reaction. He maintained that the blues need to be performed in an intimate setting, and that a sports arena was clearly not the place to cultivate this atmosphere.

I thought back to the previous year's show I saw in Davenport. Followers of Clapton now point to this Iowa concert as being unusual because he was sober and seemed involved in the performance. Many shows of the 1974 tour, they say, were sloppy and drunken affairs. Not so in Davenport; Eric gave those Iowans his best. The 1975 Madison gig is now viewed as unusual because he played "Sunshine of Your Love" near the end of the concert, which he only did twice on that tour. I doubt none of these retrospective analyses, and I have since heard soundboard recordings from both concerts. I agree that the performance Clapton gave on the Davenport race track sounds fine, and I would compare it favorably with many of his officially released concert recordings from the 1970s. It's just that when you are hot, tired, and thirsty, sitting in the dirt of a racetrack all afternoon…well, these external stimuli can't help but impact on one's enjoyment of music. As such, neither Clapton concert is a particularly pleasant memory for me. My third encounter with the man would be different.

In 2005, Cream announced that they would reunite for four shows at the Royal Albert Hall. I watched with interest as this most unexpected reunion took shape, and I read the reviews from opening night. My Texas friend Tony and I agreed that if we had unlimited wealth we would have flown to London for one of these shows. Another friend sent me a good fidelity, complete audience recording of one of Cream's Albert Hall concerts, which I listened to a lot. I thought they were playing well (if not as intensely as in the old days) and that Clapton was really hitting it.

Then came word that Cream would be playing a few New York City dates in October at Madison Square Garden. Tony got tickets; I was envious. But then his wife could not get away from work, so Tony asked me to meet him in New York for a weekend of Cream and hanging out. I went, grateful for a friend in Texas. No way I could have attended that concert on my own. The face value of the Cream ticket was $375, crazy expensive at the time. And now!

The trip itself was great, and in our urban meanderings I think we witnessed the early death throes of the New York City record shop scene. On our last night in town we saw Cream. We were on the side of the stage—up a bit high, but that was OK with me; I had brought binoculars, which really helped. Tony was disappointed that we were not closer (he had paid for the tickets, after all), but I was just glad to be there. We were very fortunate in that, while it was a side view of the stage, we were looking straight into Clapton. That is, he was facing us (while he looked toward Jack Bruce) for the entire concert. With the binoculars, I could watch him playing throughout.

It was a great show, and I loved every note, even "Toad." Tune after tune after tune saw Clapton really digging in. The soloing was all on him, and he consistently nailed it. I couldn't help but think of how generous Clapton was to be doing this; he didn't need it, but cohorts Bruce and Baker surely did. That is to say, Clapton could have sold out Madison Square Garden with his own band. There is no way that Baker or Bruce would have come close to that, or could have charged the obscene face value of the tickets. But business aside, these three guys were again producing great and powerful music. After about the third tune, Tony turned to me feigning surprise and said, "Hey! These guys are pretty good." Cracked me up. Then and now.

Besides witnessing Clapton's guitar work, I could see him when he left the stage during the drum solo. He stuck around and watched Ginger Baker's drumming from the wings, while Jack Bruce disappeared. After a few minutes Bruce reemerged and Clapton looked at him and imitated smoking a cigarette. Bruce nodded and they both laughed. I especially liked this moment because I think this off stage camaraderie showed that they did not hate each other. Further, this was not a show of friendship for the benefit of the crowd.

In a live trio setting, there is no place for the principal soloist to hide. And Clapton consistently rose to the occasion, needing no other electronics than a single wah-wah pedal to augment his lead guitar work. (Think of the sound of Clapton's concluding guitar solo on "White Room.") Jack Bruce also required no assistance in creating fluid bass lines that acted as counterpoint solos to Clapton's guitar. However, Bruce did sometimes lean on a high-backed stool for physical support.

The two-hour set was nearly identical to the Albert Hall shows, opening with "I'm So Glad" and "Spoonful," and closing, just as they had in the old days, with "Sunshine of Your Love." Tony was very pleased that they performed "Deserted Cities of the Heart" early in the night, a song they had not played in London.

Afterwards, we shared a cab back to the hotel with two enthusiastic young men. They wanted to impress us by saying that they had travelled all the way from the Bronx to attend this Cream concert. Tony looked at them and pointed to each of us, "I'm from Texas; he's from Wisconsin." The two New Yorkers fell silent. It was clear by their faces that they had *heard* of Texas but weren't sure whether it was farther away from Manhattan than the Bronx.

In the aftermath of these New York concerts, people bitched. Billy Joel said he had expected Madison Square Garden to explode. (It didn't.) Ginger Baker said it was an off night. (It wasn't.) Many watched the PBS video from London and expressed ennui; others said it was a money grab. None of that matters. I was there and it was perfect. That concert reinvigorated my appreciation for this band in a big way. I still go back to the 2005 Cream recordings, both the audience tape and the legit release; the trio is in fine form throughout. The pinnacle of the group's original music is, of course, found within the band's live recordings from the late 1960s. Listen closely to both of Clapton's solos on "Crossroads," study the guitar and bass interplay of "I'm So Glad." Then move on to the concert version of "Steppin' Out." Have some oxygen ready.

Post Script

When the two-CD expanded set of the Derek & the Dominoes *In Concert* LP was released, the compilers chose to use several alternate performances from the two-night (four-show) Fillmore East stand. As such, a full 45 minutes of music found on the *In Concert* record album does not appear on the CD release. I assume that the record company will eventually issue a set of all four complete shows, as they have recently done with Fillmore concerts by Aretha Franklin and by Joe Cocker. And when they do, of course, I will buy it.

CD Review

Eric Clapton
Back Home
Reprise Records, 2006

It's hard to tell an old friend that he has grown dull—especially if he has been an inspiration for many years. But, Eric, while my respect for your abilities as a guitarist could not be higher: the new CD is a bore. I am truly happy about your contentment in marriage and your young family, but this particular brand of parental joy doesn't translate into compelling music.

The recorded sound of a baby's cry has never been compatible with any song, whether it's on Stevie Wonder's "Isn't She Lovely" or here within *Back Home's* "So Tired," on which Clapton smilingly bemoans the duties of an aging parent. Caught up in the mood of this opening track, Eric remembers only once or twice that his guitar skills are the reason we play his records.

Clapton has increasingly become a live act. And with rare exception, maybe he always was. His most rewarding albums of the present decade are not his studious tribute to Robert Johnson or the well meaning collaboration with B. B. King. Instead, the concert release from the 2001 tour, *One More Car, One More Rider,* better documents his musical abilities, demonstrating passionate guitar work on a solid tune selection.

Fresh from his brief Cream reunion, Clapton is planning a world tour with second guitarist Derek Trucks. Rumor is that he plans to revive some Derek & the Dominos songs with their twin lead guitar lines. Nostalgia can be a dangerous thing, but Eric Clapton recreating his past has become far more interesting than his new efforts, happy home life or not.

Bonus Track

Even from the start, Eric Clapton's concert recordings stood apart. On the first Best of Cream *LP, the requisite hits of "Sunshine of Your Love" and "White Room" were included, of course. But the track that demanded the most attention was the live recording of "Crossroads," on which Clapton took two short and perfect guitar solos. At the end of this tour de force, the band members acknowledge one another. Clapton says into the microphone, "Jack Bruce and Ginger Baker!" Bruce then credits the guitarist by saying, "Eric Clapton, lead." I have a friend who, to this day, insists that this last statement was somebody at the bar summoning the guitarist: "Eric Clapton, phone call, please." Right. Hey Eric! Somebody's on the phone for you. Put that guitar down and get over here! Funny? Well, it always makes me laugh.*

Remembrance

Jack Bruce
October 2014

With the death of bassist Jack Bruce over the weekend, we are again reminded that our rocks gods are mortal. We are also reminded that Bruce belonged to a band that will be remembered as THE power trio, Cream: the gold standard against which all subsequent rock trios must be measured.

Cream played a sports arena in my home town of Des Moines shortly before disbanding in 1968. I couldn't attend, but those who went said it was nothing but bad sound and echo. Years later, a friend told me he had seen them in a Long Island basketball arena. "They played only three songs, and one was a drum solo." I didn't care about either bad report; the live material on *Wheels of Fire* and *Goodbye Cream* redefined the rock landscape for me. There was Clapton's lead guitar virtuosity, of course, but bassist Jack Bruce also seemed to be taking an endless solo. In fact, when I would think back to the stretch sections of "Spoonful," it was usually the melodic bass lines I found myself singing.

After Cream disbanded and the super group Blind Faith misfired, drummer Ginger Baker formed his Air Force big band and soon dropped out of sight. Eric Clapton, of course, became Eric Clapton. Jack Bruce soldiered on, trying some inventive lineups. I bought his first two post-Cream solo LPs—*Songs for a Tailor* (1969) and *Things We*

Like (1971). They are not bad, but I was expecting more. Even with the presence of guitarist John McLaughlin on the latter, there was nothing extremely notable about these records.

I remained loyal when Jack Bruce joined new groups, one jazz and one rock—Tony Williams' Lifetime and later West, Bruce & Laing. After both of these short-lived bands imploded, I again bought the subsequent solo LP, this one titled *Out of the Storm* (1974). I later tried one last solo effort by Bruce before giving up, an odd LP with an ugly cover from 1980 called *I've Always Wanted to Do This*. Afterwards, I lost track of Jack Bruce but still would return to my Cream albums with some regularity.

Unquestionably, Jack Bruce stands with the most influential of rock's bassists. I would mention other names, such as John Entwistle and of course Paul McCartney, but whenever one makes a list of this sort, people get touchy if it is not comprehensive enough to include personal favorites. So instead, let's just agree that we will miss the virtuosity of Jack Bruce and that he played bass in a band that took rock music to new places.

Concert Commentary

Todd Clouser's A Love Electric
The Jazz Estate
Milwaukee, Wisconsin
October 4, 2014

WHY WAS I THINKING about Cream all night? The guitarist didn't play like Clapton. The bass player didn't sing, and the drummer wasn't doing bass drum rolls. There was not a blues lick to be heard, and the group was not from England. In fact, A Love Electric comes from Mexico City! Still, this trio played with the musical interplay and intensity found on *Wheels of Fire*.

The group's compatibility might be partially explained by their itinerary. This Milwaukee date was the last of a world tour, one that had them gigging in Frankfurt, Germany, and Fargo, North Dakota, within the same week! But far from appearing exhausted, the group sounded invigorated throughout their three long sets.

Most of the night's music consisted of material that occasionally threatened to fall into musical chaos. But just as a breakdown appeared eminent, it became obvious that the players always knew exactly where they were. They were so tight that they could feign a looseness that bordered on harmonic anarchy, consistently reemerging in perfect unity.

Aaron Cruz's electric five-string bass frequently had the fat tones of Stanley Clarke, with a popping stylistic approach that also echoed this fusion master. Reminiscent of Jack Bruce, Cruz often played intense yet melodic bass lines against a counterpoint lead guitar solo. This interplay can run the risk of becoming too busy, but the intricate bass lines were always logical and tasteful. Cruz also incorporated clearly executed harmonics that rang like bells on several pieces.

The rhythm section of Cruz and drummer Hernan Hecht was locked in a groove on each number. Like the bassist's occasional flurry of notes, Hecht gave a lot of percussive background to the soloists, but at no time was he showy or disruptive; his playing always fit the tune.

Group leader Todd Clouser would sometimes flail with abandon at the fret board of his blue Gibson 335, providing a bed of sound over which another band member would solo. He also played well-executed lead lines and lots of straight rhythm patterns. He was a generous leader, and the group never seemed anything but a collective of three equals.

Foot pedals were sometimes employed by Clouser to evoke various sounds, including synthesizer tones. Mostly, though, he played his guitar without external effects, getting the notes he was after by picking and bending strings. In fact, at one point Clouser bent his low E string all the way around the back of the guitar neck to create the sound he wanted.

The guitarist was no stranger to purposeful distortion on his instrument. Perhaps this is why one of the rare non-originals covered by the band was a hot instrumental take on "Manic Depression." Hendrix influences would occasionally surface in Clouser's playing, but never in a straightforward imitation. At other times, the guitarist sounded like he had been studying some of fellow guitarist Howard Roberts' experimental albums. This made for an interesting and varied evening.

Instead of the usual high octane closer, the group was confident enough with their music to end the first set with a ballad, "Break in the Morning." The second set began with two instrumentals, including "Without a Face." Most of the pieces had lengthy and intricate heads, on which the musicians never faltered. After these two slower numbers the band kicked back into high gear as the music continued to meld from one tune into the next without interruption for more than 40 minutes. Stylistically, it was reminiscent of a 1970s set of flowing material at a Grateful Dead concert.

Vocals were occasionally included. On "Your Money's No Good," Clouser sang the solo guitar lines as he was simultaneously playing them, conjuring a young George Benson. More often, intentionally unmelodic spoken narratives were placed over a textured vamp. One selection about time spent in Chicago worked well, as did another that had the unsettling refrain, "Mr. Kahn Scratched his Ticket." On these numbers, Clouser combined delivery styles of Tom Waits' *Nighthawks at the Diner* era with Ken Nordine's "Word Jazz." The set's handful of vocal numbers showed admirable diversity, but some of the spoken pieces were more successful than others. Microphone problems didn't help the performer.

A Love Electric shone brightest on their instrumentals, and I always felt the same was true about that 1960s trio from England. Cream performed as a group less than three years. Todd Clouser's A Love Electric have been playing for that same duration but sound as if they have been together a lifetime.

Concert Commentary

Aaron Williams & The Hoodoo

Fifth Annual Paramount Records Blues Festival
Grafton, Wisconsin
September 17, 2010

AARON WILLIAMS HIT THE STAGE playing an odd little string instrument that appeared to be an electrified cigar box. It sounded a lot like a dobro. As I took a closer look, there was some metal mesh in the instrument's two F-holes. I wanted to ask Williams about it, but the opportunity didn't come up.

The appearance of this instrument was not the only curious thing about the performance. From my lawn chair in the midst of the festival crowd, Williams looked like an old guy in a fedora hat. As I approached the stage, it was clear that here was quite a young man dressed in an older style. He had studied the fashion of an earlier era, just as he had studied early music styles. And Williams could play these styles convincingly. As appropriate as his clothes were, his blues licks were just as studious—but fresh and distinctively his own.

After the first number, which Williams performed alone, two more musicians emerged and the three burned as a trio. After what seemed like a quick set, Williams introduced the band and said they had just one more tune. I was sorry to hear this, especially after the overly long set that preceded Williams. And while he told the truth, that final number lasted about 20 minutes. And was great. He did the crowd-pleasing act of walking through the audience while still playing—something that wireless technology now makes pretty simple. The Hoodoo stretched like mad and played with great energy and enthusiasm.

At the end of the set, the guitarist returned for what was clearly an unplanned encore. Again unaccompanied, Williams played "The Star Spangled Banner," Jimi Hendrix style. He didn't let it roll into the lengthy Woodstock medley, but stayed with the song's melody; he kept it brief and fine. This young man can play. I would go see these guys again tonight. Right now!

Concert Commentary

Lil' Ed & The Blues Imperials
Fifth Annual Paramount Records Blues Festival
Grafton, Wisconsin
September 18, 2010

I WAS LOOKING FORWARD to Lil' Ed, and his performance did not disappoint. Still, it was an odd situation, perhaps because of my high expectations. I had seen Lil' Ed & The Blues Imperials in 1986, when I lived in Texas. They were wild, and really tore up the small club in College Station. I remember Lil' Ed riding through the room on the back of one of the other band members while playing some hot lead guitar. As I watched the band set up at the Paramount Blues Festival, it was immediately clear that Ed's riding days were behind him. For one thing, I didn't see anybody in that band who could support Ed for a piggyback trek of any duration. That's fine. Hell—the show I saw in Texas was more than 20 years ago.

My Texas friend Tony Davidson told me I should ask Lil' Ed to play the song "20% Alcohol." So between the acts at this festival, I walked to the stage to request the song. "20% Alcohol" is a fierce anti-alcohol number that appears on The Blues Imperials' second album. It was written by Lil' Ed's famous uncle, J. B. Hutto, who taught Ed to play guitar. I had been told that Lil' Ed had gone through some substance abuse days, but (again) this was an *anti*-booze song.

Standing by myself in front of the stage, I asked if he would consider performing this song during his upcoming set. Lil' Ed looked at me for a long time in silence. I finally asked, "Do you guys still do that tune?" The rest of the band had stopped setting up and were also now looking at me. Lil' Ed said, in an unmistakably surly tone, "I'll play that song for six thousand dollars—in advance—cash." Hm. So I said, "Well, I'm sure it would be worth every dollar." And I walked away.

That was the end of our conversation. I guess Lil' Ed is not big on requests. What can you say to a response like that? I mean, the song was on one of his albums; it's not like I was asking for something associated with another artist. When I later related that story to Tony, he snapped: "Man, if I'd been there I would have asked Ed if he was too good to play his uncle's songs!" Tony was mad! Good to hear some real passion about music coming through the phone lines from Texas.

Ed is a distinctive sight, wearing a bright red turban of some height. In fact, he had donned this head gear by the time I spoke with him, a full 20 minutes before the set started. I guess he just likes wearing it. Or maybe he wants to make sure that you know exactly who is leading this group. I'm sure he has no problem letting his band know who the star is.

Lil' Ed did not play "20% Alcohol," and he did not ride around on the back of a band member. But his set was still the high point of the night, if not of the entire festival. His slide guitar was on fire, and he smoked through a fine hour of blues. My son and I were very close to the stage and we saw Lil' Ed put on a real show. What impressed me, in part, was how generous he was with the rest of his band. He had Mike Garrett on second guitar, a thin white guy who was great at holding down the rhythm section and playing single line solos when given the opportunity. Ed's huge brother (or so said Ed) was on electric bass, and drummer Kelly Littleton kept it honest with a very solid beat.

Actually, I was surprised that I did not get tired of the distinctive sound of Ed's slide, because he rarely played anything else. I think that was partially due to his willingness to share solo space with the other guitarist. Ed played an unusual guitar that looked custom made. He had three absolutely identical instruments in the rack, but played just one fire engine red and white guitar for the entire set.

At one point people behind us yelled that the sound mix was bad. It was fine where we were, but I guess his vocals were buried farther from the stage. That's OK; you don't go see Lil' Ed to hear him sing. But that's when the attitude briefly emerged that I had seen before the set. "What? You can't hear me?" asked Ed. "Listen harder!" And he then stormed into the next number. And like Aaron Williams on the previous evening, Lil' Ed closed by walking unencumbered through the crowd playing wireless guitar, then returning to the stage to conclude the set.

One final thing impressed me: after Lil' Ed had left the stage, the trio played for another ten minutes without him, vamping on the closing number. It was here that you could again really appreciate the rhythm section and especially the abilities of Garrett's second guitar. Good stuff. And I know my son had dug it, because when we got home he immediately went online to see if Ed would be returning to the area anytime soon. We'll definitely go see him again. And I'm planning to yell for "20% Alcohol" when we do.

Concert Commentary

Rahn Lawrence
Toad's Place
New Haven, Connecticut
June 14, 2010

IT WAS STILL PRETTY EARLY, and I was determined not to spend the evening alone in my Yale Campus Housing dorm room. I walked past a club called Toad's, where I saw posters announcing upcoming acts including Ted Nugent and bassist Victor Wooten. Damn, thought I, why can't there be a rock show tonight? It was pretty clear that very few participants in the conference I was attending were much into music. And I had found no takers when I suggested general walkabouts. The conference leader himself had mentioned Toad's by name earlier in the day, but it was in the form of a derogatory comment concerning the type of music played there. I looked more closely at the posters for upcoming and previous acts. They'd had some names come through. The place looked dark, but I pulled on their front door anyway. A guy thrust his head out of a window and gruffly said, "May I help you!?" "Any live music tonight?" I asked. "Upstairs at 9:30—guitar trio." No kidding! Good news.

I headed back to campus housing to get ready. I put on my *Be The Person You Want to Be* T-shirt and headed out. As I hit the front door of the dorm, three uniformed security guards were talking. I walked out, they loved my shirt, and I said I was off to see some music at Toad's. They told me to have a good time, so I figured all was safe enough. I returned to the club at a little after 9, gave the gruff guy my $10 cover and went upstairs where no band was set up yet. No matter—I got a great seat in a very small club…and waited. But then, true to form, the band slowly emerged with amps positioned and instruments placed. I was expecting jazz guitar. And while the guitar was featured, this was a hard rock trio. Fine by me. The drummer had a fairly normal kit. The keyboard player had an elaborate array of electronics and was covering the bass part. I'm not a big fan of replacement instrumentation, but I must admit that the lack of an actual electric bass was not a distraction to me, as the night belonged to the guitarist.

The guitar player was a large, very black man. His name was Rahn Lawrence, and his size made a normal sized Fender Stratocaster look laughably small. He readied his extensive foot pedal array, and off he went. Absolute smoke, burning through a variety of recognizable covers from Motown to metal. Mainly instrumentals; long and interesting guitar solos. I was pleased. His playing seemed effortless. When the band's first break was ending, Lawrence was unable to get the management to turn off the juke box music—so he just started to play along with the song and rolled for several minutes, quickly overpowering it.

The band was completely with Lawrence throughout the night as he was calling up tunes with no predetermined set list—very little down time between songs. They had an ongoing Monday night gig, and the atmosphere was one of happy regulars. That night was the birthday of two people—a black waitress and a skinny white guy.

Somebody had brought cake, which was being given out during the break. I was offered a piece, but they were small cakes and I felt like I should let the regulars enjoy them. About two songs into the second set somebody from the club leaned over to guitarist Rahn. He announced that one of the party hosts had severely sliced her finger while cutting the cake.

"She's gone to the hospital. But it's OK—she's a nurse so she knew to go." Then he laughed and tried to assure us that no blood had gotten on the cake. People started to make bets on how many stitches she would need. It was too great! Laughing, Lawrence admonished them that wagering on injuries was probably in bad taste, and the trio kicked into another tune. It was getting late and I was thinking that I should get back, but then Rahn called for the birthday girl to sing a number. I was not expecting much—perhaps this was a nice gesture to the honoree. But she was no stranger to the microphone; she sang a sultry version of Michael Jackson's "Rock with You." Wow. Fine! Lawrence next called up the birthday boy and he killed on a version of Journey's "Don't Stop Believing." Both vocalists were unexpectedly talented.

Late in the second set, Lawrence asked if anybody liked The Eagles. Little reaction. "The Eagles?" I thought. "No," he clarified. "Not the sports team! Well even if you don't, were going to play 'Hotel California'." Hm. Questionable choice for this sort of band, I thought. They then played a lengthy instrumental version of the tune that was absolutely great. That closed the second set and the night. I went up and introduced myself to the band, telling them I was in town from Milwaukee for a couple of days. They were very friendly and asked me to come back next Monday. I was flattered to be included in their circle, but I'm not sure they understood the distance between Milwaukee and New Haven. It would, I decided, be worth the drive.

Book Review

Society's Child: My Autobiography
By Janis Ian
Penguin Books, 2008

Janis Ian should hire a fact checker. Her autobiography *Society's Child* is an interesting read about New York City culture at mid-20th Century. She discusses McCarthyism, intolerance, and overt racism. The book also serves as a wide-eyed account of show business in the 1960s and 70s. But because Ian makes numerous erroneous statements about the music scene, readers may be skeptical about her other recollections.

In one early chapter she has Sam the Sham headlining a concert at Shea Stadium several years before The Beatles' appearance there. Ian also has The Blues Project morphing into the Chicago Transit Authority. Neither assertion is correct.

Janis Ian had two memorable hits, the book's title song and the haunting "At Seventeen." Like her body of work, this book has many pleasant moments, but it is a distinctly second-tier reflection.

Book Review

Kaleidoscope Eyes:
Psychedelic Rock from the '60s to the '90s
By Jim DeRogatis
Citidel / Carol Press, 1997

Jim DeRogatis makes a convincing case for psychedelic rock as an ongoing genre rather than 1960s nostalgia music. What helps *Kaleidoscope Eyes* is the groundwork DeRogatis lays. He meticulously defines his terms before diving into a readable history and analysis of the form.

Kaleidoscope Eyes neither proselytizes for LSD nor longs for halcyon days of youth, demonstrating instead the breathtaking musical achievements in this genre. DeRogatis does discuss several specific losses that music has suffered due to an over-exuberance of chemical stimulus, such as Pink Floyd's Syd Barrett. Readers will undoubtedly disagree with some of the author's choices for revered music, as well as his assessments concerning dismissible bands. DeRogatis, however, backs his assertions with thought-provoking explanations, leading to a fruitful re-examination of many forgotten groups as well as the ongoing psychedelic scene.

Book Review

The Encyclopedia of Dead Rock Stars:
Heroin, Handguns, and Ham Sandwiches
By Jeremy Simmonds
Chicago Review Press, 2008

The late comedian Bill Hicks loudly proclaimed, "I want my rock stars dead!" He would have embraced *The Encyclopedia of Dead Rock Stars*, a reference work that uses 1965 as its date of death starting point. Considering the brevity of the entries, Jeremy Simmonds explores the many hazards of stardom with impressive depth. He also stresses the reasons to remember each departed individual. For example, who knew that Little Feat's Lowell George was classically trained, and had played oboe at Frank Sinatra recording sessions? Straying only occasionally into glibness and the pointlessly macabre, this book throws light onto many names in music that would be easy to forget.

Book Review

Killer Show—The Station Nightclub Fire:
America's Deadliest Rock Concert
By John Barylick
University Press of New England, 2012.

There was a reason your third grade teacher took the school's fire drills so seriously: fire is a relentless cause of death. John Barylick's new book *Killer Show* documents the causes for "The Station Nightclub Fire, America's Deadliest Rock Concert." This 2003 Rhode Island date for the band Great White was meant to be just another gig at a crowded club, but the group's use of indoor pyrotechnics went terribly wrong.

The fire's death toll reached 100, and many of the survivors' terrible injuries—both mental and physical—linger to this day.

Barylick does an excellent job of outlining the interlocking reasons for the fire and its gripping aftermath. The clear prose never lapses into sensationalism or bombast; a straightforward account of the evening's timeline is horrific enough. Any concert patron who places himself in the midst of a packed crowd needs to read this book, as do building code inspectors and club owners.

CD Review

Elvis Costello
The Juliet Letters
Rhino Records.
2006, 2 CD expanded re-issue of 1993 release

The Juliet Letters was Elvis Costello's 1992 song cycle of correspondence. Some of these musical missives are penned to the character Juliet; others range from junk mail advertisements to suicide notes. Costello says he initiated this project after learning that many young English girls actually have written letters to Shakespeare's Juliet with their romantic concerns.

With the Brodsky String Quartet as a backing group, the record was an acquired taste at the time of its release and is no less odd today. String quartets combined with pop songs, even mature pop songs, is a marriage bound to be troublesome. Costello's audience may be better prepared for it now, however, having since lived through a multitude of Costello's collaborations, ranging from Burt Bacharach to mezzo-soprano Anne Sofie von Otter.

The 1993 *Juliet Letters* LP was Costello's last for Warner Brothers Records, and the 2006 reissue was the final installment of Rhino Records' Costello project. Each of the Rhino reissues comes with a generous second disk of collectors' dreams. This release's bonus disk contains 18 extra tracks, including five of the pieces that the group used as encores when performing *The Juliet Letters* in concert. Among them: The Beach Boys' "God Only Knows" and the Tom Waits' song "More than Rain."

In liner notes newly penned for this reissue, Costello mentions his admiration for Van Dyke Parks' early album *Song Cycle*: it didn't sell, but it should be heard. Costello could be describing his own project. Not completely successful in sound or substance, *The Juliet Letters* is worth hearing as an entry point to the various collaborative paths that Costello would travel during the next 15 years.

Remembrance

Lou Reed
October 29, 2013

I wasn't going to write anything about Lou Reed's passing. I didn't think I had followed his career closely enough to weigh in on the significance of his death. Then last night I was talking to my good friend Pete on the phone and indicated my reluctance. Pete said: "Are you in your office at home?" I was. "Look at your shelves and tell me how many Lou Reed albums you own." Um…14. "And CDs?" About eight. "Yeah, sounds like you've barely heard of the guy." And so, blame Pete for another entry into the world of Wilmeth obits.

"Walk on the Wild Side" was the unlikely Top 40 hit that introduced me to Lou Reed. I loved the sound of the record—the upright bass, the female singers, the song's concluding saxophone, and the low-keyed but clearly enunciated vocal delivery. Then my high school drama teacher told me what some of the lyrics meant, and I was intrigued. Drugs and sex had never been so simultaneously overt and covert on my radio.

This hit single led me to the album *Transformer*, which discussed transvestites and junkies in ways I found scarcely believable. But it wasn't until his next album, *Berlin,* that I really connected with Reed. These songs were depicting seriously depressing scenarios. *Berlin* took the bleakness of Leonard Cohen to new places. While Cohen could be elusive through the symbolism of his lyric portraits, Reed would put it right out there, describing a woman named Caroline getting up from the floor, asking why the man beats her. Another song, "The Bed," describes the location where the singer's children were conceived, but also as the place where the mother ended her own life with a razor. Think of George Jones' "The Grand Tour," but a tour led by Stephen King.

Among the songs' most unnerving elements was Reed's ability to depict these scenes in uncomfortably realistic settings. The lyrics were especially disconcerting, placed as they were within the beautiful orchestral arrangements found throughout the album. Lou Reed's *Berlin* was one of the very few records I was told not to ever play again when I worked at KUNI (FM) in Cedar Falls. I had included both of the songs mentioned above during the course of a Saturday afternoon folk music show. I guess there were some phone calls. I was told by colleagues and the management alike to leave that record alone. I complied.

There's no other album quite like *Berlin*. Maybe that's a good thing, but uniqueness isn't an inherent plus. Another release unique to recorded music in the Reed canon is *Metal Machine Music*. Infamous for presenting four sides of screaming white noise, it stands alone as a tribute to something; I'm just not sure what. I read at the time that Reed released *Metal Machine Music* as his sonic rebuttal to critics who accused him of a softening artistic attitude. I own the album, but I'm not sure if this is the type of record one can actually "know."

Reed played the Iowa City Fieldhouse in the mid-1970s. I didn't go, but I was told later that there were quite a few walk outs when he performed the song "Heroin." As Reed sang, he used the microphone cord to simulate the act of tying off his arm. Then he shot himself up, using the microphone as the pantomime needle and syringe. This stage act was apparently too much for some members of this hip college audience—an audience that apparently had no problem with the safer, yet more violent theatrics of Alice Cooper.

In the late 1980s Lou Reed seemed to be at the top of his game. He had released the album *New York*, and during this same era the Canadian band Cowboy Junkies made their reputation, in part, with a haunting cover of his song "Sweet Jane." I loved the *New York* record. It was both rockin' and melodic, and the lyrics were filled with razor sharp observations about the city Reed loved so much. In fact, *The New York Times* printed lyrics from one of the songs as a self-contained editorial. Even so, I was still not compelled to really get serious about following Reed's career. I bought the subsequent *Magic and Loss* CD but found it less interesting than *New York*. I read that *Magic and Loss* represented a grieving process for Reed; one of his good friends had just died. In any event, I again lost track of the man's career until very recently.

The news seemed unlikely. Lou Reed was recording with Metallica? Yep. The odd double CD *Lulu* was the result. I don't know of any Metallica or Lou Reed fan who has much good to say about this 2011 release, but I give Reed credit for trying something different. While *Lulu* already stands as an anomaly in both the Metallica and Lou Reed discographies, Reed also experimented with setting the poetry of Edgar Allan Poe to music in his take on *The Raven*. I thought this Lou Reed project would soon be lost in the shuffle, so I made sure that I held out until I found the elusive two-CD set version of *The Raven*. Didn't everybody?

Since Reed's passing on Sunday, I have been asked what I thought was his best solo work. For me, it was a tie between the rockin' and political *New York* album and the bleak, personal vignettes found on *Berlin*. When it was first released, I raved about *New York* to anyone who would listen. One friend almost sneered, "Eh; if you like Lou Reed, it's good. If you don't like Lou Reed, it's not." And while very much of a "duh" comment, there is something to it—either you were on board with this guy or you weren't.

Lou Reed was once asked if he worried about alienating his audience. "I have absolutely no idea who my audience is," he replied. Perhaps Lou Reed's own uncertainty is why I myself am only now realizing that I have been a fascinated member of that audience for a long time.

Concert Commentary

Bruce Cockburn
Shank Hall
Milwaukee, Wisconsin
August 23, 2006

BRUCE COCKBURN'S PERFORMANCE at Shank Hall on Wednesday night was more lighthearted than usual, more politically charged than usual, and definitely more talkative than usual.

Although this Canadian's albums have often included dark songs of personal and political despair, Cockburn does not always bring the heaviest of these songs to the concert stage. The second set gave a double shot of political consciousness with his 1981 composition "Dust and Diesel," followed by the recent "Baghdad," for which he switched to a 12-string guitar.

If the second set showed his songwriting at its pointed best, Cockburn's first set seemed at times to be an enjoyable but wandering sound check. He began with "Open," "Lovers in a Dangerous Time," and his one American hit single, "Wondering Where the Lions Are." He then offered two instrumentals, "Jerusalem Poker" and "The End of All Rivers." Both were well played, but the audience seemed glad when Cockburn returned to singing, with "Different When It Comes to You."

Gary Craig backed Cockburn on an unnecessarily large drum set, but his real assistance came from the many light percussive accoutrements he sprinkled throughout the songs. Frequent collaborator Julie Wolf was again present for this tour, adding moody textures behind Cockburn's acoustic guitar with her various keyboards.

As Cockburn strapped on an electric guitar and traded licks with Wolf, "Slow Down Fast" showed that the Canadian had not lost his sense of humor or his ability to rock. The evening ended with "Last Night of the World" and encores of two favorites, "Rocket Launcher" and "Night Train."

Whether focusing intently on love or on the world situation, Bruce Cockburn's ideas were always interesting and his guitar lines clean and precise. On "Beautiful Creatures," he used a thin falsetto voice that was not exactly pleasant, but it fit the atmospheric tenor of the composition.

Cockburn appeared to be having a good time throughout both sets, talking about the songs and his new CD, *Life Short Call Now*. He surprised and pleased the audience by telling them that he had arrived in Milwaukee early enough to take a bike ride near the lake that afternoon. Perhaps because Cockburn had seen more of Milwaukee than usual on this visit, he allowed the audience to peer a bit deeper than expected into his musical psyche at the evening's concert.

CD Review

Bruce Cockburn
Small Source of Comfort
True North CD, 2011

Bruce Cockburn's latest release could be called a "best of," but this term is reserved for previously released material. Let's instead call it a "culmination," for on his new *Small Source of Comfort* CD Cockburn is able to assimilate all that has been good in his catalog since 1971.

Politics have not left the singer's oeuvre, but neither has Cockburn's sense of humor. Simultaneously fearless, bizarre, and compelling—"Call Me Rose" is a first-person narrative by Richard Nixon, reincarnated as a single mother of two living in the projects. Accepting this strange premise prepares the listener for other surprises on the CD.

More unexpected than the song's transformation of Nixon is the change in the singer himself, as Cockburn reconsiders his own long-held views concerning war. Having recently seen Canadian casualties at Camp Mirage in the Middle East, Cockburn sings "Each One Lost" with an attitude reflecting far more sorrow than anger. This, from a man known for his revenge-soaked song, "If I Had a Rocket Launcher."

Cockburn's love songs are still poignant and increasingly mature, which makes sense as the artist cruises past the 60-year mark. "Radiance" and "Boundless" both address physical love, but each also moves into realms of spiritual and Jungian devotion. Another form of love is found with "Lois on the Autobahn," an instrumental work inspired by Cockburn's late mother.

Each of the CD's five instrumentals serves as islands on which the listener can pause to reflect on the album's lyrics. Most of these instrumentals were commissioned for, but not used in, various film projects. I suspect that the reason a director would refrain from including these rich pieces is that they don't behave like background music. Each is strong enough on its own to compete with a film's visual elements.

Small Source of Comfort closes with the brief ballad "Gifts," used for years by Cockburn in concert as a final encore. The inclusion of this long withheld jewel makes it clear that the performer himself regards this CD to be a special release. Last year the government of Canada honored Bruce Cockburn's career with a high-profile concert broadcast on CBC Radio from Toronto's Massey Hall. This album demonstrates why such recognition is appropriate.

Concert Commentary

The Dark Star Orchestra
Pabst Theater
Milwaukee, Wisconsin
February 3, 2012

I HAD BEEN HEARING good things about The Dark Star Orchestra (DSO) for several years. They were a Grateful Dead cover band, I was told, but much more. Fans raved that this group elevated the concept of a tribute band to a new level—that the DSO took an actual set list of songs from the Dead's own touring days and recreated a complete concert. I heard how the band was extremely attentive to detail—the physical setting of the stage, the correct instrumentation; even the number of people in the band, depending on which era of the Dead was being replicated on a given night.

Beginning with a February 1973 show in Iowa City, I had seen the real Grateful Dead six times. As such, I initially had no interest in an imitation, no matter how authentic or heartfelt. But last Friday night there I was, front row of the balcony at the Pabst Theater in Milwaukee, waiting for The Dark Star Orchestra to hit the stage. I was just hoping that the set list they chose would be from the early or middle part of the real Dead's career.

The band came out and set the mood for the evening with "Let the Good Times Roll." Fun—a good opener. The version of The Grateful Dead being presented by The Dark Star Orchestra on this night had two drummers and no female singer. Fine by me. I had seen the Dead twice during the band's Keith & Donna Godchaux era, and I didn't feel that Donna was a needed presence. I never went to Grateful Dead shows to hear vocals. Few did.

But speaking of vocals, I was immediately impressed by the similarities of the lead guitarist Jeff Mattson's voice to that of Jerry Garcia. Rob Eaton, clearly the onstage group coordinator and the man playing the role of the Dead's rhythm guitarist Bob Weir, also had a vocal timbre very close to Weir's. Neither has an especially good voice, but they sound just like Weir and Garcia! Attention to detail, indeed.

Each performer had his respective instrumental parts extremely well covered. Eaton stayed on rhythm guitar throughout both sets, except for solo breaks on two tunes late in the evening. This is similar to Weir's role with the original band, letting Garcia stretch the lead lines. And speaking of the Garcia guitar chair, Mattson played wonderful Garcia-styled solos all night. Fluid and clear. I was initially surprised that bassist Kevin Rosen played a 6-string instrument in replicating that Grateful Dead concert. The Dead's bassist, Phil Lesh, was into electronics pretty early.

The first set lasted 75 minutes and was enjoyable. DSO really hit its stride late in this set with "It Must Have Been the Roses," followed by Bob Dylan's "Queen Jane Approximately," which was one of the peaks of the entire evening. Then the first set wrapped with powerful takes on "Ramble on Rose" and "Let It Grow."

I knew my son Dylan had a tentative attitude about this show, so I was pleased that he did not consider leaving at intermission. We talked about high points, watched the audience in this sold-out hall, and readied ourselves for round two. There had been a beer tasting event prior to the concert, so numerous attendees were pretty well oiled. Good move on somebody's part. Maybe.

Also during intermission Dylan ran into a college friend who told us that the lead guitarist was a fairly recent addition to the Dark Star Orchestra. He had joined the group within the past year, after their previous guitarist had joined Further, a band that included a surviving member of the Grateful Dead. I really can't keep all of the post Garcia bands straight— Further, Phil Lesh and Friends, Bob Weir's Ratdog. Get a score card.

There were the usual concert distractions during both sets. Because this was a general admission event, the crowd was more fluid than at a reserved seat affair. Some young people sat beside us for a few minutes and talked, but soon left. Good. The people immediately around us were pretty focused on the music. Also good. I was glad we had the front row balcony seats. The main floor had turned into a large dance floor. And those who were not dancing were standing. Sit down and you would see nothing. Even in the balcony many people were standing. And as I looked to the high upper balcony of this beautiful 1895 concert hall, I noticed a lot of hard partying going on. It was a long show; I was happy to sit. The second set alone lasted a full two hours before the encore.

Maybe it had been raining the night of the actual concert, because both of the Grateful Dead's famous rain songs were performed early in the second set—"Box of Rain" and "Looks Like Rain," two numbers I had always enjoyed—and each was very well played. But as with any real Grateful Dead concert, there were slow spots. DSO's take on "He's Gone" seemed to go on forever before mutating into a very odd and interesting instrumental section, so all was forgiven. The low point of the evening, however, was the obligatory "Drums" feature. I have no problem with drum solos, but this could not even be called such. Rob Koritz and Dino English both became involved with sound boards and electronics instead of percussion, tweaking computer controls more often than playing any instrument. As my son said, "They completely lost their way." Or as my junior high band director often told us: "Practice at home!"

The rest of the band finally returned to the stage, and the Dark Star Orchestra regained momentum and caught fire in their last three numbers. "I Need a Miracle" went into an unexpected "Gimme Some Lovin'," featuring organist Rob Barraco. This eventually morphed into a beautiful and stately "Morning Dew," which closed the main part of the concert.

One of the things I found most impressive was the band's ability to burn hard at slow speeds. This was evident when the fragile vocal of "Morning Dew" gave way to a slowly building and majestic instrumental section of this song. Being able to smoke at high speed is a basic requirement of a professional rock band, but to be able to bring urgency and intensity to a slow tempo takes even greater skill. I remember a night long ago when a friend spoke about a local band's performance of "Stairway to Heaven." "They're good," he said, "but notice that they take the tempo of the last part of that tune in double time. If they were really good, they could make it burn without speeding up, like it is on the record." Good call.

By the end of the night the crowd was getting rowdy. The ballad "Morning Dew" had elicited a bevy of howls and whistles. Why? I don't know. I guess people were digging this song and wanted the band to know it. I would have preferred audience silence on this number, but that wasn't happening.

Were there disappointments during the night? Very few. I wish that DSO's lead guitarist Mattson had faced the audience a bit more. Most of the time Mattson was visible only in profile, as he was facing toward second guitarist Eaton. That's fine for musical interplay, but I like to see the guitarists fingers dance over the fretboard. Son Dylan was likewise impressed with Mattson, proclaiming that this lead guitarist "carried the band." I won't go that far, but I loved every note he played—all night long. He was reading music off a stand for a couple of numbers. This bugged some people, I was told. But I thought it showed a desire for musical accuracy. And remember, this band plays a huge number of different songs. Cut the new guy some slack. I was glad to see that he *could* read music!

I looked at the band's web site the next day. This is where I found the date of the set they replicated. I compared the show we saw with some of their other song lists from past weeks. I think we attended one of their better recent gigs; I certainly was not disappointed. Dylan asked me how the Dark Star Orchestra compared with the real Grateful Dead. I dodged the direct comparison, instead repeating that in addition to the authoritative set list, the vocals and instrumentation were all remarkably attentive to detail. And I stressed that I would go back to see them again.

And just which night from the Grateful Dead's history was The Dark Star Orchestra replicating on that Friday night in Milwaukee? It was a surprisingly late show—a September 1988 date at New York City's Madison Square Garden. Whenever I put on Grateful Dead recordings, I never pull from that late in their repertoire. And I'm glad, actually, that I did not know the original date of the set; I'm sure it would have prejudiced me.

As we drove home after this great night of music, Dylan and I talked about what songs we would have liked to hear that the DSO did not play. I said "Love Light" and he mentioned "Friend of the Devil." I thought of "Truckin';" he wanted "Uncle John's Band." I said "El Paso" and he called for "Wharf Rat" (just because he likes the name). This back and forth list continued until we stopped ourselves and said, "Hell, that would have been an entire third set!" We agreed that we were both surprisingly satisfied with the generous evening of music, just as it was. We drove further in silence, and we bid them good night.

Concert Commentary

Motorhead
with Clutch and Valient Thorr
Eagles Ballroom
Milwaukee, Wisconsin
February 17, 2011

"Motorhead? You are going to see Motorhead?"
    "Hear them, more likely."
    "Why?"
    "I'll regret it if I don't."
    "What was their big hit?
    "They didn't have one."
    [silence]
    "'Ace of Spades' probably comes closest."
    "Never heard of it."
And so the conversation was repeated with various people during the days before the concert.
    "Who are you going with?"
    "Can't find anybody who wants to go."
    "And you're going anyway?"
    "Sure."
    "Why?"
    [See above…]

SINCE I BEGAN to take Heavy Metal music more seriously a few years back, there were an increasing number of bands that I wanted to check out. Milwaukee is a good town for such explorations. The single thing that had the greatest impact on my change of attitude was SiriusXM Radio's *Liquid Metal* station, and especially Ian Christe's informative program *Bloody Roots*. I listen to this show and the *Devil's Dozen* overview of new metal releases each week, learning quite a lot along the way.

Motorhead's early 1980s live album *No Sleep 'til Hammersmith* alerted me to an area of rock that had been largely outside my experience. I knew guys who were into Black Sabbath back in high school, almost 40 years ago, but the metal genre that Sabbath ushered in did not initially grab me. But years after its release, hearing Motorhead's *Hammersmith* album, I was unexpectedly impressed. Still, I did not immediately embrace this style of rock.

For a long time I thought of metal in the same way I viewed the most avant-garde forms of jazz, as almost joke music. Not that the musicians weren't deadly serious and dedicated to their vision, but I often found the performances more amusing than engaging. Preferably taken in short doses.

Motorhead was among the bands I most wanted to see, in part, because I knew Lemmy and his guys wouldn't be around forever. I felt that I needed to witness this classic metal band. This type of music differs considerably from the elder statesman bands of hard rock, such as The Who, The Rolling Stones, or even Led Zeppelin. With Motorhead, we're talking about thrash metal. Clever lyrics, a la Pete Townshend? Why bother? A strong melody? What's that? A vocalist like Robert Plant? Unimportant at this level of metal.

This recalls another friend's astute analysis: "Some people can't get past the fact that vocals can be used as a rhythm instrument." Good one. And he wasn't talking about scat vocals. Lemmy was indeed singing lyrics, but I don't think it mattered much. Still, the guy next to me apparently knew the words to every song; I could see his lips move. Also, Lemmy introduced the songs as being about certain things, so it's clear they must have had thematic substance. But I don't think many people in the large crowd were there for the vocals, whether they could sing along or not. As I said to my wife upon returning home from the concert, "Remember Dylan's performance at the Grammys? Bob sounded like Jim Reeves compared to Motorhead's Lemmy."

I arrived at the show quite early, knowing that I would have a substantial wait in front of me—they were on rock time, after all. The venue is a beautiful old structure on Wisconsin Avenue, The Eagles Ballroom, built in 1926. Acts from Glenn Miller to Buddy Holly had played this hall in its earlier days. I had been there a few times in my 20 years as a Milwaukee resident to see varying folks—Bob Dylan, Béla Fleck, Kenny Wayne Shepherd. But I hadn't been there in several years.

Maybe it was because I scanned older than the target audience, but everybody working the place could not have been nicer. "Use the side door please, sir." "Do you *have* a ticket or do you *need* a ticket?" Professional folks. And because I was early, there was not a mad crush to get in. I was frisked by a large security guard at the entrance. He hit a solid mass in my coat pocket and looked at me quite surprised. "Binocs," I said. He smiled and nodded. I was not the droid they were after.

I wasn't really sure how well Motorhead would draw. They are highly respected by the Metal community, but they had played Milwaukee just over a year ago, at this same venue. Were they exhausting their drawing power? Part of the reason I felt comfortable in attending this show was due to a review I read of their previous appearance, which stressed the aging nature of the audience. I expected a large motorcycle contingent of tough guys and lots of leather. There was some of each, but not nearly as much leather gear as I had seen at an Emerson, Lake, & Palmer concert in Milwaukee a few years back.

Entering a smallish bar in the building's basement, I was surprised to find a quartet already performing. Bag of Balls was the band's name, and I was pleased—at least there was some live music to kick things off, and they were working hard. The room was crowded and too warm, but not terrible on either front. After about their sixth of several interchangeable numbers, Bag of Balls' singer said something about Motorhead playing later in the adjacent room. Made sense—this was a pretty small stage for headliners.

I wandered over to the main room, a cavernous area that made up most of the building. This was the original, 25,000 square foot oval wooden dance floor, now a standing area for those wanting to be near the bands. Because I was there when the doors to the main room opened, I walked to the steel mesh fence that separated the crowd from the stage, where there was space for security and photographers. I was arguably too close to the giant stacks of amplifiers.

The guy next to me had his earplugs in place, so I thought I would follow suit. Mine worked best if I had my stocking cap on, to keep the plugs from popping out of my ears. Before long the first of the advertised groups took the stage. I was glad that they were making an effort to be on time—with three bands, I knew this would be a long night. The group's name was Valient Thorr. I thought at first it might be sort of a joke name, a band with a sense of humor—willing to gently mock the very genre they also embrace. After all, they seemed clueless about the correct spelling of their own name and claimed to come from Venus. Then I thought that with a name like Valient Thorr, they might be a gay metal band. That would be cool—and something different! I'd welcome it. But I was wrong on that front, too. Everybody was very serious and starkly hetero about this music, Venusian or not.

Valient Thorr had the most stereotypical metal look of the night: very long, very greasy hair, prominent tattoos, and a flying V guitar! They employed the standard lineup of two guitars, bass, drums, and vocalist. These guys looked the part of a metal band and sounded like one. I was directly in front of the lead guitarist, but the other guitar at the far end of the stage also seemed to be constantly soloing. The sound was loud, of course, but I was unable to distinguish what each instrument was playing.

Lyrics were largely unintelligible, but before the last song, the band's vocalist directed the audience's attention to the banner hanging behind the stage. "That's not just some band logo," he shouted. "That design symbolizes 'Peace through Rock and Roll'!" OK—his heart was in the right place, it seemed. This impressed me much more than the unorthodox ideals that some metal bands claim to embrace. Copping an attitude, as we used to say; or, I hope it's just a promotional act. Maybe this is where a lack of intelligibility in the lyrics is an asset to my enjoyment of this music.

As to musical genres and subgenres, even the most popular of the so called Alternative Country acts recently admitted that labels were immaterial; they were struggling bands just trying to get their music heard. Jeff Tweedy, now of Wilco, said that his seminal band Uncle Tupelo never billed itself as Alt Country, but they weren't going to argue if this tag helped sell records and get people to their concerts. Ralph Stanley never called his own music bluegrass, but if you bought a ticket he wouldn't dispute the point with you. Perhaps the same is true of some metal musicians. If a band can sell records or fill concert halls by implicitly riding the tail of Satan, what the hell (literally). Even so, none of the three bands on this bill were actively proselytizing the audience on behalf of the devil.

Valient Thorr's front man seemed very appreciative of having the opening spot on this leg of the tour. More than once he said how nice it was to "play the big stage" and to be opening for Motorhead. He told us to hold tight for Clutch and then left to the same great enthusiasm which the crowd showed for their entire set. Even so, no chance of an encore on a night that had such a tightly packed schedule as this. That's fine; I'd heard what Valient Thorr could do. The roadies were efficient—monitors and drum sets switched out, the banner replaced at the rear of the stage. Mikes checked, and here we go!

Clutch sauntered into view looking more like well-groomed construction workers than a metal band. Short hair, black T-shirts and black baseball caps, both without logos or demarcation—normal attire that would have been considered conservative in its own audience that night. These guys came to play and, like the previous bands, they too were deadly serious about what they were doing. A quartet, Clutch ripped through a 45-minute set that I probably enjoyed more than Motorhead's. These guys were...well, if a metal band can be subtle, they sometimes were. Still positioned near the front of the stage, I noticed that this guitarist took interesting, even thoughtful solos on his Les Paul. That, and he was dripping sweat from beneath his baseball cap from song one.

Unlike most of his metal guitar contemporaries, Clutch's Tim Sult had a very dark tone. Not dark like a Kenny Burrell fat note jazz sound, but Sult played almost all of his solos down on the low E and A strings. This is very different from most guitarists who go screaming up past the high octave range on the B and high E strings. Refreshing. Restrained. Also, Sult was not speedily trying to play every note or every lick he knew on each solo—they were well paced, and I could actually hear what he was doing.

Clutch had a better mix than the first band. At least, it sounded better to me through my ear plugs and wool cap. What an odd way to experience music. I felt sorry for some of the folks around me who had no ear protection. Live and learn. It took me a few days of ringing ears after several concerts in my youth to become convinced that ear safeguards might be worthwhile.

Speaking of which: This concert was certainly among the loudest shows I have attended, but not THE loudest. The top concerts on that front belong to Grand Funk Railroad in Des Moines 1970, and The Doobie Brothers in St. Paul 1982. But the dubious winner (surprisingly) must go to Earth, Wind, and Fire in Ames, Iowa, 1977. That was a true soul review lineup—The Emotions, The Brothers Johnson, and Earth, Wind & Fire. I wanted to enjoy it, but the sound at that concert was like having ice picks stabbed into my ears.

I was a little concerned about my current situation: If Clutch and Valient Thorr were this loud, then they might be saving the really high wattage for headlining Motorhead. And Lemmy's band WAS loud, but they didn't seem that much louder than the others. Of course my ears were already numb by this point. I briefly removed an ear plug once or twice during the opening bands' sets. Wow. The high end of the sound spectrum returned, but at what cost! So I replaced the plugs and lived with a muffled but tolerable sound level. I do wonder what the decibel level measurement would have been. Just as I wonder about the size of the crowd—at least a couple thousand enthusiasts. The place was packed.

Both of the main stage opening bands were absolutely traditional in gear: Fender basses with four (not five) strings, all cords plugged into amplifiers (no wireless connections), drum sets with a single bass drum, and the requisite Gibson Les Pauls. No doubting the pedigree of the equipment! I also liked the fact that the guitarists stayed on one instrument all night. They had racks of other axes sitting nearby, but each guy had a guitar he liked and played it throughout the set. No switching around for special sounds or alternate tunings. No need. I interpreted that (rightly or wrongly) as performers who had few pretensions. Just play the damn thing. And while Les Paul guitars are a gold standard for many players, Marshall Amplifiers are the long-favored weapons of choice for assaulting a crowd with loud music. And this stage had stacks galore of Marshall amps. In fact, it seemed that each player in every band had his own double stack of Marshalls. Visually impressive; aurally frightening.

The other, more important similarity Valient Thorr and Clutch shared was each group's ability to hit some grooves at various points of their sets. They straddled the fence between Valient Thorr's competence and Clutch's more accomplished musicianship, as exemplified by guitarist Sult. Clutch was not a newcomer to the field, as I had supposed—they were on tour supporting their *ninth* studio release! Although quite stable in personnel make up since 1991, they had just dropped their organist, returning to a four-piece band and to their original guitar-dominated sound. That was OK, really. The presence of keyboards at this show would likely have been too exotic for most of the crowd.

As the singer for Valient Thorr had earlier enthused, Clutch's front man Neil Fallon also indicated the group's great pleasure in being on this tour. "When you wake up every morning and realize that your band is going to play with Motorhead that night…it's amazing!!" He may have dropped an f-bomb or two in there along the way. I just can't recall. Clutch played its last song and departed. Their set had actually sped by for me.

The roadies again took the stage. This break lasted quite a bit longer and the crowd grew somewhat restless. When I had initially entered the hall, I grabbed a place on the far side of the stage. My choice was unintentional, but turned out to be fortuitous. The center section had become a mosh pit of sorts, with some pretty fierce slam-dancing breaking out during Clutch's set. Now, between bands, with the recorded music on the sound system, the frenetic dancing continued. I didn't mind watching it, but had no desire to participate.

One good thing about being so close to the stage was the lack of beer in my area of the hall. It was a long walk back to the bars, especially through the densely packed crowd. As such, drunks seemed few and nobody was spilling drinks on each other. That is, on me. There were photographers taking pictures of the excited and happy crowd. It was still a good, if intense vibe.

Huge security men positioned themselves in front of the stage—not so muscular as just plain large. Lights dimmed and Motorhead hit the stage. Yep, this was different. The cords were gone; this was a wireless outing all the way. The drums stood on a highly raised pedestal—and this time it *was* a double bass drum set up. Loud? Yes, but not that much louder than the other bands had been. I was relieved, but I don't want to downplay the intensity of the volume. Even though I became resigned to the stunning sound levels, I still couldn't help but notice that my blue jeans felt at times as if they were being blown by a pretty stiff breeze around my ankles. Sounds waves and shock waves. Too much. Just as I had expected.

Lemmy's bass guitar looked to be a modified Rickenbacker—a large, beautiful instrument wrapped in tooled cowhide. It resembled the trappings of country artist Hank Snow's acoustic guitar. Very cool. Lemmy came to the microphone and announced, "We are Motorhead!

And we play Rock and Roll!" The crowd screamed approval, and with that the trio roared into their anthem "We Are Motorhead!"

What struck me immediately was how healthy Lemmy appeared. I was expecting a road-weary, bedraggled presence. But Lemmy looked great and he alone was completely running this show. The huge, thick sound of his bass carried the songs. The rest of the band also made their presence felt. Unlike Clutch's Sult, who stood still and played guitar with head bowed beneath his cap, Motohead's guitarist Phil Campbell was a showman, striding the boards and repeatedly coming to the very lip of the stage to engage the crowd. In fact, I could have reached him if he and I had both stretched out our hands.

But I had no desire to touch Campbell, and I'm sure the security guards would have taken exception to this. Campbell had the more traditional style, playing fast licks high on the fret board. He wasn't playing a Les Paul, but the design of his white guitar was similar. And, as with all of the guitars that night—the strings' tuning pegs were where they were supposed to be—that is, at the visible end of the fret board. No weird, modern, empty-ended guitars. Not in the world of Metal, which is traditionally conservative in its own way—but they would likely cut me for saying that.

I didn't recognize the types of drums that Mikkey Dee played; probably custom jobs. Dee was an energetic drummer who would have been a more positive presence if we could have actually seen him play. But with such a huge drum set, he was largely hidden from view—although the few glimpses I got of his face indicated that he was having a great time. A drummer who kept things surprisingly interesting and a hot guitarist who added energy and color to the set were both indispensable. But this was Lemmy's band and Lemmy's show all the way, all night—the undeniable focal point of the stage.

After their eponymous opener, I did not know any of Motorhead's songs, but I assume many were from the new CD that the band had released that very week, *The World is Yours*. Earlier in the night, I heard two guys quoting a recent interview with Lemmy about the new album. The interviewer had asked, "Lemmy, why do all of Motorhead's albums sound alike?" To which Lemmy answered, "It's the same band." Those two guys loved that response, as did I. And this comment summed up the evening. The songs were very similar, but also exciting and well executed.

At one point Lemmy announced, "Here is an old one. It's from 1983—before you were born!" A girl's voice behind me protested that this did not apply to her, but she (and I) were among the exceptions. The song was admittedly unfamiliar to me, but I thought it was good that the band was acknowledging their older fans by playing some of its back catalog. I took a pen and paper with me, planning to take a note or two, but there was no chance of having enough room to do this. I was pretty packed in, increasingly pushed into the unyielding steel mesh fence. At one point I gallantly moved sideways so a young girl could throw her room key at Lemmy—hoping for a post-show rendezvous, I assume. Witnessing that act was by far the creepiest part of the evening.

The crowd was changing, the mosh pit expanding. I felt two hard blows. These were not accidental shoves, but some of the folks a few people away were starting to flail recklessly into others. I was the indirect recipient of what was passing for dancing. I had already checked the exits, and it looked like it would be a slow road out of the hall. Having experienced uneasiness at the size of the departing crowds during last year's Summerfest gathering late one night, I had planned to make my exit before the encore. But now I thought that maybe 45 minutes of Lemmy would suffice for the evening. A couple more strong body blows convinced me—time to leave. I made slow progress down the fence to the edge of the crowd. There was a green exit sign close to the edge of the stage. The crew behind the fence, although still very polite, pointed me away from this escape route, around the periphery of the crowd to the distant doors. OK—probably illegal and undoubtedly a fire department violation, but OK.

In fact, that exit strategy was fine. Being stageside for the whole night, I hadn't the opportunity to do much people watching. Now I slowly wound my way around the outer edge of the large ballroom that was crowded, but not impassible. I was amazed to see a coat check room in operation. I stopped at the merchandise alcoves for all three bands, but didn't really see anything I wanted. I almost bought a Clutch CD, but they all looked pretty beat-up for being new copies. As is true at all such gatherings, quite a few people were there only for the event and not to hear the band. I looked a little more in line with the age of many of these back-of-the-room folks at the bar and of those just hanging around. However, I had come for the music.

I wanted to get out before the set ended, so I kept moving. I knew I would miss Motorhead's song "Ace of Spades," which I did want to hear. But that would be near the very end of the show, and I was ready to go. I returned to the side door where the same people who had welcomed me when I arrived were still there. I told the woman that I had had a fine time, but it was getting just a wee bit violent near the stage. She didn't seem especially shocked at this, but was glad I had enjoyed myself. She thanked me for coming to the show, and I was out the door. Once on the street, I was surprised at how little of the band's sound could be heard outside the hall. That Eagles Ballroom was one solid building, now on the National Record of Historic Places. That recognition seemed appropriate to me as I drove home. After all, it was the historic nature of Motorhead that got me to come to this very "unWilmethian" type of gig, as good friend Pete proclaimed it.

I enjoyed the night; I was not above it; I wanted to be there. I was guilty of raising a fist in the air once or twice in pure excited metal joy and of occasionally pointing at a guitarist in admiration. As Motorhead's set progressed I saw body surfing up close and almost became an unwilling member in a mosh pit. And I escaped unscathed. Who could ask for more?

The next morning, I woke up feeling like I had been in a minor car wreck. My body ached. My head throbbed; I felt pretty hung over. What the hell? I knew that I had absolutely nothing to drink the previous evening. Ah yes. The Motorhead concert! Of course. My ears rang a bit, especially the left, but not terribly—similar to the aural aftereffects of a rough plane ride. I went to school to teach my classes. The few colleagues who knew of my plans were intrigued as to whether I really, actually went. I showed tangible evidence by taping the ticket stub to my office door.

"Well?"

"*What?*"

"So how was it?"

"*What?*"

"HOW WAS IT?"

"Oh. It was great—had a good time. Glad I went."

"Do you plan to write something about it?"

"*What?*"

"Never Mind!"

Post Script

Lemmy died unexpectedly during the last week of 2015. The metal world continues to mourn. As I say at the beginning of this piece, I am glad to have been at this show. I would have regretted not seeing this remarkable band.

Bonus Track

I saw The Clash near the end of their run, in August 1982. They played the same St. Paul hall where a Bruce Springsteen concert had changed my life two years earlier. I liked the Clash's show and was impressed by the tremendous amount of energy coming from the stage. I had several friends who were rabid in their devotion to this band, beginning with the group's first UK release. But even after seeing them live, I was not transformed into a true believer. And after their double LP London Calling, *followed by the triple,* Sandinista!, *I thought they were just throwing out anything and everything they had recorded.*

Two things I liked best about The Clash: the cover design of the London Calling *album is a purposeful nod to the first RCA album by Elvis Presley. Second, they recorded a version of Bob Dylan's lesser known "The Man in Me" for that album, but this song did not make it onto the record. I guess this shows I was wrong—they were not releasing everything that had recorded, after all.*

Concert Commentary

Anthrax
With Death Angel and Testament
Eagles Ballroom
Milwaukee, Wisconsin
November 19, 2011

WHATEVER HAPPENED to Punk Rock? I think I know: It changed its name and is now alive and well, living a full albeit incognito life as Thrash Metal. I am probably not the first to say this, but it has only recently dawned on me that Metal is not that far in lineage from its 1970s musical ancestor, Punk. I don't think any true, first wave Punk bands are still playing gigs and recording, but the healthy resurgence of various forms of Metal takes Punk's aggressive, in your face attitude, and amps up the intensity. Or at least the volume.

Some differences exist, of course. Punk was initially a musical reaction to the complacent world that rock music had become by the mid-1970s. The huge arena concerts and the overblown concept albums were so much garbage to bands like The Sex Pistols and The Ramones. Today's Metal seems not to be crusading against anything so focused; its world is too insular to care much about other areas of music, not even its sister genre, traditional Hard Rock.

The Metal school of rock music predates Punk. It is usually traced to 1970, specifically to Black Sabbath's first album. The Metal of today has gone through various incarnations. The current Metal bands on the road—be they Speed Metal, Death Metal, Black Metal, Brazilian Metal—likely include far superior musicians compared to the originators of Punk rock (which is NOT to be viewed as an insult to Punk bands). And these Metal musicians are probably in better physical shape than the first wave of Punk players; they would need to be, just to sustain the intensity of their music in concert. I can't imagine Richard Hell or Johnny Rotten keeping the frenetic pace of the lengthy high energy Metal sets I have recently enjoyed by bands such as Anthrax, Clutch, and Testament. (Mr. Rotten, I know, would take issue with this.)

From whence came these staggering (and overly simplistic) musical insights about Punk and Metal? Well, since you asked…

I kept going back and forth about whether to attend Milwaukee's recent Anthrax show. Part of my hesitation sprang from a performance video I had seen. I still liked the excitement of the live music atmosphere, but when I looked at the immense crowds in their part of *The Big 4* DVD, taped in a Bulgarian sports coliseum in 2010, I wasn't sure I really wanted to put myself back into that type of confined audience setting. I had been ringside for the Motorhead show the previous February and had a fine time. But I was a bit fearful that the Anthrax audience would be more intense than Motorhead's, and I didn't relish an evening of physical rigor in order to hear a band.

But music won the day, and I headed down to Milwaukee's *Rave* concert hall to have a go at Anthrax. The support acts sounded like interesting road veterans as well, especially Testament. Death Angel would open the night.

As with the Motorhead show, there was a live band playing in a side room when I arrived, but because the security check had taken a while and this early crowd was larger than I had expected, I passed immediately into the main hall to get positioned. I was about five rows back from the stage, but space was somewhat fluid since there were no chairs. Several tall people with large hair stood right in front of me, but I knew this would make little difference. And sure enough, they soon departed for a beer run.

Hitting the stage a few minutes early, Death Angel played a fast and furious 35-minute set. The lead singer Mark Osegueda often indicated that this was a special night for two reasons: it was Metal heaven for them to be in Milwaukee, and this was the final night of the tour. I knew that the latter was fact, but assumed the shout-outs to Milwaukee were standard stage patter—passionately praising whatever town they happened to be in on a given evening.

But as I learned at the conclusion of Death Angel's set, maybe front man Osegueda was not just blowing smoke about Milwaukee's reputation as a midwestern Metal Mecca. I started talking to a guy next to me—shouting with him, actually—and he said that Milwaukee regularly had far more Metal shows than where he lived—in Minneapolis! I was surprised. "Even with First Avenue there?" I asked. Yep. And he had driven in from Minneapolis for this concert! Wow. I think he said he had come for the previous evening's show by Kiss' Ace Frehley and stayed over for Anthrax. He told me that neither tour was hitting

Minnesota's Twin Cities. Wow again. Maybe we are special after all, but this also perhaps speaks to Milwaukee's lost moniker as "Workshop to the World," where blue collar was the predominant job opportunity. Metal is a Working Man's music.

Just as I used to say about The Clash's live shows: expect no ballads. In fact, when there was anything approaching a silence between songs during Death Angel's set, the mood in the hall felt odd. There were no resting tunes during these shows or even intentional down times. Front men would often speak to the audience, but only to whip them into frenzied readiness for the next song, or to indicate appreciation for the local crowd's intense support.

As the music played, I thought I felt water dripping on the back of my neck. What the heck? But as I looked around, I saw that what I had been feeling was the long hair of a young man slapping me rhythmically as he violently shook his head to the music. I pulled my stocking cap lower onto my neck. Problem solved. Still, this type of unexpected involvement was not welcome.

Death Angel ended with a flurry, and drummer Will Carroll threw out two broken drum sticks. One came near to where I was standing. When I saw that no one was scrambling to retrieve it from the floor, I thought, "Hell; I'll take it." And so I did, and I'm glad. That broken drum stick came in handy later in the night.

During the first break between bands I also talked to a young man about the new Metallica CD, a collaboration with Lou Reed called *Lulu*, which has been getting hostile reviews. He wanted to know who Lou Reed was. I tried to offer a quick tutorial but found it tough to do so. I was becoming increasingly hoarse trying to shout above the din of the crowd and prerecorded music. Soon the lights dimmed, Testament appeared, and—like concert days of old—the smell of pot became suddenly noticeable. I was surprised, since I don't recall *any* such smell wafting through the air at the Motorhead show.

The lead singer for Testament was a drag, I thought. Not that Chuck Billy sang poorly—that doesn't really matter so much in a band like this. (And that's not a shot.) It's just that he was a visual distraction. He took air guitar to a new, problematic level. It's one thing to play your microphone stand as if it were a guitar fret board, but to play it *constantly* and mimic the guitarist's solo note for note—now that's one frustrated singer, and a wanna be player. The column of the mike stand lit up blue, and many in the audience probably thought that he *was* playing the solos on a strange instrument. Maybe Billy wanted them to think it.

What this performance also says is that, for a lead singer to mimic the guitar lines with such perfection, the solos must be identical at each performance. Repetition is not necessarily a bad thing, but singer Chuck Billy unintentionally made it clear that there was no musical improvisation happening here. Having said this, I still plan to search out some recordings by the band—they have a box set retrospective that looks good. After all, I don't have to watch the singer while a CD is playing.

As Testament got deeper into their unexpectedly long set, most of the mosh pit area had stopped moving. That was surprising, but fine by me. But then one young man decided to create his own area of slam dancing, right in front of me and the guys I had been talking with. We exchanged a couple of grimaces. I even pulled out my recently acquired drum stick to ward off the unwelcome mosher's large body as he bounced my way. We hoped he would move on or fall or simply stop. But it was clear that this guy was not going to be dissuaded. Damn. And unlike the soft albeit irritating hair of a fellow patron hitting the back of my neck earlier, this guy's waist length hair was literally whipping into my face as he convulsed in front of us. This would not do.

About that time two people were cutting their way through the crowd to get to the side of the hall. I think one person was leading a sick friend. They passed right behind me so I decided to add myself to that short human train. I would have liked to talk with the Minnesota guy some more, but *c'est la guerre*. I took advantage of the pair's parting of the crowd—more tightly packed than I had thought—and made it to a stage-side bar. This was actually a good call since I was becoming weary and very thirsty. So I ordered a drink and leaned on the bar; both problems solved. And from that vantage point I could see the band surprisingly well. I had to look between large beams that supported this huge old building. But I could see the entire stage. And I could certainly hear Testament just fine.

One thing that I had noticed during the sound check between bands was a distinct stereo separation for the hall's mix. This is why, during my previous metal encounter, with Valient Thor, I could see a guitarist soloing at the far end of the stage, but I could not hear him well. I find this mix for a concert hall odd. But I have been at many such shows over the years with distinct sound separation. This audio approach means that only a small number of patrons will hear all of what is happening on stage—just those in the middle of the audience seated (or moshing) between the speaker columns. Why not just mix the whole thing to mono? Then everybody would get the same sound and be able to hear it all. Just who does the sound man have in mind for that mix? I'd give worlds to know.

Testament played a little longer than I needed, but I was impressed by their drummer, John Tempesta. The next day I was raving that Tempesta was the best drummer I had ever seen. I myself am surprised by this proclamation as I write this, but I know I meant it. And he *was* great! Tempesta was sitting in with Testament on this six-week tour because their regular drummer had some mysterious ailment that kept him off the road. Whatever. Tempesta had formerly been Testament's regular drummer for a short stint in the early 1990s. He is now in a band called The Cult. No matter the lineage, this cat could play and make things interesting throughout. I rarely single out drummers for praise, but this guy was amazing.

It looked like some cash transaction business deals were going down around me as I stood at the bar. I guess I did not strike anyone as a threat, and was duly ignored. Good. I remained at the bar for the duration of Testament's set. After this, I knew a crowd would approach, seeking beer, so I left my perch and had a walkabout toward the back of the hall and the milling throngs. I did not feel particularly old in this crowd. It included young people, to be sure, but there were lots of members of the post-40 set. What did irritate me was that so many of the men in the crowd had kept their hair—and had grown it long! My own thick black hair abandoned me some years back.

I walked over to the merchandise area, but it was pretty lame. They were selling the new Anthrax CD and a couple of other items, but nothing special. Maybe it was because it was the final night of the tour, but everything looked pretty beat up and worn out—even the people selling the stuff. I found a place at the back of the hall where I could lean on a wall and still see the stage. I just waited for the headliners while observing the people.

The various shirts worn by the audience told an interesting story. Many sported designs of the bands performing that night, Anthrax and Testament. Other than these, the only bands represented were Metallica, Iron Maiden, Motorhead, and a smattering of old Black Sabbath shirts. Based on numbers, Pantera was the band with the most followers. What also struck me was the *absence* of many of the staples of hard rock. Nowhere to be seen was anything like Led Zeppelin or even The Clash. One guy had on a Kiss shirt, and even this was wildly out of place. I assume he had been at the previous evening's Ace Frehley show and had just kept it on. Nothing close to Pearl Jam or Nirvana attire, either. Anyone in a Grateful Dead shirt would have probably been denied entry to this concert.

Early in the night I saw one guy in the lobby with a Beatles baseball cap on, but he looked truly lost. I wore a nondescript brown sweatshirt, my blue jeans torn at the knee, and a stocking cap. The jeans tear was for cred and the cap was to keep the earplugs in place—a fashion statement with a purpose! Vanity—the constant striving to be cool and to fit in. Metal audiences are not immune. Nor am I.

Tattoos were commonplace, as was the vagabond appearance of most attendees. Much like Holden Caufield's vexation over the winter whereabouts of the ducks from the pond in New York City's Central Park, I have often wondered where the homelessly attired people I would see annually at the Iowa State Fair go for the other 11 months of the year. I think I now know—they are attending Metal shows. And couldn't be happier about it!

Anthrax hit the stage and played a solid set. They too talked about their love for Milwaukee and that this was a special, final night of the tour. As the young man said to me earlier in the evening, these are all essentially Battle of the Bands shows. And mainly fun outings, in spite of some inherent annoyances.

I recognized some of Anthrax's older songs and a few from their latest CD, *Worship Music*, including one called "Fight 'em 'til You Can't," a song about trying to battle zombies. This had been getting airplay on XM's Liquid Metal station. Lots of fun, especially if you don't take the subject matter too seriously.

Impressed again by the faded splendor of this venue, I decided to hit one of the men's toilets, just to see if this too had at one time been a regal room. Once inside, waiting in a short line, I witnessed a very drunk man trying to tear the paper towel dispenser from the wall. He did not succeed. I went into one of the stalls, which was uncomfortably dark and very narrow—built a long time ago. Don't drop your keys in here, I thought. Just then I heard a *woman's* voice yell, "Jimmy! The bus is leaving! We are going *now*!" I couldn't see her, but the woman must have been *in* the men's bathroom. No response from Jimmy, and I think the woman quickly left. A couple of patrons chuckled and one guy spoke out, "Anthrax is on stage and the bus is leaving? I don't think so!" Poor Jimmy. Poor woman.

I was starting to wear out. After about an hour of Anthrax intensity, I began to head for the door. As I walked through the back of the hall I put my hand flat against one of the building's main support pillars. It was vibrating heavily, but I'm sure it had been through worse. Solid structure, I thought. Approaching the exit, I saw that a side-stage area was accessible through a bar. It was fairly clear, and so I walked as close to the stage as I had been all night. There was a man trying to take pictures with a professional camera (not a cell phone), being hassled by a band security thug. There was a pair of overly well-dressed women who I had seen earlier at the far end of the hall. Still looking for customers, I guess.

Heading more determinedly for the exit, I passed by the small, now deserted alcove where the local metal band had been playing as I entered. They seemed competent and eager, but I really couldn't tell more than that. As I glanced at the empty stage, I saw that their set list remained on the floor. I retrieved it read the names of the songs that this departed, unknown group had played that night. The one title that has stuck in my mind is "Fuck Your Sister's Eyes." I smell a hit!

Bonus Track

Speaking of rock music and hit songs, one hard rockin' radio hit that stood apart in the fall of 1967 was The Who's "I Can See for Miles." Several people, including my son, have told me that this tune does not do much for them. But at that time, "I Can See for Miles" was the heaviest thing on radio. It showed the power of the band in a 3-minute package. This was not the group's first American chart entry, and many would follow. But curiously enough, "I Can See for Miles" remains The Who's only song to make it into the Top 10.

The aural ferocity of "I Can See for Miles" may have

*opened the door for the following spring's intense hit version
of "Summertime Blues," by Blue Cheer. This old Eddie Cochran song would subsequently be recorded by The Who. It's
all connected.*

Remembrance

Bobby "Blue" Bland
One Night in Bryan, Texas, 1986

My wife looked at me, trying to be a good sport. "You know," she
said slowly, "Most baby girls wear little tops that have flowers on them.
Or maybe ducks or bunnies." She paused. "Our Cindy is wearing a
T-shirt that says, 'Bobby 'Blue' Bland: World Tour.'" And she was right.
But my daughter came by that shirt honestly. And, it was a quality
shirt. Like Bland himself, it was constructed of superior materials,
made to last many years. Cindy wore it until she outgrew it; then her
brother inherited it.

I don't really remember what songs Bobby played in Bryan that
night, but I'm sure they were the hits. Truth to tell, I didn't know Bobby
"Blue" Bland's catalog very well in the spring of 1986. I was a recent
transplant from Minnesota to deep in the heart of Texas. In mid-1980s
St. Paul, a black vocalist who fronted his own band meant Prince.

What I do recall about that Texas night was how my friend Tony
told me that he would not be taking his nice car to the gig, and that it
would be a late show. We parked in a mud lot and made our way to
the door. People stared. The club itself seemed to be made of rusted,
corrugated tin. Once inside, I saw that we were the only white faces
in the crowd. That didn't bother me until Tony began to insist loudly
that we were on the guest list. Maybe we were, but I was happy to pay
the cover to keep the escalating voices from going to the next level. No
problem. Tony got us in.

We moved to the side of the stage, where we were very close to the
band. The flock of middle-aged women who crowded in front of Bland
had to be gently cleared from time to time by the singer's body guards.
I think they would have welcomed something more strenuous to do.

The crowd was very segregated that night, but in an unexpected way. The women were together in a cluster admiring Bobby, and the men stayed at the tables and drank. There were a few minor fights on the dance floor, but not many. Maybe the separation of the sexes helped with that.

As the set continued, sweat pooled on the stage floor like rain on asphalt. Smoke obscured the view, even feet away from the bandstand. Bobby wore gold chains, heavy and numerous. By his demeanor, the singer appeared to be weighed down by some larger burden. Maybe it was just part of Bland's persona, but it fit. Here was a weary man who had the blues. And here was a true soul show, in music and in setting. Distorted guitars through long blown amps and pulsating rhythm purveyors who couldn't remember the last time they had been off the road. The band settled into a groove. Everybody got comfortable. This longed-for feeling was why the room was packed. Time and music became elongated, stretching into the night.

Then, without fanfare, it was over. The lights came up, just slightly. As we left, I looked down at the merchandise that was arranged on a card table with one leg missing. Tony already owned all of the artist's CDs they had on display (and many more). I picked up a small, pale blue T-shirt that said "Bobby 'Blue' Bland, World Tour." I thought that wording was smart, because he could use it in any location, forever. I stared at the tiny image of Bobby's face in the logo. "I'll take this," I said. My Cindy was about six months old. It would be perfect. The older woman operating the concession was pleased to see that I was thinking of my daughter. My wife, however…well, this is where we began.

Post Script

This piece was written on the occasion of Mr. Bland's death, June 23, 2013.

CD Review

James Hunter
People Gonna Talk
Rounder Records, 2006

Is it culturally risky to say that James Hunter has the voice of a talented black singer? I'm inclined to take the risk. Hunter is at turns elegant and gritty on *People Gonna Talk*. Before examining the artist's photo on the CD cover, discerning ears could point to various black American antecedents for both his vocals and his guitar work. Given the photo, they would undoubtedly be surprised at the performer's pale complexion.

In numerous glowing reviews, much has been made of the recording process of this British bluesman's first U.S. release. And true, the sound has a warmth that only the older analog process seems able to capture. The only reason we care about the way this CD was recorded, however, is because of the consistently high quality of Hunter's singing and playing.

Although his blues influences are many, Hunter is no clone. He shows impressive originality, writing all 14 of the tracks on this CD, without a weak sister among them. He comfortably leads his quintet through numbers sometimes reminiscent of Robert Cray, at other times of Sam Cooke, or occasionally even James Brown. Let me amend my opening statement: James Hunter doesn't have the voice of a talented black singer. He has the voice of *several* talented black singers.

Bonus Track

While still in high school, I would occasionally visit a friend in the hip college town of Iowa City. It was sort of our area's version of radical Madison, Wisconsin. On one outing, we saw Gil Scott-Heron play a show at the university union. It was a long and rhythmic evening. The thing I recall best is not the music, however, but Scott-Heron's lengthy spoken piece "We Beg Your Pardon," which condemned the political scene of the time, and especially the recent pardon that President

Ford had bestowed on Richard Nixon. It was entertaining, but also an extremely pointed political statement.

CD Review and Book Review

James Brown   and   *The One: The Life and*
James Brown Jazz   *Music of James Brown*
Verve Records, 2007   Gotham Press, 2012
                                     By R. J. Smith

When James Brown died on Christmas Day 2006, record companies rushed to do their usual thing—each of Brown's former labels repackaged the music they owned by this artist and issued it with a new cover. One of the more unexpected collections was called *James Brown Jazz*. For me, this title conjured unpleasant memories of Jimi Hendrix's troubled posthumous recording legacy. One former producer tried to champion Hendrix as a frustrated jazz guitarist on releases like *Nine to the Universe*. Even less likely, some said that The Allman Brothers Band would have become jazzers had guitarist Duane not died.

I bought *James Brown Jazz* but didn't play it much until recently, when I encountered Brown's new biography, *The One*. In it, R. J. Smith shows the diverse elements that made up James Brown: R&B, funk, gospel and grit; hard driving grooves and those heartbreaking ballads. All this, and more, were a part of Brown's bag. Regardless of form, at no time was his sound indistinct. Whether hearing "King Heroin" or a Christmas hymn, you immediately knew this was James Brown working the room. He was incapable of aural anonymity.

But jazz? As the CD title says so clearly—this is *James Brown* jazz, the genre as seen through this performer's unique musical lens. He solos repeatedly on organ during these largely instrumental tracks from the Smash and King labels, all recorded in the 1960s. In a telling side note, when the *James Brown Jazz* CD is called up on the *All Music Guide* site, the "sounds like" category for this release includes records by Wes Montgomery, Joe Sample, Jimmy Smith, and Ray Charles. I can't argue.

Brown's connections to jazz (on his own terms) explain part of what makes reading the 2012 biography *The One* so worthwhile. But Smith's title does not refer to its subject. Instead, "the one" is a reference to the way Brown orchestrated his music, with an unyielding emphasis on the first beat of every measure. The book's title is as a fitting as the text, for in it Smith focuses on Brown's music. At times, in fact, within these 450 pages, James Brown the person sometimes remains a frustratingly unknowable figure.

We do get glimpses of Brown as a difficult boss, insisting on perfection from his players, yet obsessed with visual style as well as sound. Unafraid to examine the little known and unflattering aspects of his subject's life, Smith indicates that physical abuse and unyielding dominance was business as usual for Brown, both on and off the bandstand. But so was an extraordinarily community-minded outlook, along with unflinching generosity. Smith doesn't downplay lurid episodes from the road or trials on the bandstand, but these are not central to the narrative. The business side of James Brown is not ignored, either, as Smith describes the singer's involvement with his early record labels. The account includes eye-opening passages during a career that takes Brown from being an abused artist to having absolute control over his records.

Still, it is Brown's music that holds center stage in this book. Although readers wouldn't need great expertise in music appreciation to read *The One*, some musical background would help. Smith includes discussions about Brown's rhythmic intricacies and the part they played in creating various grooves. These passages help to explain how Brown consciously formed his specific rhythmic *sound*, which was usually more important than his specific *songs*.

Smith does an excellent job of appealing to a wide audience in *The One*. Tales of relentless touring are here, as is an in-depth examination of the mid-century America society which produced this artist. Influences on Brown include high level politics, stateside protests, and foreign entanglements. The description of Brown's successful insistence that he perform for American troops in Viet Nam is a highlight of the book. Smith also shows the performer thrust into various unrequested roles during this turbulent era. Brown served as a *de facto* peace keeper in Boston after Martin Luther King's assassination, and he (warily) endorsed Hubert Humphrey's 1968 presidential bid. Both of these tasks were accomplished on Brown's own uniquely specific terms.

Brown's battle with King Records to release *Live at the Apollo* is fascinating and frustrating by turns, as is Smith's depiction of business dealings in the world of small record labels. The artist's struggles to connect and then desperately reconnect with a black audience are recounted, as is his relentless determination to remain in control over all aspects of his career. For example, fearing that he could become too dependent on a single person to play a gig, Brown often took five drummers with him on the road!

The One tells how Brown built his stage show element by element over several years, discarding what didn't immediately excite his audience, and cultivating what did. He knew the importance of his set's musical structure, but also knew that this was a SHOW! Stage performance was a critical element in the James Brown experience. Brown's precise dancing, along with his caped and exhausted exit from the stage each night, projected memorable images and generated excitement among his audiences.

It was no accident that Brown succeeded at such a high level. Smith's narrative leaves us with a portrait of "the hardest working man in show business," no matter what the genre. While jazz music will not be the primary element in Brown's legacy, Smith's account of the part it played in this artist's career helps to show that very few things were beyond the reach of James Brown.

Bonus Track

As Smith's book and the film biography of James Brown both stress, this artist was an astute business man and protector of his own interests. Brown was the first artist I ever heard to address the practice of audio "sampling." This is where one artist takes a section of a recording by another artist to use in some way on his or her own recording, usually without permission or payment. I once heard Brown complain during a radio interview, "How about if I just take a part of you and use it? How about it I take your toenail and use that? You like that? That OK with you?" Funny. But the heavily sampled man had a point.

Book Review

Prince: Chaos, Disorder, and Revolution
By Jason Draper
Backbeat Books, 2011

Must tremendous talent always be accompanied by startling strangeness? Perhaps not, but Jason Draper's new biography of Prince portrays equal doses of prodigy and poser.

Draper does a good job of chronicling Prince's rise from a Minneapolis basement to the world stage. The book also stresses Prince's early awareness of the power of the Internet, only to later miss various web-based opportunities and ultimately remove himself completely from artistic ventures in cyber space. The infamous battle with Warner Brothers Records is recounted, and the reader can see why both artist and label could claim legitimate reasons for unhappiness.

The author meticulously discusses Prince's numerous side project recordings of the *Purple Rain* era, many of which were released under pseudonyms. Also tantalizing is Draper's description of Prince's vault in his Minneapolis home, where various unreleased masterpieces are said to reside. What undercuts the desire to open this vault is found in the latter part of the book: if so much wonderful Prince material lies dormant and unheard, why does he insist on releasing unremarkable music at this point in his career?

Draper is not afraid to criticize Prince's missteps, but the author also never loses sight of why The Purple One is worth an exasperated fan's devotion: this is one very talented cat! The book is sometimes repetitive, but descriptions and assessments are clear and fair throughout. A useful "Career Timeline" appendix is included. A complete discography would have also been welcome, but such a list for this extraordinarily productive artist would necessitate a second volume.

Post Script

Prince died in May 2016. In typical fashion, the aftermath saw mourners who proclaimed to be Prince fans rushing to buy his recordings. The real fans already owned them.

Concert Commentary

Stevie Wonder

The Forum
Los Angeles, California
December 20, 2014

FANS OF STEVIE WONDER were becoming increasingly impatient as the fall of 1976 began. It had been more than two years since the release of his last album, in a day when two years was a gaping stretch of time for an artist to go between records. Wonder himself was aware of his audience's increasing anticipation—anticipation bordering on irritation.

The release date of the new album was delayed and then delayed again. Rumors swirled that Stevie wanted to record more music; then it was said that he wanted to remix the whole project. Some began to worry that there was no album to release, that Wonder's creativity had run dry. That fall, in an effort to assuage growing unrest, Motown Records ran a full-page ad in *Billboard Magazine*. It showed a defiant woman standing in deep shadows, holding a reel of tape. The caption at the bottom of the page read simply: "We're almost ready."

Reasons for the heightened expectations were well founded. The three previous albums by Wonder had taken this artist from the realm of a talented Top 40 pop singer into the more adult world of album-oriented music. Instead of producing hit singles, Wonder was now creating art in the form of record albums. But he made this transition while still being able to place songs on the radio. Marvin Gaye had already made a similar switch, successfully going from hit singles to concept albums like his masterpiece *What's Going' On*. But unlike Gaye, Stevie Wonder began to release albums of audio jewels like clockwork.

For those paying attention, Wonder's first real breakthrough album was *Music of My Mind*, from July 1972. The back cover states, "This album marks a milestone in the development of a great artist." Liner note exuberance isn't unusual, but in this case the statement about the artist's greatness was absolutely true. Wonder had written every tune and played virtually each instrument on the record. Although a tour de force, *Music of My Mind* produced no sizable hits. "Superwoman" peaked at #33 on the singles chart, in spite of containing one of Wonder's finest melodies. A strong album but without hits, it was overlooked by Wonder's radio audience and did not sell well. Motown owner Barry Gordy could not have been pleased.

Some will say that Wonder's breakthrough started with his previous release, *Where I'm Comin' From*, in 1971. Perhaps so. But no one disputes that the album that caused the music world to refocus its collective attention on Stevie Wonder was *Talking Book*, from October 1972. *Talking Book* contained two #1 singles—"Superstition" and "You are the Sunshine of My Life." The album includes other memorable songs, including "Blame it on the Sun" and "I Believe (when I fall in love it will be forever)."

Wonder followed *Talking Book* in 1973 with *Innervisions*, an even more mature album. With *Innervisions*, Wonder found the perfect balance of artistic expression and hit singles. The album included "Too High" and "Livin' for the City," both Top 10 hits. The upbeat rhythms of the first song seemed to mask its dark theme of drug abuse, while the second took a pointed look at life in an American ghetto. Like Marvin Gaye's "Inner City Blues" and "Mercy Mercy Me (the ecology)" from two years earlier, Stevie Wonder was getting songs of social consciousness onto the radio.

In 1974 Wonder released the third of his amazing trilogy, *Fulfillingness' First Finale*. Although nobody realized it at the time, the album's title was completely accurate. With this record, Stevie Wonder brought down the curtain on the artist he had become since beginning his focus on albums as art forms. Like *Talking Book* and *Innervisions*, this collection also had two big hits: "You Haven't Done Nothin'," which went to #1, and "Boogie on Reggae Woman."

Because of his annual release schedule, the fall of 1975 found people expecting Wonder's next album. But no record was released. At the subsequent Grammy Awards for 1975, Paul Simon publically thanked Wonder for not putting out a record that year. It was a humorous and candid remark; the two previous awards broadcasts had seen Simon (and others) eclipsed by Wonder's virtual sweep of popular music Grammys.

No one begrudged this artist some time to breath, certainly, but when the fall of 1975 turned to spring 1976 and then to summer—concerns were voiced. Still, nothing was forthcoming. No stopgap singles, no placating collection of hits or unreleased live material. Just silence.

Finally, during the last days of September 1976, Motown sent out promotional copies of the sprawling double album titled *Songs in the Key of Life*. The orange cover was unmistakable, and the packaging included a large folio of complete song lyrics, performance credits, and various notes of thanks from Stevie.

The two-album set also included a 7" record (the size of a single) that played at 33$^{1/3}$ rpm. This was termed "A Something Extra" at the time of its release, four songs that would be called "Bonus Tracks" in the CD age. In the 1950s this extra record would have been called an EP, an Extended Play. By 1976, the format had been long abandoned by the American record industry. But here was Stevie Wonder resurrecting it to make sure his four extra songs were included. This "Something Extra" contained an additional 18 minutes of music and featured some of the strongest material of the entire set. It was inconvenient to play this small disk on our then modern turntables, but well worth the effort.

Essentially, then, this was two and a half albums worth of music. It began to make sense why it took the artist so long to get this set prepared for release. Wonder had a huge amount of material, and he didn't want to pare it down to a double album. But expanding it to a three-record set would take more time, and he was already getting pressure from fans and his record company alike to get the record out.

Some would say—especially in later years—that Wonder should have shortened some of the lengthier grooves, making room on the main album for the four relatively brief songs from the extra disk. Does "Another Star" really need to be eight minutes long? Couldn't both "Black Man" and "Isn't She Lovely" be truncated a bit? Undoubtedly. But that's not the way Stevie wanted it. Looking at the album as originally released, sides one and two are a series of concise songs. Even at seven minutes, the opening "Love's in Need of Love Today" has a structure that never slips into a jamming groove. This is true of each of the ten songs from these first two sides.

The jam party starts on the second record. Each of the previously mentioned songs provide a stretch for the musicians (that is, Stevie) as does the latter part of the transcendent song "As." However, long tunes had been a fairly common canvas on Wonder's album tracks for some time, as with "Maybe Your Baby" from *Talking Book*. To trim the grooves of sides three and four in order to accommodate the four bonus songs on this release would undermine Wonder's overall vision for the set. Love it, tolerate it, ignore it, hate it; but this is the way Stevie Wonder wanted you to hear his *Songs in the Key of Life*.

The album was a triumph. It was rewarded with accolades, Grammys, enthusiastic reviews, sky high sales figures, and two #1 hit singles: "I Wish" and "Sir Duke." The wait had been more than worth it. All doubts were cast aside. Wonder seemed unstoppable.

And then...a complete retreat by this prodigy turned mature genius. He did not tour after the release of this remarkable record, even though he could have sold out any hall on the planet many times over. Stranger still, Wonder's subsequent albums seemed to be almost afterthoughts. It was a full three years later that he finally released his next project: the odd, largely instrumental album of soundtrack music for a movie that nobody saw, called *The Secret Life of Plants*.

Hotter than July was released in the summer of 1980. It's a good, if largely unremarkable album, saved in part by the inclusion of "Master Blaster (Jammin')." After that, another soundtrack—this time for *The Woman in Red*. Both records yielded hit singles, but Wonder appeared to have abandoned his desire to be an album artist and was now again satisfied with placing songs on the radio. This is something he could still do, seemingly at will. "Send One Your Love," "Part-Time Lover," and "I Just Called to Say I Love You" were all big hits in the years and decades following *Songs in the Key of Life*. But these singles were not culled from cohesive album projects, as his hits had been in the 1970s. Instead, Wonder had gone back to recording and releasing mere collections of songs.

It was never the same for many of us after *Key of Life*. Our respect for Wonder could not have been greater; his music was absolutely on a level all its own. Yet something had gone out of the artist once this album was finally released. If *Fulfillingness* was the end of his powerful trilogy, then perhaps *Songs in the Key of Life* could be viewed as the curtain call.

So it was with some amazement when I learned that Stevie Wonder had launched a brief string of concert dates on which he would be performing the entire *Songs in the Key of Life* album. I discovered this fact the night before Wonder was to play Chicago, a mere two hours south of my Milwaukee area home. I investigated. The hall was sold out; scalpers were charging high dollars for poor seats. It was final exams week; going anywhere would be problematic, much less a foray into downtown Chicago. I resigned myself to playing the album that night at high volume.

Then my wife saw that Stevie was ending the brief *Key of Life* tour in Los Angeles, where our son lives. We were planning to visit him in December, so it was arranged that I could stay and attend the concert. My son bought us tickets for the show, which had not yet sold out, to be held at L.A.'s recently refurbished Forum.

The mood in the sports arena that night was of high expectations. Many had arrived well dressed. I thought that my son would scan on the young side, as he has at so many other concerts we have attended together. But to our mutual surprise, the audience covered a wide age spectrum. It was also clear that Wonder had not lost his African American audience. That sort of loss had been a major frustration for some popular musicians of the past like Louis Armstrong and, later, James Brown and Jimi Hendrix.

Audience members found their seats at a casual pace, discussing both the holiday season and the evening's event. At precisely 8:30 the Forum's house lights went dark and the stage was illuminated. Stevie Wonder made his way to stage right, closest to our balcony seats, and addressed the crowd. His opening remarks were spiritual and hopeful. Wonder thanked the audience for attending and he thanked God for giving him the 21 songs that made up the *Songs in the Key of Life* album. He was inclusive in his acknowledgement of many religious beliefs, but his remarks centered primarily on Christianity, stressing that this season was to be remembered for the birth of Christ.

Wonder said he would like to do a little Christmas music but was aware of the large amount of material they were scheduled to perform, so would defer for the moment. He introduced a beautiful woman named India.Arie, who had led Wonder to the lip of the stage for the opening remarks, saying that she had been with him for many tours.

As Wonder again thanked the audience for attending, he surprised many by sincerely stressing that his own performance would be superior to that of his most recent Forum concert. "Three years ago I was having trouble with my voice. That won't be a problem tonight." Honest and accurate, as we would soon discover.

Wonder retreated into the wings while the 40-member KJLH Radio Free Gospel Choir entered and took their places. This Los Angeles singing group was positioned at four different spots on the vast stage, in clusters of 8 and 12 members. The director gave the down stroke and the beautiful sound of choral music filled the Forum. My son recognized their opening selection as one he himself had sung with the Gospel Choir of the University of Wisconsin-Milwaukee. The piece was called "Total Praise," composed by Richard Smallwood. This 25-minute set by the KJLH choir concluded with Donny Hathaway's moving "This Christmas." The spiritual matters that Wonder had spoken of were being clearly incorporated into the performance, beginning with this gospel prelude to the evening's program.

As most of the choir departed, the night's working band settled in for the main event. Two percussionists, one on each side at the rear of a wide stage, were separated by a six-piece horn section. In front of the horns were two drummers with full sets. On either side of the drummers were platforms where two separate quartets of singers stood. At center stage were two electric guitarists, who would switch instruments depending on the song being performed, as did several of the horn players.

A Yamaha grand piano was positioned at center stage, in close proximity to Wonder's surprisingly concise keyboard array. Electric bassist Nathan Watts stood positioned stage left, by one set of background singers and in a cluster with two electric keyboard players. Greg Phillinganes, the Music Director/Conductor, played a single keyboard, not far behind Stevie's own set up. Electric guitarist Ben Bridges was also on this level, near the conductor. These three players, Watts, Bridges and Phillinganes, each had the distinction of appearing on the original *Songs in the Key of Life* album.

The fact that his band included horns and a grand piano indicated that the leader wanted the sound to be real and right. Although Wonder was an early advocate of electronic synthesizers, which he still uses to great effect, these songs called out for other, non-synthesized sounds. It was no surprise, but still very impressive, that Wonder also had an eight-piece string section at stage right.

Throughout the evening, players would quietly come and go. For most numbers, only one of the two drummers would play; only occasionally were both men simultaneously performing. With this configuration, Wonder was usually backed by a 16-piece core band that had a certain amount of fluidity. And while I earlier called Greg Phillinganes the conductor of the large ensemble, it was no secret that the night's true conductor was Stevie Wonder. Every music cue and each intonation began with him.

And begin they did, with a full-bodied sound on the opening of "Love's in Need of Love Today." It filled the Forum and caused a unified gasp throughout the audience. After listening to the record for so many years, it was remarkable that this piece could sound new and fresh. But it did. And that was one of the keys to the success of the entire evening—that Wonder could make these songs retain their relevance, both in sound and in lyrical content.

The audio mix was perfect; background singers could be heard distinctly, as could each instrument. The tempo was not hurried, not sluggish. It was a magnificent performance of a full-length version of the song, which set the bar high for the rest of the night. The band immediately began the funky rhythms of "Have a Talk with God," which included guest vocalist Denise Williams. Multiple keyboards and numerous rhythm players gave this song the distinctive Stevie Wonder feel.

As the audience expressed prolonged appreciation for these two opening numbers, Wonder slowly made his way, sans assistance, to an empty area of the stage near the string section. A spotlight on the performer, now standing, was the only illumination; the strings the only sound as Wonder began an impassioned version of "Village Ghetto Land." Deep into the second verse he faltered. Wonder stopped; his head sank. Was his voice not as strong as he thought? This was very early in the night for throat trouble.

Then it became obvious: Stevie Wonder had become profoundly saddened by his own words. The disturbing portraits painted in "Village Ghetto Land" are among the bleakest in his canon. Sad vignettes of underprivileged children, especially during Christmas, briefly seemed to overwhelm the singer. If there was any doubt about Wonder's sincerity concerning his own lyrics' subject matter, he dispelled it here.

"Contusion" followed. After the stark nature of tales from the ghetto, this joyful and upbeat instrumental provided needed relief for audience and performers alike. Some were hoping that Wonder would use this number as a point of departure for extended solos and funk exercises. Instead, Wonder held this piece to the exact lines executed on the record. It's clear that Wonder thinks of "Contusion" as a true composition to be played with precision, and not as a groove vamp.

Then came the double shot. Wonder counted off and the horns took the band into "Sir Duke." The audience began to dance. The party was officially under way! Without a break, bassist Watts started the recognizable lines of "I Wish." The ovation was prolonged as Stevie made his way from electric keyboards to the grand piano. After the intense bass of "I Wish," the sparse instrumentation and lilting melody of "Knocks Me Off My Feet" served as a perfect counterpoint to the previous three hard edged numbers.

It was during Wonder's performance of side two of the record that the set list started to take on a life of its own. "Pastime Paradise" and "Ordinary Pain" were performed in their entirety, but within these numbers Wonder also featured members of his backing ensemble. First, he challenged a background singer to a contest, of sorts. Wonder would sing a line of scat vocal syllables, and the singer would try to match him exactly. In this, the singer succeeded two, three, and on the fourth time of increasingly intricate challenges, Wonder conceded: "OK; you're good." The audience loved it.

Wonder then introduced the vocalist as Keith John, the son of Little Willie John, who had a big hit with "Fever," later covered by Peggy Lee and many others. Wonder asked John to sing a bit of it, and of course he complied. After this, Wonder challenged members of the string section to the same matching contest. He would sing a line and they would have to play it back exactly. It was clear by the reactions of the string players that this was not a canned exercise; they were on the hot seat. Wonder told the audience that all musicians love to jam, and then encouraged two of the violin players to take solos on their own. Each one did so, with grace and ease as the rhythm section vamped behind them.

After generously featuring some of his backing musicians, Wonder made good on his word. He stood alone by the grand piano and sang a moving version of "The Christmas Song." Beautiful. He reiterated his thanks for the audience's attendance and stressed the reason for the Christmas season. But as entertaining as these unexpected sections of the concert had been, it struck me that there was a heck of a lot of music yet to be performed if they were really going to get all the way through the four album sides and EP of *Songs in the Key of Life*.

Concluding the ballad "Summer Soft," Wonder next introduced Shirley Brewer to sing the woman's "reply" on the song "Ordinary

Pain." Brewer sang this rebuttal on the original recording, and she was greeted warmly by the audience. With a background singer flanking Brewer on each side, the trio provided a powerful vocal response to Wonder's first section of the song.

Using Shirley Brewer to recreate her part was an extremely classy move by Wonder. Earlier in the night, when Denise Williams had been included on "Have a Talk with God," I was briefly worried that the concert might become one of multiple guest stars, at the expense of hearing Wonder performing his own songs. An unappealing scenario, maybe more likely to unfold in Los Angeles than at other venues. But my fears were for naught; this was Stevie's show through and through. He was gracious in sharing the stage with his band, to be sure, but Wonder remained in control and was the focal point throughout the evening. And after all, Shirley Brewer was not really a guest—she was a part of the album!

"Ordinary Pain" concludes side two. I had heard there was a planned intermission so was surprised when the band began the powerful chords of "Saturn." As with the album, this song describing a Utopian society was among the highest peaks of the night. Stately, majestic; a beautiful reading of this uplifting song. Then came the uberfunky "Ebony Eyes." Wonder sat at an upright piano that had been brought to the stage specifically for this song. The instrument's striking mallets had thumbtacks added to them, so the sound was extremely crisp, like a barrelhouse bar piano. A good-time feel was set within multilayered rhythms, and this celebratory love song had the audience dancing again. As the number reached its conclusion, Wonder leaned into the microphone and said, "See you in 15 minutes."

I looked at my watch. The group had just presented two solid hours of music. The first part of the album itself had taken 90 minutes. Stevie was giving it the full treatment, and I was glad that he didn't appear to be in a rush to get through it. Nothing was truncated. These were all complete versions of each song, and more. No medleys. The lights came up and we had a few minutes to reflect on what we had just witnessed. Even during the intermission, I was still finding it somewhat difficult to believe that I was attending a concert where Stevie Wonder was performing the entire *Songs in the Key of Life* album.

During the past few years, many acts have adopted the idea of playing some of their older albums all the way through in concert. I first heard of it when Cheap Trick announced their plan to do this, about seven years ago. Bruce Springsteen picked up the idea and in recent years has performed *Born to Run* and *Darkness on the Edge of Town* in their entirety. Springsteen is known for long shows but (at the time of this 2014 concert) Bruce had just once given a complete live performance of his own double album *The River*.

Before this trend became fashionable, the only time I ever attended a performance where an artist ran through an entire record was at The Guthrie Theater in Minneapolis in 1979, when jazz violinist Jean-Luc Ponty played his then recent release, *A Taste for Passion*, all the way through. He didn't make a big thing of it; he just performed the four selections from side one of the album. Ponty talked to the audience a bit about the music, and then played the pieces from the record's second side. Fine. Logical. If an artist likes the way the record is sequenced, why not present it that way in concert? But as I say, Ponty was the only performer I ever saw do this. Until fairly recently.

As the house lights dimmed at the Forum and the *less* than 15 minute intermission concluded, I thought Wonder would probably become diligent in presenting the rest of the record. The stage lights rose, showing Wonder standing next to one of his female backup singers. But this was not just any backing vocalist. This was Stevie's daughter—Alisha Morris—the woman about whom "Isn't She Lovely" was written. They spoke to each other a little and laughed. "What was it I said on that record?" Wonder asked her. "Get out of the water, baby," replied his daughter. She retreated to be with the other vocalists, sound effects of a baby crying came through the sound system, and the band launched into "Isn't She Lovely."

Two noteworthy things about this song's performance were omission and inclusion. Wonder opted to leave out all of the subsequent baby sounds after the opening bars. The welcome inclusion was Stevie Wonder's most extended harmonica solo of the night. Chorus after chorus, with the band popping behind him, the man reminded the audience of just what a versatile musician he is. The song was long, but the solo never faltered.

Wonder moved back to the grand piano for "Joy Inside My Tears," another absolute pinnacle of the concert. During the evening's opening, Wonder talked a little to the audience about how he had not toured after the 1976 release of *Key of Life*. Because of this, he said, there were several songs on the album that he had rarely performed live until deciding to present the entire record. "Joy Inside My Tears" was one of these lesser heard songs. If anything, Wonder took the number at a slower tempo than the recorded version. He soaked in it. It was magnificent. A double stop that I feared had prematurely signaled the end of the song only served to underscore the fact that Wonder was taking his time. If I had thought he would be rushing through this second set, I was happily mistaken.

"Black Man" concludes side three of the record and is a funky, upbeat history lesson. In one of the very few missteps of the program, Wonder decided to include the album's recording of teachers' and students' voices that shout the names of famous Americans. A well executed live performance of this element would have been more successful, I believe. But the other problem was that the recorded voices were too loud, getting in the way of the band's groove. A minor criticism, to be sure, and one that emphasizes just how perfect the rest of the concert was presented.

I was again surprised at the order of the set list when the band next went into the introduction to "All Day Sucker," from the Something Special EP. This infectious and funky number was followed by "Easy Goin' Evening (My Mama's Call)." Then I understood why Wonder had programmed these two songs between sides three and four. As a conclusion to the lengthy album, "Easy Goin' Evening" was appropriate and gentle—an instrumental goodnight. But for the end of a concert, it might not be the right closer for the main set. "Easy Goin' Evening" was given a lovely trio performance with Wonder, joined by Frederic Yonnet recreating Stevie's harmonica part from the record, and Ryan Kilgore on tenor saxophone, all huddled around Wonder's keyboards in a single spotlight. The Forum took on an intimacy that belied the huge sports arena's normal atmosphere.

The lights came up full for the sprightly "I am Singing," a joyous celebration of life offered in Spanish, Zulu, and English, on which Wonder was again joined by the resplendently dressed India.Arie. This number also featured the Marcodi harpejji, a stringed instrument similar to the sound of a dulcimer, with the appearance of an autoharp. Placed in the performer's lap, played by tapping the strings with one hand and fretting the fingerboard like a guitar, the harpejji brought a unique melodic and percussive voice to the song. At one point the instrument began to slip from Wonder's grasp. Quickly reestablishing control, he began to play "The Little Drummer Boy" which gave way to Michael Jackson's "The Way You Make Me Feel."

A final ballad graces side four, just prior to the two stretch vamps that close the album proper. The setting described in "If It's Magic" is located across the tracks from "Village Ghetto Land," certainly. But Wonder asks why life can't be positive. Why are we more concerned with clothing styles than with taking care of our children? The message is pointed and harsh, yet encased in this beautiful musical setting it is never strident or preachy.

With this number Wonder again demonstrated what a generous performer he is. During the intermission, my son astutely noted that he had not seen a harp on the stage—an instrument that would be needed to present "If It's Magic" true to its recorded version. Before beginning this selection, Wonder told the audience that he would be accompanied by a tape recording of Dorothy Ashby's harp performance, taken from the *Keys of Life* record itself. The reason, he said, was that shortly after completing the song, Ms. Ashby was diagnosed with cancer and subsequently died.

Wonder stressed that Ashby had played the part perfectly, and also wanted to use her recording as a tribute. Wonder told one interviewer that she "had made the harp sing." A photo of Dorothy Ashby was projected onto the hall's large screens at the end of the number. And speaking of visuals, there were almost none. The stage itself was far more interesting to watch than the occasional projection of moving shapes on the back wall of the concert hall. Large video screens on each side of the stage were used well for close ups of soloists and, of course, were often focused on Wonder. But extraneous stage designs were unnecessary. The musicians were the show, musically and visually.

Applause subsided and the ensemble began the song "As," a long groove that proclaims the singer's everlasting love. This number showcased the background singers. It also gave Wonder the opportunity to use a variety of his own vocal styles during one song. And as with so much of *Songs in the Key of Life*, this selection contains another strong statement of faith.

Although it is lengthy, "As" came to a surprisingly abrupt end, just as it does on the LP, and the band went immediately into "Another Star." The party had been in full swing for some time, but now it reached a new level. All of the musicians were on stage, including the KJLH choir from the evening's opening set. I initially estimated there were about 60 performers involved. Then I took the binoculars and decided to do a specific count. There were 83 musicians on the stage during "Another Star"! I don't think that even George Clinton, in his largest Parliament/Funkadelic days, used 83 musicians at one time. It was remarkable.

During the second half of the concert, more and more shouts were called out from the audience. These were not requests, but exultations of encouragement. The atmosphere became increasingly reminiscent of a gospel meeting, especially during "Another Star."

After this type of generous and extended performance, I was expecting a brief encore and a heartfelt, if hasty farewell. Wrong again. Wonder does not physically leave the stage before performing an encore. It is logistically impractical. So as the applause subsided, the crowd began to sit down and hear what the night's star had to say.

Wonder thanked the audience for their continued support throughout his career and touched upon some of the spiritual themes that had become important motifs for the evening. He then said, "OK, that was the Stevie Wonder part of the concert. Now I am your DJ, Tick Tick Boom." He insisted that the audience repeatedly shout "Tick Tick Boom" until we acknowledged that this was now his name. He good naturedly taunted the Los Angeles audience for being too hip to play along, saying that "the women of Toronto" had yelled louder than this crowd.

Using this alter ego, the performer-cum-DJ continued to toy with an audience still eager to hear more. Using prerecorded backing tracks, Wonder tantalized the crowd with an excerpt from "Master Blaster." Wonder sat at his keyboard and played along with the taped music for a bit and then abruptly stopped the recording. The audience moaned and shouted and laughed. He did the same with "Higher Ground," "Do I Do," and one or two more. He was messin' with us, but we loved it. This odd little section also served to remind me of just how deep this man's catalog goes. We had just witnessed Wonder the album artist; but he is also the master of the hit single, with over 25 Top 10 entries!

Finally, Tick Tick Boom seemed to evaporate and Stevie Wonder again addressed us. While the band members readied themselves, Wonder told The Forum audience that he hoped we would enjoy our Christmas, but that there would be no Christmas joy for some people.

He mentioned Jefferson, Missouri, and Michael Brown by name. The singer told the audience of his belief that most law enforcement officials were good and just people. But whenever someone is placed into a position of authority and power, stressed Wonder, it is essential for the person to use that power justly. Softly spoken "Amens" were heard throughout the arena.

These were not casual comments; Wonder spoke passionately. He did not lecture the audience, but he wanted us to know where he stood on matters of faith and social justice. Wonder's beliefs are repeatedly spelled out in his music, but this artist obviously wanted these ideas to be expressed in clearly articulated speech as well.

Wonder then said that he was going to sing a song that he wished he didn't have to perform any longer, but he felt he must since it is still relevant. The opening chords of "Living for the City" filled the hall. It was a great rendition, with Stevie's voice still in peak form. After playing this song that cries out for justice, Wonder got funky one last time and burned slowly through "Superstition." He thanked the crowd, and the night was over.

Stevie Wonder had just completed a four-hour concert! Maybe this should not have come as such a shock. After all, *Songs in the Key of Life* has always been closely associated with the concept of time. It had seemed an eternity for the album to even be released. Then when completed, the amount of music ran too long to be included on a conventional double album.

Time has proven to be Wonder's friend. His masterwork album has resonated with audiences since its release in 1976, and will surely continue to bring joy and inspiration to those who choose to listen. As highly regarded as many of his albums and radio hits have been, this project is unlike any of his others. Wonder himself recently told an interviewer that *Songs in the Key of Life* was "more than just a bunch of songs put together." So true. And this was more than just a concert.

Book Review

Paramount's Rise and Fall:
A History of the Wisconsin Chair Company and its Recording
Activities
Mainspring Books, 2004
By Alex van der Tuuk
June 15, 2004

One of the American people's least proud traditions is that we are quick to discard those things which no longer fascinate us. This is not a recent trend: in 1900, Mark Twain complained about America's fickle obsession with new artists, comparing it with other countries' ability to bestow lasting honors on their older performers. Evidence of this mindset can be found in the modern era when one is forced to search out releases from foreign lands in order to locate older recordings by American musicians. Germany's Bear Family record label leaps to mind for its dedication in making our own past available to us.

Now we gladly credit another international source, Holland's Alex van der Tuuk, for providing Wisconsin with a focused and thorough look at its own legacy of recorded music. The story of Paramount Records, like most history, is complex. But in essence, the Paramount label was an appendage of the Wisconsin Chair Company, a major manufacturing firm based in Port Washington; at one time it employed most of the town. The recording studios for Paramount were located just south of the chair plant, in neighboring Grafton.

Spanning a mere fifteen years (1917-1932), the Paramount label released 78 rpm records which are now feverishly sought on a global market. Blues legends like Blind Lemon Jefferson, Skip James, and Ma Rainey all made some of their first records in Grafton. Son House and Charley Patton also recorded on the banks of the Milwaukee River in this long-closed studio. The Paramount discs were cheaply made and the sound inferior, even by standards of the day. Still, low fidelity notwithstanding, these Wisconsin made recordings contained sounds found nowhere else, before or since.

Details about the Wisconsin Chair Company's label have remained stubbornly elusive. Various attempts to list all of Paramount's releases have proved incomplete. But Alex van der Tuuk has unearthed a wealth of fragmented information about Paramount. He has put the pieces together and contextualized them in an act of reconstruction akin to the recovery of deleted scenes from a damaged film. More than that: van der Tuuk's history of a single label also serves as an overview of the entire recording industry from the late teens through the 1930s. This was a tremendously important time, as the business of making records was experiencing huge changes in its technology while simultaneously struggling economically to stay alive.

With more than 150 photographs, *Paramount's Rise and Fall* is visually appealing. The well reproduced graphics range from advertisements for the label's latest releases by its now famous artists to rarely seen photographs of the Port Washington and Grafton areas. While interesting, the book is not a casual read. The painstaking nature of van der Tuuk's solid research is evident throughout, but occasionally makes for some dry sections. The book also is hindered in places by a static writing style, with some passages sounding stilted and academic. Yet the depth of information and its straightforward presentation are also the book's great strength, with no detail about the Paramount label too small for inclusion.

Van der Tuuk is quick to give credit to his many stateside colleagues and resources. But it was he who pieced together often sketchy information into a valuable book-length tribute to our region's place in recorded music. Historians of both music and the Wisconsin region owe this author a great deal. Alex van der Tuuk says that he plans to return to the area to continue his research on the Paramount label. Make him welcome when you see him.

Book Review

Do Not Sell at Any Price: The Wild, Obsessive Hunt for the World's Rarest 78 rpm Records
By Amanda Petrusich
Scribner Press, 2014

Amanda Petrusich emerges from one of the music world's darker corners to share barely believable findings. She describes collectors of prewar blues records who are so focused in their pursuit as to make Dylan obsessives appear normal. Paramount Records of Grafton, Wisconsin, is a touchstone throughout, and this book does a good job with its brief overview of the label's importance. Non-collectors might think that the level of competitive intensity described here is hyperbolic. Petrusich assures us that her encounters are not only real but, more importantly, that the remarkable music being preserved by these devotees is absolutely worth the effort.

Bonus Track

Peter Buck, the guitarist for R.E.M., is a true record collector. He recently stressed to Portland journalist Matthew Singer that he actually plays the records he buys; he does not just file them away. Buck once told author Brett Milano, "I know every Elvis Costello B-side, but I don't know anything about my own, even which [R.E.M.] single came from which record." Buck remains obsessive about music but not about himself.

CD Review

Girls
Broken Dreams Club (EP)
Fantasy Trashcan / Turnstile Records, 2010

Wow. A cross between a pop group and a jam band! With horns, no less. And a steel guitar. And a mellotron. And an ethereal voice appropriately buried in the mix. And interesting songs. And guitars that sounds like they are on loan from Chris Isaak's Silvertones at their most atmospheric. This all adds up to a moody and memorable collection of music.

Brief and to the point: *Broken Dreams Club* by the band Girls is a musical high mark for 2010, arriving just in time to make the onset of winter seem a little less glum. Christopher Owens is clearly the driving force behind the group—principal songwriter, guitar, vocals; he is even responsible for the CD's cover art. Still, producer Chet Jr. White is also inseparable from the success of this 30-minute studio set. It is appropriate that White, as producer, is listed immediately under Owens on the CD's list of credits.

Girls know the sound they are after, and they nail it with seeming effortlessness. Like waking slowly from a dream, the ethereal and compelling closing track "Carolina" drifts through your brain for nearly four minutes before Owens' first vocal line emerges. White's production takes the sound from phantasmagoric blend to crisply delineated sounds with the expertise of a man well acquainted with his sound board. Fine songs, well recorded—the six selections on this EP are often haunting, beckoning one to return for repeated listenings.

Remembrance

Trish Keenan, vocalist for the band Broadcast
January 19, 2011

I do something each week about which I rarely speak. It is almost a ritual, except that rituals often fall into the realm of empty actions. Instead, my weekly exercises perform an ongoing and important function that I am convinced keeps me happy and stable. It culminates each December in a flurry of activity that becomes obsession itself, followed by a return to the norm of a relatively brief weekend activity.

Since the late 1970s I have recorded the Top 40 pop charts each weekend and then listened back to the taped programs during the course of the following week—in my car, in my office, while doing dishes. Although I do fast forward over the commercials, I listen to every song on the countdown, all the way through. I went through a brief period of fast forwarding over songs that I didn't want to hear or skipping songs that were on the way down the chart. However, I soon found that I was jumping over most of the songs. So I now listen to it all. And I do mean listen. If I leave the room or if the phone rings, I first shut off the tape. It's rare that I ever want to skip over a song. Not that they are all good—God knows—but because I am invested in hearing the countdown. And I greatly enjoy the process (or I wouldn't do it).

What began with a weekly walk through of Casey Kasem's *American Top 40* would expand after I left the Midwest. When living in Texas,

I started also taping the weekly *American Country Countdown,* with host Bob Kingsley. Like Casey's chart, this too is a four-hour weekly program. Each is about three hours of listening time if you jump the commercials, the Long Distance Dedications, and other non-chart extras.

After I moved to Wisconsin in 1991, other programs became part of my weekly radio diet—Nick Spitzer's *American Routes* chief among them. *Little Steven's Underground Garage* also became a priority. But even with this additional four hours of weekly audio, things were manageable and I still made plenty of time for listening to my own record collection and other songs I sporadically felt like hearing. I was not and am not a slave to the charts. Or so I tell myself.

Things took an unexpected turn when my lovely wife Ellie gave me an XM Radio subscription four Christmases ago. Although it began slowly enough, I soon found myself taping other weekly countdown shows including *A Rack of Blues,* Slim Shady's *Hip Hop Countdown,* Liquid Metal's *Devil's Dozen,* Verge's *Alt Nation Countdown,* the *Octane Countdown,* and (the most recent addition) the *XMU Download 15.* The length of these countdowns ranges from barely 30 minutes (*Hip Hop* and *Devil's Dozen*) to an hour or more (*Rack of Blues*). What I find remarkable is that virtually no musical overlap exists within these programs. Even *American Top 40* rarely duplicates any of the songs found on the *Octane, Alt Nation* or *XMU* charts.

I love them all, to varying degrees, depending on the week and on my mood. But what I have repeatedly noticed is that I must listen to these charts by myself. It is not the same experience if I am not listening alone. If anyone is with me—be it wife or son or daughter, all extremely well versed in music, I find that can't enjoy most of the countdown. For some reason I feel that I am responsible for what the chart holds. I think it is my job to justify and explain and entertain the person with me. As such, I don't enjoy the music nearly as much. So I simply don't try to share the experience.

Why do I listen at all? As I say, I still enjoy the experience, and when I no longer find pleasure in hearing these new songs, I will stop taping. Over Christmas, making the seven-hour drive back to Wisconsin from my parents' home in Des Moines, son Dylan and I were (as usual) playing with the car's XM Radio. Dylan came across a countdown mentioned above—the *XMU Download 15,* a chart based upon how many times a song had been downloaded from the web during the previous week. I was unaware of this countdown, but was struck by many of the songs. None hit me as hard as a selection called "Carolina." In fact, after returning home, I taped a rerun of this countdown and then went to Milwaukee's Exclusive Company record store to find it.

The fact that I didn't just download it says worlds about me, I know. But I'm glad I didn't, for the song came from a brief EP called *Broken Dreams Club*. It is by the San Francisco group Girls; as far as I can tell there is nary a girl in the band. The entire CD is good. In fact, I was so impressed that I wrote a review of it the following morning. I have played that CD more in the past month than anything else. All of the songs are fine. I gave it a very positive review, and my opinion of it keeps going up!

I admit that the above example is unusual. It is rare that a song hits me that hard, but I would have been completely unaware of "Carolina" or of Girls had I not listened to that countdown. Would I have lived without it? Sure, but my life is better for experiencing the song.

This week, the *XMU Download 15* chart started on a somber note. The announcer began by saying that the singer on the first selection had just died unexpectedly after a two-week bout with pneumonia. Rough stuff. And at age 42! The singer was Trish Keenan. The name rang absolutely no bells with me. The tune started and I was again knocked out, much as I had been by "Carolina." I was impressed not because she was no longer with us, but because of an unmistakable and beautiful voice. I was angry that I had never heard of Trish Keenan before, and that it took her death to make me aware of her. I did some research and discovered that Keenan had been singing with her band Broadcast since the mid-1990s. How had I missed this?

Most of what I have read about Broadcast and Trish Keenan indicate that record labels and radio formats did not know what to do with them. They fit no readymade niche. And as we survey the landscape, we see so many others who were musically talented but fit no single genre—Charlie Rich (more talented than Elvis, said Sam Phillips), the Louvin Brothers (too country for the gospel crowd; too gospel for the country audience), Doug Sahm, Todd Rundgren, and many others, from Prince to Bobby Darin. These are the type of talented artists who have and will continue to slip through existing radio charts—no matter how many exist and no matter what the format.

I mentioned at the start of this piece an obsession which hits me each December—the annual taping of the year-end charts. Last December I recorded over 75 hours of these countdowns, from pop to hard rock to techno to Latin. I have listened to each program at least once. At no point did I hear anything by the group Broadcast. I would have remembered.

Why do I tape the countdowns? I am searching for Trish Keenan.

JAZZ

"If people don't know what to call a type of music, they call it jazz."

—*Ray Marklund*

Book Review

What a Wonderful World:
The Magic of Louis Armstrong's Later Years
By Ricky Riccardi
Pantheon Books, 2011

I was born in 1955. Like most of my generation, I had grown up with little awareness of Louis Armstrong. Although I was around at the time, I don't recall his Sunday evening appearances on *The Ed Sullivan Show*, any of his television commercials, or his guest spots on *The Tonight Show with Johnny Carson*. My main point of interest with this musician had to do with a Beatles-related fact: his "Hello Dolly" somehow managed to knock the Fabs out of the #1 spot on the *Billboard* pop chart early in 1964.

The first time I heard any serious discussion of Louis Armstrong came in 1981, when I was working backstage at a jazz concert in St. Paul. A few of the older horn players were relaxing between sets, and at one point the conversation turned biblical. One trumpet player mentioned how much he was looking forward to someday hearing Gabriel play his horn. Another musician immediately countered, "Gabriel? You've already heard him. He's been here! His name is Louie Armstrong." And as if on cue, the men in the room all nodded their heads as one and mumbled in agreement that this pronouncement was accurate. I waited for the punch line, but nobody laughed. No one even smiled. These guys were serious; Armstrong was heaven sent.

I was moved by this collective expression of devotion. Other loyal attitudes about Armstrong occasionally came forth. I heard a radio interview with Tony Bennett where the singer archly defended Armstrong against various criticisms of the interviewer, who insisted that the trumpeter projected a demeaning racial image. Bennett was also the first person I ever heard who distinctly pronounced Armstrong's first name as *Louis*, not Louie.

In fact, I think it was Bennett's repeated use of the word *Louis* that made me purchase my first Armstrong record. The album cover caught my eye because of the single word LOUIS boldly spelled out in white against a photograph of an older Armstrong, trumpet engaged. Upon closer inspection, the words "Chicago Concert" also appeared at the bottom of the sleeve. I had no Louis Armstrong albums in my collection at this time, only a random track on a compilation album here and there. This was a double album from 1956. I had always heard that the early studio material was his best, but I figured this album would fill a gap in my collection, even if I didn't play it a lot.

Man, was I wrong. Oh, it filled a gap all right. But as to not playing it much...I played it all the time! I couldn't *not* play it. Sometimes I thought I just needed to hear a single tune, as a pick-me-up. The album side would invariably track through to the end. Here was the rare record on which a needle could be placed on any spot of its four long sides, and the music would be great. Tune after tune after tune. I especially loved the numbers I had no idea Armstrong recorded, such as "The Gypsy," a haunting lament I had previously known only from an obscure Willie Nelson album.

Every part of the set list offered high points: "Do You Know What It Means to Miss New Orleans?" into "Basin Street Blues" into "Black and Blue" into "West End Blues." It just killed. Also, it was a recording from a single night's performance. This is the kind of live album I respect because it shows what an artist can do on a given night, as opposed to a cobbled-together collection of good performances taken from many concerts.

On the strength of my love for that 1956 recording, I took great interest in Ricky Riccardi's recent project, a biography of Armstrong that focuses on his later years. During those years, Armstrong incurred especially strong criticism: he had presented himself as a caricature, some said. He was a traitor to his race, said others, and that his music no longer mattered.

Riccardi's book is a work of love and devotion, but it never becomes a valentine. The author takes a clear-eyed view of the charges of artistic abandonment leveled against Armstrong, carefully exploring the reasons behind each. The book methodically analyzes these attacks, exposing important weaknesses in the critics' arguments. The research here and throughout the work is excellent and, overall, the writing is strong. There are a few times when clarity falters and redundancy creeps in, especially near the end. A discography of Riccardi's recommended releases would have made for a welcome appendix, as would a selective list of worthwhile unreleased Armstrong recordings from the artist's later years. But these are inconsequential concerns when this extremely readable and engaging book is taken as a whole.

Most of all, the work is convincing! Authors who set out to rescue a diminished hero or offer a reevaluation often become shrill and defensive. Not Riccardi. He presents his assessments and insights even-handedly, relying on evidence rather than rhetoric. Some of the author's source materials have been unavailable to previous biographers, including private documents and a voluminous number of audio recordings made and cataloged by Armstrong himself.

Reading this book, I became convinced that Louis Armstrong had been short changed, in his later life and in death. Near the conclusion of *What a Wonderful World*, as Riccardi describes several of Armstrong's albums released during the 1960s, I began to realize just how slighted this artist has been on so many different levels. The second edition of the respected *All Music Guide to Jazz* does not even list (much less review) many of Armstrong's later albums, including *Louis and the Good Book*, *Louis and the Angels*, *Ambassador Satch*, *Country & Western*, and *I Will Wait for You*. The fact that so many original albums (not compilations) can be ignored by the very resource which calls Armstrong "the most important and influential musician in jazz history" is telling. It tells us that, true to Riccardi's premise, here is yet another voice wanting to acknowledge only the artist's early years. Thankfully, Ricky Riccardi has a far wider view of Louis Armstrong's artistry and has shared it with us.

Book Review

Louis Armstrong's New Orleans
By Thomas Brothers
Norton Press, 2006

Context. This is the sole reason Thomas Brothers has dedicated years of his life to writing books chronicling the world and art of Louis Armstrong. His mission is to provide context concerning the emergence of a musical genius into American culture.

In 2000, Brothers published *Louis Armstrong: In His Own Words* (Oxford University Press), a selection of interviews with, and writings by Armstrong. Now comes *Louis Armstrong's New Orleans*. Brothers' newly published research complements his previous book, attempting to contextualize many of the specific references made by Armstrong. Although not a traditional biography focusing solely on one person's life, every page is in some way connected to the great trumpeter.

With New Orleans continually receiving headlines for sad events, this is a welcome narrative. Often celebratory in tone, it gives a fascinating history of the cultural makeup of New Orleans 1900-1920, the epoch from which Armstrong emerged. Brothers' vivid descriptions invite the reader to walk the century old streets of an often dangerous world, observing lifestyles both intriguingly strange and oddly familiar.

Just as it surprises many to learn that Babe Ruth was a great pitcher before acquiring his fame as a slugger, Brothers makes the case that the cornet (and *then* trumpet) became Armstrong's main instrument only because there was no venue for his preferred musical choice: singing. Brothers suggests that vocal groups were nearly as predominant as instrumental bands during Armstrong's youth, with Louis organizing four-part harmony vocal quartets for street corner performance. The author also strongly argues that Armstrong's later vocals, both scat and traditional lyrics, were neither novelties nor used for crossover appeal. Rather, they were the expression of his earlier musical love.

Brothers convincingly demonstrates how New Orleans' many parades led Louis to a brass instrument. Parades gave the young Armstrong a way out of his rigid confines, literally expanding his vision of the world. A marching band, by its very nature, had to move—often through parts of the city which were otherwise taboo for a black child. Before gaining the musical skill to join the marching band, young Louis was already traveling alongside the group, acting the part of roadie for the performers' instruments.

Once he became a respected local musician, parades would also lead Armstrong toward unaccustomed interaction with residents of mixed ancestry. Many of the Creoles encountered by Armstrong possessed a formal music education, which Louis lacked. It is one of Brothers' great accomplishments that he can effectively connect topics as seemingly disparate as marching band parades and race relations, as well as showing how the music of the African American Sanctified Church relates to what would soon be named *ragtime* and then *jazz*.

The author admits that some of his theories about undocumented turn of the century New Orleans life require leaps of faith on the part of the reader. This is an honest admission, but Brothers makes his case well for many aspects of what Thomas Wolfe termed "lost time." Some of Brothers' social theories are easier to accept than others, but he is quick to indicate when his otherwise solid research drifts into personal speculation.

Brothers is not afraid to make some startlingly large statements. Socially, the author repeatedly stresses that Armstrong "was not the least bit interested in cultural assimilation of any kind." Musically, Brothers insists that were it not for his remarkably strong understanding of a soloist's use of harmonic precision in relationship to a song's melody, Armstrong would have been "a footnote in jazz history." Big claims, to be sure, but this book argues well for these, and many speculative points.

Unfortunately, the author is also quick to criticize Armstrong's previous biographers—of which there are many. Brothers is right to remind his readers that there has never been a consensus about the origins of jazz, but he sometimes forgets that his is not the only valid voice on the topic of Louis Armstrong.

Assumed exclusivity aside, *Louis Armstrong's New Orleans* is an important book for readers seeking to understand the world from which Armstrong emerged. Just as Robert Caro's biographies of Lyndon Johnson describe the entire state of Texas to better portray an individual man, Thomas Brothers successfully writes of a vast and complex New Orleans culture in order to place Louis Armstrong's talent into sharper relief.

Book Review

Louis Armstrong: Master of Modernism
By Thomas Brothers
Norton Press, 2014

Thomas Brothers' *Louis Armstrong: Master of Modernism* continues an investigation into the fascinating life that began in the author's previous volume, *Louis Armstrong's New Orleans*. *Master of Modernism* discusses 1922-1932, a pivotal decade in Armstrong's life that saw him depart New Orleans for Chicago, where he began to make the recordings that would keep his music alive to the present day.

The author shows that while many of these records demonstrate brilliant performances and should be heralded as genius incarnate, there is a lot more to Armstrong's story. The author rightly says that, for today's audience, the records of Louis Armstrong are the "main event." It's all we have of him. But to the artist himself, "These commercial recordings were," argues Brothers, "merely a side show." Armstrong lived for live performance.

Brothers dissects each of the various elements in these recordings with specific notations worthy of an archeological dig, examining Armstrong's music of this era with the care it deserves. Not content merely to explain his findings, he also wants the reader to have first-hand awareness of the specimens under discussion. To that end, Brothers cites various places where the original recordings can be heard, pointing to Armstrong's own demonstrations of the innovations and musical elements being described.

In spite of his meticulous parsing of Armstrong's playing, Thomas Brothers never loses sight of the reason why these records were first purchased and enjoyed. The music was exciting, inspirational, and life affirming. Here's hoping that Brothers plans to continue his excellent work, taking Armstrong's story into the 1940s and beyond.

Bonus Track

Louis Armstrong is rightly credited as a musical innovator. Although he did not initiate the session, in the summer of 1930 Armstrong played (uncredited) on a recording date with country music superstar Jimmie Rodgers. The song was Rodgers' "Blue Yodel #9," also known as "Standing on the Corner." This song is now seen as an early cross-pollination of two distinctive American musical styles—jazz and country. Other genre-crossing collaborations would follow, including those between Stan Kenton and Tex Ritter, Béla Fleck and Chick Corea, and Willie Nelson and Wynton Marsalis.

Book Review

Bing Crosby: A Pocketful of Dreams— The Early Years: 1903-1940
By Gary Giddins
Little, Brown, 2001

While in Milwaukee last winter to discuss his Elvis Presley biography, Peter Guralnick stated that, with the passing of time, Presley's popularity would decline. Gary Giddins wants to rescue Bing Crosby from the backwater of faded cultural icons. Giddins' challenge will be difficult; the decline that Guralnick foresees for Presley took place decades ago for Crosby. Fortunately for author and subject alike, this new work is extremely successful, and with *A Pocketful of Dreams* Giddins may do for Bing Crosby what Ken Burns did for Louis Armstrong. He may succeed in exciting new audiences about a long-silent talent.

Crosby is remembered today primarily as a singer, often associated with the Christmas season. Giddins writes to correct this narrow view. He chronicles Crosby's dominance not only of recordings, but also radio and movies. The young man who emerges from the text is one of tremendous talent, capable of excelling in various fields of entertainment. However, the scene also describes a self-imposed and self-serving isolation that began early, as well as Crosby's insistence on getting every ounce of what he felt was his—from top billing for secondary roles to a generous cut of every royalty percentage possible.

As this first volume nears its conclusion, the career parallels with Presley become striking. Like Elvis' post-army days, many of Bing's recording sessions were a waste of the singer's talent, capitalizing on the demand for anything bearing the Crosby name. Also like Elvis, the focus of Crosby's career soon turned to movie roles. The music suffered, often due to poorly or hastily chosen material, or because of the record company's misguided attempts to push the singer away from jazz material in favor of bland and widely marketable pop songs. But also like Presley, Crosby's natural talent saved many of what Giddins acknowledges were "dreary arrangements" with his consistently interesting voice.

Giddins obviously loves his topic; he describes with great clarity what transpires during the artist's life. Various media projects are discussed, along with what lies in the grooves of his best recordings. These detailed descriptions are welcome, since most readers of the book (as Giddins wisely acknowledges) will be unfamiliar with all but the biggest of the crooner's radio hits. Along the road to Bing's cultural dominance, Giddins chronicles Crosby's stints with Tommy and Jimmy Dorsey, and the Paul Whiteman Orchestra. Other notables from the arenas of jazz and film provide fascinating vignettes, as do Bing's own comments on his one-time roommate Bix Beiderbecke.

At one point in the narrative the author recounts various Crosby artifacts that have gone missing. Lamented are lost studio takes, unsaved radio broadcasts and, especially, some destroyed performance footage from an abandoned film project. While these items are apparently forever gone, Giddins is determined to save the rest of the Crosby legacy, making it available and even enticing in this successful biography.

Post Script

Although this biography does not explicitly have "volume one" in its title, it does say "The Early Years." It was assumed by most that this 2001 portrait of Bing Crosby would be the start of a multivolume work by Giddins. And maybe it is. But 15 years later, we are still waiting for the second installment.

Remembrance

Mitch Miller Memories
August 4, 2010

Mitch Miller died this week at age 99. He was the Jack LaLanne of song. Just as the exercise guru led workouts by means of early television screens, Mitch Miller led his own glee club of viewers. As with the gymnast's approach, Miller insisted on an active audience.

News releases said that Miller had experienced only a brief illness before his death. I'm glad for that report, but I have read the numerous articles about Mr. Miller's passing with increasing skepticism. For example, I have yet to encounter an obituary that heralds Mitch Miller as probably the finest classical oboist that this country has ever produced. Which he was. I have also read that Miller was responsible for signing Bob Dylan to Columbia Records. Which he wasn't.

Obituaries mention in passing that Mitch Miller was in the record business and that he conducted orchestras at various junctures of his long career. The notices have, of course, focused smilingly on Miller's *Sing Along With Mitch* sensation of the very early 1960s. Certainly these popular albums and his corresponding network television show put Miller on America's cultural landscape, and the *Sing Along* series is why he is remembered today. Still, it saddens me to see the man reduced to a gently mocked, stiff-armed caricature.

Having worked briefly with Mitch Miller in the early 1980s, I'd like to offer another voice. Miller had agreed to participate in a series of programs describing his career as a record producer. Interviews for these programs were conducted in St. Paul with Minnesota Public Radio's longtime jazz host Leigh Kamman. I served as the board operator, recording the conversations.

Mitch Miller was an impressive presence. Dressed in flamboyant colors with a cravat and beret, this was a man absolutely confident and extremely at ease. His trademark beard was neatly trimmed into the point on his chin that made his visage unmistakable. He was friendly, outgoing, and willing to talk about any topic. In fact, the interview session originally planned for a single afternoon stretched into three full days! Smoking was not allowed in studios, but no one ever considered asking Mitch Miller to extinguish his ever-present cigarette in its lengthy, ornate holder.

Here are a few of the things I recall from those sessions, held nearly 30 years ago. Miller was not afraid of failure if you could learn from it. He had experienced numerous failures in the recording studio as a record producer, but his only regret about these instances was that he didn't go back and try the same thing again. Miller lamented that he saw others succeed with some of his failed experiments only because he hadn't the time to rework some of his unsuccessful ideas. Although he did not get specific about the artists he had in mind, I doubt that Miller was referring to the problematic recordings he made with Frank Sinatra or with Aretha Franklin.

He did get specific about his role in convincing Johnny Mathis that he possessed an exceptionally good voice. But it was a voice well suited for ballads, and not for the jazz that Mathis wanted to sing. As Mathis himself has often said, he started to record "Wonderful Wonderful" as a syncopated romp. Miller confirmed to Kamman that he stopped the session and instructed the singer to sing the melody as straight and as unadorned as possible. Mathis reluctantly agreed, believing this unhip arrangement to be a waste of time. In 1957, "Wonderful Wonderful" would be Johnny Mathis' first hit single, a record that started the singer's lengthy career as a purveyor of romantic ballads. Mathis still praises Miller's insight.

This story about Johnny Mathis led Mitch Miller to indicate, in more general terms, that he often had to convince certain artists of their own talent. They were frequently unaware of their potential, he insisted. He mentioned Rosemary Clooney in this category, as I recall.

There was not a lot said about rock and roll. It is well documented that Miller, as a record company executive, was responsible for keeping rock acts off Columbia until somewhat late in the day. Once Miller left the label and could no longer strenuously object to the genre, Columbia Records took the plunge and signed some rock bands. The Byrds would sell a boatload of records for the company, and this fully opened the gates for rock music onto the staid Columbia label. But this was not until 1965. Even then, Columbia probably yielded only because they envied the fortune that The Beatles were making for their competitor, Capitol Records.

Mitch Miller and Leigh Kamman were of a mind about the subject of rock and roll. As Miller said, "Rock is dumb music for uneducated listeners. I knew that the kids would get tired of it. I was simply wrong about how long it would take. I thought it would be over in ten years, but it has held on a bit longer." He was very convinced, however, that rock music was winding down now and that it would soon be dead. Remember, this was 1982. Mr. Miller was a true believer in what he saw as refinement and taste.

Years later I again met Miller, but this time only in passing. In the late 1990s he was the guest conductor for a Christmas concert with The Milwaukee Children's Choir, to which my daughter belonged. By this time I had spent several years in Texas and had become extremely interested in country music. As Miller was signing album covers and programs after the dress rehearsal, I asked him if it were true that he had been responsible for convincing Tony Bennett to record "Cold Cold Heart" in 1951. This Hank Williams composition would prove to be Bennett's breakout pop hit, and it simultaneously introduced Hank Williams' music to an entirely new, non-country music audience.

Continuing to autograph various items, Miller laughed and answered, "Oh yes. Bennett wanted nothing to do with that song." Dropping into a low growl, Miller mimicked the singer's reaction: "I'm not recording that cowboy crap!" He laughed again. I asked what gave him the idea to have Tony Bennett record Williams' "Cold Cold Heart." He stopped signing, looked up at me and replied as if the answer were obvious: "It was a good song!"

At the conclusion of the concert, Miller thanked the audience for attending the event and said that he hoped to see them "many, many more times." This, from a man who was not close to being young, even ten years ago. I was impressed that he clearly embraced what he was doing so thoroughly that the thought of slowing down or (God forbid) of dying was simply not on his radar. I envied his attitude.

I have friends who are rabid in their enmity toward Mitch Miller, calling him one of the great enemies of rock and roll. Perhaps true, but the genre seems to have circumvented his opposition and thrived. Sitting across from him in a recording booth in St. Paul or talking with him at a concert in Milwaukee, it was difficult not to be captivated by his every response. He was passionate in wanting to deliver quality music to people, whether from the oboe chair, the podium, the recording studio, or the television screen. In my experience, that depth of commitment is a very rare thing.

Remembrance

Leigh Kamman: Portrait of a Jazz Broadcaster
June 27, 2011

Leigh Kamman is alive and well and living in Edina, Minnesota. Now recently retired from the airwaves, Leigh (rhymes with *say*) had been a fixture on jazz radio for many years before I met him. That was in the summer of 1980, when I was interviewing for a position at Minnesota Public Radio in St. Paul. Kamman was speaking to the person who was interviewing me, suggesting that the station should record an upcoming jazz event. Leigh's program *The Jazz Image* was the late-night show that aired on the statewide network of radio stations each Saturday from 10 P.M. until 4 on Sunday morning. Leigh's voice was well known to me long before this encounter, and I quickly realized that this polite man was its source.

More striking than Kamman's familiar and well-articulated speech patterns was his professional attitude, clearly evident in his manner and his clothes. While most everyone I encountered on that hot July day had on shorts, T-shirts, and sandals, Leigh Kamman wore a tailored three-piece suit. Since this was a job interview for me, we were the only two in sight who were formally dressed. Leigh's professional attire fit his voice perfectly and, as I think back on it, I'm not sure I ever saw him in anything *but* a suit and tie.

I landed the job and was soon fulfilling the various functions of a radio station board operator. Before long, Saturday's late night shift fell my way. Most thought this an unenviable position, but I was glad for the opportunity to serve as Leigh's engineer. The deserted station and Leigh's jazz selections created a very relaxed atmosphere when compared with the frenetic pace of the broadcast day.

Leigh is a Minnesota native who spent some time as a broadcaster in New York City in the early 1950s. He returned to St. Paul to work in radio and for the 3M Corporation. That's about all I knew about his past. Not surprisingly, his taste in jazz at that time was a bit different than mine. Leigh was deep into Johnny Hodges and the big bands.

I liked Paul Desmond and fusion. But to pigeonhole either of us by these narrow overviews would be a disservice, as I quickly came to see. As the weeks went by and the number of my Saturday night shifts mounted, my interest in older jazz increased. Leigh played a mix of old and new, but largely stayed with the music of the 1940s and 1950s, which his listeners had come to expect.

Because my father prized arrangements over solo virtuosity, I grew up hearing the music of Tommy Dorsey, Harry James, Benny Goodman, and especially Glenn Miller. Leigh played a little of the Dorsey Brothers and less of Miller. Leigh liked Benny Goodman, but he was even more interested in bands that I knew little about. I was aware of the bigger hits of Duke Ellington, of course, and had even participated in two high school jazz clinics run by Stan Kenton, but Leigh played material from these artists that I had never heard before. Deep catalog stuff. I learned a lot about music on those Saturday nights, but was usually ready for 4 A.M. to arrive so I could start the network's pre-recorded *Jazz Alive* reels and head home to bed. It wasn't until Leigh was assigned the task of recording individual programs that my master class in jazz appreciation really began.

By the early 1980s, the expanding Minnesota Public Radio empire had multiple FM stations positioned around the state and one AM station located in St. Paul. I think the AM station had been a donor's gift, but it was sort of a white elephant for us. We filled the signal with news and some simulcasting, but the FCC demanded that the station not be merely a "repeater" of the FM signal. Leigh was asked to put together a series of one-hour shows that could be broadcast on the AM station at night. These were to be self-contained jazz modules that would fill time while providing original content. Leigh agreed to come in to record these shows after his 3M day was over, and I asked to be his board operator.

We were well aware that these were production line shows, and we would crank out three or even four of them a night if we could record them in real time; that is, without stopping. "Sausage links," is what Leigh called them, but he also knew that there was precious little space given to jazz on any area radio station, so he was glad for the opportunity to fill this void. Because of repeats, the shows could ultimately have a larger audience than his Saturday night statewide broadcasts. As such, Leigh took the task of producing these programs very seriously.

Every module needed to be exactly 55 minutes in length in order to allow for the five-minute newscast from the Associated Press network at the top of each hour. This format was no problem for Leigh, and neither was finding content. We started with some basics, recording four hours on Louis Armstrong. Featuring only one performer per show helped Leigh to give his listeners some depth on each artist. While rolling tape in the control room, I learned much about artists I had never heard in my youth: Jimmy Lunceford, the Sauter-Finegan Orchestra, Jack Teagarden, Benny Carter. Fascinating material, with each selection augmented by Leigh's informative but concise commentary. Sometimes he was reading liner notes, sometimes jazz reference books, but most often he was giving information from his own knowledge of jazz and from years of living with the music.

Leigh was open to suggestion, direct or circuitous. At a break between tapings, I once asked about baritone sax man Gerry Mulligan and his unexpected tenure with Dave Brubeck. After answering my question, Leigh decided that we would next do a series of Mulligan modules. Fine. I think we did six hours. I even provided a couple of albums. And then we did two more hours of less well-known material by the classic Brubeck quartet. It was work for both of us, but also a luxury to be able to record as many shows as we wanted on whichever artists struck Leigh's fancy.

We were recording one of these shows when the wire services reported the death of Earl "Fatha" Hines. We assembled a four-hour special on the great pianist that very night; it was picked up the next day by the NPR network and distributed nationally. Leigh had the knowledge and the recordings; I knew how to operate turntables and tape machines. We flew.

Leigh Kamman was successful in providing jazz to the Minneapolis/St. Paul region and beyond. As I suspected from the outset, those modules were aired frequently during the following years, but because there were so many of them we never had a listener complaint concerning duplication. Also, each hour would stand up to repeated listening. This is because Leigh would play some well-known material by an artist from the station's music library, but he would also dig into his personal record collection and into that of his friend Ray Marklund. They would regularly come up with worthwhile recordings for the programs from deep within their own archives.

Leigh consistently kept the focus on the music, never on himself. He had spoken to Duke Ellington on numerous occasions, first as a 17-year-old fan at a train station! But he wouldn't think of dropping this fascinating nugget into a conversation in order to impress. I had worked with Leigh for nearly three years before I heard him mention, in passing, about once having spoken with Charlie Parker. I froze at the tape deck with reel in hand. I asked him to expand a bit, but he intentionally drifted to another subject.

It makes sense that Leigh would not stress his conversations with Charlie Parker. For one thing, hard bop was not his favorite form of jazz. And there weren't a lot of upbeat aspects to address in Parker's life when they met in the early 1950s. Leigh played Parker's records on the air, but not frequently. Once when I pressed him a bit, Leigh did tell me that he had talked to Charlie Parker, Billie Holiday, and Oscar Pettiford. As I recall, Leigh said they were all together at his New York City apartment one night after their respective gigs. I asked if Leigh recalled any overall impressions of the conversation. He paused for a long while and finally said, "They were all quite bitter about money." "You mean," I asked, "They felt cheated?" "Yes," was all Leigh replied, but this short response said worlds.

Leigh had very little to say about various musicians' public struggles with substance abuse or their detrimental personality quirks, unless these things had to do with the music itself. During his time in New York, I'm sure he had seen the darker side of the music alley up close and had no interest in lingering there.

If Leigh was a jazz fan first, he also knew the realities of the business side of music. He was slow to get involved with anything which might infringe on the rights of musicians, keenly aware that paying gigs were a professional musician's life blood. I never knew Leigh to take a comp seat; this would hurt ticket sales and the bottom line for the performer. He was also very aware of who owned the rights to which recordings and was determined that no one was to be cheated out of a fair share. One night I showed Leigh a recent Joel Whitburn book which listed a record's peak position and overall statistical performance on the *Billboard Magazine* charts. Leigh examined it for a while and proclaimed it of limited use because the book did not include listings for the copyright holder of each song. Wow. But that's what he wanted to know! Chart position and sales figures can be manipulated. Ownership is ownership.

Leigh was responsible for helping keep jazz not only on the airwaves but also on the stages of the Minneapolis/St. Paul area. Whether from weekly promotion on the radio or actual involvement with booking artists, he remained among the greatest supporters of jazz in the area. One time Leigh told me that an old friend from New York was coming to town to give a lecture and that he wanted the station to record the talk. I didn't think much about it until he later casually mentioned that the name of his friend was John Hammond!

Some younger jazz aficionados, especially those new to the genre, were critical of the playlist heard on Leigh's Saturday night show. True, it did not always reflect the latest trends, but that wasn't because Leigh was unaware of them. I would regularly see him investigating the Minneapolis jazz scene, enjoying local performers like the Natural Life band and the talented Peterson family. Leigh made certain he was present for jazz artists passing through Minneapolis while on tour—individuals like Phil Woods, Howard Roberts, and Jon Hendricks. I saw Leigh at Minneapolis' famous First Avenue club when Wynton Marsalis first played there in 1981, checking out the newest young lion. He was easily identifiable in the packed house by his suit and tie, the only person in the place so dressed except the band. As with the radio show, Leigh's focus was always on the music. He had a very open mind and a broad musical perspective, but he also knew what would and would not work well on his own weekly *Jazz Image* broadcast.

Crunching the numbers, we had recorded a total of 187 modules, and I worked at least 150 Saturday night broadcasts with Leigh. After that, the MPR network acquired a long sought after deal with the Canadian Broadcasting Corporation, and the need to fill time with original programming became less critical. We would plug into the CBC's feed for long stretches. The jazz modules project was suspended, and even the length of Leigh's Saturday night show was scaled back. Formats shifted.

In the fall of 1983 I made plans to depart Minnesota for Texas. I didn't have direct contact with Leigh for several years after that. Even so, it was clear that he was keeping his ear to the ground. When I received an academic accolade, he sent congratulations through mutual friends. On the rare occasions when our letters did form a pre-email conversation, he repeatedly encouraged me to return to radio, even going so far as to point out jobs he thought appropriate. His confidence was encouraging, of course. But I left radio, in part, because I had already enjoyed the good fortune of doing everything in broadcasting that I wanted to do; things almost exclusively related to music. I would later have other fine teachers in various fields of study, but Leigh Kamman's lessons on jazz and on personal grace have stayed with me the longest.

Post Script

This piece was written at the time of Leigh Kamman's retirement from radio. Leigh died in October 2014.

Commentary
Stubborn Isolationist: Jazz on the Radio
January 14, 2013

Why can't jazz broadcasters offer their listeners year-end specials showcasing the genre's new releases from the previous 12 months? Such a retrospective would offer a useful overview. From a personal standpoint, it would remind me of the music I liked, alert me to the music I missed, and prompt me to place a number of recent releases onto my "Must Buy" list.

I'm a devoted follower of radio charts, and late December is my busy time. As I recount elsewhere, I record year-end specials on music forms which interest me. Between the FM dial and my XM radio, I annually record quite a number of countdowns and overviews. From Alternative to Pop to Country to R&B to Metal to Folk, each of these formats take the opportunity to present the previous year's finest recordings and brightest moments.

So why not Jazz? As independent jazz radio stations become rare in American broadcasting, I point to SiriusXM as my primary object of dismay here. If SiriusXM's *Real Jazz* station would offer such an annual wrap-up of the year in music, it would help the current crop of jazz artists who are struggling to be heard and to make a living in music.

Perhaps *Real Jazz* does not offer a year-end overview because they do not have a weekly showcase of new releases. Scroll down the program descriptions on the *Real Jazz* site: "roots of jazz," "jazz from the early 20th Century," "traditional New Orleans jazz." OK, but couldn't a current-release show fit into the format? SiriusXM's *Watercolors* channel is the only other satellite radio station which plays newly released jazz recordings, but these are all focused on the Smooth Jazz format.

John Coltrane's importance to jazz is undisputed. But when there are three separate references to this saxophonist on the *Real Jazz* programming page, it's clear that air time for recordings by newer artists such as Brad Mehldau and Jenny Scheinman will be taking a back seat to music from the past.

God bless the *Real Jazz* station for recording and airing live concerts. However, these usually feature either the Jazz at Lincoln Center Orchestra or music from San Antonio's Riverwalk, which again focuses on "traditional jazz from the early 20th Century." Nowhere is there a live program in the style of National Public Radio's long abandoned *Jazz Alive* series, which programmed weekly live sets by veteran performers and virtual unknowns, side by side. And these were true field recordings, often taped at low profile gigs across the country.

Jazz is certainly not the only radio format to ignore the opportunity to present annual overviews. I once asked the Program Director of SiriusXM's *Bluesville* station why they didn't have a countdown of the previous year's most popular blues records. He told me that too many people would get angry at such an evaluative chart listing. And besides, the Blues are above such trivial things as countdowns. When I pointed out that his station's weekly "Rack of Blues" program was exactly the type of countdown he was disparaging, I received no reply. Similarly, I recently asked the Program Director of *Real Jazz* about my concerns regarding a year-end overview but have yet to hear back.

Let me suggest that SiriusXM's *Real Jazz* station open its schedule to a focused, two-hour program each week dedicated to artists who are making inroads on industry charts, whether it be *Billboard Magazine* or any other recognized industry standard. (I am available to host, by the way.) I also envision a weekly program focusing on unsigned jazz artists. But one step at a time.

Commentary
Rough Times for Smooth Jazz: Ed Roth and the Radio
October 25, 2012

What happens to a music format when the audience abandons it? Once vibrant genres that leap to mind include Disco, Fusion, and Folk. These styles still exist, but certainly not in the same form and not with anything close to the same popularity that they once enjoyed.

I'm convinced that part of the decline in popularity for some music can be traced to the confusion brought about by labeling. Disco has been renamed Dance Music, and Folk is now usually termed Alt Country. Fusion music has retreated farthest from the scene, even though some Techno tries to fill the void.

David R. Adler has published a pair of interesting articles in *Jazz-Times* describing the state of jazz on the radio. Smooth Jazz was his primary focus, with an emphasis on a pair of related problems: nobody likes the label "Smooth Jazz" and, no matter what it's called, this music is rarely found on the radio. Even the genre's most recognizable name, Kenny G, was candid in his assessment of the public's limited access to his style of music on the radio, and how this has hurt his career.

When radio programmers turn away from a once-successful format, what becomes of those artists who are recording quality music within a genre that is in remission? Fortunately, many dedicated musicians remain true to their personal love of music, regardless of current styles and industry trends.

L.A. keyboard session man Ed Roth cares little for labels. He has just released the self-titled *Ed Roth* CD on Warrior Records. No matter what genre tag is applied here, this is as fine a set of electric instrumentals as I have heard in a long time. But I did not learn of its release from radio airplay. At a California Transit Authority gig this summer, near the end of a very hot set of originals and reinvigorated Chicago tunes, that group's original drummer, Danny Seraphine, introduced his band. He told the audience that keyboard player/band director Ed Roth had the tune "Summertime" climbing the Smooth Jazz charts.

This single comes from the *Ed Roth* CD, which, although a studio recording, is constructed as a well-paced live set. The selections consist of a good balance of original material, familiar old tunes, and unexpected melodies. "Summertime" placed into the same set with both

The Champs' "Tequila" and The Who's "Who are You?" doesn't seem logical. But it works. Throw in War's "Low Rider" and Stevie Wonder's "Higher Ground" and you have an array of recognizable themes played by monster L.A. studio cats.

Roth wisely takes the role of equal partner here. He gives his talented colleagues a lot of room to solo. But when the group leader's keys *are* featured, he plays the hell out of his Hammond B-3, Fender Rhodes, clavinet, Wurlitzer, and acoustic piano. Between the hard edges of this new CD's "Who are You" and the...well, I'll say it: the smooth sound of "The Biggest Part of Me," *Ed Roth* is a welcome addition to this summer's jazz releases. The Smooth Jazz demarcation may be in decline but, fortunately, musicians such as Ed Roth are making great music with little regard to labels.

Concert Commentary

The Don Ellis Orchestra
Hoyt Sherman Auditorium
Des Moines, Iowa
November 1, 1970

IN HIGH SCHOOL I was pretty open to suggestions about music, so when our band director got excited over the fact that Don Ellis was going to be in town soon, I organized a foursome to go see him. One member of the outing later told me that this Don Ellis concert changed his life; he put away his Steppenwolf records after that show and switched to jazz. And true, it was great. Ellis was a trumpeter known for playing in unusual time signatures. Odd meters that built on Dave Brubeck's 5/4 and 12/4 time experiments. But Don Ellis would take this concept to places like 23/14 alternating with 29/7: strange, literally uncharted territory.

His was a large group (or orchestra), playing at Hoyt Sherman Place, a nice old hall which rarely booked live music. Unlike my friend, I did not abandon my rock albums, but I liked the concert enough to go out the next day to find Don Elllis' latest release, the double album *At Fillmore*. This record was a somewhat successful attempt to court the rock crowd. Two things about this record would appeal to a rock audience: the band was loud, and the album cover had the word *Fillmore* on it. The use of that venue's name, alone, would sell records in those days. I played this LP a few times in my upstairs bedroom, quite loud, thinking that because it was a horn band, my dad would dig it. He didn't.

I saw Ellis the following year at a dilapidated movie theater. And while I still liked the music, the evening didn't have the first-time magic that the Hoyt Sherman show held. I remember his T-shirt that night read, "Cure Virginity," which I found fairly shocking. Still, I must not have been put off by the show, because the next year I went to see him again at a beautiful theater in Ames. In fact, it was a two-night event; the first was a workshop and the second was the concert. In addition to odd meters, Ellis was interested in electronics, playing his trumpet through an early synthesizer device called a ring modulator. Strange and often just noisy. Very experimental. Off-putting to most of the audience, but Ellis certainly enjoyed it.

Don Ellis followed the success of his *Fillmore* set with another live double album, this one called *Tears of Joy* (1971). That too was a strong record. I lost track of Ellis when I entered college, which is sort of surprising to me now because during those years I followed big band jazz releases through my musician friends. Like my own interest, it seems that Ellis' crossover success was not lasting, although he continued to create quality work. An album from very late in his run, recorded live at the Montreux Jazz Festival in 1977, is quite good.

Don Ellis never had a hit single like fellow jazz trumpeters Chuck Mangione ("Feels So Good") or Maynard Ferguson ("Theme from *Rocky*"). Too bad. What was even sadder was that Ellis died of a heart condition in late 1978, at only 44. Many of his records hold up well, but I very rarely put them on.

Post Script

During his brief career, Don Ellis encountered some great successes and some bad luck. In 1967, Ellis is signed to the prestigious Columbia label and soon records the album *Electric Bath*. It is heralded as a breakthrough of early jazz/rock, and wins many awards. In 1968, Ellis records an anticipated follow-up album, *Shock Treatment*. However, Columbia mistakenly issues the wrong tapes! Ellis is able to get Columbia to fix the many problems of the initial pressing of this release, but I have always felt that some of his momentum was lost in the process.

Concert Commentary

The Stan Kenton Orchestra
Ingersoll Theater
Des Moines, Iowa
Fall 1973

ALTHOUGH MY DAD had no time for Don Ellis, he had once been a fan of Stan Kenton, another jazzer (albeit from an earlier generation) who was also deep into experimentation. I always found my dad's interest in this bandleader surprising because Kenton was a tough listen. Not that my dad couldn't listen, but Kenton got quite weird at regular intervals (so to speak).

In about 1973 Kenton's band was playing a gig at Des Moines' Paramount Theater, an old movie house which had been converted into a concert hall. It was a well-done renovation with intimate seating. We were very close to the band. I remember liking the show and I was impressed with the playing, but I didn't know many of the tunes. Dad seemed to know quite a few. We stayed for both of the long sets; the room largely cleared between shows, but the band did not repeat tunes. My father still talks about it.

One of the few things I recall about this night was Kenton's promotion of cassette machines, urging young people to record their parents' old 78 rpm records onto tape and actually listen to them. Good advice, Stan. The other thing that stuck with me was his admonition to the audience not to applaud as he said the names of the band members until he had finished the roster. He lamented that he had one of his very best ensembles break up over egos and applause. Odd, but I could certainly believe it. Performers. Billing!

I learned of Kenton through several high school jazz clinics. He was not hawking his LPs at these student gatherings; he seemed to be there strictly for the purpose of jazz education. My high school crowd talked a lot with the members of his large band, who were usually nice and accessible. Kenton had a double live LP that a lot of us knew well thanks to our high school band director. The record was a concert recording from Redlands University; it included an experimental version of The Beatles' "Hey Jude" (as did the Don Ellis *Fillmore* set).

We asked some of Kenton's musicians about that record and about that tune in particular. But the band with Kenton at our workshop didn't have much to say about the Redlands set because few of them were on it. In fact, the bassist told me that Kenton had insisted he *not* listen to that recording of "Hey Jude" so he would not be influenced by the previous bassist's featured solo on it. Band personnel changed constantly in those big band organizations during the 1970s, but we didn't realize this at the time. For me, if you were in a band, that meant long-term commitment. Like The Beatles or The Who: four guys, and that was it. This concept, I would learn, is the exception with music groups, and it's almost unheard of in jazz.

The fact that Kenton even recorded "Hey Jude" spoke volumes, as this was a band leader who had crusaded against the multitude of evils inherent in rock music. He had even lectured on this topic in Des Moines only a few years earlier. Now he was covering Beatles songs and performing a long arrangement of numbers found on Chicago's third album. That night with my father, I recall Kenton giving high praise to horn bands Chicago and Blood, Sweat & Tears. I also remember thinking that they had chosen material from the wrong Chicago album for their lengthy medley.

I have very few recordings by Kenton, even though his early Capitol releases get reissued with some regularity. I recall Mosaic Records issuing a limited edition box set of these recordings, but the Creative World material from Kenton's own label must still be in the vaults. Or so I think, but I really haven't searched it out. As interesting and innovative as Stan Kenton's music charts could be, I always got the impression that he was jealous of Duke Ellington's talent. Kenton was probably not alone on that.

Bonus Track

I find Kenton's 1960s crusades against rock music even more interesting when examining some of his lesser-known projects. In 1962, Kenton released an album with country music star Tex Ritter! That same year, Kenton charted with a single called "Mama Sang a Song" that included a narration by country star Bill Anderson. The record went to #32 on Billboard's Top 40 chart, and Kenton thought enough of the track to rerelease it on his own Creative World label in 1970.

Interview
Eddie Harris
Minneapolis, Minnesota
December 1979

I really didn't know Eddie Harris' music well. Just a track here and there. I did know the tune "Compared to What" (a record that had actual swearing in it). And I knew "Freedom Jazz Dance," which had been recorded by several artists, but I'm not sure I connected that piece with Harris the night I spoke with him.

I had the opportunity to interview some touring performers after becoming the overnight DJ at a jazz station in Anoka, Minnesota, in 1979. I had arranged to speak with Harris before his show. I was taken downstairs into a cold, dreary cellar beneath the club. It had been snowing hard all day. Harris had a bad cold, and as I look back on it now I am surprised that he even talked to me, much less showed me as much tempered kindness as he mustered. Harris was scheduled for two shows and was wondering aloud whether there would much of a crowd at either. We sat at a rickety wooden table; he blew his nose a lot.

Some of the things Eddie Harris said that night have stayed with me for a long time. He talked about the propaganda of press releases, and especially the liner notes of albums. "What are they going to say on the back of a record?: 'This is not a good album and you should not buy it'? I don't think so."

He was fairly bitter about the format of the club scene. Because the management cleared the house after each show, he was obligated to play anything that had been even close to a hit from his career during each set. He had scored in 1961 with an instrumental take on the "Theme from *Exodus*." It had gone to #36 on the *Billboard* singles charts, but that counts as big fame on the jazz circuit. It had given him work, but he was tired of playing it at every show. "It deprives the audience, too," he complained. "They can't sit in the club for a couple of sets and enjoy the evening and a variety of styles. They are herded in and out and I am required in my contract to play 'Exodus' and whatnot during each set."

I knew of his LP at the Montreux Jazz Festival with Les McCann. Even though this was a well-received album, Harris had nothing special to say about this release. At one point, I asked Harris what was his personal favorite of his own records. He declined to answer that because (he said) of the tremendous variety of music he had recorded. "I even have a comedy album out there, which you may not know about." Actually, I had seen it, called *Why I'm Talking S**t*, but I hadn't heard it. The album cover showed Harris holding a broken saxophone, flattened by a truck. He listed a variety of styles he had tackled—blues, fusion, bebop, and lots of experimental, with a focus on electronic and free. This, he said, was the point of music: to try new things.

Then it made more sense to me why he resented playing the same stuff each night. If he really did like taking chances, he had little interest in repeating himself. Harris seemed to be bluntly honest throughout our conversation. No band members around; no management; just the two of us in the basement on a winter's night in Minnesota. He was not what I would call friendly, and he surely wasn't trying to butter me up for a positive review. Just very straightforward and very interesting. He would have been in his mid-40s when we spoke. He died from cancer in November of 1996 at age 60. That seems young to me now.

What follows is a transcript of our conversation on a night in late December 1979, prior to Harris' first set. I began by asking him how much time he spent on the road.

> Eddie Harris:—How much time? Too much. Really, though, I only play about four to five months on the road each year. Many times I'm ghostwriting for people in the television world or ghost arranging for rock, and rhythm and blues groups. I'm making records and working on different inventions and

books. Many times I'll be sitting around getting all tied up with that…what I call 'overtaxing' work. Then I'll go out and play a job. I'll play solo piano; I won't even play the saxophone.

Tom Wilmeth:—When you say 'ghostwriting and arranging' you mean work that you don't take credit for? Your name never appears on any of these arrangements?

EH:—That's right. Someone solicits a job, and in many instances maybe he or she can't do it. Or maybe they can do it but they have too much work, and they get me. You'll generally know it's my music because mine sounds a little funny. Lots of intervals is the way I write.

TW:—You were into electronic saxophone very early. Would you consider yourself an innovator as far as writing or playing?

EH:—It's up to others to consider what I am. I've been a pioneer in electronics. I'm just an experimentalist, and people have been taking my experiments to heart and they've been copying me throughout the world, so…I don't know. I guess you say you're an innovator when people copy you. Other than that, you're just a guy that's experimenting a little different and if nobody copies you then I guess you're not an innovator.

TW:—When you perform, do you prefer a club setting like you are in tonight?

EH:—Many of my fellow constituents in the industry tell me they like to play concerts. I've never been a concert type of guy because I like to *play*! But it's rough on you out here if you start traveling. At one time, years ago, you could play the clubs. Consequently you could play three, four, up to six nights in one locale. But what's happening now, you play one night here, one night there.

Many clubs I play, they empty the audience out before the second show. I'm playing concerts in a club, and that bugs me because I like to play a club where I don't have to play the same thing at the second show; I can stretch out and play. That's what I got in the music business for: to play! But when you play concerts, the way I see it, you really have to play the same thing.

TW:—We have a couple of local performers who point out during their sets that they are playing a wide variety of tunes every

night, and that a lot of people on the road, in a concert setting, play the same dozen numbers night after night. Do you
think this is a necessity when you are in a tour situation?

EH:—Most definitely. That's why I say I like clubs. If many groups
had to play clubs nowadays you'd find out they are not as
good as you thought they were.

TW:—Because they only have those certain tunes down so cold—
they run the risk of falling apart if they try playing tunes
other than what they are totally familiar with?

EH:—Yes. In other words, you can check them out. If someone
appears here at a concert they might next go to Rochester and
that might be near enough for you to go see them, and they'll
have the same show and the same encore. It's not music then,
to me. Then it's more like a play. You've seen it once and if it's
good you might see it twice, but more than likely you're not
going to see it three times.

 You're not going to last many years [doing that]. You have
to work up a new *show* to come around when you should be
able to just come out and perform. Like many plays on stage:
guys could improvise lines; change it up and have people just
cracking up in the audience. You know, this makes you come
back to see it five, six times if he was a very good actor or
actress.

TW:—But applying that to music, would you say that among the
big names or well-known players, not everyone is able to do
that in performance? You've got 8,000 bootleg recordings of
Charlie Parker doing one tune and you can point to differences. That is an extreme case, but would you agree that not
many players have that flexibility and are able to make those
numbers come alive in a different way each night?

EH:—You're absolutely correct, because many guys that I would
call well-known improvisers, making records under their
own name, leaders, are really not leaders. They're very good
musicians who, in many instances, have played [with] other
bands and gotten solos and gained recognition and someone
decided to record them. But they're not leaders in the true
sense of the word, as an improviser. They take solos, but an
improviser can control his audience. He does more than just

run up and down his horn. Improvising is just like speaking. There are many people who have a large vocabulary, but that doesn't mean they're saying anything!

    There are some people who can stand up and speak and they can reach people. They have that inward gift to improvise. That's improvising verbally. It is the same way when you're playing music. You've got to be an improviser of this nature to be able to control an audience. On records, a lot of times, it's a little shady because a guy can go over his solos and write them out and learn them. Then you have what you call souped-up backgrounds, enhancement, embellishment, and everything. But in person [at a club] you can tell the truth on him. Where if he's playing a concert and you only catch it one time, you have mixed emotions. You don't know whether he's that good, but he's gone. But if he had to play a club you can catch him the next show, catch him the next night. Then you can figure out for yourself whether he's that good or not.

TW:—I understand there are riders in some of your contracts concerning the style you can play for a given gig.

EH:—Yes. This happens with me quite frequently due to the fact that being as diversified as I am, there are places I go where people have what are called pure jazz clubs, or I play with orchestras where they say that I won't play any "funk licks." I'll just play straight ahead, legit. Because I've played with five orchestras. And if I accept a job, I'll do that. In fact, I played a job just last week where I was at Chicago's Jazz Showcase, in which I played no electric, no singing, just straight ahead, hard core jazz.

TW:—As far as tonight's show is concerned, you can play pretty much what you want?

EH:—Yes, I really can. But primarily, knowing the city where a club is situated and knowing the other type of music acts that pass through here, common sense would lead me to believe that this is more or less a funk/blues oriented room and audience. Although I don't have a specific rider which states what I should or should not do tonight, I still know that straight-ahead jazz, like I played last week, wouldn't go over too well here.

TW:—You feel you have to basically play what people expect?

EH:—I think everyone does. If he or she doesn't, I think they won't have an audience very long, regardless of what they play. The people who come to see you like what you've done, I gather. That's why they came to see you. So for you not to play that, you're really insulting the few people who like you, because they took time to spend their hard-earned dollars to see you. Now that doesn't mean you have to cater to their every whim, you know, [and] try to make it just like the record or play this tune whenever the person hollers it out. I mean, you can't just be arbitrary and say, "Well, I'm not going to play that. I don't care what you want to hear. I'm going to play what I want to play."

TW:—You're saying that you can't just thumb your nose at the audience or you will lose them.

EH:—Well, yes. But you may develop a new audience following… but I'd like to clarify that. I don't believe an audience should dictate to you [about] when and what you should play. You should have control over that. But when a guy comes in and he's a singer, well maybe he don't feel like singing. Let's face it, he was supposed to sing because that's what got him there. So he should sing one or two numbers if he's going to do the gig. If he's that sick or something, he shouldn't have shown up that night.

But what I'm trying to explain is that there are many artists who say, "I'm into a new bag and I'm not going to do anything of the old bag." Well, until your new bag catches on you have to infiltrate it with the old bag because you can't just come out with your new bag and say, "I'm into this now." You've known groups who've come in and said, "I've changed personnel. This is what I'm doing now." And they have a current record out that didn't do anything, and their other record has gotten them there and was the old bag. So you don't make a total switch like that on a tour. That's kind of rough.

TW:—There are a lot of good musicians who are not able to play what they want. You've been in the business a long time and are on a different level from someone just starting in the field, but do you ultimately feel fortunate that you are able to usually present your music to an audience in the style you want?

EH:—Well, you hit upon a very key phrase. There are a lot of "good musicians" who can't present their music in the way they want. But they have to stop and realize that they are not exceptional musicians. They are good. And when they are good they have to understand that they are good. Consequently they can go around and be good.

See, what is happening in this country, I've found after living abroad for several years, is that people can't accept the fact many times that they are just good; and that's an achievement within yourself, being good. But here everyone wants to be exceptional. It's like a very attractive woman, very pretty; she don't get as many dates as a nice looking woman. Everyone assumes she's got a date, so she sits home on Saturday night.

Guys look at me and say, "Hey, you can play what you want." I paid dues. I've been playing since '49. Guys don't even call me. Guys used to have sessions. They say, "Let everybody play. Don't let Harris. He sounds too weird." If you read the life story of Charlie Parker and all these different guys…Coltrane, Bud Powell…they were the worst before they were accepted. Billie Holiday. "Aw, she can't sing. Looks like she's out of tune." People were giving her trouble in the big bands. But many guys don't stop to realize that I was the worst before I am now considered one of the best. Do you understand what I'm saying?

TW:—It's like criticizing Miles Davis because he doesn't always hit a straight note.

EH:—That's correct. They used to talk about him, be on his case. There are guys who've been good since they were teenagers, but I was always different, wasn't good. Then all of a sudden they say, "Hey, listen to what he's doing there. Before, it was too weird; it didn't sound right." So that's what I'm saying when guys [complain], "I can't get my music across and I'm *good*." They should think about the guy that's *exceptional* that can't even get a job!

There are guys who work frequently and they want to

be geniuses in music, but they don't really have anything different to say. But they are very good. And that's what is happening in the music business; they are pushing everybody as individuals and saying that the other guys are copying them. I don't want to name the names to prejudice people's minds, but all they have to do is go around and listen. Then start looking at the dates on the records and they'll see where guys are getting their material from.

TW:—Speaking of recordings, looking back through your catalog of albums, could you point to any specific one that you are most proud of? [A long silence.] Or any few of your albums that particularly stand out to you?

EH:—No, not really, because I have a lot of work out there and, you know, I have many different facets of works. If I'd been doing the same thing since I did "Exodus" then sure, I could say, "This one is the best." But because I tend to delve into a lot of different areas, how can I say *good, better, best*? I'm playing bop, I'm playing funk, experimental, avant-garde, electric. I'm going into singing the blues, singing the pop, I do antics with my voice, yodeling, growl singing…so how can I compare it?

I just hope people get an opportunity to hear the different facets of my music, where I play very fast, then play very pretty, very funky, then play abstract, then sing. I want people to know that I attempt all these things. Some of them, people probably won't like. Some of them *I* don't like, but I only do them because I didn't know I didn't like then at the time I was doing them.

TW:—So you are ready to try anything to test the water to see how you like something new?

EH:—Well, that's what music is about. If I wanted to be safe I would just continue to play "Exodus."

Concert Commentary

Toshiko Akioshi/Lew Tabakin Big Band

Guthrie Theater

Minneapolis, Minnesota

April 1980

EDDIE HARRIS HAD his frustrations, but he expressed them only to a young interviewer, not to his audience. When some of us went to see the Toshiko Akioshi/Lew Tabakin Big Band at the Guthrie in the spring of 1980, we attended the second of two shows held that evening. To begin the concert, pianist Akioshi openly complained that each audience that night had been less than half the hall's capacity. So much for the welcome.

The performance of the band members paralleled their leader's attitude, playing like they had zero interest in being there. Somebody from our group later talked about how every note that saxophonist Tabakin had played was golden. Maybe, but the vibe in the room was dismal, and I thought hostility permeated the music. That is the only show I can remember attending where the band was aggressively packing up their horns DURING the last number. Damn near leaving the stage, clearly with their boss' approval. Unsurprisingly, there was no encore.

Concert Commentary

Stanley Clarke

Orchestra Hall

Minneapolis, Minnesota

September 30, 1979

ONE-TIME JAZZ BASSIST Stanley Clarke came to town last week and brought along his rock band. Several ads for the concert ran with Clarke's name spelled incorrectly. This turned out to be appropriate. The concert seemed to be performed by a Stanley Clarke totally different from the one who first came to the music world's attention playing on such albums as *Child's Dance*, by Art Blakey, and on Joe Farrell's

Moon Germs. Most famously, Clarke enhanced the recordings of Chick Corea's group, Return to Forever.

During Clarke's tenure with Return to Forever, electronics became prominent. Corea expanded his own sound from a Rhodes piano to banks of diverse keyboards, and Clarke added an electric Alembic bass to the act. This group, like the early 1970's Mahavishnu Orchestra, could play electric music and still make it viable jazz. Clarke has evidently forgotten much of what he learned under Blakey and Corea, or he chooses not to display this knowledge. There was very little jazz included at Sunday night's show.

The set opened with promise as the band sped through a flawless reading of "Beyond the 7th Galaxy." This number comes from the peak era of the first electric Return to Forever band. But from this point onward, the concert went downhill quickly. And loudly. The music became single riff based, causing redundancy and boredom to become the rule, as few pieces were less than ten minutes in length.

Al Harrison, trumpeter for the backing horn quintet Lips, briefly brought some actual jazz to this evening of hard rock. Clarke played acoustic bass behind Harrison on Charlie Parker's "Confirmation." But even while making this gesture toward versatility, Clarke seemed in a rush to return to the rock numbers. Once Harrison retreated to the role of backup musician, the show again featured interchangeable and deafening vamps.

At another point of this 90-minute set, it looked like an electric ballad might break the frenetically paced tedium. Hopes ran high when Clarke introduced Charles Mingus' "Goodbye Pork Pie Hat." Unfortunately, Clarke used the opening of this number to mug heavily to the audience while he and the keyboard player desperately attempted to be cute. Once past the intricate melody of this standard, the group did not play the number's actual chord changes, but allowed the music to dissolve into a simplistic two-chord pattern. Atop these inaccurate changes were lengthy solos that had nothing to do with the composer's intention for this piece.

There can be little doubt that Stanley Clarke is, or can be, a truly great bassist. Why he hid it so completely at Orchestra Hall is anybody's guess. The rock world already has enough adequate bassists. Sadly, Clarke is now content to be just another showy player, leading a competent rock group through numbers that are void of substance, serving merely as showcases for fast finger exercises played at high volume.

Commentary
"All About the Bass"

Like many of my music obsessive contemporaries, I was guilty of looking away from other bassists when Jaco Pastorius came onto the scene. Most obvious, of course, is the comparison of Pastorius to the great Stanley Clarke. Before I became aware of Jaco, I had seen Chick Corea's band Return to Forever on half a dozen occasions, beginning with the era when Bill Connors was the group's guitarist. The common saying is that after Jaco arrived, everybody forgot about Stanley. True, and yet…not quite.

The real problem for me was that I was already losing interest in Return to Forever about the same time Jaco arrived. RTF's *No Secret* album had not clicked with me, and the elaborate arrangements of *Romantic Warrior* nearly eliminated the improvisational sections that had made *Where Have I Known You Before* and, especially, *Hymn of the 7th Galaxy* so interesting.

I always felt that tension between band members could actually be heard on the later Columbia releases by Return to Forever, especially after Stanley Clarke's solo records started outselling the RTF group albums and Chick Corea's own solo LPs. When no less than three of a quartet's members are intent on solo careers while also keeping a band together, something has to give. Just ask Ringo.

CD Review

Christian McBride
Live at Tonic
Ropeadope Records, 2006

The ongoing release of Miles Davis box sets might make one think that jazz/rock fusion experiments existed only in the early 1970s. Bassist Christian McBride demonstrates the form's continued vitality on his new live release, leading a powerful quartet through determined funk and fusion grooves that never lose sight of melody.

McBride is an inventive musician, accomplished on both acoustic and electric bass. He sometimes cross-pollinates, using a bow on his electric instrument! McBride also wrote most of the music on this affordable three-disk set. Original compositions that occasionally give a nod to influences such as Weather Report's "Boogie Woogie Waltz" make *Live at Tonic* an inspired recording that sounds like the future even as it acknowledges the past.

Concert Commentary

Ron Carter Quartet
Whole Coffee House
University of Minnesota
Minneapolis, Minnesota
January 16, 1980

ALTHOUGH THE STRING BASS is not generally thought of as an instrument to lead a jazz quartet, Minneapolis/St. Paul has seen two groups led by bassists in the last few months. The first was in October, when German bassist Eberhard Weber performed at the Walker Art Center. More recently, Ron Carter and his quartet played three nights at the Whole Coffeehouse on the University of Minnesota campus. These two quartets differ in many ways, but the similarity lies in the uniqueness of a bassist taking the role of primary soloist.

Both leaders seemed to recognize that a full-sized acoustic bass will not be able to cut through the sound of the rest of the group's instruments if played in its customary manner. Weber resolved this situation by designing his own electric version of the upright bass, adding a high C string for extended upper range. Carter remedies the problem by playing what is known as a piccolo bass: smaller than a contrabass and larger than a cello.

In fact, the beautiful sound of the piccolo bass comes very close to that of the cello, Ron Carter's original instrument. In a range somewhat higher than that of the contrabass, the piccolo bass gives Carter results similar to Weber's, but in a more traditional and purely acoustic manner. In addition to Carter's own piccolo bass, the quartet includes a full-size acoustic bass. Clearly, the leader sees himself as a soloist, and not a part of the rhythm section.

Carter led his quartet through what he called its "great American composers" program. The concert's five performed works spanned 90 minutes, featuring selections from the leader's recent albums. The quartet brought an unmistakably somber feeling to each of these traditional numbers, exemplified by the opening piece—25 minutes in length, largo tempo.

Following this low-keyed beginning, I thought the mood might next swing to a lighter vein. But Carter was intent on cultivating a reflective atmosphere, for the following composition was Thelonious Monk's sedate "'Round Midnight." This recognizable work was welcome, as always, but it seemed as if the group had forgotten to play the up-tempo selection that would have been expected between these two slow numbers.

This anticipated faster number, in fact, was never played. The entire evening's set consisted of ballads and slowly evolving dirgeful pieces. I was not waiting for the screaming guitars or cheap theatrics that were hurled at the audience by fellow bassist Stanley Clarke at his recent Minneapolis concert. But an occasional number to demonstrate how the band could handle a hot tune would have been a welcome, and in fact needed contrast.

Carter has great respect for the musicians he brought with him. Although the leader took most of the solos, he gave the piano and the contrabass a chance to engage in lengthy explorations of their own on nearly every number. Drummer Ben Riley frequently ceased playing, and the group became an intimate trio. Less often, bassist Buster Williams or pianist Kenny Barron would also remain silent, leaving only a duet.

Barron is an excellent musician, whose piano work was outstanding throughout the evening. Except for the piano, however, the only solo voices heard here were piccolo bass and contrabass. After an hour of primarily bass solos, I found myself wondering if the group's horn man couldn't make the gig. A saxophone or trumpet not only would have been an additional voice in the instrumentation, it would have made Carter's own solos more enjoyable by contrasting them with the timbre of a horn or reed instrument.

Hearing the featured basses less often would have made a great difference, even if no solos had been eliminated. Carter's 1979 release *Parade* is a quartet recording, but the group is more balanced than the one that played the Whole Coffeehouse. The piccolo bass occasionally is present on *Parade*, as are the piano and drums, but Carter's inclusion of saxophonist Joe Henderson provides the spark that enlivens the album.

Ron Carter is undeniably one of the greatest living bassists in the world. His name seems to appear on every other jazz album currently issued. The man is successful, and rightly so. This means he has the luxury of putting together whatever kind of group that pleases him. While wanting to promote his records and have his music heard, he is not interested in paying the least bit of lip service to any audience but true jazz fans.

Two basses, piano, and drums is undoubtedly one of the most unusual instrumentations of any quartet that we'll see in Minneapolis this year. It's doubtful that anybody but Ron Carter could get away with this setting. But because of Carter's reputation, on his own and as an important part of the Miles Davis legacy, he could fill halls with a quartet comprised *only* of basses. And if Carter does come to town leading this sort of group, I'll be there.

Post Script

That Ron Carter concert was unusual in another way. Early in the program, the group leader spotted someone in the audience who was tape recording the performance. (No—I was not the guilty party.) After the first selection, Mr. Carter requested that the person refrain from using the cassette machine. He said that sometimes these tapes would be issued in foreign countries as legitimate albums. Carter indicated that he had no control over such recordings and received no payment for them. He was calm as he explained this, but also insistent that the person stop recording his set. After the second number, Carter told the audience that the person was still recording, and that the band would not continue if it did not cease. There was a brief scuffle between two audience members near the stage; one man shouted, "Shut it off!" The quartet resumed playing, so the situation must have been resolved to Ron Carter's satisfaction. I remember this instance well, since it was the most energetic moment of that entire concert.

LP Review

Dexter Gordon
Best of Dexter Gordon
Columbia Records, 1980

A quick glance into a record shop might lead one to believe that Christmas is close, since Columbia Records has released yet another in their series of *best of* albums. A repackaging of an artist's better-known material is a favorite trick that record companies use before the holiday season in order to get more of their product into the bins. This encourages sales of a "new" album, and it sometimes helps the musician fulfill a recording contract.

Columbia Records' recent *best of* series showcases a diverse group of jazz artists including Eric Gale, Maynard Ferguson, the group Return to Forever, and drummers Tony Williams and Billy Cobham. Saxophonist Dexter Gordon is included in the label's seasonal attempt to make fresh dollars from old sessions, and *The Best of Dexter Gordon* now resides in the racks beside the rest of his large library.

Considering the length of the man's career and the number of LPs in the Gordon catalog, this new collection's title is a little misleading. Certainly not a comprehensive representation of his work, the album ignores all of the artist's recordings on record labels other than Columbia. This means Gordon's playing on the Inner City label, during his Copenhagen residency, as well as the earlier Prestige recordings, are all omitted. What we have are five numbers from a period of time spanning less than two years. A more accurate title for this release would have been: *A Few Fine Selections from Dexter Gordon's Post Expatriate Years, 1976-1978.*

While Gordon has been heralded as a "sophisticated giant" for many years by the jazz world, it has only been since his return to the United States that many have rediscovered his playing and recordings. Credit where it's due: some of the renewed interest in Gordon's art is due to his recent, excellent Columbia recordings.

The tunes on this new conglomerate are pulled from three different sessions: two studio dates and one live encounter. The LP opens with two pieces in a quartet setting, "LTD" and "Body and Soul." The first gives us a breezy, catchy tune, while "Body and Soul" is Gordon's search for the heart of the ballad. Being in no rush, the saxophonist explores the melody of this standard in a lengthy solo first with the group, and then unaccompanied. It is during this solo segment where, as is his wont, Gordon liberally quotes other melodies, including that of "'Round Midnight."

If this brief excerpt from "'Round Midnight" isn't enough for a listener, the record can be turned over and a full-length version (at thirteen minutes) can be heard with Gordon backed by trumpeter Woody Shaw's quartet. "'Round Midnight" shows what this musician is like in a jazz club setting: unhurried and melodic soloing within a unified small group structure. "'Round Midnight" is taken from *Homecoming*, Gordon's first LP for Columbia after his return from Europe. The double album was recorded live at New York City's Village Vanguard in December 1976, and stands as the artist's definitive domestic recording.

The remaining two selections on the *Best of Dexter Gordon* return to the studio for a larger ensemble atmosphere. "Moontrane" and "Red Top" feature a 10-piece group sharing the spotlight with the tenor man. It is a welcome contrast to hear how this saxophonist reacts to sessions with more than four or five players. Even so, the highlight of this collection is when Gordon is at his most inspired, and that takes place in front of an audience.

The Best of Dexter Gordon is an arguably superfluous repackaging of selections from relatively recent releases, true. Even so, the record provides an enjoyable, if narrow, cross section of the man's work in three distinct settings. For the uninitiated, this is a fine introduction. If it leads the listener to a deeper examination of this artist, so much the better.

Hangin' with the Stars #6—Two Views

Dexter Gordon and Woody Shaw
The Village Vanguard
New York City
October 26, 1982

My wife and I were in New York City on our honeymoon. Earlier in the day we had seen Pavarotti refuse to sing a number with Paul Shaffer's band at a taping of *Late Night with David Letterman*. Now we were seated in The Village Vanguard, waiting to hear Dexter Gordon and Woody Shaw!

I spotted Dexter at the back of the room. He was starting to make his way toward the small stage, carefully weaving through the narrow passage of tables on a path that would take him right by us. As he passed our table, I stood and told him that we were from St. Paul and on our honeymoon. I myself was still impressed by this remarkable situation. The saxophonist must have been too stunned by the news to react, for he just kept walking toward the bandstand.

Woody Shaw was immediately behind Gordon, trumpet in hand. He said to me, "Did I hear you say that you two are on your honeymoon? That's great, man!" Shaw shook my hand and waved to Ellie. He joined Dexter, and the music soon began.

Both men are gone now and both had great talent.

Woody Shaw was a nice guy.

LP Review

John Coltrane
The European Tour
Pablo Records, 1980

By this time, one would assume that the recorded shreds of late saxophone legend John Coltrane would have been totally picked over. Pablo Record's owner Norman Granz proves again that this is not the case, as fresh versions of old tunes surface on *The European Tour*.

It has become an annual surprise to see what the Pablo label can find of Coltrane's unreleased works, and once again neither performance nor fidelity disappoint on this latest glimpse into the man's artistry. Like last year's *The Paris Concert*, specific recording information is sketchy for *The European Tour*, but Granz seems confident that these selections come from November 1962.

The Coltrane-ologists will be happy for some new material to add to their bulging collections, and the players with "traned" ears will be thankful for new tenor solos to transcribe. But this record is not merely for hardcore fans who already have numerous versions of these pieces.

Nor is its value only historical. *The European Tour* is a great album in its own right. Remove the legend, the mystique, and all thoughts of, "What would he be doing now had he lived?" Take this new LP at face value: it contains superb musicianship that translates into joyful listening.

McCoy Tyner's melodic piano introduces "The Promise," one of Coltrane's own compositions. This leads to what was surely one of Trane's personal favorites, Billy Eckstine's beautiful "I Want to Talk About You," which this group performed often. Although Granz is unable to provide exact recording dates for these four selections, it is fairly easy to place the recording of "I Want to Talk About You" as coming from late in the tour, based on the length of the saxophone solo and the complexity of ideas Coltrane presents here.

Another Coltrane original concludes side one, a piece he wrote for his first wife (which bears her name), "Naima." Drummer Elvin Jones and bassist Jimmy Garrison help Coltrane to give this traditionally low-keyed number a surprisingly energetic performance. As with all of these tunes, "Naima" here is quite different from the studio version. This is one of the trademarks of a musical giant: not being content to simply copy the studio versions of their own recorded music. For Coltrane, it's obvious that the concert hall was a place for new ideas and experimentation.

This is one reason why these albums keep appearing—Coltrane lovers realize that they can hear 14 versions of "Impressions," and each one will be worth examining for subtle and sometimes even substantial musical differences. The central reason for such a close study, of course, being that Coltrane is on the bandstand. Like Charlie Parker, Bob Dylan, Miles Davis, and other exceptional performing artists, Coltrane was uninterested in repeating himself. There was something fresh and different about each rendition.

This new LP also includes a tribute to the late bassist Paul Chambers, "Mr. P.C.," which fills a complete side here, as it did on *The Paris Concert*. But while lengthy, this up-tempo version of "Mr. P.C." is less drawn out, as members of the quartet are not allowed the expansive solos found on last year's entry to the Coltrane canon.

John Coltrane's latest posthumous release should not be relegated to the collector's corner. To someone unaware of this saxophonist's powers, the set shows what this man could do. *The European Tour* contains great music from a gifted musician, and as long as Norman Granz and his Pablo label keep discovering these high quality performances by Coltrane, they will be tapes well worth releasing.

Concert Commentary

Sonny Rollins
Children's Theater
Minneapolis, Minnesota
April 1980

SONNY ROLLINS PLAYED the Children's Theater in mid-April and did not disappoint two packed houses of enthusiasts. Saxophonist Rollins has been a leading figure in small-group jazz for over 20 years, and the Minneapolis concerts showed the reason for his lasting influence. Rollins expresses emotion through his instrument in a way few can.

Opening with an original composition from the 1950s titled "Strode Rode," Rollins led his quartet and the audience through a wide spectrum of instrumentals, ranging from a lyric feature on Duke Ellington's "In a Sentimental Mood" to an unashamed reading of a disco number to an encore of Stevie Wonder's "Isn't She Lovely?" A gifted soloist, Rollins is also a strong composer. With the exception of the Ellington and Wonder numbers, the evening's compositions were all by Rollins. Many were vehicles over which the group would stretch into lengthy solos, yet there was still something about the melody of each tune that made it stand apart from the others. This individuality gave the concert a continual feeling of freshness. Rollins paced his set with an expertise reflecting his many years of leading groups through countless nights of performances. Each tune had something different to say, and Rollins made sure you didn't miss any of his points.

Helping Rollins to get his music across were Jerome Cooper on electric bass, Mark Soskin at the piano, and drummer Al Foster. The leader obviously enjoyed the solos his sidemen were taking. Contrasted against the brilliant solos by Rollins, however, Cooper and Soskin were simply outclassed. They were onstage to accompany Rollins, and this is what they did best.

Foster was Rollins' drummer the last time he came through town, on an all-star bill with McCoy Tyner and Ron Carter. This time the stage belonged to Rollins, but Foster remained important throughout. Though the drum isn't usually thought of as a melodic solo instrument, Foster was—with the exception of Rollins—the most interesting player of the night. Foster goes beyond the role of timekeeper; he is a true percussionist, complementing soloists and never getting in the way of the other musicians.

Predictably, one of the brightest spots of the set came during an extended saxophone solo. Playing in a variety of styles, Rollins and his horn seemed to sum up the reason why so many had turned out to hear this performer: pure music played by one who possesses real talent. There was no need for devices such as ring modulators or phase shifters to enhance what this musician was doing. Every note Rollins played was heard clearly, with the audience hanging on each phrase.

Electronics *were* incorporated at times, although the quartet still retained an acoustic quality for most of the show. After a few numbers, Soskin turned from his grand piano to have a go at the electric Rhodes piano. Cooper played electric bass all night, but both fit well with the overall texture Rollins obviously had in mind. It was only during the brief and uncharacteristic disco selection that the group began to lose its acoustical quality, creating a highly produced sound.

Sonny Rollins featured his tenor saxophone for well over an hour during each of his two shows. The group was hot, the audience receptive, and the message was clear: music can be listened to on many levels, but it is there to be enjoyed.

LP Review

Stanley Turrentine
Inflation
Elektra Records, 1980

This is safe music. Stanley Turrentine's latest album, *Inflation,* cannot possibly offend a listener. Once a leader of notable jazz sessions for the Blue Note and CTI labels, this talented saxophonist continues his slump toward Muzak. *Inflation* offers a mere shadow of Turrentine's substantial abilities. Each of these overly orchestrated pieces is played at the same tempo, without peaks or valleys. It is the equivalent of musical wallpaper. On second thought, maybe I am offended by this album.

Remembrance

Gerry Niewood
February 2009

Gerry Niewood was on his way to just another gig when the plane crashed. The multi-reed jazzman was scheduled to play his various flutes and saxophones with Chuck Mangione in Buffalo, New York. Niewood first joined flugelhorn player Mangione in 1968, with the group reaching its artistic peak on two LPs released in 1972—*The Chuck Mangione Quartet* and *Alive!* Niewood's alto saxophone would sometimes evoke the spirit of Paul Desmond, while his sound on the flute was warm and melodic.

In 1976, Niewood left Mangione to start his own jazz group, named Timepiece. A fine, eponymous album was issued on the short-lived A&M/Horizon label. I spoke with Niewood when he was in Cedar Falls, Iowa, not long after the *Timepiece* album came out. He told me he was happy with the record, but was not currently touring with that quartet. Niewood was in town to perform as guest soloist with the University of Northern Iowa Jazz Band. I asked about future plans with Chuck Mangione, but Niewood indicated that his musical association with Mangione had concluded. From his reserved demeanor, it was hard to gauge whether his departure had been amicable.

No matter the reason for the split, by the 1990s Niewood was again playing with Chuck Mangione. Having seen Niewood perform with Mangione and on his own, I can attest to the jazz community's sad loss of a well-rounded musician.

Concert Commentary

Ella Fitzgerald and **Cleo Laine**
Northrup Auditorium   Guthrie Theater
Minneapolis, Minnesota   Minneapolis, Minnesota
March 1980   March 1980

THE MONTH OF MARCH saw two of the finest female vocalists alive today honor the Twin Cities with their talents. The first was Ella Fitzgerald at Northrup Auditorium and, more recently, Cleo Laine at the Guthrie. These women performed with small backing ensembles to full houses at their respective concerts. And while there were other similarities, the differences between them point to the unique qualities that make Fitzgerald and Laine stand far above the majority of today's singers.

It took Fitzgerald until about the fourth number until all the variables fell into place, but fall into place they did. After a couple of up-tempo openers, Lady Time took the audience through two ballads so emotional that they put the crowd at her feet for the rest of the engagement. "'Round Midnight" is usually known as an instrumental number, but after hearing it interpreted by Fitzgerald, it is impossible to listen to that tune again and feel it is complete without lyrics. Unlike so many jazz standards, the words actually fit this melody; they do not seem to be tacked on as an afterthought for the benefit of a vocalist.

Ella next took her audience to Broadway, as she performed Rodgers & Hart's "Bewitched, Bothered and Bewildered." Together, "'Round Midnight" and "Bewitched" encapsulated the strong emotions and moods of most of the evening's selections. The lady is a romantic, without question. Most of the songs she performed were of broken love, like "You've Changed," or of whimsical reminiscing, as with Duke Ellington's "Don't Get around Much Any More."

Fitzgerald sings with sincerity about the human heart and soul. The numbers she keeps in her current repertoire do not just happen to be mostly torch songs and ballads of love gone astray; she is concerned and intrigued by the condition of the human heart. So strong were the readings of these numbers that some of the set would have made an appropriate prelude for one of Eugene O'Neill's darker plays. Fitzgerald was not acting a role, but she continually evoked feelings that are often experienced through an intense evening at the theater.

While Ella Fitzgerald could have been an appropriate *introduction* for a drama, Cleo Laine performed her pieces *as* an actress for most of the night. The setting of Minneapolis' famed Guthrie made Laine's theatrical stylings seem all the more fitting to the audience, and perhaps to the singer as well. Although she brought the theater to her performance, Laine did not go to the Broadway stage for much of her material. Her opening, a largely a cappella performance of Rodgers & Hammerstein's "It Might as Well Be Spring," was all that she drew from the American stage. She did use a well-known English playwright for some words when she performed Shakespeare's "If Music Be the Fruit of Love, Play On," set to music by instrumental group leader and husband John Dankworth.

Laine's fluid vocals were a constant amazement throughout her set as she hit low notes with a full-bodied, rich voice and, in the next measure, reached the upper end of her wide range. Laine hit both ends of this vocal spectrum with such apparent ease that it seemed there were no limits to this woman's singing abilities. Laine's delivery was impeccable and all lyrics were clearly understood. From "My Love Belongs to Somebody Else," to articulating like lightning during a Mozart variation, her diction was perfect.

Fitzgerald did not have to worry as much about her enunciation because, for the most part, she performed songs with which the audience already was quite familiar. Ella was at somewhat of a disadvantage as she played Northrop Auditorium. While the acoustics were good, this large hall could not hope to compete with the intimacy of The Guthrie Theater. During both performances, however, the sound was exceptional. Every instrument was clearly heard, each singer's voice always cut through the band to lead the way.

Where Fitzgerald improvises by scatting, Laine leans more toward singing close variations of the song's melody. Laine uses syllables in place of the words, but she can't really be called a scat singer in the same sense as Ella. While a solo should usually not altogether abandon the original melody, Laine is content to confine herself to minor melodic changes. Hers is a theme and variation approach; it shows a matter of artistic preference rather than any lack of ability.

At both concerts, the vocalists' accompanists opened each program with half-hour sets of largely recognizable instrumentals. Pianist Paul Smith headed the trio that backed Fitzgerald. The rest of the group showcased Bobby Durham on drums and Keter Betts on upright bass. Pianist Smith explained to me that he, and not Fitzgerald, set the order of the songs for a given night. "She'll look over the list I give her and OK it or change it up a little. Like tonight, we were going to do one number, and she said we'd done that so much lately; she said let's do "'Round About Midnight" instead, so of course we did. I decide the order, but she approves it."

Similarly, Laine counts on Dankworth to put the evening's music together. This was clear when, at one point of the Guthrie recital, she turned to her husband and asked if a particular tune had been cut from the set. If it had been cut, her question implied, Dankworth would have been the one doing the cutting. This dependence is not surprising. Professional vocalists must place great trust in their backing musicians. Putting together the evening's fare is just one more item for the band leader and one less job for the singer.

While Smith led his trio for Fitzgerald's concert, Dankworth had a quintet of "merry men" to back Laine. The rhythm section was made up of Kenny Clare on drums and Daryl Runswick on electric bass. Paul Hart had the unusual distinction of doubling on keyboards and violin, and Bill LeSage had rejoined Dankworth's group recently to play vibraphone. The group leader played soprano and alto saxophones as well as clarinet. It was Dankworth's clarinet that was particularly welcome during the performance.

Fitzgerald and Laine each gave an outstanding evening of entertainment. While these women were predictable in their performances, this is to their credit. Singers who are consistently exceptional within their chosen genre, no matter what number they choose to perform, possess true talent as musicians and as interpreters of songs.

Concert Commentary

Grace Kelly
The Deer Head Inn
Delaware Water Gap, Pennsylvania
June 12, 2010

I CONFESS THAT BEFORE last summer I did not know who Grace Kelly was. OK, I mean I knew that she was the lovely actress from Alfred Hitchcock's *Rear Window*. But I had no idea that the name lived on in a talented young saxophonist. So when my wife told me we were headed to Delaware Water Gap to see musician Grace Kelly, I was skeptical. What sort of performer takes her name from a departed movie star? I had flashbacks to a club in Texas where I once sat through a set by another recognizable name: Yogi Bear, the Fiddling Contortionist—an act every bit as odd as it sounds. But on this night in Pennsylvania there was no gimmick, no bait and switch, no ploy. Instead, Grace Kelly offered the most enjoyable jazz club date I had experienced in years.

A smallish, comfortable restaurant and club set on a winding residential street, The Deer Head Inn has been booking live jazz since around 1950. We had dinner and then moved to a spot that gave us a better view of the band. I was stunned as an 18-year-old Korean American woman with an alto horn ascended the stage. This was Grace? Yep. Giving an immediate downbeat, the quartet swung into their first number.

Kelly played alto and led a combo of drums, acoustic bass, and electric guitar. But the focus never strayed from Grace, the musician clearly in charge. She was obviously enjoying herself, absolutely delighted by the sound of her colleagues, tune after tune. Kelly told the audience that she had a recording session with Phil Woods scheduled for the following day, a session which was subsequently released as her acclaimed *Man with the Hat* CD. Even with such an important date only hours away, it was clear that she was not saving herself. Grace was playing hard all night.

The pairing of these alto players made sense. Kelly comes from Phil Woods' post hard bop school, in both sound and selections, but she was not a slave to the past. During the two long sets, Grace played several tunes that she had written. They were all good; really good. And they did not sound derivative of her heroes. She occasionally sang, but it was the sax playing that remained her great strength.

A man came in shortly before the music started and took a seat at the bar. The band all clearly deferred to him at the set break. In the dim light, I thought at first that maybe it *was* Phil Woods, but no. Still, he seemed familiar. The protective tarp was removed from the baby grand piano, and early in the second set Grace introduced this guest to the bandstand. It was the acclaimed pianist Monty Alexander! He performed several numbers with the group, providing beautiful texture and voicings to an already accomplished quartet. Alexander clearly considered Grace a worthy colleague.

Even in in this informal club setting, the audience was respectful and quiet throughout. Late in the evening a woman called out a request for a specific ballad. Grace was surprised: "How do you know that tune?" she asked. The woman told her that she owned all of her CDs and was a big fan. Ms. Kelly first begged off. "Gee, that's from an early CD and this band doesn't know that one." Then she clearly decided: What the hell. She found the lead sheet in the guitarist's book and taught it to the group on the spot. You would never have known it was their first time through the number as an ensemble, and it had some odd time changes to it! A trooper of a performer, Grace was willing to take musical risks in public for an attentive and appreciative audience.

Of the evening's backing trio, Bill Goodwin (drums) and Evan Gregor (bass) both appear on *Man with the Hat*. Monty Alexander was also present for every track on the CD, save one bass and alto duet. The evening's guitarist Matt Stevens is not on the CD, but he was working hard at the live date, sounding fine throughout. Stevens seemed the most nervous of the players and was often hidden at the back of the small stage. Seen or not, I could hear that he was handling his part with the professionalism of the guitar veterans he had obviously studied. He sounded like he had listened to a lot of Pat Martino. I said this to him after the gig, and Stevens took it as the compliment I had intended. Asked about his guitar, Stevens was happy to show me his vintage hollow body Gibson ES 335, the instrument that had produced those broad notes and dark sound.

As with all new bright lights in music, critics are divided about Grace Kelly. Most disturbing to me are those who expect her to be the savior of jazz. This is an unfair albatross to hang around any musician's neck. Even if the artist seems willing, as Wynton Marsalis was in the early 1980s, it will usually lead to vicious backlash. And if the person appears uninterested in leading movements, a la Jaco Pastorius, a different sort of promise is dashed. This is a vast oversimplification, of course. But my hope is that we can step back and allow Grace Kelly to develop her abilities as a musician without drowning her in a sea of unrealistic expectation. Enjoy her music and her attitude. Both are uplifting.

CD Review

Grace Kelly
Live at Scullers
Pazz Records, 2013

This live CD is a reminder of why I still go to concerts. I recently enjoyed a performance by alto saxophonist Grace Kelly, whose hard bop jazz sensibilities showed impressive maturity. So my expectations for this concert release were high. Sadly, Kelly's new live recording in no way resembles the performance I had admired. The CD seems to be a conscious attempt by her record label to recast this remarkable saxophonist as a singer who occasionally picks up a horn. There are backing vocalists, a cello, a trumpet, and a ukulele. All of this is clutter which severely obscures a clear view of Kelly's talent as an instrumentalist.

I stress that my disappointment may not be the fault of the artist. I had the opportunity to speak with Tom Waits a few times during the early part of his career. More than once, Waits voiced frustration over how little input or control he had over what his record company released. Waits told me that the only way to put out a live album that represented the artist was to release bootleg tapes of a regular gig.

Kelly would have been better served on her recent live CD if she had subscribed to Waits' philosophy. One problem, based on this release, is that the listener is unable to tell where Kelly's primary musical focus lies. Buried by so many extraneous backup singers and strings, Kelly is often a stranger on her own stage. Jason Palmer's trumpet only adds to the confusion, offering pandering quotes from the theme of *Sanford and Son* instead of contributing an appropriate solo.

Grace Kelly has chops. And late in the set, on "The Way You Look Tonight," some actual blowing does occur. This superior selection, however, serves as a frustrating indicator of what the album could have been.

It's hard to know whether her label is pushing this performer to be the next Norah Jones, or perhaps Alison Krause. Grace Kelly writes her own material and she sings well. But like the great Eddie Harris before her, she or her label may be diversifying herself out of an audience.

Concert Commentary

The Manhattan Transfer
Minnesota State Fair
St. Paul, Minnesota
August 1980

I WAS THERE to see Martin Mull. I wasn't even sure who he was opening for, but I went to the dusty grandstands on that hot August afternoon specifically to see Mull. At the conclusion of his matinee performance, I decided to stick around for the headliner. I had paid for the ticket, after all.

The Manhattan Transfer played a great set and had a hot touring band. I was won over by the four vocalists and was impressed by how much they allowed their backing group to shine. I knew the hits, of course: "The Boy from New York City" and the more recent "Birdland." But every song was fine. The harmonies were perfect, as were the solo features. Even when Janis Siegel wrenched every possible note of romantic despair out of "Guess Who I Saw Today," it worked.

After performing "Birdland" as the encore, the musicians departed. There was a long stretch before the four vocalists returned sans band to harmonize around one, hastily placed microphone at center stage. They closed with what seemed to be an impromptu, yet perfectly executed version of "A Nightingale Sang in Berkeley Square." Beautiful.

I managed to get backstage after the concert ended. My priorities had changed. Martin Mull was no longer my prime interview target. This was good, since he shouted to me from his trailer that he would not be interviewed. Instead, I had the opportunity to speak briefly with the Transfer's tenor vocalist, Alan Paul, who was nothing but gracious and cooperative. I asked how long they had been out on the road, and my usual tour questions.

Being so struck by the last number, I was certain that the group had added the selection as a treat for this appreciative Midwest audience. I asked Paul how often they sang "A Nightingale Sang in Berkeley Square" as a second encore.

"Almost every night," he said.

And so my education continued in the art of stage performance, and how the pros are able to make an audience feel special. I arrived at the state fair unaware of who was playing. Afterwards, I stayed aboard The Manhattan Transfer until its last stop.

Post Script

This piece was written October 16, 2014, after learning of the death of Tim Hauser, the founder of The Manhattan Transfer.

Concert Commentary

Stan Getz
Minneapolis Jazz Society's Inaugural Concert
Orpheum Theater
Minneapolis, Minnesota
Fall 1979

ARRIVING IN MINNEAPOLIS in early 1979, I was eager to become involved in city life. Finding a job was important, but I also wanted to establish myself as a concert and record reviewer for the local press. I searched out a few things that I felt had promise, including the Twin Cities Jazz Society. This organization was just getting off the ground. Even at the time, I thought it odd that there was no existing jazz society in a thriving metropolis like Minneapolis. But I was happy to become involved with its fledgling efforts.

I met a few people through this organization, but it led nowhere close to a job or a date. Most of the people I encountered were well-meaning head cases, including one frantic woman who was the society's de facto organizer. After a few fundraising shows that featured local musicians such as guitarist Mike Elliot and members of the Peterson family, the society was ready for a concert that showcased a nationally known jazzer. The big name hired to headline this concert was tenor saxophonist Stan Getz.

I watched the concert from the elegant old theater's balcony, going alone in case I had to take tickets or work some other detail. I had my eyes opened that night in a couple of ways. First, the audience was really dressed to the nines, going with the theme of an opening night. I was hoping and assuming that the performer would also be in that spirit. He wasn't; Getz couldn't have cared less about where he was. It was a gig, period. In no way did he acknowledge the crowd or the special aspect of the evening. I don't think he announced the title of one tune or bothered to introduce his quartet to the audience. Rude, thought I. He played 75 minutes on the nose, and gone; contract fulfilled. Good tunes and fine playing, but a bit of congeniality would have gone a long way that night. Wynton Marsalis has described Getz as a man with a beautiful tone and a hard personality. Seems right, from what I saw.

The other thing I found strange was how most of the organizers of the event appeared to have no interest in seeing Getz perform. They were all talking and drinking in the balcony lobby throughout his set. I needed to run to this lobby to check something once or twice, and I even announced to the gathering: "Hey; he's on!" Stares. The frantic woman was counting receipts, which I knew was a necessary business aspect of the evening. Still, it all struck me as being odd. I have subsequently had the distinct feeling that people involved with music societies aren't always the biggest fans of the music.

Interview
Gary Burton
Orchestra Hall
Minneapolis, Minnesota
1976

Manfred Eicher would probably cringe to hear it called a "package show." Perhaps even more insulting to him would have been the term "Battle of the Bands." But in retrospect, I think that's exactly what was happening. In 1976, ECM Records put together a concert tour featuring several of their current acts. After individual sets of music from groups led by bassist Eberhard Weber and drummer Jack DeJohnette, plus a duo performance from guitarists Ralph Towner and John Abercrombie, the evening concluded with one of the label's highest profile performers, vibraphonist Gary Burton.

Some of the music was pretty dense stuff. I was familiar with Weber's *The Colours of Chloe* LP, so I knew what to expect with his quartet. I had followed Ralph Towner's trajectory from The Paul Winter Consort through the group Oregon and to his most recent solo and duet recordings. I had been a longtime fan of Gary Burton, thanks to some upperclassmen from college.

But even for the initiated, this was challenging material. And what I recall of that night is not only the concentration needed to appreciate the music, but also how some audience members, while sincerely trying, were lost from note one. I frequently heard well-meaning but intrusive smatterings of applause at inappropriate times, plus other signs of bewilderment. It was as if there should have been a jazz appreciation seminar offered prior to this show, which I don't mean as a criticism of the artist or the audience.

The set by Gary Burton's quartet was the evening's most accessible, by far. His pieces were relatively short, between four and six minutes each. It struck me that he was consciously concerned with reaching the audience through his music. After the concert, I waited backstage for an opportunity to interview Burton. It was cold that night in Minneapolis; those of us trying to get interviews were tired. Nobody knew who to approach about getting backstage. But down the hallway came Ralph Towner and John Abercrombie. The other journalists didn't appear to recognize them, so I waited until they had passed by before addressing Towner. I wanted him to myself, and the chances of getting the interview with Burton were looking increasingly dim.

"Mr. Towner, I enjoyed your set tonight," I told him. He turned and smiled. He too looked tired. He was patient, but I could tell he wanted to escape. So I just lobbed a fan's question, yet one that I genuinely had wondered about: "Which recording of 'Icarus' is your favorite?" Towner had closed his set with this well-known, melodic composition. He thought for a moment and then said, "The live one we did with Paul Winter." I was glad, for this was the version that had introduced me to the piece: the opening track on The Paul Winter Consort's beautifully performed and unusually well recorded live album from 1970, *Road*. After a pause he added, "And I like the version on the duet recording with Gary Burton." This was from a very recent LP, titled *Matchbook*. In fact, I thought that Burton and Towner might perform "Icarus" as a duet to close the night. But there were virtually no cross-pollination performances between group members at the concert.

I thanked the guitarist and walked back to the huddled group, which had begun to dwindle. Then a man came out and said, "The guy from National Public Radio should come with me." Hey! *I* was the guy from NPR, or at least one of its affiliate stations. I was led downstairs into some concrete dressing rooms, one of which held Gary Burton. He was immediately pleasant and strikingly articulate. What follows is a transcript of our conversation.

I began by asking if he adapted his performance to the audience each night. As he answered this and several other questions, Burton gave examples about how music parallels the spoken word, viewing his performances as a form of improvised storytelling.

> Gary Burton:—The storyteller tailors the work to that particular audience situation. And his main goal is to get this all communicated to the audience and put it across. And the improvising musician is in much the same position. He's playing these tunes that he knows and is sort of interpreting them… according to his usual style and all, but he tailors it in a lot of subtle ways for each individual performance, so that it sort of fits the situation and has a certain amount of spontaneity apparent to it that makes it…unique…compared to written music or rehearsed music.
>
> And so I am very conscious of trying to strike this conversational rapport with the audience, as if I am out there talking to them and telling them these various stories which I believe in very much. These songs that I have chosen to play for them, I like them a lot and I want the audience to feel as strongly about these pieces as I do. I'm there to try to convince them of that.
>
> Tom Wilmeth:—When you improvise, you know where you're going. It's a matter of taking certain paths and certain directions.

GB:—Well, there are a couple of ways to go about that. We [his quartet] tend to play organized structured songs on which to improvise. And that is the most familiar type of improvisation in jazz music that you'll hear. There are also freer circumstances where there are fewer predetermined structures, and everybody just sort of listens to each other and reacts and lets it wander wherever it may, not adhering to a set number of measures or a format or predetermined circumstances.

And there is a parallel to that, I'm sure, in public speaking as well, where you are just going to talk off the top of your head. And if you're clever enough and quick enough and imaginative enough, I'm sure that works. You can sit there and talk all evening with nothing planned, and drift from one thing to another and still get a lot across. It would depend on one's style.

TW:—A friend of mine tells me that you have an unpublished book on a subject, and forgive me if I am off base on this, but you have a concept that if one *thinks* about practicing, this is the same as practicing. Do I have that right?

GB:—Uh, yes and no. This is a confusing issue. It's not a book. There *are* books on these subjects, but I haven't done one. But I often go into these sorts of things when I am doing workshops and clinics at universities. These sort of...rather esoteric points will come up. And it has a lot to do with understanding how language works. I mean, we don't practice speaking in order to keep our conversational skills up. We don't go home and workout for a couple of hours just practicing words and sentences or anything. In fact, if we did it would probably stultify our speech and make it seem less natural. And the same problem exists with the improvising musician. So he has to be careful *how* he practices and *what* he practices, because he's trying to keep it spontaneous and flexible and natural sounding. And *not* prepared and rehearsed, and *not* repetitive and mechanized.

So for most players, who are experienced players, they get to the point where they don't practice in the normal sense of playing an hour or two each day, exercises and whatever. As long as you play regularly, your technique continues to stay under your control and even continues to grow and evolve without using the normal kind of training materials that you think of are necessary for technique.

TW:—So you and your bass player Steve Swallow don't run scales to practice?

GB:—No…if we're going to play, I'll usually wiggle the mallets around just to get my hands loosened up, so I'm not stiff. Otherwise the first tune or two tends to be a little clumsy. But I don't have access to my instrument—it's either in shipment or down at the club or at the concert hall or at the airport or somewhere. So I've just learned over the years to go without practicing on that regular basis. Something that you have to do when you're learning to play in the beginning, to acquire this basic technique.

Again, like language: I mean, if you came from a foreign country and had to learn this language you'd probably have to study it for a few years, and then you could continue to improve your use of the language by using it on a normal basis. And then if you continue to develop you would be able to write poetry and novels, or whatever. And that's what the musician *hopes* will happen. He learns it mechanically first and then just tries to make it a part of his ability to express himself, as if another language.

TW:—You've been involved with college-level jazz education for quite some time in Boston. Do you ever get the feeling that music majors, and particularly people who are going into jazz, are being cranked out on an assembly line, much like business majors? That they are not really able to express themselves as jazz musicians?

GB:—This is…possible…to a certain extent. But I don't think it will ever affect the music scene. What it means is that there will be a lot of people who may have notions of going into music, who will not have the slightest chance of ever finding a career. Twenty years ago [ca. the 1950s] people often did not even find out about jazz until they were in their mid-20s, or at least in college. And one of the big changes is that with jazz bands in the schools, everybody tends to find out about it, at least, at an earlier age. And a lot more people are coming into direct contact with it. So it means that a lot of people now who would have missed out on this completely, had it been 20 years earlier, are now being introduced to this type of music and perhaps get an interest in it.

It *doesn't* mean that there's a job for everybody that has some experience at playing in a jazz band at school, any more than it means that there would be for all the people playing in the concert band in school. I mean, there aren't that many symphonies around. It's sort of the same kind of thing.

Those who are outstanding will undoubtedly make it, as has always been the case. It's just that there are more people considering it for a career now. That's where the misleading thing may be going on. I think that it should be made clearer to the student that there are 20,000 jazz bands in the schools around the country. If even one, let's say, out of each band thinks about going into that as a career, then from each graduating class there are 20,000 going into a field where there is maybe a handful of big bands. So there's just more competition.

At this point Gary Burton's guitarist, Pat Metheny, sticks his head into the room and asks if Burton is planning to go get something to eat with the rest of the band. Naturally, I take the hint and begin to wrap up the interview.

TW:—You said that, undoubtedly, the people who are good will always make it. But what about somebody who is really gifted and puts together a band and just gets upset to the point of quitting because of the business aspects—the agents and the clubs.

GB:—Well, everybody has to deal with that. The only final judge is the court of public opinion. And if you can find enough people to support your music for you to continue playing it, then you've succeeded. And for some people it's a fairly small, but loyal following. But it's enough for them.

Like if certain…more experimental composers and so on manage to have careers…that are not flamboyant or even that noticed by the music business at large, but nonetheless,

[you] look at them ten years later and they're still composing music for a living, getting it played, and managing to have a family and a normal life, even though they may not be major stars at it. So, it just depends. [long pause] It's not as it seems in the press, I guess is what I'm saying.

TW:—On this tour, are you travelling as a package?

GB:—Right. We are doing altogether 16 cities; we've already done seven or eight as of now, and we have another batch to go.

TW:—How do you like this sort of arrangement?

GB:—Oh, just fine. Of course, no group gets to play what would be considered their whole concert's worth of material. But as long as we didn't do this year round it isn't a problem. In this case you introduce the music to a lot of people who may not have heard it before, particularly in this case the groups from Europe and the musicians who are not normally touring here. So it gives a lot of identification to the [ECM Records] label and all of our record output. It's generally good to do this sort of thing if it's handled with decent taste and everybody's compatible.

TW:—How long have you had this band with this personnel?

GB:—Different lengths of time, because our new drummer [Danny Gottlieb] has only been with us for about six weeks. So in that respect it's a fairly new combination, but actually we've had this instrumentation and this general concept of the music for quite a while. Our bass player Steve Swallow has been with me since the beginning, because we were together in another band before we started our own. And Pat Metheny on guitar has been with us three years.

TW:—And lastly—being a teacher, do you find it difficult to write music yourself?

GB:—Yes, to some extent. I also must point out that I don't think that teaching, per se, will keep someone from writing. For me, it happens to. And I think it's partly because I'm not much of a writer to begin with. I certainly don't want to blame it on teaching completely. I was the type who only wrote a song or two a year, anyway. It may just mean that I would have stopped writing anyway.

Teaching does make you much more analytical about

everything you do, much more observant about things you're doing. And therefore, it makes you that much more self-conscious about what you do, if you're not careful. That's the danger of trying to do both at the same time. So it takes a certain amount of strength and belief in your style in what you're playing and what you're doing to not get psyched-out by that sort of thing—getting so self-conscious about it. And doing your own tunes, it's that much harder. You start to write and the next thing you know you've rethought what you've already written and changed it four times and lost the thread of it.

And with that, I thanked Gary Burton for his time, as I finally allowed him to depart and join his colleagues for dinner. I have been in contact with Mr. Burton in recent years and, just as with this conversation, I have never found him anything but pleasant and accommodating.

Bonus Track

Before interviewing Gary Burton, I had a brief hallway conversation with Ralph Towner about his "Icarus" composition. I later learned that Towner was in Tim Hardin's band when Hardin played Woodstock. I would have liked to have asked Towner about the Woodstock gig and about playing with Hardin in general. Tim Hardin wrote "If I Were a Carpenter," "Hang on to a Dream," and "Reason to Believe," among several other very good songs. He is remembered now as a pure folky when he is remembered at all. This "folky" tag is not really accurate, as his Live in Concert *album shows. On this April 1968 recording, Hardin is backed by what is essentially a jazz quintet, including Mike Mainieri on vibes, Eddie Gomez on upright bass, and Warren Bernhardt on piano. Hardin's versatility is also demonstrated on some of his earliest recordings, from 1964, which feature him as a solid blues vocalist. I think of Tim Hardin when I hear Neil Young's "The Needle and the Damage Done." Great talent; great sadness.*

Commentary
"*The Tennessee Firebird:* Gary Burton in Nashville"
May 2014

Gary Burton plays an instrument rarely heard in Nashville recording studios—the vibraphone. In fact, the scarcity of this instrument is the reason Burton got his first break in becoming a professional musician. In 1960, session guitarist Hank Garland was preparing to record a jazz album. Garland wanted a vibes player for his group, but there were none in Nashville. Saxophonist Boots Randolph was a well-respected Nashville session musician and a colleague of Garland's.[1]

Randolph had been impressed by a young man who played vibes at afternoon jam sessions in Evansville, Indiana, where the saxophonist often visited family. So when Garland put out the call for a vibes player, Boots remembered the kid from Indiana, 17-year-old Gary Burton. Randolph returned to Evansville, found Burton, and drove him to Nashville. There, in a studio with Owen Bradley overseeing, Gary Burton played a few tunes with Hank Garland, who immediately encouraged this high school senior to move to town. Garland had his man.

Burton had already made plans to attend Boston's Berklee School of Music that fall, so his time in Nashville was limited to the summer of 1960. Burton went specifically for the Hank Garland sessions which produced the influential album *Jazz Winds from a New Direction.* But during his brief stay in Music City, Burton found himself becoming an increasingly welcome studio side man, playing on various sessions. Perhaps most notable was an invitation to participate on pianist Floyd Cramer's first recording session as a group leader. The request came from Cramer himself.

In addition to his studio work, Burton performed on weekly jazz dates with Garland at Nashville's Carousel Lounge. The club was frequented by some big names, including Jim Reeves and Chet Atkins. After Atkins heard Burton play at The Carousel, he arranged a record contract for him with RCA. Burton's debut as a group leader was a 1961 jazz trio album titled *New Vibe Man in Town.* Recorded in New York City, the music held few hints of Burton's time spent in Nashville

---

1   Boots Randolph had a Top 40 hit record, in 1963, with an instrumental titled "Yakety Sax."

the previous year. This would be true of his next several records. Releasing albums under his own name while touring as a sideman for saxophonist Stan Getz, Burton now concentrated on his jazz career. His Nashville days were over, at least temporarily.

After spending the summer of 1960 working with Hank Garland, Chet Atkins, and the cream of Nashville's session players, Burton did depart to attend college in Boston. However, it seems clear that when he left, the young man who played the odd instrument left on good terms. Six years later, in the fall of 1966, Burton returned to record in RCA's Nashville Sound studio with an idea for an album that would combine jazz and country music. He enlisted many of his former colleagues for the project.

The record that came out of these genre-crossing sessions would be titled *Tennessee Firebird*. But unlike Hank Garland's earlier *Jazz Winds from a New Direction*, Burton used country players and chose numbers from the country music repertoire. In addition to his own vibes, Burton had Charlie McCoy on harmonica, fiddler Buddy Spicher, the Osborne Brothers on mandolin and banjo, Buddy Emmons on steel guitar, and Chet Atkins himself, who also co-produced the record. The selections, too, were unmistakably country, including Bob Wills' "Faded Love," Leon McAuliffe's "Panhandle Rag," and two written by Hank Williams, "I Can't Help It If I'm Still in Love with You" and the lesser known "Alone and Forsaken."[2]

Burton had high hopes for the *Tennessee Firebird* album and even travelled to country music radio stations to promote it.[3] Burton

2   Perhaps Burton felt that the public might accept this style amalgam because of Ray Charles' success with *Modern Sounds in Country & Western Music* (1962). This groundbreaking and hugely popular album combines country songs with Charles' soulful arrangements and vocals. Burton even used one number that Charles had successfully adapted, Ted Daffan's "Born to Lose." Burton told Rich Kienzle in 1988 that he was "partly inspired" by Stan Getz's blending of Brazilian music into his repertoire. Burton brought the idea for the album to Chet Atkins, who approved the project.

3   RCA Records did issue a 45 rpm single from the album in 1967, credited to Gary Burton and Friends. The A-side is an edited version of the album's title track, "Tennessee Firebird." The B-side, "Black Is the Color of My True Love's Hair," is another truncated number from the album. Burton's promotional visits to radio stations had little impact. The single failed to generate enough sales or radio airplay even to enter the Top 100 of *Billboard Magazine*'s "Country Singles" chart. To be fair, instrumental hits are rare in country music. Perhaps Burton thought his upbeat "Tennessee Firebird" single could replicate part of the success Buck Owens enjoyed in 1965 with his #1 instrumental hit "Buckaroo." [The record

thought the hybrid of styles would interest both jazz and country music audiences. It turned out that the project was embraced by neither. In fact, the record sold poorly—even by jazz standards. In 1988, Burton told music journalist Rich Kienzle that he "probably did [the album] two years too early."

Perhaps Burton is right, and *Tennessee Firebird* was ahead of its time. Maybe this album will belatedly spawn a jazz/country fusion movement. And maybe not. But I did find it interesting that, in 1966, Burton would so openly acknowledge the influence that Nashville had on him with the *Tennessee Firebird* release.[4] And concerning influence—it may have run both ways. That is, I wonder if Chet Atkins was at all influenced by the memory of Burton's vibraphone when he was working to smooth out the sound of country music.

In 2013, Burton published his autobiography, *Learning to Listen: The Jazz Journey of Gary Burton.* As the title suggests, it focuses on the artist's life in the world of jazz. However, early in the book Burton discusses his time spent in Nashville. By the tone of the writing, it is clear that this era is still important to Burton and is fondly remembered. Nashville helped break down Burton's musical prejudices, making him open to new ideas. He admits that, before leaving Evansville, he "had become a jazz snob," with little time for any other type of music. In his autobiography, he states that his summer in Nashville "opened [my] eyes to a world of truly talented people."

In *Learning to Listen*, Burton outlines the similarities between country music and jazz. Both genres are "rhythmically powerful, both feature improvised solos and, in both, the musicians have an enormous respect for instrumental skill and creativity." Having said this, he is also

---

number for Burton's single is RCA 47-9133. The length of the A-side is 2:14; the B-side is 1:50. The songwriter's credit for "Tennessee Firebird" misspells the artist's name, listing him as Gary Burrton.]

4   Like the rest of Burton's RCA catalog from the 1960s, *Tennessee Firebird* has been long out of print. Bear Family Records reissued this title on CD in 1989, but this too is now deleted. Burton's next album after *Tennessee Firebird* was called *Duster.* This 1967 release used Burton's working quartet at that time, including guitarist Larry Coryell, John Coltrane's former drummer Roy Haynes, and longtime Burton collaborator Steve Swallow on bass. *Duster* is now considered to be an early step toward the jazz/rock fusion genre. In 1969, three years after the disappointing reception of *Tennessee Firebird*, Burton released an album called *Country Roads and Other Places.* In spite of the album's title, this was not a second attempt at combining genres; it included neither country songs nor Nashville players.

quick to indicate that the skills required for these different genres are not interchangeable. One hastily arranged recording session recalled by Burton in his book involved country musicians "doing their best to play jazz, although it wasn't their usual thing."[5]

After reading the autobiography I had some questions about a few of the topics Burton briefly addressed, so I tried to contact the author for details. Since he does not hesitate to take colleagues to task in this book, especially if he believes them to be musically lacking, I thought that Burton would be honest with me. He was kind enough to reply by e-mail, and his answers to my questions were candid and illuminating throughout.[6]

I first asked about the book's repeated assertion that Nashville studio musicians were not readers of music when he was there. In his response, Burton stressed that people who could read music in Nashville at that time—even in the studio setting—were the exception. He didn't say this in a critical or dismissive way, but this fact had clearly surprised him when he arrived there in the spring of 1960.

Burton wrote, "There was a certain amount of more commercial studio work, jingles, etc., in Nashville, with arrangements written by Cliff Parmenter and others, and reading was required on those dates. The Anita Kerr Singers were often involved in those projects. They could read music, too."

I followed up with what I thought were potentially sensitive questions about specific musicians. I asked whether Hank Garland and Chet Atkins read music. Burton responded, "Yes, Hank Garland could read music, as could a few others of the studio regulars. Floyd Cramer could read music. [I'm] not sure about Chet's ability to read music. I suspect the answer was no in Chet's case." Burton continued in more general terms: "For a lot of the guys, technically they could read the notes and chord symbols, but not very well, and such a skill was not really needed that much in their usual day-to-day calls."

I also asked Burton if he saw the Nashville Number System used,

---

5   This specific recording situation could be a paper unto itself, but to summarize: Several country players found themselves involved in an impromptu jazz session after their performance was cancelled at the Newport, Rhode Island, Jazz Festival in 1960. The resulting album is called *After the Riot at Newport*.

6   Unless otherwise indicated, all of the subsequent Gary Burton quotes are taken from e-mail exchanges between Mr. Burton and the author.

in the studio or when he attended the Grand Ole Opry with Garland.[7] While he did not comment directly on the Opry, Burton wrote, "I didn't see anyone using alternate systems in the studio, including when I worked with some of the guys myself. I once saw a guitar player ask what chord was being used at a certain part of a song, and the answer was 'four hand holds down,' meaning count four frets down on the fingerboard. That was at a Hank Snow session I witnessed. But as for a set of hand signals, I didn't see any of that, though it's easy to imagine that such a thing could have existed." Burton recalled, "They did have some of their own descriptive terms for things: such as the term 'drop beat' instead of what most musicians would describe as an 'off beat.'"

Because Hank Garland had been so important to Burton's arrival in Nashville, I wanted his reaction to the movie *Crazy*, the 2007 film biography about Garland's career. I told Burton that I agreed with the brief, negative assessment he gave of *Crazy* in his autobiography. Burton had written that he was disappointed with the movie, which he called "distorted" and filled with "factual inaccuracies."

Burton talks briefly about the sad fate of Hank Garland, including a telephone conversation he had with the guitarist several years after Garland's debilitating 1961 car accident. He recalls how Hank was very confused, but that he seemed aware of his own confusion. Garland said things like, "I spoke with Hank Williams yesterday. But he's been dead for 20 years! How was that possible?!" Garland also spoke to Burton as if they had just recorded together the previous week.

Garland had been good to Burton. He took time off from his busy schedule as a first-call studio guitarist to find the young musician an apartment. He also introduced the newcomer to many of Nashville's most prominent players. Gary Burton says he will always be grateful to Hank Garland, but found it very difficult to speak with him after the accident.

---

7   The Nashville Number System consists of the group leader holding up fingers to indicate what chord was to be played next, operating like a living Fake Book for the Opry house band. One veteran Opry performer told me that if the leader is calling out chord changes from the bandstand during a song, the word for a D chord could be confused with the sound of C for a C chord or B or G for those chords. Also, hand signals make less noise than shouting out the names of chords to your musical colleagues while someone is performing. I have been told that this system was needed during live broadcasts, in case a singer called up a tune that the band didn't know.

I asked Burton if he placed any credence in the movie's conspiratorial elements concerning the car crash that ended Garland's career. Burton sort of sidestepped a direct answer by saying that he had "heard about Hank's accident and what happened from Boots Randolph, a year or so after" the wreck. Burton concludes, "I have no idea how accurate Boots' version of events was. I always meant to ask Harold Bradley what he remembered of the incident, but never did."

Strained race relations were among the themes of *Crazy*. One of the movie's scenes portrayed Nashville musicians telling Garland that he was costing white players jobs. Specific anger was focused on the use of bassist Joe Benjamin from New York City. I asked Burton, "Was Hank Garland criticized, and even physically threatened by area musicians for hiring African American players, as the movie maintains?"

Burton's pointed response made me wonder whether this question alone was the reason he responded to my e-mail—in order to go on the record about this specific topic. He replied, "Definitely not. That was a part of the movie that angered me. There was no racial attitude involved at all. In fact, there was already a prominent black musician—violinist Brenton Banks—who worked regularly in the [Nashville] studio scene. And, in the case of our record, that was the only time Joe Benjamin, the bass player, worked with Hank Garland. He came down to Nashville with drummer Joe Morello to make *Jazz Winds from a New Direction*, and returned to New York afterward. He was never in a [performing] band with Hank [or the others]."

Burton continued, "The only bassist locally who could have possibly been considered for the record, Bob Moore, wasn't bothered in the least by having a famous guy from New York play on Hank's record. Everyone knew Hank was making a jazz record, and there were no experienced jazz musicians in Nashville." Burton concludes by saying that the lack of jazz players in Nashville at that time was the same reason that *he* became involved with the album.[8]

From these unlikely Nashville studio experiences, Gary Burton became a premier jazz artist. He is highly respected in his own right and has recorded albums with some of the biggest names in music, from

---

8   Jim Reeves regularly used a vibes player named Marvin H. Hughes on his sessions during the same time that Garland was looking for a player. However, as Burton notes, many Nashville musicians were unaccustomed to jazz charts. I assume that Hughes, although in Nashville, did not fit with the music style Garland wanted. It also appears that vibes was not Hughes' primary instrument.

pianist Chick Corea to violinist Stephane Grappelli. Even so, Burton says he is always a bit humbled when recalling that the largest selling record he has ever played on, by far, is Floyd Cramer's instrumental hit "Last Date." But if Burton is humbled, he is certainly never dismissive of his brief time spent in Nashville, or of Country Music as a genre.

Concert Commentary

Chick Corea and Gary Burton
Orchestra Hall
Minneapolis, Minnesota
October 14, 1979

TWO HEROES of the current jazz scene passed through town recently, vibraphonist Gary Burton and pianist Chick Corea. While the instrumentation may seem inherently limited in scope, there was little room for boredom during the performance by these artists.

This duo has recorded two albums for the ECM label, the most recent titled *Duet*. While Burton and Corea would probably admit that their current tour has something to do with promoting the record and selling albums, one did not feel pressured to buy a new product. Some recent concerts have become one long advertisement for an artist's latest album. Although all of the numbers from *Duet* were performed, the LP was mentioned by name only once from the stage, when Burton referred to it almost as an afterthought when introducing a piece.

Corea and Burton have gone through many musical changes since coming into the public eye. Corea has moved with ease from his involvement in free jazz with his group Circle, to light melodies played by the original Return to Forever quintet. This band subsequently abandoned reeds and vocals for a dense, intensely electronic sound, with Corea retaining the Return to Forever name. He has most recently written for fully orchestrated settings, still keeping a quintet as the core of his music.

Since disbanding Return to Forever, Corea has embarked on a series of concerts with fellow jazz group leader Herbie Hancock, during which they play duets and solo pieces on two acoustic pianos. Corea has again released electric recordings since the celebrated Hancock tour, but this Minneapolis date found him at home at the grand piano, bringing forth from it all the color and diversity of any moog synthesizer.

While Gary Burton's vibraphone itself hasn't changed, his music has frequently evolved. By the early 1970s his group, featuring Roy Hanes on drums and guitarist Larry Coryell, had dissolved. Burton began working in a variety of settings on the ECM label. Among the most notable of these releases is his *New Quartet* record of 1973, featuring Michael Goodrick on guitar. Other outstanding recordings of this era are Burton's two duet albums, one with the longtime bassist Steve Swallow and the other featuring guitarist Ralph Towner.

Burton and Corea are not strangers to change or to the duet setting. Their obvious comfort was quickly transmitted to the audience as the two 45-minute sets passed rapidly. Burton chose several Steve Swallow compositions for the duo to use as departure points for their improvisations; Corea, himself a prolific writer, drew from his own repertoire. After closing the first set with an inspired workout on Corea's "Senor Mouse," the two returned for solo numbers. Burton devised a medley of "I'm Your Pal" and "Hello Bolinas" for his musical monologue. Like a jazz version of Pete Seeger, Chick Corea was insistent on recruiting the crowd for audience participation, including complicated harmonies and rhythmic hand clapping. The idea had merit, but the length of the piece dampened any feeling of spontaneity.

The concert concluded with the "Duet Suite," a lengthy piece written by Corea, but one that gave Burton the lion's share of improvisation. This balance might be said for the entire performance. Corea was certainly heard, but it was Burton who proved to be the night's strong man. Vibes can cut through the sound of most other instruments when played in an ensemble, but mere acoustic balance was not the culprit. Burton's music was simply more interesting, and he seemed to bring more energy to his part. Only on the encore of "La Fiesta" was Corea taking the role of equal partner instead of side man for Burton. The fact that Corea often placed himself in the shadows did not lessen the excellence of the evening's musical content; it was simply unexpected.

Concert Commentary

Chick Corea and Béla Fleck

Uihlein Hall; Marcus Center for the Performing Arts
Milwaukee, Wisconsin
April 2, 2013

IN A CONCERT BILLED on the artists' own websites as "a collision of musical worlds," Chick Corea's piano and Béla Fleck's banjo never once crashed during two hours of duets last Tuesday in Milwaukee. Instead, the duo travelled together beautifully on a path of musical inventiveness.

As the house went dark, the musicians immediately dove for deep water, beginning the concert with lengthy versions of Corea's "Senorita" and Fleck's "Menagerie." The first set was well under way before they surfaced long enough to greet the crowd and then offer Fleck's uxorial ballad, "Waltse for Abby." This was followed by Corea's oddly titled, but exquisitely played "Joban Dna Nopia."

It may sound strange to say that an act is on the road promoting an album released seven years ago, but most of the compositions performed in Milwaukee were taken from the one collaborative CD that Fleck and Corea have recorded, *The Enchantment*. Based on their musical communication skills, a second project would be welcome. If nothing else, they should consider issuing a live album from a night such as this.

Deep rooted stylistic leanings of each player often came through their instruments. Even on the ballads, Corea's unmistakable Latin rhythms would surface, just as the occasional bluegrass lick would emerge from Fleck. The first set concluded with the evening's only overt nod to the stylistic background that is inseparable from Fleck's instrument. The appropriately titled "Mountain" offered touches of the Appalachian music so associated with the banjo. Corea added to the mood of this number by occasionally suggesting the theme from Dave Brubeck's "Unsquare Dance."

After a full hour of music, many in the audience were surprised and pleased when Corea took the microphone, not to announce a final number but an intermission. The evening of music continued with more of the performers' own compositions, including their CD's title selection "The Enchantment" and Fleck's set-closing "Spectacle." The one non-original work of the evening was a version of Stevie Wonder's melodic "For Your Love." At one point, the duo reached back to Fleck's first *Tales from the Acoustic Planet* CD for "Bicyclops." This 1994 piece had special meaning, as it was the first number Fleck and Corea had recorded together.

Corea played a Yamaha concert grand piano, and a seated Fleck stayed on one closely miked (not electric) Gibson banjo. One might think that two musicians would run out of ideas in such a setting. But the variety of sounds and styles that filled Milwaukee's Uihlein Hall was always fresh. A perfect sound mix allowed the audience to hear exactly what each man was doing, whether it was the subtle harmonics played by Fleck on "Children's Song #6" or in Corea's emotive piano voicings.

At times the pair traded improvisational measures of 4; at other times it seemed they were trading 36s. Each musician created breathtaking solos, but they also played unison lines so seamlessly that the sound was that of a single instrument. Often Corea and Fleck would improvise simultaneously, reminiscent of a *shout chorus* from an earlier era.

A final number from *The Enchantment* served as the concert's encore, "Sunset Road." Perhaps it was because of the warmth of an appreciative audience on a strikingly cold April night; or maybe it had to do with this Wisconsin show being the final date on a brief, nine-city tour. Whatever the reason, the duo graciously performed what seemed to be an unplanned second encore, creatively improvising near the borders of Corea's "Spain" without actually entering the terrain.

The two men thanked the audience and departed to pursue other concert commitments. Fleck begins a series of bluegrass dates with Abigail Washburn. Corea will now play a week of jazz sets with Stanley Clarke and Marcus Gilmore. Even though Béla Fleck and Chick Corea left Wisconsin bound in different musical directions, each has indicated that he wants to record further collaborations. Might I suggest a concert recording? Their generous evening of music in Milwaukee demonstrated stylistic cross pollination at its best. Musical worlds should collide more often.

Concert Commentary

Pat Metheny
Children's Theater
Minneapolis, Minnesota
November 14, 1979

THE NAME PAT METHENY may not leap to mind when the muddled term *jazz* is used. He is not of the Jim Hall, Charlie Christian, or even George Benson schools of guitar. At times, his echo-laden sound comes closer to the rock he was weaned on than to the style of the aforementioned guitarists. But Metheny cannot easily be written off as jazz/rock. That term is unfair if one includes such groups as Chicago into the fold. So where does this guitarist fit in? He doesn't. Metheny's music is distinctive and truly his own, which is perhaps his greatest asset, and at the same time occasionally proves to be a liability.

Metheny's echoing lines are immediately recognizable among today's numerous guitarists. Few instrumentalists can match Metheny for his ability to evoke a unique and totally controlled voice from an instrument played by so many. But the problem with this extremely identifiable sound is its tendency to make much of his music seem similar. After several selections, this specialized sound has had its say and can only repeat itself. This is a flaw that Metheny could resolve easily by occasionally playing without the constant echo effects. Until he turns that switch off now and again, his distinct sound will become increasingly redundant.

The evening began with "Phase Dance," which, as the guitarist pointed out, has been the group's standard opening since its formation. Although Metheny is the ECM record label's best selling artist, he has only led a touring band for a few years. As late as 1975, Metheny was on the road and recording with vibraphonist Gary Burton, who brought the young guitarist to the spotlight. Metheny did not begin his solo recording career until December 1975, releasing the refreshing trio LP, *Bright Size Life*, featuring the best pieces he had written while working with Burton.

Metheny scarcely touched his first release at this Minneapolis date, preferring instead to pull a major part of the show from the *Pat Metheny Group* album and *American Garage*, which had yet to be released the night this concert took place. Even though the audience could not have yet heard the latest record, new music was expected and eagerly awaited by Metheny's enthusiastic followers. They were not let down. The group performed the majority of *American Garage*, in addition to a pair of compositions written within the last two weeks, making the new *Garage* material almost dated in comparison. Predictably, Metheny did not dwell on his solo guitar recording of last year, *New Chautauqua*, preferring instead to feature his outstanding quartet.

Danny Gottleib is the group's drummer, playing the role of background man who usually rejected flash for tastefulness. The obligatory drum break came late in the set and, as with most drum solos, seemed plenty long enough. With Gottlieb, however, it was not the sound of drums for their own sake. The solo made sense and definitely was headed somewhere throughout its duration.

The same could be said of the solos from keyboardist Lyle Mays. Although there were some predictable moments of tension and release, May's playing doesn't take a back seat to Metheny's guitar, even though the pianist is not given as much solo space as the group leader. Mays is responsible for co-writing the quartet's material and for giving the band some needed balance by means of his outstanding solos. Several times Mays' acoustic piano work came as a welcome relief from the constant electric echo of Metheny's guitar. This echo became most out of place during the ballad "Old Folks," a number that cried out for an acoustic, non-reverberating guitar. This, along with Gottlieb's surprisingly inconsistent tempo, made "Old Folks" a piece with great potential that never was realized.

At one early point in the set, Metheny took a lengthy solo spot that combined two numbers. The solo was just getting to the point of being uncharacteristically flashy when he broke into chord changes much on the line of "House of the Rising Sun," showing the leader's sense of humor. At the conclusion of the solo spot the band went into a Keith Jarrett composition, which became the peak of the performance. This medley demonstrated another strength of the quartet, their awareness of dynamics. Although this might seem simple enough, it is amazing how many groups seem to have absolutely no variation in their dynamic range.

The Metheny ensemble performed with attentive respect for one another's playing during the nearly two-hour concert. The group has obviously logged many hours of listening to their colleagues' musical thought processes. They knew what to expect from each other, but their playing never became stale. The sound was crisp and the ideas were fresh and full of energy. This is part of the musician's goal: not only to be valuable as an improviser but to breathe new life into tunes played at countless other gigs. On this night, Metheny's group succeeded; twice, in fact, during this night's two sold-out shows.

Concert Commentary

Herb Ellis
William's Pub
Minneapolis, Minnesota
1981

I SAW HERB ELLIS at a small club in the Uptown area of Minneapolis. I didn't know much about Ellis other than he was a respected name. It became clear early in the set that he didn't want to be there that night. He was a good player, to be sure, but negative attitudes overshadowed the music.

He pointed to something on his guitar which was designed to reduce distortion. I think he was playing a large, hollow body Gibson, which may be prone to feedback. Ellis made a real point to tell the audience that his attachment to the neck of his guitar was NOT a capo. A capo is a bar placed across the strings of a guitar. It allows a guitarist to play in different keys, using alternate fingerings. "If you ever see me with a capo," he snarled, "you can call the morgue because I'll be dead."

He could have made this comment about capos in a less challenging way, but he didn't. Even so, for many years after this comment, I always thought that players who used capos didn't really know their instruments and were inferior musicians. Then one night I saw Chet Atkins on *Austin City Limits*; he used a capo on one tune, and I suddenly realized that Ellis was just being elitist, or worse.

I don't have many recordings by Herb Ellis—just, a couple of live dates on the Pablo record label, including a duet with fellow guitarist Joe Pass. Good, certainly, but there are guitarists I like better. I later bought some live Oscar Peterson Trio material with Ellis from the

1950s. That material really burns! Probably his best playing, and he likely knows it. I have one later CD by Herb Ellis as a group leader that includes some distinctive acoustic guitar work by Willie Nelson, called *Texas Swings*. I have been told that Ellis was not happy with that CD, but I like it fine. It's a collection of traditional Texas tunes and a few spirituals. "The Old Rugged Cross" comes to mind as a high point. *Texas Swings* would be the guitarist's last release. Ellis died in 2010 at the age of 88, suffering from that cruel disease, Alzheimer's.

Concert Commentary

Jim Hall
Walker Art Center
Minneapolis, Minnesota
March 5, 1982

PIANO AND GUITAR have always been the two jazz instruments I enjoy most. Or at least I consider them to be the starting places for melodic exploration. Dave Brubeck and Kenny Burrell have long been my go to performers for these instruments, respectively. Another guitarist I find simultaneously melodic and interesting is Jim Hall. The first album I got to know by Hall was a live recording from 1975 for the short-lived A&M/Horizon label.

I was able to see Hall in a small room with good acoustics at the Walker Art Center. Just as I find a seated rock guitarist to be an anomaly, I was surprised that Hall played standing up. And Hall didn't just stand, he sometimes paced the stage as he played, at least within the limits of his guitar cord. He led a trio through tunes that people knew—standards, that is. They were complicated arrangements, but his playing was accessible and constantly interesting. Early in the set he explored the beautiful melody of "Baubles, Bangles, and Beads," a show tune from *Kismet*.

The trio's drummer had broken his arm the previous week, but he played the gig anyway with his incapacitated arm in a cast. This approach would be a forerunner of Def Leppard's one-armed drummer, Rick Allen. At one point of Hall's set, both the bassist and drummer left the stage for two or three tunes and Hall played solo. What irritated me was that the drummer had left his snare engaged, so it continually rattled while Hall was playing alone. I remember this especially well because I was taping the concert and I didn't want that rattle on my recording.

Concert Commentary

Howard Roberts
William's Pub
Minneapolis, Minnesota
August 17, 1982

HOWARD ROBERTS is another name on a lengthening list of now departed jazz artists who I had the opportunity to see perform. Roberts made his living as a Los Angeles first call studio musician. It was rare for him to perform live dates, much less outside of the L.A. area.

I enjoyed the two hours of music he played that night, but can't say I understood—at the time—what set him apart. It was only after I got home and, during the following days, repeatedly listened to the recording I had made at the show that I began to relate a bit better to his music.

Roberts' studio releases of this era as a leader were very odd affairs. He had abandoned the traditional small group approach to jazz that he had embraced on his Capitol albums of the mid-1960s, such as *Guilty*. By the early 1970s, Roberts had released two highly produced and multilayered recordings called *Antelope Freeway* and *Equinox Express Elevator*. An interviewer once asked Roberts if these records were elaborate in-jokes for musicians. Roberts responded that he was dead serious about the music on those albums and had worked hard on each project.

In spite of these experimental studio releases, Roberts' live set in Minneapolis that night was a traditional trio format. I liked Roberts' playing, but the evening's music didn't blow me away. After my earlier complaints about guitarist Herb Ellis' treatment of his audience, it's worth mentioning that Howard Roberts' stage demeanor was personable and respectful towards the audience.

Having few recordings of Ellis, I have even fewer by Howard

Roberts. The only traditional jazz set is *Color Him Funky*, from 1963. I do own both *Antelope Freeway* and *Equinox Express Elevator;* I don't understand the music on either one of them. I am told that they are part of a trilogy. Naturally, I would buy the third one if I saw it.

Bonus Track

A friend of mine attended a guitar seminar led by Howard Roberts in about 1978. One of his main recollections was of Roberts stressing the importance of a professional musician's sight-reading abilities. This was because time equals money in the studio; the quicker the number is recorded the less expensive the date. The guitarist also talked about the follow-the-leader attitude that was prevalent in the studio scene. Roberts said that if he and a couple of his first call session guitarist colleagues suddenly started playing a certain type of guitar, the demand in L.A. for that brand of instrument would change overnight. Players want what the pros are using, even at that level.

Concert Commentary

Anthony Cox and Mark Waggoner
The Night Train
St. Paul, Minnesota
March 28, 1981

CREDIT MUST BE GIVEN to one of St. Paul's newer trendy restaurants, The Night Train, for offering live jazz. Bassist Anthony Cox and guitarist Mark Waggoner were there recently and presented an evening of extraordinary music. Cox will soon move to New York City, making this gig one of his last in the area for some time. After Saturday's performance, the Twin Cities jazz community can be proud of this musical export to the Big Apple.

Cox's acoustic bass laid the groundwork for the pieces and provided a departure point for Waggoner's guitar. There was no attempt to give Cox as much soloing space as his partner enjoyed, for while the bass was the occasional center of focus, this was an evening of guitar features.

The guitar work of Mark Waggoner is well established on the Minneapolis music scene. He appears regularly with drummer Eric Kamau Gravatt's group, Mystic Harbor Bridge. Gravatt's band shows off Waggoner's talents, but not as well as in a duo setting. Attention was consistently drawn to the guitarist's treatment of a piece's melody line and the subsequent improvisations growing from these themes. The varied set included Cole Porter's standard "What Is This Thing Called Love?" as well as classics of a different era, such as Wayne Shorter's waltz, "Footprints."

Waggoner's precise guitar work stood out, even at low volume in a bar packed with conversing patrons. Often the single line solos would resolve into full chords; at other times chords were the main base of operation for solo passages. Waggoner's melodic style was unusual too, in that the inherently dark sound of his large guitar was never lost in the range of his partner's bass.

This guitarist does not subscribe to the "more notes is better" school of playing; his self-editing was appropriate, as the music flowed with no extraneous pyrotechnics. None were needed. Waggoner and Cox said with their instruments what was necessary to get their ideas across, which is what performance is supposed to be about.

One might have expected the set to close with an upbeat number. Instead, Cox and Waggoner ended the evening with their most gentle ballad of the night, Billy Strayhorn's "Chelsea Bridge." This subdued choice again demonstrated the duo's awareness that quality music can stand on its own.

Concert Commentary

Alex de Grassi

Peck Recital Hall
University of Wisconsin—Milwaukee
September 27, 2014

TWO HANDS, TWO GUITARS, and a seemingly infinite number of ideas. This is all Alex de Grassi used to keep an audience spellbound for 90 minutes last Saturday night on the campus of the University of Wisconsin-Milwaukee, where he also served as visiting teacher/performer in the school's Guitar Studies Program. Each selection was a springboard for innovative explorations. Placing his own mark on such diverse pieces as The Carter Family's "Single Girl" and Jimi Hendrix's "Angel," Alex de Grassi traversed a remarkably wide musical map with accessible flair and imagination.

When a recital opens with a number about a cat called "Blue Trout," one is wise to suppress further expectations. An original number about James Brown taking a walk in the rain came next. The title piece from de Grassi's *Water Garden* work followed, which melded into The Beatles' "You Never Give Me Your Money." Later in the program, de Grassi played another selection from *Water Garden* called "Cumulus Rising," which he dedicated to his deceased friend and fellow acoustic guitarist Michael Hedges. Both musicians were among the first artists signed by Windham Hill, a record label prominent in the 1980s that still holds an unusually strong bond with its early audience.

De Grassi showed a spiritual side with "Lay This Body Down" and "Swing Low Sweet Chariot," and he gave a nod to country and western music with "Bury Me Not on the Lone Prairie," which somehow found itself on a Jamaican landscape. A few standards were revisited, including "St. James Infirmary" and "It Ain't Necessarily So."

Part of what was so refreshing about this solo performance was de Grassi's keen awareness of his audience. Although often playing complex figures, he was never self-indulgent in the length of his selections. He was gracious and funny throughout the evening, offering useful information about each piece. His sense of humor extended to his repertoire, which included an unexpected version of "Shortnin' Bread" in a section of the concert he dedicated to "death and food."

Alex de Grassi's guitars were, not surprisingly, custom jobs. For most of the evening he played a prototype of the Lowden Guitar Company's forthcoming de Grassi signature model. The other instrument came from California guitar maker Jeff Traugott. The first four selections were played in standard tuning. After this, alternate tunings were frequent. He also took full advantage of the two guitars he alternated between, adding percussion by striking the hollow body of each instrument, and occasionally strumming the short strings near the tuning pegs for some lovely Autoharp effects.

No amps, no picks; just those guitars and his two hands. Hands that were surely busy, for in the palm of one of them he also held an audience spellbound.

LP Reviews

Kenny Burrell   and   **The Heath Brothers**
Live at the Village Vanguard   *Live at the Public Theater*
Muse Records, 1980   Columbia Records, 1979

Two live releases have just hit the record shops that show, for the most part, what small group jazz can aspire to on a good night. The first, appropriately titled *Kenny Burrell Live at the Village Vanguard*, features a jazz trio in the intimate ambience of this famous New York City club. The set comes from one night in December 1978, and it shows Burrell to be a guitarist who never ceases to improve his skills.

Like many performers, Burrell seems to do some of his best work in front of an audience. As Burrell points out in the album's liner notes, he finds the Vanguard a comfortable place to play. More than this, perhaps, is the almost family atmosphere provided by club owner Max Gordon, who has shared a working relationship with Burrell for more than 20 years.

"Second Balcony Jump" opens this refreshing record on an upbeat note. While the entire set is memorable, it is this opening number that stays with you after the album has been put away. The following ballad, "Willow Weep for Me," shows Burrell's range of tempos. He can be a hot and fast player when the occasion calls for it, and he is able to make a slow standard sound fresh, as if you are hearing it for the first time.

Burrell is a gifted player whose melodic phrases never become muddled; every note is clear. The superior technical quality of this recording allows one to appreciate the nuance of Burrell's playing. This is thanks to Helen Keane, longtime record producer of many jazz artists, including pianist Bill Evans. Keane knows what goes into high fidelity recordings, just as Burrell knows about high quality performances.

Burrell frequently goes it alone here. But these segments are so fully orchestrated by the solo guitar that the bass and percussion are not initially missed. It is only after the other two players return to a given piece that the listener realizes just how long Burrell has been handling all aspects of the music by himself. Few jazz guitarists are willing to let their instrument stand naked in a live setting. Joe Pass is not reluctant to perform alone, but the vast majority of this genre's guitarists seem to feel uncomfortable without a rhythm section. Those that do attempt solo settings rarely succeed as well as the gifted Burrell.

Backing Burrell is the upright bass of Larry Gales and drummer Sherman Ferguson. These players are given some time to show what they can do as soloists, and they handle their parts well. But most will play this record to hear Burrell. *Live at the Village Vanguard* is his finest release in some time because the guitarist is given the freedom that comes from working with, and apart, from a trio. Here, the listener is able to discover how the artist uses that freedom.

From Burrell's trio we move to a quintet setting for *The Health Brothers Live at the Public Theater*. These new Heath Brothers and Kenny Burrell LPs share some common ground. They are both small-group live albums of longer than normal length. Further, Burrell and the Heath Brothers are Duke Ellington fans all, and they show their dedication by performing compositions from Duke's vast library. The Heath Brothers perform "Warm Valley." Burrell, known for years as a leading interpreter of Ellington, chooses to make a medley of "Don't You Know I Care (or Don't You Care to Know)" and "Love You Madly." Another similarity: it could be argued that these Ellington numbers are the peak of each record.

Since The Heath Brothers' appearance in Minneapolis a few months ago, two percussionists have been added, and Akira Tana has replaced Keith Copland on drums. Other changes also seem to have occurred within this group. One installment of last season's *Dick Cavett Show* saw bassist Percy Heath denouncing current trends in music—especially disco. He was smug as he told Cavett that their group came from the school of mainstream jazz. It did not cater to or depend upon the latest musical whim of the industry or the taste of a fickle public.

We can now disregard all of that nobility, as this release includes the Heath Brothers' answer to Mangione's "Feel So Good" and Herb Alpert's "Rise": a disco flavored number titled "For the Public." The brothers seem proud of this track and obviously hope it hits the pop charts, since the album cover prominently states that this collection features "For the Public." So much for scorning commercial potential.

The rest of this release presents the Heath Brothers as you expect to find them. Jimmy Heath blows a smooth tenor saxophone, but we also hear more flute from him than on recent recordings. Brother Percy is the solid bottom, on the acoustic bass. While it is the brothers' band, two other members of the group have the potential to steal the spotlight. Tony Perrone is a fluid electric guitarist who never seems to run out of interesting lines. He is featured several times on these half dozen numbers, but not quite enough to do the man justice. And speaking of justice, it is nothing short of a crime how Stanley Cowell's keyboards go almost unheard for the entire set.

The Heath Brothers Live at the Public Theater is a good album, but it has some problems. The record pales in comparison to their performance last fall at the Children's Theater, or even the numbers performed on the Cavett show. It seems strange the group would release these tapes when it's obvious that the band can produce more satisfying jazz than what is represented on these sides.

Concert Commentary

Kenny Burrell Trio
The Back Room of The Carlton Celebrity Room
Bloomington, Minnesota
December 12, 1981

BY THE 1970S, almost every recording artist in pop and country had released a Christmas record. If not an entire album, then at least an individual song: Bruce Springsteen, Prince, Willie Nelson, Eagles.

No one seemed exempt. But in spite of the expanding market for holiday fare, Christmas albums by jazz musicians were still somewhat unusual.

Guitarist Kenny Burrell was one of the first jazz artists to release such a record. His *Have Yourself a Soulful Little Christmas* was, and remains, a landmark album. Recorded in October 1966 and released a few weeks later, it provided a mix of old and new music, including both sacred and secular pieces. Expected Yuletide material like "Away in a Manger" and "Silent Night" is found here, but so are gospel numbers, such as "Children Go Where I Send Thee" and especially "Mary's Little Boy Chile." A blues number closes the record, with Burrell's take on the Charles Brown hit "Merry Christmas, Baby."

When Burrell played a suburban Minneapolis date in December 1981, *Have Yourself a Soulful Little Christmas* had been out of print for years. This would not be remedied for another full decade. Clearly not striving to promote an unavailable album, Burrell's trio seemed happy to feature selections from this Christmas album in each of their sets. In fact, Burrell was aware that some audience members were there specifically to hear his Christmas arrangements, for early in the program he indicated that they would indeed be playing material from his *Soulful Little Christmas* album. The audience was quiet and respectful throughout the entire performance; Burrell was just letting them know that he was aware of the season.

An hour into the set, Burrell pulled his acoustic guitar from its case and proceeded to play three unplugged numbers with gentle backing of bass and brushes. He acknowledged that he was not really known as an acoustic player and didn't often pull out "the guitar with the big hole" for club dates. But when listeners were as attentive and appreciative as this Minnesota audience, he said he was glad to get the chance. One of the acoustic numbers he performed was the title number from his 1979 release, *Moon and Sand*.

Returning to his large electric Gibson, Burrell led his trio through the promised set of holiday fare, beginning with "My Favorite Things." The following three selections flowed together, but I hesitate to call it a medley since these renditions were not at all truncated. Full versions of "White Christmas," "Have Yourself a Merry Little Christmas," and "Santa Claus Is Coming to Town" were presented as the nostalgic and joyful songs they are. The group acknowledged the applause of the audience as drummer Sherman Ferguson softly started what would become his percussion feature on "The Little Drummer Boy."

Burrell began to close out the evening with a two-song Ellington tribute, "Love You Madly" and "I'm Just a Lucky So and So," on which he not only took a hot, chord-driven solo but also sang! The trio began their closing break theme, Kenny Burrell thanked the audience for coming out, and the evening was over. A generous set, to be sure, especially since this was his second show of the night. More generosity was still to come, however, as the group returned to the stage for a little more Ellington, with "Take the A Train" and a final encore of "The Christmas Song."

As the audience thinned I took a seat at the bar, hoping to speak with Mr. Burrell. It wasn't long before he came out of the dressing room. He was happy to talk, even though his manager wanted to get him back to the hotel. During our short conversation I recall telling Burrell that he was an "important" jazz guitarist. He smiled at this and thanked me, but disagreed. He stressed that he was fortunate to have a lasting audience. This had allowed him to make a living playing music, but to be called "important" seemed to make him uneasy.

"I'm 'historically important' maybe, as a continuation of a musical heritage," he said, "but that goes far beyond me as an individual." I indicated how much I enjoyed the *Have Yourself a Soulful Little Christmas* LP, and that I had been in the audience to hear him twice during the past week. I probably strayed over the fence a bit when I told him that I had searched out both a stereo and a mono copy of his Christmas album. He looked somewhat vexed at this unexpected compliment (or so I meant it), but offered no real comment. I thought it best not to mention that I had recorded that evening's music on my portable cassette machine. Instead, I asked him when he thought the *Soulful Little Christmas* album would again be available.

He hoped it would be back in print soon, but also told me that he had little input over such things. When I looked surprised, Burrell explained that this was normal in the recording industry in general, and that jazz artists probably had even less control than most performers. He considered himself lucky because he had experienced some tangible success with one album in particular, which had earned numerous critical accolades as well as making money for the record label. "The success of my *Midnight Blue* record [1963] opened a lot of doors that remain important for me to this day," he said. "Lots of fine musicians don't have the opportunities I've had, and I am grateful for the way things have worked out." It seemed that he really did consider himself "a lucky so and so," as he had told the audience in song just a few minutes earlier.

I thanked him for his time and his music. I said again how much I enjoyed his Christmas album and the live versions he had offered that week. Knowing he was headed to the next town for the next gig, I asked one final question of Mr. Burrell as we parted, while his manager again pointed to his watch.

"Being constantly on the road, does it even seem like the Christmas season to you?" I asked.

"It does now," he smiled.

Bonus Track

Jazz guitarist Kenny Burrell was in The Back Room of The Carlton Celebrity Room. On the main stage that week was Andy Williams. My father had some of Williams' records. Dad would often reference Williams' Iowa roots and how he used to sing with his three brothers in a vaudeville act. One of my older cousins was a big fan; she had seen him at the Iowa State Fair grandstand in the 1960s. I didn't feel strongly about Williams either way, but I really liked his single "Can't Get Used to Losing You." Still do.

During one of Burrell's breaks, I wandered around the Celebrity Room complex. Seeing no ushers guarding the door, I walked up the carpeted slope that led to the establishment's big room. There was Williams. I don't recall what song he was singing, but I distinctly remember the way he commanded the large stage. His presence filled the room. Suddenly, I saw the appeal. He could sing, absolutely, but he could also perform! That audience was enthralled. I saw maybe two minutes of one song that night, but I was extremely impressed. Miles of stage presence.

I didn't think about Andy Williams again for many years, until a relative gave me a book she found at a rummage sale, Williams' autobiography—Moon River and Me. I recommend it highly. It is well written and offers glimpses of an ensemble style of live entertainment that was about to go extinct shortly after World War II. Williams recounts climbing the show business ladder with his three brothers, taking a well-rehearsed act from the corn fields of Iowa to a very corrupt Las Vegas and beyond.

LP Review

Jean-Luc Ponty
A Taste For Passion
Atlantic Records, 1979

Jean-Luc Ponty's new *A Taste for Passion* LP is the successful culmination of electronic experimentation and the hummable popular song. The album consists of ten pieces that fluctuate between simple vamps and intricate chord patterns. Both work well here.

Unlike Ponty's previous efforts, there is no lengthy violin feature on this record. The spotlight shines on the group as a cohesive unit more than as a combination of five soloists. On more than one selection, various members of the group are featured briefly before Ponty even makes his musical entrance. Saving himself for the latter part of a piece might be an old trick as far as a tension builder or star status is concerned, but Ponty knows that he is playing with other excellent performers. This is not a one-man show, and the leader uses the talents of his band members accordingly.

Ponty has retained electric bassist Ralphe Armstrong from their time spent together in a later incarnation of The Mahavishnu Orchestra. A wise decision on Ponty's part, as Armstrong is among the finest young electric bassists in the field. The band also includes Allan Zavod's keyboards and drummer Casey Scheuerell. Joaquin Lievano's talents as a guitarist enhance most every number. Lievano's electric guitar begins to sound a bit like a violin when he plays in the upper register, at which point Ponty usually takes over with his real violin and we hear how the group leader handles a solo.

Ponty seems to realize that, after a while, electronics can turn into a toy, making sounds that are interesting only to the musician creating them. (I think here of trumpeter Don Ellis' experimental Ring Modulator.) When this occurs, the use of an instrument as a conduit for music is lost, becoming its secondary purpose. Fortunately, *A Taste for Passion* does not include electronics used for open-ended audio experimentation.

Ponty lets go of his classical and jazz schooling to become, for this release at least, a practitioner of outstanding pop music—pop music in the finest sense of the word. The numbers included on *A Taste for Passion* are melodies that are retained in your head after the album is over, which is saying something for a set of instrumental fusion pieces. The tunes are simple melodies, often using a two-chord pattern. Upon these basic ideas Ponty and his group weave some of the most approachable soloing of the year. *A Taste for Passion* is first-rate musicianship set against the backdrop of electric instrumentation and readily accessible song structures. The results are successful.

Concert Commentary

Jean-Luc Ponty and **Eberhard Weber**
Guthrie Theater   Walker Art Center
Minneapolis, Minnesota   Minneapolis, Minnesota
October 7, 1979   October 7, 1979

AN UNINTENTIONAL COMBINATION of international jazz bookings occurred one night last week. The Guthrie Theater hosted a concert by the French jazz violinist Jean-Luc Ponty. Literally across the hallway at the Walker Art Center Auditorium was German bassist Eberhard Weber. I went to see Weber's performance, but a late show had been added for Ponty, and I was able to buy a ticket on the street for this sold-out concert.

Weber's group played several of his new and very long compositions, such as "T on a White Horse." It was clear that some of this music was very new to the group, for they were sometimes reading from lengthy pieces of sheet music that their music stands would scarcely hold. Having learned of this bassist when I was living in Iowa, I knew some of the older pieces he played, including "Yellow Fields."

I was able to interview the soft-spoken Weber after the concert. The bassist was gracious and pleasant, but said he really did not care to tour. He acknowledged that he was an unusual musician; most players, said Weber, after they have a really hot set, they want to keep playing. "Yes, again. Let's play some more." Not Weber. He told me that after he has played a satisfying set of music, he really doesn't want to play his instrument for a while—perhaps a week. Maybe let the tank refill.

After my brief interview with Weber, I rushed over to the late performance by Jean-Luc Ponty. I was working as the overnight jazz DJ at the time, at a radio station just north of Minneapolis, so had already heard Ponty's new record, *A Taste for Passion*, which I thought was quite good.

I had never seen a concert quite like this. Ponty entered the Guthrie stage with his crack band (the same as on the record) and proceeded to play the entire new album, complete and in the tracking order of the LP. I guess Ponty was happy with the record. They performed the tunes beautifully, clearly making a conscious attempt to replicate the album. And succeeding. After a performance of the entire album, Ponty encored with a couple of his better-known numbers, including "Egocentric Molecules." The night was a fine twin bill of European jazz.

Concert Commentary

Daryl Stuermer
Cedarburg Performing Arts Center
Cedarburg, Wisconsin
January 26, 2013

LET ME SUGGEST that Chick Corea give Daryl Stuermer a call next time the guitar chair opens up in his group Return to Forever. Before being tapped in 1978 for his lengthy tenure with the prog rockers Genesis, Stuermer says his playing was more oriented toward the fusion genre. His three mid-1970s albums as Jean-Luc Ponty's guitarist certainly prove this point.

When Stuermer now tours as group leader, he acknowledges that the evening will include a healthy amount of Genesis material. But this is no tribute band or oldies review. As he told the hometown audience last Saturday night in Cedarburg, Wisconsin: "Most of these Genesis numbers did not receive much radio exposure."

The quintet opened with instrumental scorchers: "Duke's End" and "Just a Job to Do." Over two hours later, a stretched-out version of "Firth of Fifth" closed the main set, with "Turn It On Again" used as a satisfying encore. Between these pillars of deep catalog Genesis were several numbers from Stuermer's most recent solo CD, *Go*.

Whether playing Genesis tunes or his own compositions, Stuermer effortlessly melded his crisp and muscular lead lines onto the strong melodies and complex arrangements. The music from the evening's generous set sounded strikingly fresh and vital throughout.

Happy to discuss the music with an appreciative audience, Stuermer recalled how his first assignment for Genesis was to work up the song "Squonk" from a tape the group had sent. At that time, he said he found it interesting how "Squonk" was "a simple tune, yet difficult to play." His performance showed that he was still intrigued by the song.

Throughout the night, on pieces such as "Heavy Heart," "Deep in the Motherload," and "The Quiet Earth," Stuermer demonstrated a mastery of technique on his instrument and, occasionally, included some restrained pedal board synthesizer and experiments with sustained notes. His lines were fluid and clear, with a perfect sound mix allowing the audience to hear each intonation and harmonic. Surprisingly, the audience showed little recognition when Genesis LP titles such as *Trick of the Tale* or *Wind & Wuthering* were mentioned. Still, they were extremely receptive to all of Stuermer's music, for which the guitarist warmly thanked them.

For the guitar heads: Stuermer played his Godin LGXT for all but two numbers, switching to a blonde Godin Multiac steel string solid body electric for "Your Own Special Way." At one point he held aloft a large-hollow body Montreal Premiere, which he had just received for Christmas from the Godin Guitar Company. He then played this beautiful crimson instrument on "In Too Deep."

Milwaukee native Eric Hervey played five-string electric bass, and St. Petersburg transplant Kostia Efimove has been Stuermer's trusted keyboard man since 1990. Alan Arber only recently joined on drums but demonstrated a comfort level that made it seem like he had been with this band for years. Guest performer Woody Mankowski played tenor and soprano saxes throughout the evening and was also an occasional vocalist. A diverse group of musicians but, as Stuermer was happy to note, each band member had his own Wisconsin connection.

Daryl Stuermer was a welcoming and engaging front man who articulately led the audience through the evening's music. However, he seemed most at home while playing those remarkable guitar passages. At this point, Stuermer doesn't need to be anybody's side man; he is busy with his own career and is a first call studio session cat. But given the opportunity, I believe Stuermer might also make time for a chance to revisit the fusion genre that he put on hold back in 1978. Hey, Chick Corea, are you listening?

Interview
Bobby Lyle
Minneapolis, Minnesota
April 1980

Pianist Bobby Lyle returned to his hometown of Minneapolis this past February to give a spirited concert at Orchestra Hall. At 35, Lyle has travelled a long way from the Land of 10,000 Lakes. His decision to leave this area a few years ago and relocate to Los Angeles marked him as one of the many aspiring musicians from around the country hoping to succeed in the swirling west coast music business.

First making his name in L.A. as a sideman and a studio session player, Lyle soon impressed his California contemporaries as a performer in his own right. Among his earliest gigs were dates with Sly and the Family Stone. In 1978, Lyle performed with Pharoah Sanders at the Montreux Jazz Festival, a live session released on the album *Beyond a Dream*. Such jobs exposed him to a wider audience; many were quick to note, in Lyle's words: "Hey; there's somebody new in town who can *play!*"

A contract with Capitol Records soon followed his L.A. apprenticeship. With three LPs behind him as a group leader, Lyle recently returned to the concert stage as a solo pianist. While this shift away from his previous activities as group leader and session player constitute a new direction, Lyle sees the change as part of his musical and creative growth. He plans to release an acoustic piano album that will offer a potpourri of styles, from impressionistic works to familiar standards to some spirituals he learned as a child.

The following interview was conducted in Lyle's home, prior to his Minneapolis engagement in the spring of 1980.

Tom Wilmeth:—Looking back to your days as a player in the Minneapolis area, what was the jazz scene like from the early sixties through your departure in 1974? Were there many live jazz clubs in operation at the time?

Bobby Lyle:—Oh yeah. There were definitely places to play. When I was coming along as a late teenager and in my early twenties, the Minneapolis club scene was very healthy. The Blue Note, over north of town, and The White House on Olson Highway were both booking jazz. There was The Ebony Lounge and The Take Five in St. Paul. A club called The Red Feather goes back quite a few years, to the late fifties and maybe real early sixties. That was one of the first places I can remember going to sit in.

Then there was Big Al's down by the railroad tracks. Over on Washington Avenue was The Key Club, which was where I first saw the old Miles Davis group with Coltrane and Cannonball. St. Paul's American Legion Hall booked a lot, and I understand they are still providing live jazz. The Marque Club in downtown Minneapolis was the first place I met Thelonious Monk. I had a chance to sit in with his group; he walked around with his overcoat on and his big furry hat and stood over the top of me while I was playing; made me nervous as hell.

TW:—Do you come from a musical background?

BL:—Yes. My father doesn't play an instrument but is very much a music lover and exposed us to all kinds of music: classical, jazz, Latin. My mother actually plays; she has been a church organist and pianist and also plays classical music. She has a brother who used to come through town in the summer with an armload of the latest jazz albums. I really got my first exposure through him as far as the west coast scene: Chet Baker, Dave Brubeck, and that whole thing. He was responsible for my Miles Davis era. I've had a varied musical background, and I guess it comes out when I play.

TW:—Do you still go back and put on *My Funny Valentine* and those albums by Miles?

BL:—Definitely. Those records still sound just as good as they did 15 years ago.

TW:—What variety of recent performers do you listen to when you put on an album?

BL:—Well, you hit the nail on the head when you said "variety" because when I'm away from performing, or away from the studio, my taste might run from listening to Art Tatum and Oscar Peterson to listening to Horowitz play classical pieces. I like some singers like Sarah Vaughn. I love Miles Davis of course, and Coltrane; so there's a variety of things I listen to, depending on what mood I'm in.

TW:—The people you've mentioned mostly play acoustic pianos. Do you lean more towards listening to an acoustic piano, as opposed to the sound of an electric Rhodes?

BL:—Yeah, I think I really do, even though I appreciate the work that people like Chick Corea and Herbie Hancock have done with the Rhodes. There is something about the [electric Rhodes] sound that sort of neutralizes everybody in comparison to the acoustic piano, which is much more expressive to me. The Rhodes has a fairly locked-in sound and it's hard to really establish an individualistic thing on it. I feel the acoustic piano has a much wider range.

TW:—Do you think the traditional piano is making a comeback after the number of electronic keyboard albums we saw flourish during the seventies? Corea and Hancock became well known for their electric work, but even they have again embraced the acoustic sound and are on tour together playing concert grand pianos.

BL:—Yes, I definitely feel their tour is kind of an indication that interest in the acoustic piano is coming back, though some people have been out there with it all the time, like McCoy Tyner and Oscar Peterson. The acoustic is here to stay; people who thought that electronics would replace it were just crazy.

TW:—You are beginning a tour of strictly solo acoustic piano performances.

BL:—Right. I'm striking out on this new format, and The Minneapolis Orchestra Hall concert is the maiden voyage into this realm. We're going to focus primarily on colleges, but we're going to do some concert halls as well as we really get the acoustic sound out to the people. Solo acoustic piano is definitely my strong point, musically.

TW:—Right now, do your priorities include more studio work or would you prefer to be on the road in front of an audience?

BL:—I would like to concentrate on performing now because I've done a lot of the Los Angeles studio scene and the ratio of studio to performing has been overbalanced toward studio recently. It's kind of nice to get back in front of an audience again and get my performance juices flowing. But I'd also like to get back to the studio and record a totally solo piano album. That would help to facilitate what we are trying to do with the solo concerts.

TW:—You've done most of your recording in Los Angeles?

BL:—Right; that's one of the reasons I did leave the Twin Cities to move there. I realized there was a lot of recording opportunity out there, and that kind of influenced my decision not to go to New York.

TW:—When you moved to L.A. did you have anything to go to, or did you just head out there to see if you could hit something?

BL:—Not really. I laugh sometimes when I think about leaving like that. I didn't really have a whole lot of money, and I didn't have a definite job lined up. But I did know a few musicians out there who I thought could probably get me into the right circles, in time. But when I think of leaving like that now, the way the economy is…boy, there's no way I would attempt it. But I'm glad I tried it at the time I did.

TW:—What does it take to make it? Is it pure persistence—hitting your head against that wall one more time?

BL:—Well, everyone speaks of the "clique syndrome" of the Los Angeles and New York music scene, and there's a reason for that. A person who produces a record has quite a bit of responsibility. A record producer handles a lot of money, and the company is watching to see how he handles that money. More often than not a producer is going to hire players that he knows something about, who are tried and true professionals. These are the studio cats who will take the least amount of time in the studio, but will give the most creative effort. So you can kind of see the reasoning why certain players are used over and over in recording sessions.

For a new player to break into that, you have to have your chops together. You have to definitely be on your axe; but more importantly, people have to like you. You have to be a good, dependable person; that is very important. Word of mouth travels, so after a couple of producers use you and you do a good job for them, word gets around and all of a sudden you're getting more calls. That's exactly how it happened with me, sort of a snowballing effect after some lean early months.

TW:—Speaking of acoustic piano concerts, do you listen to Keith Jarrett?

BL:—Yeah, I've listened to Keith's approach to the piano and there are some similarities in his and my approach, but there are also a lot of differences. I feel like I cover a wider range of musical areas than Keith does. He seems like he staked out a certain musical territory; and even though he is free and impressionistic, he is free and impressionistic within his territory. I suppose on various occasions through his career he has ventured outside of this territory, but it seems to me that when you become a solo artist, you are a sum total of your musical experiences, and it seems like he would draw from some of his other experiences when he plays like this. He is melodically oriented; every now and then he'll get into some nice rhythmic things and you'd like to hear him do that more, or even play through some changes.

TW:—What do you think of his rapid release of so many albums in the past few years?

BL:—I feel that a true artist is trying to establish a sound and a musical identity through which he can develop an audience. This audience will come to rely on the performer for certain things. Through all of this, however, I think you have to allow for your individual growth. I've been playing professionally for almost 20 years but I still feel that I am a student. I have a student's attitude toward my work. I am constantly learning; I am constantly shaping and honing and experimenting.

I think an evolutionary thing happens with a musician. You want your listeners to experience each period as you are experiencing it, but I don't think you should saturate them with any one period. This is what Jarrett seems to have done in putting out so many releases in so short a time; like the *Sun Bear Concerts*, a 10-record set. I mean that's a lot of sides—a *lot* of sides. How many times can that formula work?

TW:—Listening to your records, it sounds like you are interested in a strong melody, such as the Cole Porter tune you include on *Night Fire*. Do you think the total abandonment of a head, or the melody, can lead to problems?

BL:—The songwriters of the Cole Porter era created a lot of tunes that are now standards. They have stood the test of time. There's a reason for that. Like you say, there's a strong melody; there are very logical arrangements of chord progressions. These things offer quite a feast to the improvisationist. People who ignore this I think are really ignoring something very valuable because it takes a lot of thought to improvise over a structure such as that, and the structure should be within the piece at some time. I've played the free thing and the impressionistic thing. I've done the whole spectrum and I feel that the area of strong, melodic, structured pieces is not an area I should ignore. I also think the listeners appreciate a little structure in at least some of an evening's music.

I believe that good music in general and lasting melodies will always prevail. That's why Duke Ellington's music is still with us. People should be made aware that this is the type of music that was written in another generation; but look, it still sounds good. Still fresh. Still valid.

Concert Commentary

Bobby Lyle
Orchestra Hall
Minneapolis, Minnesota
April 1980

WHILE BOBBY LYLE was visiting his hometown of Minneapolis last week, he performed a concert at Orchestra Hall that demonstrated his gifts as a solo pianist. Lyle has been into many different styles of music, as his albums showcase. He mentioned his Hammond organ years from the stage and drew immediate recognition from this enthusiastic, if not huge, audience. But there was no organ on this night, no vocals or funk licks. It was Lyle and the grand piano. Nothing more was needed.

Lyle has been a sideman on numerous west coast recording dates, but the Orchestra Hall audience saw Bobby Lyle as sideman to nobody. This was his own evening, to shape as he pleased. This came more easily to Lyle than it might have to a structured group, for with the solo piano the performer is able to read the audience and spontaneously tailor the music to it.

The audience discovered several things about Lyle during his set. The influence of gospel music on this pianist was evident as he opened with an "impression of the black experience—from Africa to the States with a spiritual influence." This was not an attempt at history through music in the style of Duke Ellington's "Black, Brown, and Beige." Instead, this was a beautiful reworking of "Swing Low, Sweet Chariot" and "Sometimes I Feel Like a Motherless Child" into a medley.

By the conclusion of his first piece, it was already easy to see why Lyle had chosen to embark on a tour of solo performances. In the hands of the right artist, the acoustic piano can be one of the most expressive outlets in the family of musical instruments. Lyle has the touch to make the piano speak a variety of languages, from his opening spiritual medley through the classic "Someday My Prince Will Come" and "Autumn Leaves" to the conclusion of the first set, a tribute to the late saxophone pioneer John Coltrane. Lyle's medley covered most of Coltrane's diverse career, from Richard Rodgers' "My Favorite Things" to Coltrane's own unusually structured "Giant Steps." This section of the concert served to spotlight both Lyle's musical talents and personal tastes.

It is not uncommon for a city to overlook its own talented offspring. Fortunately, Lyle's audience was warmly receptive to this Minneapolis man and his music. Rightly so. Lyle showed expertise and precision at the grand piano. He knew how to pace his set and demonstrated a deep awareness of his musical heritage in the repertoire he chose. Because of these combined abilities of technique and taste, Bobby Lyle should soon establish himself on the national stage within the top tier of solo pianists.

Interview
Leroy Jenkins
"This music swings, all right—but not the way it used to!"
Minneapolis, Minnesota
February 28, 1980

By the winter of 1980 I had been interested in jazz for several years, but nothing had prepared me for the far reaches of the music universe that Leroy Jenkins explored one night in Minneapolis. I was told that Mr. Jenkins would have a few minutes to speak with me before his solo concert at The Walker Art Center. I had heard his latest album and looked forward to speaking with this unique artist, an avant-garde jazz violinist.

If the music of the avant-garde is often purposefully formless, the same cannot be said of Jenkins' thoughts, which were always focused and articulate. He possessed an unhurried and reflective attitude, choosing his ideas and words with care. Jenkins was patient with the limitations of a young man from the Midwest that night. I think he knew that I was trying, that I had listened to some of his records, and that I was sincere in my interest in jazz.

As of 1980, Leroy Jenkins had been a professional musician for well over a decade. He would continue to be a leader of the avant-garde jazz scene for another quarter century, until his death in 2007. The following interview captures a brief encounter with this artist on his musical journey.

Tom Wilmeth:—You have been associated in the 1970s with ensemble performances. How long have you been giving solo concerts such as the one you are giving tonight?

Leroy Jenkins:—I've been performing concerts solo now for about two years. Probably before that it was a little more…spaced. It was now and then, but now they are coming a little more frequently. I do a lot of them.

TW:—So you are on the road quite a bit of the time.

LJ:—With solos, yes. Or the trio that I use—piano, drums, and violin.

TW:—I admit that I am not aware of many of your solo albums except the newest one on the Tomato label. [*Space Minds, New Worlds, Survival of America*, 1978] Have you made many solo LPs?

LJ:—Yes. I have a recording on India Navigation a couple of years old [*Solo Concert*, 1977]. I also have a trio on Black Saint called *Ai Glatson* [1978]. And *For Players Only* is a JCOA recording [1975]. And then of course I recorded about five records with the Revolutionary Ensemble.

TW:—That group broke up a while back…

LJ:—It's been two years ago now.

TW:—Was it because people wanted to pursue their own interests, like your solo concerts?

LJ:—Yes. It ceased to be a cooperative.

TW:—It would be best for everybody to go their separate ways.

LJ:—Seems like it.

TW:—Your latest album—the first side is a lengthy piece and is the title selection. You use Richard Titelbaum on synthesizers. He was here with Anthony Braxton not too long ago. Have you been associated with Titelbaum for very long?

LJ:—Well, he's on the New York scene. He plays with a lot of my contemporaries and friends. He has sort of the same musical sensibilities that I have. And being that I was going to make records dealing with the synthesizer: not necessarily electronics but *synthesizer!* I could think of no better player than Richard.

TW:—Do you have any preference as far as the acoustic side or the electric side of the new album?

LJ:—No, I don't really. I planned them both as they were, one to be one thing and one to be the other. I probably like both sides.

TW:—When you recorded that album, did you have any plans to

tour with either of those groups, or was that strictly a studio session?

LJ:—No, no. I perform with Andrew Cyrille [drums] and Anthony Davis [piano] regularly right now. They belong to my group that I regularly travel with when I do trios, and also George Lewis, the trombonist. We play a lot together. Richard Titelbaum was the only one that I got to play for me on the recording only. We hardly ever play together.

TW:—You spent some time with Ornette Coleman's group…

LJ:—No. I never played with Ornette. I just lived at his house when I first came to New York. He was very instrumental in helping me out when I first came there. He sort of put me into the mainstream of the music business. And of course I was influenced by a lot of his musical discoveries.

TW:—*New York Times* music critic Robert Palmer says that you play the violin *like* a violin and don't try to make it sound like a saxophone. Could you comment on that?

LJ:—Well, I've studied the violin and I think that instrument has more…things that can be brought out other than just the saxophone sound. I mean, I'm not necessarily playing any particular type of music except *improvised* music. Of course it's necessary to be able to play the violin to get out all these different qualities, effects, and techniques I bring out. And I was fortunate enough to have a good background; good training.

TW:—Concerning the importance of improvising to your approach to music: Tonight when you go out, will you have set pieces in mind?

LJ:—Oh yeah.

TW:—Pieces that you're going to be improvising around.

LJ:—Oh yeah.

TW:—So it's a…

LJ:—Motifs, mostly. Some are melodies, some are motifs. Then there are others…just an abstract improvisation.

TW:—There are not very many violin players doing what you're doing. In fact, there are very few violins in jazz music. Do you have any opinions about Jean-Luc Ponty's approach to the violin?

LJ:—Well, he's sort of like…well, I don't relate to him except that he plays the violin and people often mention him to me. But I don't relate to him because, you know, he's not…well, we are completely two different types of players and all. Hard to listen to his music. I mean, his music is the type of music that I really don't listen to that much. It's fusion, and the fusion stuff I don't really listen to.

TW:—Do you enjoy being out on the road or is this a necessary evil?

LJ:—Oh yes: a necessary evil. You know, I sort of enjoy it. The fact that I do have to make a living. And the fact that somebody *wants* me. It's a great feeling to be wanted. And yes, it gets boring a lot of times. *Off* the stage.

TW:—Like exactly what we are doing now—talking to someone who is not totally familiar with your career. I'm sure this gets old after so many…

LJ:—Well, I'm in the business of education. Being the music that I play…most people who know about it, they usually have *been* educated by one of my contemporaries or myself. Or, they are the type of person that has…who has their ears on the ground, so to speak. And are really music lovers…who like good 'listening music' and good 'modern contemporary music.' And so I understand that there are *a lot* of people in this world that don't know about me. I understand my position in the spectrum of the music society, and I go along with the problems and the good parts of it. So sure, I've repeated what I've said. And I'm sure the questions that you've asked have been asked of me a million times, but I've been a million places.

TW:—Speaking of music that *you* listen to when at home—do you ever play something like [the free jazz trio] Air? What type of albums would you put on?

LJ:—Well…I don't listen to records a lot. I listen to radio a lot, mostly FM stations. I listen to traditional jazz. I listen to all… all jazz. I listen to classical music. I sort of can concentrate better on classical music because I'm not too involved in it. Or let's say bebop; I can sort of read and probably even write music with it on. It's background. Now, I wouldn't dare listen to Air or The Art Ensemble [of Chicago] or to [Anthony] Braxton. I couldn't concentrate.

TW:—Is that because you can't…

LJ:—It's because I'm too close…I'm too close to it. I understand what's happening. It's very…a lot of feeling to it. It's really not the type…this music is like television. You have to really…it demands your attention. Not only me, I mean everybody. It demands your attention. It's not the kind of thing…it's cerebral. It's about listening, and trying to find out some corners that may attract you or may remind you of something in your life or may guide you to some point where you would like to be…or where you wouldn't like to be. You know, it's not like music that has a finger popping effect, or that music that they say swings on two and four. This music swings, all right, but not the way it used to. There's a mental swing about it now—one that you feel, rather than snap your fingers or tap your feet.

TW:—So, correct me if I'm wrong here: You say that you put on classical and bebop music because it *doesn't* demand the attention that Braxton…

LJ:—The classical does demand attention from people that are really interested in it. But I mean it's passé with me. And bebop is also passé with me. I used to snap my fingers to it. I can put the volume down low and listen to it. But not my music—I mean Braxton. I can't do it! You know, my ears are out listening for things. Because I know there's always something out there to be heard. No matter how many times you hear it, with this particular type of music that we are doing.

TW:—As an educator, do you have roots in things such as Duke Ellington's work?

LJ:—Oh yeah. Oh yeah. I'll probably be playing one of Ellington's tonight. I'm rooted in all the masters. Ellington, sure.

TW:—So with Ellington you could put it on low and not worry about it, you could also still turn it up and get something new out of it.

LJ:—Oh yeah. But I mean it wouldn't affect me…well, Ellington may be an exception. He's so strong, you know? Ah, and he's so modern. It's something that I respect greatly. I respect Bach.

Mozart. Those guys. Any *great* master. In the Master Class. I respect them all. It's just that they're passé now. Where maybe some stuff by [Philip] Glass or somebody like that, man…it's *too disturbing!*

TW:—It makes you sit up and pay attention.

LJ:—*Sit up and Pay Attention!* If I'm doing some [writing] I wouldn't…I wouldn't *dare* put on a Glass or Braxton record.

TW:—Do you have any comments about the ECM Record label? It seems to be bringing a new type, or at least a recently un-heard type of music more prominently to the states.

LJ:—Well, the only thing ECM has been doing is that they have a big distribution. That way they would get the records to more people. But there were many other record companies before them. I mean he [ECM owner Manfred Eicher] happens to be lucky enough to have gotten Warner Brothers as a distrib-utor. And that's why you can say he's bringing out all these people. These people were not brought out by ECM. They were brought out to the general public, more or less, by ECM. There were other record companies who introduced them to ECM.

TW:—I don't want to take up too much of your time. As I said earlier, I know this gets old for you—an endless stream of people with microphones.

LJ:—Well, that's OK! It's part of the job. I mean it is a job…that I enjoy. You *do* have access to people's ears here. I just hope that the people will enjoy what I do tonight and…maybe they can bring back somebody else—one of my contemporaries, or even me again.

TW:—Great. In some ways it comes down to what Gary Burton has said—So much is ruled by the great court of public opinion: Is there an audience? I mean, you are here tonight, obviously, because there is an audience for your music.

LJ:—Yeah! An audience! Some person who knows about the mu-sic wants to *bring it* to the people! That's where it is! That's how we are educated. That's how we find out things!

Concert Commentary

Leroy Jenkins
Walker Art Center
Minneapolis, Minnesota
February 28, 1980

I WALKED OUT. I'm not proud of it, but I walked out. Not in anger or disgust. Not because the concert started late or because the band was too loud or because of a poor sound mix. I walked out of Leroy Jenkins' solo violin concert because, after 40 minutes, I had not understood one thing of what was taking place on the stage.

Jenkins was playing music on his violin, but it was such nonlinear free jazz that I was lost from the start. I had interviewed Jenkins before the concert. He indicated that the upcoming performance would be centered on "motifs and themes," and would likely include a nod to Ellington's music. I was not expecting "Take the A Train," but if there was any Ellington in that set, I missed it—just as I had missed any motifs or themes to hang onto. I openly concede that the breakdown in musical communication between performer and audience was undoubtedly with me, the listener.

Acceptance of unfamiliar music, or even of new forms, can be an admirable thing. This open-mindedness was displayed at the beginning of George Harrison's benefit, The Concert for Bangladesh, in August 1971. Indian musician Ravi Shankar began an introductory set of music by welcoming the audience and then tuning his sitar for about a minute. His two fellow performers likewise readied their instruments. During the brief interlude that followed, many members of the Madison Square Garden audience began to applaud. When the clapping subsided, an amused Shankar said, "Thank you, friends. If you appreciate the tuning so much, I hope you will enjoy the playing more." But at least this young audience was receptive to music that was completely foreign to their collective background.

Music operates on an undefined emotional level more frequently than on an intellectual plane, so I didn't mind that the Leroy Jenkins performance was over my head. But I was keenly aware that his music did not engage me at all. In fact, and I am embarrassed to say it, I was bored.

In early 1978, Chick Corea and Herbie Hancock toured together, each playing a concert grand piano. The musical interplay was remarkable. On a live LP documenting these dates, the duo performs George Gershwin's "Liza." The number has an infectious melody—one that Corea and Hancock clearly enjoy playing and soloing upon. It is a nine-minute performance, with the pianists taking several choruses of improvisation.

I have always enjoyed the first half of this number, while the last half leaves me cold. Not long ago, when listening to this piece, it struck me why my attention would stray from this music at a specific point: it was when I no longer understood what the musicians were doing. On each chorus, the jazz improvisations would go further and further into experimental realms of soloing. I am able to relate to several choruses of traditional solos, but I find the more advanced musical concepts less interesting, probably because I don't understand what's going on. I still play this record, even though I know that the last part of "Liza" will again either distract or confound me, depending on how closely I am listening.

So, while I don't think I am above, below, or afraid of that 1980 solo violin performance by Leroy Jenkins—it was simply beyond my level of comprehension and (especially) my tolerance level. At least at that time and on that night.

Post Script

Several readers of this concert review have recently told me that I am too kind here in my remarks about the genre of music that Jenkins represents. They insist that the breakdown in musical communication was the fault of the artist, not the audience. Some have told me that they too would have left the hall. Others expressed pointedly negative comments about free jazz and the avant-garde as an art form. They may be right. But having lived parts of my life believing that I was above certain styles of music, I now realize that I have missed out on some good things. As such, I am hesitant to condemn Jenkins or his music. I can think of some album purchases that I initially regretted, only to later find that the artists I once dismissed had become a mainstay of my musical diet. I don't see myself embracing the music of Leroy Jenkins anytime soon, but I am slow to dismiss it out of hand. I still feel that Mr. Jenkins was sincerely striving to communicate with his audience that night in Minneapolis. But it was in a language I did not at all understand.

Interview
Oscar Peterson
Ruminations and Rebuttals
Minneapolis, Minnesota
March 23, 1980

I spoke with the great jazz pianist Oscar Peterson on a winter afternoon in 1980 in his Minneapolis hotel room. He was in town to perform his extended composition, "Canadiana Suite," with the Minnesota Orchestra. Peterson originally arranged this 1964 work for his jazz trio, reviving it later for a large scale concert performance. Peterson's renewed interest in long form jazz works culminated with his 1981 album *The Royal Wedding Suite*, "a celebration of the union of Charles, Prince of Wales, and Lady Diana Spencer at St. Paul's Cathedral." Although both suites show Peterson's abilities as a composer and arranger, each work is now largely forgotten.

In spite of his concert with an orchestra only hours away, Peterson seemed happy to discuss his own solo and small group performances. He was also quick to draw parallels between jazz forms and classical music. As we began, I pointed out which of his albums I liked best and asked him to comment on some of his newer Pablo label releases.

As we neared the end of the interview, I used one of my mainstay questions, one concerning his interest in Duke Ellington. I asked this specifically because of the major orchestral jazz piece that he was about to perform, and I compared it with some of Ellington's extended works. This discussion about the Duke led to some intense reaction, as did my inclusion of the names Art Tatum and Keith Jarrett in the same sentence.

As with any interview situation, there were conversational threads I later regretted not following. In hindsight, what strikes me is how Peterson went out of his way to stress that he is "not a musical bigot" about the electric piano. I can't help but wonder what he thought of Chick Corea's or Herbie Hancock's use of the Rhodes as their primary instrument for several years in the mid-1970s. I would also have liked to hear what he thought of Miles Davis' later records, *Bitches Brew* and beyond. But even if some of this had occurred to me during our discussion, I might have held back. Questions of this sort can seem confrontational. Also, I have learned that not every artist has heard all of the music they are questioned about; they can't be expected to. Still, as the following transcript makes clear, we made our way into some controversy I hadn't sought. Fortunately, I don't believe that any of Mr. Peterson's hostility was directed at me.

I began by asking about his work with his various trios and if he missed that setting.

> Oscar Peterson:—For over 20 years I've had trios of one type or another. And as much as I've enjoyed them, it's quite a long time to spend with one format. With jazz being the creative and improvisational music it is, the solo [performance] gives me a chance to do whatever I feel like doing at the piano without having to worry about somebody coming with me. I'm not saying this to deride any of the trios, because I have loved each one for various reasons. The solo setting is selfish, but it gives me a chance to really get with my instrument and do my own personal thing.
>
> Tom Wilmeth:—You like having everything left up to you—the entire responsibility for the music.
>
> OP:—That's right. And I think it's no different for people going to hear a classical music recital. It's a piano, it's a player, and it's a presentation of their thoughts together.
>
> TW:—Do you ever go back and listen to your trio's Verve label recordings? I really enjoy the *We Get Requests* album.
>
> OP:—Oh yeah, that's a favorite with a lot of people.
>
> TW:—And your adaptation of the strong writing from *West Side Story*.
>
> OP:—That is strong music, you're right. That was a challenge for us because the music is different. It doesn't lay like ordinary jazz selections of that particular era. I like that album.
>
> TW:—I also like *Trio Live From Chicago*.
>
> OP:—I think that is one of our most powerful albums because it was [recorded] at a time when that particular trio of me,

Ray Brown, and Ed Thigpen had become saturated within itself, and the trio had the confidence of its own professional quality. We all knew what we could do within the trio context and it worked well at that particular time. I'm hoping that recording will be reissued soon.

TW:—Could you point to any of your more recent albums on the Pablo label that you are particularly pleased with?

OP:—I like the *Nightchild* album. That's the one where I use the electronic keyboards. There were questions asked about that because it was a departure. I thought it was time to put the question to rest and musically show that I'm not a bigot about the electric piano. I think it has its place, obviously, by all the marvelous things that have been done, not only with electronic piano, but with some of the other electronic instruments as well. It's just another musical statement in a different medium, that's all.

TW:—Bobby Lyle maintains that the Fender Rhodes has a very locked-in sound.

OP:—He's right. That's the problem with electric piano. You're dealing with so many overtones and they are forever there. The acoustical piano has a much cleaner deliverance from an audio standpoint. When you hit a note, you hear the note. When you hit a note on an electric piano, it can filter off into other overtones and will roll on you, so to speak. No matter what you do it has a tremendous layover, note for note, that you don't have on the acoustic piano unless you make it play that way. I feel I can do a lot more with the deviation of sound with an acoustic. As I say, I have nothing against the electric piano; once in a while it's a nice change and it's fun to play. They're fine for the pop players who just use it for certain effects, but not for continual, serious playing in a jazz group.

TW:—When you get the time, whose albums do you put on at home?

OP:—I listen to everybody. I am a fan of certainly most of the pianists. That's the broadest field of all. Guitar, I find, is a wide field. I like to listen to everybody from Lester Young and Dizzy right up to Freddie Hubbard. I love Hank Jones and what Joe Pass does. I'm not a musical bigot, totally. I have my likes and dislikes as everyone else does, but I listen to a wide range of music.

TW:—Do you find yourself going back and putting on Ellington?

OP:—Of course. You have to. I always try to include some Ellington in every concert that I do. I think it's almost mandatory.

TW:—Ellington's major work "Black, Brown, and Beige" drew a lot of criticism for trying to stretch the boundaries of traditional jazz. You have written some pieces for jazz and orchestra, including "Canadiana Suite," which you will be performing tonight. Do you have any thoughts on the idea that jazz should stay away from serious musical structures and only be considered light music?

OP:—You have all kinds of heavy works [in jazz]. You can go through the Gil Evans book and find some pretty heavy pieces in there. Without getting into [listing] a vast number of players—Cecil Taylor's work is pretty heavy, if you want to go that way. You get writers the magnitude of Ellington and Strayhorn: you can't get much heavier than that for writing, I don't care in what medium you want to write it. There are classical composers who admire these men. You're talking about the validity of two geniuses that elect to [compose] that type of lengthy work. It has definite credibility.

TW:—Leroy Jenkins came through town a while back and said that, to him, everything is passé except new, free jazz. I mentioned Ellington and he stopped and admitted that Ellington was perhaps the one exception.

OP:—He said, "*Everything*"?

TW:—It was a blanket statement that, for him, almost all jazz from the past is passé.

OP:—Well, that's a stupid statement. You can't wipe away all that talent by saying that. That shows an inadequacy in his own makeup. One thing I teach new players is to respect those who have gone before them. They never would have arrived if the others hadn't first paved the way. The easiest way to become a talented artist, if you have that kind of talent, is to be very open and receptive to what has gone before you. That gives you a bigger vocabulary and a larger understanding. When I had the Jazz School, we insisted that all of the students listen to what had gone on before—whether it be Miles or Bird. You can't negate a talent like Charlie Parker or Dizzy Gillespie and say it's passé. It's the fundamentals of jazz! And to be ignorant enough to say that this is passé… [long pause] You know, it's people like that I can't tolerate. I get very upset about that because it's a form of musical racism that doesn't exist with true artists. If you were to talk with any of the greats—certainly Duke Ellington or Dizzy Gillespie and so forth—they don't look around and say, "This isn't any good from here to here." They just won't do that. They are very intelligent and discerning in their likes and dislikes, and I think that's what helps to make them great artists.

After this impassioned rebuttal to Leroy Jenkins, whose attitudes I may have unintentionally misrepresented, I thought it best to return to the safe turf of discussing one of Peterson's major influences, Art Tatum.

TW:—You are spoken of as the natural successor to Art Tatum. You certainly don't need to be called the next *anybody*, but do you have any comments about this comparison?

OP:—They probably say that because they know of my total involvement with the piano. I don't know what being the next Art Tatum means. There never was and never will be another Art Tatum. If I'm an extension of his thinking, fine. But I didn't set out to be that. It's like who will the next Dizzy be? There won't really be a next Dizzy, but there are people who are greatly influenced by him. If you were to ask me who the next Oscar Peterson will be, I really don't know. I am aware of exerting some influence on some of the young pianists, but I believe in the individual. Consequently, I believe everyone is influenced by the people that precede them, whether they realize it or not. And this is why I say that it is important that you listen. Eventually, if you have talent, you shed that shell of influence and come out on your own. I hope that what I've been doing has helped to revitalize interest in the grand lady of the acoustical piano, which is sort of the definitive instrument.

TW:—Speaking of Art Tatum, we can thank Norman Granz for recording Tatum heavily during the last three years of his life, the 13-album solo set and the eight-record group masterpiece set.

OP:—That was Norman's major project, a fantastic project, and I think the whole world owes him a debt for that one! Art, in many cases, was very hard to find on records. This was a concerted effort certainly by Art Tatum and by Norman to put together this group of recordings.

TW:—Speaking of expansive projects: You are a pianist who often gives solo concerts. Do you have any thoughts on Keith Jarrett and, specifically, his recent 10-record set of solo performances? Art Tatum is a different story…

OP:—He sure is!!

TW:—…but does anybody warrant a 10-record set like that?

OP:—I don't think Keith Jarrett does. I don't happen to be a Jarrett fan, I'll be very frank with you. I think it's a fad. Dizzy had a very astute saying that I quote many times. Before a concert one time, Norman Granz asked the horns to keep their solos short because of time limitations. I remember Dizzy looked up and said, "Listen, I can play everything I know in four bars." That is a comedic saying, true, but I watched a solo Keith Jarrett television special and…it was not necessary. He didn't do anything. I don't like to come down on somebody, but he's kidding. I would sooner hear 15 minutes of Art Tatum than to listen to two hours of Jarrett. There is just so much you can do. I can play the piano and I can sit down and go through that kind of performance and buffalo 'x' amount of people. I'm not trying to nail him to the cross; I just don't believe in that type of performance. You have to be a little more concise, a little more selective in what you decide to do. Anything you have to say that bears saying, you don't need two hours to say it in. You can say it very concisely within five minutes, believe it or not. This is what the great orators of the world maintain, and the same thing applies to music.

TW:—Just to reiterate: you feel that Jarrett is kidding, and he plays as he does because it's currently popular.

OP:—It *became* popular, and as a one-shot thing I don't put it down. But is this going to be a continuing thing? Are we going to have to listen to ten more albums to find out what he does? With the exception of Tatum, who was such a magnanimous talent that he certainly deserved…well, if he did 13 albums, he deserved 40. I wouldn't want to sit down with Jarrett's 10-record project. I really wouldn't. I think I'm fairly productive and I know how much thought has gone into each of my albums, and I wouldn't hesitate to sit down and play against Jarrett on that same kind of thing. I think I could do a much better job than that if I really wanted to, but I wouldn't *want* to sit down for two hours and ramble along the piano. I don't see where it is any way necessary. [pause] Keith Jarrett is the Liberace of Jazz. I'm not trying to hurt him, but it's true—he doesn't play anything!

Post Script

The televised solo piano performance by Keith Jarrett that Oscar Peterson saw was probably the August 1977 concert filmed in Shelburne, Vermont, and subsequently broadcast by PBS.

Keith Jarrett's expansive box set of solo piano recordings mentioned by both Oscar Peterson and Bobby Lyle is *The Sun Bear Concerts*, recorded in 1976 and issued by ECM Records in 1978. This release prompted reaction in the press such as *Musician Magazine's* review headline, "Would You Buy a 10-Record Set from This Man?"

LP Review

Keith Jarrett
Nude Ants
ECM Records, 1980

Pianist Keith Jarrett's aversion to the single-disc album is again on display. His new two-record set *Nude Ants* is a live recording from a May 1979 concert at the Village Vanguard in New York City. Jarrett is joined by his European sidemen: Jan Garbarek on reeds, Palle Danielsson playing acoustic bass, and drummer Jon Christensen. After Jarrett's 10-record solo piano set, *Sun Bear Concerts*, the pianist evidently feels that it's again time to spotlight his backing group. As expected, though, it is Jarrett's iron fist as a group leader that controls the music on these four long sides.

Nude Ants includes lengthy percussion workouts. Jarrett himself participates on timbales when he is not at the piano. But he fails to translate the same creative ideas to percussive instruments. From his tenures with the Charles Lloyd Quartet in 1966 to that with Miles Davis in 1970, Jarrett has proven his keyboard skills, and his piano work on this set is consistently engaging. Jarrett is, however, simply not strong enough as a percussionist to sustain interest in his lengthy solos showcased on *Nude Ants*.

As is his wont, Jarrett takes a lot of room to present his musical ideas on these six numbers. When his piano solos are concluded, however, he often insists on initiating a single note bed of sound for Garbarek's soprano and tenor saxophones. If Jarrett would simply get out of this soloist's way, we might hear what Garbarek has to say in a less constricted setting.

Jarrett remains in need of an editor. This is particularly obvious on the album's 30-minute "Oasis." There are moments of greatness in this piece, but they are weakened by the number's overbearing length. This could be said of the entire set. The quality of *Nude Ants* is obscured from all but the few who choose to wade through these sides in the hope of finding the exceptional music Jarrett is capable of producing.

Commentary
Keith Jarrett
Let Us Now Praise the Art…and respect the artist
November 3, 2013

Over the past decades I have purchased and become familiar with 27 albums by Keith Jarrett as group leader or as solo performer. I own his releases on the Vortex label, most of the ABC/Impulse material, and many of his recordings from the voluminous ECM catalog. I have Jarrett's albums with Miles Davis and his work as a member of Charles Lloyd's quartet. My collection also includes radio and television broadcasts by this artist.

I have been hearing about Jarrett's onstage peculiarities since the mid-1970s, when a group of my college friends travelled to Iowa City for one of his solo, acoustic piano concerts. They returned with tales of an artist frustrated with the audience. At one point, somebody in the crowd yelled, "Get a Rhodes!" Jarrett responded to the suggestion that he play an electric piano by walking to center stage and seating himself in a Lotus position; this lasted for some time. When he returned to the grand piano, Jarrett told the audience that "electricity should run through those who are experiencing the music, and not through the instruments." Jarrett may have played great that night, but no one ever talked about the pianist's actual performance. The music had become completely overshadowed by confrontation.

Jump ahead 35 years and we find an artist still at odds with his audience. At the 2007 Umbria Festival, Jarrett became irate and abusive because some patrons were taking photographs of his trio. The pianist was quite nasty to the audience and threatened to end the concert. The festival organizers swore he would never be invited back. However, fences were mended and Jarrett did return to Umbria in July 2013. Unfortunately, he brought his attitude with him, resulting in an encore performance of questionable behavior. This recent episode was less boisterous, yet somehow even stranger. Jarrett insisted that his trio perform for the large crowd engulfed in near darkness—the stage illuminated only by the small light from his bassist's music stand.

Keith Jarrett is not unique among those artists who bring to the stage specific expectations about their audiences. And the numerous frustrations inherent to public performance are not confined to jazz musicians. Country singer Jim Reeves was an audio perfectionist. Reeves would openly chastise concert hall management from the stage because of a venue's inadequate sound system. Classical pianist Glenn Gould quickly tired of concerts because he felt that the individual audience member was unable to focus on the music in such a setting. This, in an age before cell phones.

Gould solved the problem for himself by retiring from the stage to concentrate on making albums. He also performed regularly on radio broadcasts from the Toronto studios of the CBC. In fact, Gould found radio the perfect medium for his art: pure audio, free of extraneous distractions. In his article describing Keith Jarrett's performance in the dark, Thomas Conrad notes that one audience member astutely related the experience to being "sort of like radio." Maybe this was Jarrett's intention in Umbria.

Jarrett's working trio of Gary Peacock and Jack DeJohnette is often compared to pianist Bill Evans' great trios. This comparison goes further than the music. Evans too could show his great displeasure with a concert setting. During a 1979 taping of *Jazz at the Maintenance Shop* for Iowa Public Television, Evans pointedly criticized the sound man because of the audio mix. "So glad we had a sound check," Evans sarcastically intoned between numbers. At another point of the broadcast he said that he would play another piece because "that is our *job*." This remark is clearly a shot at a previous discussion with someone involved with the broadcast. Or so I interpret it.

Keith Jarrett is a slave to his talent, but perhaps to some self-inflicted demons as well. I had a tangential experience with the man that I still find telling. In 1981, Jarrett was scheduled to be the guest on an episode of a network radio program called *St. Paul Sunday Morning*, a 90-minute weekly showcase for classical music performers. Jarrett had previously been the guest soloist with The St. Paul Chamber Orchestra, and he seemed a logical choice for this informal interview and performance broadcast. I worked for Minnesota Public Radio at the time and was hoping that I would encounter Mr. Jarrett when he arrived to record the show in our Studio A.

I did not meet him. Jarrett apparently entered and left our studios in a clandestine manner. This did not surprise me. But he also departed without recording a program for the popular radio series. Producer Tom Voegeli later told me, "Jarrett sat in the studio at the piano and talked to us for nearly two hours. He thought about playing now and then, but it never happened. Jarrett finally told us, 'My muse is not with me tonight,' and he got up from the piano and took off. So we were left with no program. He was friendly enough, even chatty; but he never played anything." Forever the archivist, I asked if the engineer had saved the tapes of the studio conversation. Voegeli seemed irritated, "We never bothered to turn on the machines."

Jarrett has become (or remains) an artist who is more famous for his personality than for his music. We have long been accustomed to this situation in the rock music world, with performers such as Elton John, Prince, and Madonna. It is less common in the jazz world, and it saddens me that Keith Jarrett would allow his music to be placed into the shadows because of his insistence for perfection. But since he is well known for being potentially erratic during concerts, it should surprise no one when this occurs.

Neil Young is renowned for his short fuse during performances; George Jones was notorious for extremely brief sets and missing dates entirely. But none of this is news. If you were paying to see "No Show Jones," you took what you got. When purchasing concert tickets, the patron must decide whether it is worth the risk of being chastised by Young, or take the risk of Jones not showing up at all. The choice belongs to the patron: be willing to accept the possibilities or stay home.

When he was a young man, Ernest Tubb had the opportunity to see his idol Jimmie Rodgers in concert. Tubb purposefully avoided the performance, fearing he would be disappointed. And while this unusual vignette used to strike me as ludicrous, I think Tubb might have been onto something. For me, as a member of the audience, the music created by Keith Jarrett is remarkably transcendent on a regular basis. Why would I risk bringing ruinous or negative elements to my enjoyment of his art? Especially when knowing that the man has a reputation for dismantling his own concerts!

In a way, I feel like the mirror image of Glenn Gould's reaction to his audience. With Jarrett, I am the patron who has retreated from the concert hall. I can listen to his music whenever it pleases me, without being held hostage to the demands of the performer. I can hear the music in total darkness or bathed in bright lights. I don't need to worry about my fellow audience members inciting the temperamental artist into abusive language or embarrassing behavior. I can even take flash photographs of my stereo as a Jarrett record plays, without fear that the proceedings will be stopped or that I might be publicly called out for it.

There are a large number of concert recordings available by Keith Jarrett. In fact, there are many that I have not yet heard. For me, these recordings must now suffice in fulfilling my concert experience for this peculiar artist.

Bonus Track

I was recently struck by the parallel paths taken by two famous piano players—Keith Jarrett and Elton John. Beyond the fact that each musician has based his career on the acoustic piano, these guys are similar. Both Jarrett and John built their following on solid performances and quality recordings. They found success early and their name recognition filled concert halls. Then, both became better known for their personalities than their playing. Descriptions of Elton's flamboyancy filled space in the press where accolades for his music had formerly resided. Jarrett's reviews discussed his attitude more than his playing. I listen to and enjoy the music of these pianists, especially when I am able to ignore their eccentricities. I don't think Elton John would mind this comparison; I think Keith Jarrett would punch me in the mouth.

Concert Commentary

Miles Davis
Orchestra Hall
Minneapolis, Minnesota
November 11, 1981

ABOUT TEN DAYS before I had my single encounter with The Rolling Stones, I experienced my one Miles Davis concert. While I found The Stones' performance to be a happy surprise, Davis fell short of what I had hoped for. Instead, the concert was more in line with what I had feared.

I have been a fan of many of Miles' distinct musical eras for a long time. Even by 1981, I owned 33 Miles Davis LPs, with *My Funny Valentine*, *'Four' & More*, *Bitches Brew*, *Jack Johnson*, and, of course, *Kind of Blue* all being among my favorites. I was willing to let Miles be the eccentric artist he is known to be, and to play whatever he chose. Even so, the music that night in Minneapolis did not engage me. Miles played lengthy electric groove tunes that never really clicked. I was often bored, but it could have just been me. Some of my friends later said that they saw God during his set. Maybe, but I think these people were projecting the performance they were hoping for, rather than what was really transpiring on stage that night.

The live LP *We Want Miles* was recorded in the months preceding this fall 1981 concert. That album represents what Miles was doing when I saw him, but on more inspired nights. The Minneapolis concert was not especially long, maybe 75 minutes, but that was enough. I love Miles' melodic material as well as the hard-driving tunes of his second great quartet of the 1960s. I was aware that he would not be playing those older tunes, although he did perform George Gershwin's "My Man's Gone Now" from his remarkable *Porgy and Bess* album. Even so, I was disappointed by the concert.

Bonus Track

> One time in 1979, my Minneapolis roommate, Mike, had two odd musician friends visiting from New York City. These guys were obsessed with Miles, going on about him at length in a romanticized way. One visitor told us, reverently, "They say that if Miles invites you over to his house for dinner, and if he likes you, he'll play his trumpet." To which Mike immediately responded, "And if he doesn't like you, he'll play the organ." Funny.

Commentary
Huge Hunk o' Herbie: Hancock on Your Radio
May 2, 2012

SiriusXM satellite radio recently completed its four-day "Herbie Hancock Radio" special. It was a success. Beginning on Friday morning, the network turned over its *Real Jazz* station to playing nothing but Herbie Hancock recordings. Hancock as group leader, as a sideman, with ensembles, and solo; on famous recordings and on near-forgotten tracks, on electric keyboards, and on the concert grand. The special was inspirational for its range of recordings and for the stunningly high level of musicianship heard throughout the weekend.

From the station's introductory announcement, it was clear that the *Real Jazz* programmers would have their work cut out for them. A fluid voice called Hancock a "pure jazz artist" who is "also a bona fide rock star." Is that possible? And could a traditional jazz radio format really do justice to the many parts of Hancock's career? Short answer: Yes.

For SiriusXM, giving an existing channel a tightly focused four-day special such as this is different from creating a completely new outlet for one of their "Limited Engagements" broadcasts. Because regular listeners to the *Real Jazz* station have expectations when they tune in, making radical format shifts is risky. This special was successful in representing numerous works and styles of Herbie Hancock while still maintaining the established personality of the station.

The programmers wisely leaned more towards the pianist's traditional jazz selections during the day, letting the electronics flow a little more heavily during the overnight hours. There were exceptions to this, of course, and the station must be given credit for being willing to stretch the boundaries of their regular programming. Even so, Hancock's Blue Note label catalog as a group leader got a solid workout during the day, as did his recordings as sideman.

Announcements about the music were kept to a bare minimum, as is usual with the *Real Jazz* station. This, too, was a smart decision. If listeners wanted to dive more deeply into a specific selection, they could easily see what was playing by looking at their SiriusXM radio screen. They could then search the web for information on the track, including the title of the album, the year of recording, and the work's featured players. Occasionally, guests such as Chick Corea and Terence Blanchford gave brief, informative introductions to specific selections.

For those wanting a live announcer as a guide to the music, bassist Marcus Miller offered "Electric Herbie," an appropriately titled program that aired twice a day, during which Miller would give background on the selections being broadcast. The station's long running "Blue Note Hour" fit perfectly with the focused programming by offering music from Hancock's tenure with that label, chosen and discussed by host Bruce Lundvall. Two live programs also fit the format: saxophonist Wayne Shorter's performance at Lincoln Center had natural links to Hancock, as did bassist Ron Carter's 75th Birthday Concert, which featured Hancock as a performer.

And while these self-contained programs offered some commentary and context, "Herbie Hancock Radio" was nearly four days of uninterrupted music. Credit the station's programmers for not taking short cuts on this project. With just under 90 hours to fill, it would have been easy to rerun sections of programming, taking a four-hour set of music from one part of the day, for example, and broadcasting it again 12 hours later. This never happened. While popular tracks such as "Watermelon Man," "Chameleon," and "Rockit" were played more than once, the station did not repeat blocks of programming except for the *Blue Note Hour* and the two concerts.

Only one or two portions of Hancock's lengthy career were down-played, if not sidestepped completely. For example, I don't recall hear-ing any tracks from the two overtly disco LPs, *Feets Don't Fail Me Now* and *Monster*. At another end of Hancock's catalog, the experimental fusion piece "Hornets" was aired only in the middle of the night, at least in its full, 20-minute version. Both decisions are understandable for the *Real Jazz* station format, if for very different reasons.

Because this special often showcased Hancock as a sideman on other artists' albums, it would have been easy to let the weekend tilt too far toward his days with Miles Davis. But balance was maintained here as well. Tracks by Miles' 1960s bands were only occasionally played, and it was not until late one night, deep into the special, that Davis' lengthy "Right Off" was heard in its entirety. Sparse use of these Miles tracks kept the focus firmly on Hancock.

I greatly enjoyed the Herbie Hancock Radio weekend. Listening to some of the selections was like reconnecting with an old friend, and I heard some things from this man's career that were new to me. The station and its programmers should be commended. And as much as I applaud the outcome, what follows are two suggestions that I would like the station to consider for their future specials dedicated to a single artist.

First, because there are no on-air announcements about most of the selections being played, ongoing track-by-track information could be offered at the SiriusXM *Real Jazz* channel page. This could be con-stantly updated, much like the Twitter feeds which are posted on some other station pages. The effort would be labor intensive, to be sure, but it would provide useful information for both the uninitiated and the longtime follower.

Second, the weekend did feature two recent concerts focusing on Hancock's colleagues Ron Carter and Wayne Shorter, and both were excellent. But I also wanted to hear some unreleased concerts by Hancock himself from varying points of his career. If these tapes are not available for broadcast because of performance rights, some of Hancock's import-only live disks could be played as concerts sets, such as 1977's double LP *Flood* (available only in Japan) or the double live LP recorded around the time of *Sextant*, both on CBS Records.

A concert could easily be recreated by using the two live double LPs issued from the 1978 tour featuring Hancock and Chick Corea, both on concert grand pianos. This era boasted a much-publicized return to the acoustic piano for both performers and was not often represented during the weekend.

The "Herbie Hancock Radio" special was a worthy tribute. *Real Jazz* and SiriusXM should be congratulated for successfully presenting the unique career of this deserving musician. The special could easily have come across as a promotion for his new releases or a self-congratulatory weekend over his Grammy winning *Joni Letters* album, and his more recent *Imagine Project* CD. This never happened. The focus was on Hancock's ability to create a wide variety of jazz music in multiple settings. Even though "Herbie Hancock Radio" concluded last week, I still have his albums sitting right by my turntable as I continue to rediscover his music.

LP Review

Jeff Lorber Fusion
Wizard Island
Arista Records, 1980

Some younger jazz musicians are encountering a dilemma that struck many rock groups of the mid-1960s: they are competent musicians badly in need of well written material. Jeff Lorber is a prime example. This keyboardist's performance is well-executed, his band well-rehearsed, but there is little substance to many of the compositions on his new *Wizard Island* release

Most of these tunes are based on worn-out funk riffs that are twice-baked remnants of earlier fusion works. Lorber presents nothing new here, and boredom sets in soon after the needle is placed onto the record. This album could be faded in and out at most any point, and the cuts would be indistinguishable from one another. The liner notes stress that Lorber is using numerous keyboards. Even so, the result is a lackluster sameness, as there is little substance here. The similarity of sounds and weaknesses of the tunes bring me full circle: this player needs someone to write music for him.

After The Beatles and The Rolling Stones became successful with their own compositions, every pop group thought it could pen its own original tunes—and some could. For the most part, however, the British Invasion bands were at a distinct disadvantage if they had no original material of quality. A parallel situation is now heard in the music of Jeff Lorber and others artists on today's jazz scene. The new breed that Lorber typifies can usually play, and these group leaders can assemble tight bands. This is simply not enough. Unless Jeff Lorber can find a writer or develop his own composing skills, he is destined to the same fate as the many dimly remembered bands that flourished briefly in the mid-1960s.

Post Script

Few, including the group leader, could know what this band would soon bequeath to the jazz community. The saxophonist for The Jeff Lorber Fusion was Kenny Gorelick. You may have heard of him by another name: Kenny G.

Concert Commentary

Weather Report
Orpheum Theater
Minneapolis, Minnesota
February 14, 1980

ANY ACCOUNTS of Weather Report resting on its collective laurels were proved unsubstantiated when the band took the stage at the Orpheum Theater on Valentine's Day. The concert did not feature the string of obvious crowd pleasers that might have been expected after the group's recent live, hits oriented album.

Instead, new music flowed for the greater part of the evening. With the exception of Duke Ellington's "Rockin' in Rhythm," which led beautifully into the obligatory performance of Weather Report's own "Birdland," the program was largely recent and unfamiliar works.

Except for these two pieces, the oldest material of the night came from the studio side of Weather Report's latest album, *8:30*. The new compositions were unexpected and welcome, coming from a band that has been known to play it safe by filling concerts with their old tunes.

Surprises were in no short supply, as the group warmed up on a hard-driving swing piece that featured saxophonist Wayne Shorter playing more notes on one number than he has been known to play during some entire concerts. Shorter's sax sometimes gets lost in the electronics of Weather Report's music, but this was far from the case in Minneapolis, as he took numerous solos on tenor and soprano. The solo spot accorded him in earlier tours was unnecessary on this night, as the saxophone was featured continually within the structure of the group.

Shorter's longtime collaborator and group cofounder is Josef Zawinul, who played a variety of keyboards. The sound was a mix of textures that varied slightly but always remained interesting and fit the moment. Many bands now use electronic equipment, but only a few engage in any sort of meaningful expression through these instruments. Weather Report has been and remains the prototype for true electronic experimentations. The band continues to employ various new keyboard instruments, but always allows the sound of Shorter's saxophone to cut through the electronics. It is this distinctive combination of Shorter's traditional sound with Zawinul's modern keyboard passages that places Weather Report's music above today's glut of nondescript fusion and jazz/rock groups.

Weather Report is a collection of fine players from several different schools. Shorter and Zawinul have diverse musical backgrounds, but both musicians have played with Miles Davis during different periods of the 1960s. Then there is Jaco Pastorius, who seemed to come out of nowhere and become instantly acknowledged as the most talented electric bassist in music today. While it is difficult to say 'best' about any musician, in the case of Pastorius it is simply a case of 'no contest.'

Pastorius performed flawlessly, laying down solid foundations for Shorter and Zawinul to solo over. When Pastorius stepped into the limelight, however, he reveled in the opportunity to show unique control and mastery of his instrument, a worn and dilapidated Fender. Pastorius is able to produce unbelievable sounds from his unadorned electric bass, proving that the talent lies in the performer, and not in some instrument that has a plethora of special effects. Pastorius did use some electronic devices during his solo segment, but they were not the basis of his performance, nor were they employed to disguise any lack of technique.

A couple of tours ago Pastorius allowed his solo segment to become somewhat tedious in its length and repetition. He has disciplined his delivery on the bass and in his stage presence. In the past his physical antics sometimes upstaged other performers and diminished his own playing. Although he still danced on this occasion, his presence was subdued compared with that of earlier shows. Here was Pastorius, an entertainer, but an entertainer as musician and not as athletic court jester.

Peter Erskine was the other half of the rhythm section. This drummer fit the band well and, with percussionist Robert Thomas, Jr., gave band members a backdrop against which they displayed their musical virtuosity. Erskine's drumming was the constant that allowed Pastorius flexibility in his bass lines, letting him hang distinctive harmonics in the air.

A collective sound was what this group achieved. Although there are three well-known performers in this band, the quintet was a model of unity throughout the show. In fact, I found the camaraderie between the members surprising, as they are not known to be humble musicians. This was an ensemble performance by talented instrumentalists that featured three brilliant points of light: Shorter, Zawinul and Pastorius. Each shone individually at times, but it was the blending of these talents that produced the richest hues and most satisfying performances.

The group members joked among themselves and were obviously enjoying what must have been a hot night on the tour. It was fascinating to observe the group's nonverbal interaction: Pastorius would egg on Zawinul to try a different approach during a number; Shorter would watch the keyboards closely to complete Zawinul's melodic phrases with a single saxophone note. The feeling that the band was having fun spread to the audience. And although not a word was spoken from the stage, the rapport between patron and performer was intimate.

Near the end of the concert the group ran through two numbers from the studio side of the concert album *8:30*, though they stretched out so hard on both that neither of these remarkable pieces much resembled its studio counterpart. "Brown Street" was played without

Pastorius, as Zawinul handled all the bass lines on his keyboards. The ending of this number was one of the peaks of the night, a duet between Shorter and Zawinul. This provided a prelude to the evening's up-tempo finale, another recent number called "The Orphan."

Remembrance

Four Nights with Jaco Pastorius
September 2011

Jaco Pastorius is dead. I mean no disrespect by this statement. I point here to the eternal condition of the departed bassist neither to celebrate his birthday nor to lament his death anniversary. This article remembers Jaco because his was a talent that deserves continuing accolades. It might become easy to take him for granted or, worse, to neglect his memory. But it must be said and said often: Jaco Pastorius possessed a musical gift like no other. Ever.

What makes me think of Jaco today are my recollections concerning the death of George Harrison. At the time of the guitarist's passing, nearly ten years ago, I asked my college-age students if any of them knew who Harrison was. A hush fell. Absolutely no name recognition. I then told them that he was a member of The Beatles and asked if any of them knew what instrument he had played. Silence. I asked the question that day to three different classes. In the third, a young man sincerely ventured, "George played the trumpet?" I did not continue asking. I couldn't stand it.

Some years back I quizzed an elder statesman of country music on how it was possible that so many great artists had been forgotten by modern fans. It particularly surprised me that this was happening in the world of country which, like jazz, is an American musical style that supposedly reveres its own past. I had recently seen an *Austin City Limits* broadcast on Public Television by Hank Thompson & His Brazos Valley Boys. To its credit, the show gave him the entire hour. But as Thompson ran through his biggest numbers, it was clear that even Texas music fans were unfamiliar with many of these songs. It was an uncomfortable set to watch, as Thompson, with over 60 *Billboard* chart entries, drew only polite applause for even the largest of his many Top 10 hits. Before Rick Rubin, Joaquin Phoenix, and the Grim Reaper had restored his legacy, Johnny Cash also had an hour on *Austin City Limits*, with only a slightly better reception. This was in the mid-1980s, shortly after Cash had been unceremoniously dropped by Columbia Records.

When asked about this epidemic of amnesia concerning music's recent past, the country musician told me, "These performers are forgotten because they have no drummer." After realizing that the assessment had nothing to do with percussion, I pondered this theory. Certainly high profile supporters, or "drummers" of promotion, could do wonders for a fading or forgotten career. Dwight Yoakam gave Buck Owens a complete reboot, even coercing Buck back on the road with him to reestablish his respectability after Owens' uncomfortably long, if lucrative association with television's *Hee Haw*.

Willie Nelson's numerous duet albums gave new, if fleeting attention to the careers of his musical heroes, from Hank Snow to Webb Pierce. For performers who were no longer available to collaborate, such as Lefty Frizzell, Willie recorded tribute albums, just as Merle Haggard had previously done for both Bob Wills and Jimmie Rodgers.

Similar album-length tributes are found in jazz. Louis Armstrong plays the music of Fats Waller. Sonny Fortune invokes the spirit of John Coltrane. Kenny Burrell honors Duke Ellington. Both Burrell and Herb Ellis emulate Charlie Christian on separate recordings. The avant-garde trio Air remembers Buddy Bolden (if only for one surprisingly linear tune). And in a most unexpected genre-crossing example, Rolling Stones drummer Charlie Watts offers his tribute to the *Charlie Parker with Strings* album!

This personal recognition of inspiration can be noted in other areas of music: Bette Middler honors Rosemary Clooney. Jeff Beck pays homage to Cliff Gallup. Eric Clapton respects Robert Johnson to a fault. Phish performs full albums by The Beatles and The Who. I can offer Jaco Pastorius no tribute album or collaboration project, but I can shout his name out loud in an effort to be *his* drummer.

I had the great fortune of seeing Jaco in concert on four occasions. At no time was he less than brilliant. It was impossible for me to look away from him for very long, even when he was not soloing. The first time I saw him was simply good fortune. We were college students excited about a road trip, with the intent of going to see John McLaughlin. We knew that McLaughlin had abandoned his electric guitar, but we were excited nonetheless for a journey from Cedar Falls, Iowa, into the great northern city of Minneapolis, Minnesota. We were going, all later admitted, on the off chance that McLaughlin would renounce his new acoustic band Shakti and plug in his old twin-necked Gibson guitar and turn it up! Just for that one night.

We knew it couldn't happen, but we were such fans of the original Mahavishnu Orchestra that we made the trek anyway. Also on the bill was Weather Report. That was fine with us, but Weather Report was not the reason for this trip. Most of us knew their early records. Some thought they might perform "Orange Lady." I wanted to hear "Boogie Woogie Waltz."

We bought tickets at the door and were told that we were purchasing good seats. Actually, they were at the far end of the large hall. No matter. We had good sight lines of the stage and we were excited to be in the city! The fact that so many tickets could be sold for such music is telling. An acoustic Indian music quintet playing an arena? Clearly we were not the only Midwesterners eager to see John McLaughlin, no matter what style he played.

McLaughlin's Shakkti opened the night, with the group members emerging to sit on the stage floor. I like Ravi Shankar as much as the next guy; maybe more. I owned two of the Yehudi Menuhin/Ravi Shankar *West Meets East* LPs. I would actually *listen* to the Shankar side of Harrison's *Concert for Bangladesh* benefit album (if only occasionally). And I had the obscure *Ravi Shankar Live at the Woodstock Music & Arts Festival* LP. As such, I wasn't completely out of my element with this instrumentation. I liked it fine, but it soon became clear that there would be no "Noonward Race" played this night. So we sat back to hear what McLaughlin's new direction was all about.

In retrospect, however, acoustic music wasn't completely new for him. If one returns to McLaughlin's second album as a leader, *My Goal's Beyond*, from 1970, there is acoustic music aplenty within. And even some tracks on the studio Mahavishnu LPs, such as "A Lotus on Irish Springs," show that at no time in his career had McLaughlin been a complete stranger to his acoustic guitar.

As expected, John McLaughlin was lightning fast, and the sound was surprisingly clean considering the booming acoustics of the large room. But at the time, like most attending the concert that night, I was bound to be disappointed with McLaughlin's new endeavor. And I was.

Shakti concluded their set. We all thought: yep, Johnny's still fast. Then we waited for the stage to be reset. Somebody leaned over and said to the collective row, "I hear that Weather Report is supposed to have some hot new bass player with them." What had happened to their former bass man, Alphonzo Johnson? Nobody knew. The lights dimmed. Weather Report kicked into their first tune. The group included the expected co-leaders Joe Zawinul on varied synthesizers and Wayne Shorter on tenor sax. But who was that electric bass player? Some were even expecting an acoustic bass, but of course that never happened. Nor did they play "Orange Lady" or "Boogie Woogie Waltz" that night.

In fact, I can't tell you what numbers they did play—probably "Elegant People and "Scarlet Woman." But individual selections didn't matter. For me, the *sound* was the focus. My clear, indelible memory is one of an odd looking young man bathed in a white spotlight. He was center stage holding a beat up Fender bass high on his chest, playing like it was an instrument on loan from Mount Olympus. I kept hearing these amazingly fluid solo runs. But that couldn't be the electric bass. Still, Zawinul wasn't even playing at this point. It *had* to be the new guy! Playing those crystal clear harmonics. On a *bass*? And the speed and cleanliness of each line, even in that fidelity-challenged hall.

I was stunned. Time became meaningless; it seemed to me that they played about ten minutes, but I'm sure they performed a full set. The lights came up and I said something articulate like, "Wow." Then I gushed about how that was the best bass player I had ever heard. Some of our group quietly agreed, clearly knocked out by what they had just witnessed. Others dismissed his playing as "all show." It completely blew my mind. I couldn't stop thinking about that bass man: his stage presence, his sound, and especially his chops. Like many others in the audience that night, the flame of my casual interest in Weather Report was immediately fanned into a blaze.

The next time Weather Report came though the Midwest, Jaco Pastorius had become a star. They were to play Iowa City's Hancher Auditorium in November 1977, and I had good seats, about 14 rows back with Jaco directly in front of me. I came prepared for this one and taped the show; a typical mono audience recording of its day: low fidelity, but listenable. Even with questionable fidelity, that tape demonstrates the power of the entire band and Jaco's place in it. "Black

Market" and "A Remark You Made" were high points. Since this was after the release of *Heavy Weather*, they of course played "Birdland" near the end of the set. The use of prerecorded tapes to set distinctive moods, such as the sound of ships leading into and out of "Gibraltar," may appear trite now. But these sonic settings worked well that night.

Midway through the concert Jaco had a solo spot. Watching him perform this segment, seeing how engaged he was, and how he obtained sounds from his dilapidated Fender bass, added a new element to my admiration for this musician. His physical antics were fun to watch, but none of these visual elements would have mattered if Jaco had not been a monster player.

Even at this point, however, a backlash was setting in. I recall a review in *Billboard Magazine* of a solo New York City performance by Pastorius. The reviewer took Jaco to task for too high a ratio of stage antics and showboating to actual playing, something that famed promoter Bill Graham had criticized Jimi Hendrix for, to his face, only a few years earlier. The reviewer could have been right, but nobody in the Iowa City concert hall that night minded Jaco's theatrics. If he wanted to embellish his playing with some gratuitous showmanship, fine by us.

Jaco played in a few other music settings; Zawinul even encouraged him to do so. The only time I saw Jaco outside the Weather Report realm was when he played on the tour of Joni Mitchell's excursion into jazz during late summer 1979. (This beat Sting's celebrated dip into these waters by half a decade.) Joni's ringing electric guitar and open tunings were accentuated by Pat Metheny's distinctive electric guitar voicings and Jaco's unmistakable bass. Lyle Mays' keyboards and Michael Brecker's tenor sax rounded out this high-priced backing band. I have been told that Peter Erskine was originally slated to drum for the tour, but this would have violated a section of the Weather Report contract, which stated that Zawinul's side men could not depart en mass to form another band. Smart guy. Because of this proviso, Don Alias was on drums for Mitchell's tour.

Each of the band members had a solo feature, but this was Joni Mitchell's show and she was the focal point. The set consisted mainly of tunes from the era of *Hejira* through her latest LP at that time, the heartfelt but problematic *Mingus* album, a genre-crossing tribute that cost Mitchell much of her longstanding audience. The touring band was excellent, of course, but during the concert there were times when Jaco's physical acrobatics seemed to draw strained smiles of tolerance from both Metheny and Mitchell.

The last time I saw Jaco was a February 1980 Weather Report concert. Some critics have viewed this tour as a holding pattern for this immensely popular lineup. Jaco's talent was starting to be taken for granted; some said he was coasting. I disagreed strongly. The band was playing harder than any time I had seen them and were presenting a lot of new material. I had balcony seats, and watching the band operate as a unit was actually better than staring at a single part of the whole. Breathtaking to the last!

This concert also served as my own finale with Jaco and Weather Report. I began to lose interest in the band shortly after the largely live *8:30* album and the follow up, *Night Passage*. This is odd, in retrospect, since I felt the studio material on *8:30* was some of the strongest in the band's catalog. Weather Report continued to record and tour with, and then without, Jaco Pastorius. But I ceased to search out the group's new releases, even before Jaco's departure. I heard that Zawinul retooled the band and changed the name to Weather Update, but I never checked that out either. Even the later days of Weather Report itself were off my radar. In fact, I recently came across an 8-track tape of their album *Domino Theory*, a post Jaco release I had never even heard of.

Many defend the band's music after Jaco's departure, and I don't disagree. It was I who dropped out. I never felt too guilty for drifting from Weather Report, if I ever thought about it. I believed that I had "band cred" for being somewhat into them in their pre-Jaco days. I owned the import *Live in Tokyo* double album and had even interviewed drummer Eric Gravatt about his days in the band. But that's another story.

In hindsight, the Jaco era amounted to only one portion of this great band's timeline. It's clear that Joe Zawinul felt this way, for when the 2002 *Live and Unreleased* overview of his band was issued, Zawinul made sure that this two-CD retrospective covered many (but not all) eras of the band's performance spectrum. This approach is laudable, as the collection could easily have become a Jaco Pastorius tribute. In fact, it probably would have sold better in that guise. And concerning sales figures, Columbia Records clearly has limited economic interest in the later Weather Report LPs, as the company has allowed several of these releases to go out of print.

Speaking of Jaco recordings that would sell: I have been assured that many high fidelity concert recordings remain locked away in various vaults. One that comes to mind is the performance by Jaco's Word of Mouth big band at the Kool Jazz Festival of 1982, which was professionally recorded by National Public Radio for their *Jazz Alive* series. Most of the concert was broadcast, and these tapes are definitely worthy of official release. I'm certain there are others.

Jaco Pastorius does not need me to be his promotional drummer. His recordings say it all. As time passes, I become increasingly aware of how fortunate I was to have attended concerts during the short era when this virtuoso was storming world stages. But since no artist can really promote himself from the grave, even an incandescent light such as Jaco provided might not be clearly seen by subsequent generations. Individuals like Duke Ellington and Miles Davis enjoyed lengthy careers and have ample aural documentation for later admirers to pore over and posthumously appreciate. Jaco Pastorius, much less so. But the collection of music he did leave is worthy of continued rediscovery, by those of us who know it well and especially for the uninitiated.

Five Recommended Starting Places:
Jaco Pastorius – *Jaco Pastorius* —(Epic Records, 1976)
Weather Report – *Heavy Weather* —(Columbia Records, 1977)
Weather Report – *8:30* —(Columbia Records, 1979)
Joni Mitchell – *Hejira*—(Asylum Records, 1976)
Joni Mitchell – *Shadows and Light* —(Asylum Records, 1980)
The albums 8:30 *and* Shadows and Light *are concert recordings.*

CD Review

Wynton Marsalis
Live at the House of Tribes
Blue Note Records, 2005

If any musician has done a thorough job of documenting his working live bands, it's Wynton Marsalis. In the mid-1980s he released the lengthy double LP of his quartet *Live at Blues Alley*. In 1999 came a seven-CD set featuring three different Marsalis-led groups, all recorded at the Village Vanguard from 1990 to 1994.

On the new *Live at the House of Tribes*, Marsalis' quintet plays a program of expected composers. But give credit to the often-maligned Wynton for keeping these renditions challenging and fresh. It would be easy for the heralded trumpeter to take a café society approach to jazz at this point of his career. He could play it safe, creating chamber jazz for audiences often drawn to his concerts by cultural name recognition, rather than by a love of the music. Marsalis clearly enjoys the celebrity he has gained over the years, but he is still leading a jazz group that strives for exciting improvisation, as this CD repeatedly shows.

Opening the set is Thelonious Monk's composition, "Green Chimneys," which gets a quarter-hour workout, as does "Just Friends," which follows. Charlie Parker's "Donna Lee" seems positively brief here at a mere seven minutes. The set is rounded out with the Cole Porter perennial, "What Is This Thing Called Love?"

Marsalis has been criticized for being too studied in his playing, too reverent regarding the music's history, and too opinionated in his promotion of jazz. Perhaps the truth behind much of the criticism is that he is just too successful for the medium. It has been five years since Ken Burns' *Jazz* series was broadcast, starring Wynton in the role of Shelby Foote. For those sharply critical of Marsalis, for whatever reason: can we give it up now and hear his horn? Just listen!

Concert Commentary

The Jazz at Lincoln Center Orchestra with Wynton Marsalis
Wynton in Winter
Milwaukee, Wisconsin
December 1, 2014

WYNTON MARSALIS came to Milwaukee this week to give a history lesson. But instead of using PowerPoint for instruction, he brought along the 17-piece Jazz at Lincoln Center Orchestra as his teaching tool. Marsalis offered background and context for each piece, yet at no time were his remarks dry or didactic. In fact, once the format was established, Marsalis' brief comments before each selection became a welcome and expected part of the evening's performance.

The night began with the march "Peanut Brittle Brigade" from the *Nutcracker Suite* as arranged by Duke Ellington and Billy Strayhorn. This powerful opener had echoes of Ellington running all through it, sounding at times like it wanted desperately to meld into Duke's "Rockin' in Rhythm." With Tchaikovsky and Ellington as the starting point, the evening's lesson had begun.

"White Christmas" came next, on which Wynton took one of his few extended trumpet solos. In fact, Marsalis was a confirmed section player for most of the evening. At no time did the concert become a star vehicle for the leader. The focus stayed firmly on the group as an ensemble and on the music it produced.

If any musician was in the spotlight more than the others, it was Milwaukee native Dan Nimmer. Marsalis introduced pianist Nimmer as the "home boy" more than once and even called on Nimmer's parents to stand and be acknowledged for providing an example of what music education can produce. It was interesting to watch band members watch Nimmer when the pianist was featured on a trio arrangement of "Santa Claus Is Comin' to Town." Even while accustomed to hearing him every night, the other players appeared enthralled with their colleague's abilities.

Vocalist Cecile McLorin Salvant joined the orchestra for several numbers, including "Have Yourself a Merry Little Christmas." While striving to make the song her own, Salvant could not escape the long shadow of Judy Garland's definitive performance of this number. The singer was at her most engaging on the spiritual "Mary Had a Baby," followed by "Easy to Blame the Weather." On this Sammy Cahn song, Salvant used her lower register to explore some wonderfully slow scat vocals. This selection, which also featured Wynton's trumpet and a bass solo by Carlos Henriquez, was a highlight of the night.

Another pinnacle was saxophonist Ted Nash's unexpected arrangement of "We Three Kings." In addition to unusual chord voicings, this piece inverted the format of improvisation. Almost all jazz tunes start with the melody and then stretch into different areas of experimentation before returning to the melody. Nash's version of this Christmas song started and ended with exploratory sections, with the middle of the tune reserved for the most recognizable melody lines. It was a successful new approach to a very old work.

If "We Three Kings" offered the night's furthest stretch, the take on "Zat You, Santa Claus?" was probably the most traditional. On this Louis Armstrong tribute, the orchestra had the sound of a true big band, with unison section playing leading to individual solos. They swung hard here, and Satchmo would have approved.

Well known melodies dominated the concert's conclusion with "What Child Is This" and the Count Basie arrangement of "Jingle Bells." But if the works were familiar, the approach was always fresh and energetic, with the orchestra members breathing renewed holiday spirit into every selection.

Wynton thanked the appreciative audience for coming, and the band walked off stage. But as the lights began to come up in the hall and the audience started to leave, Dan Nimmer's piano was unexpectedly heard, with Henriquez's bass and then the drums of Ali Jackson falling in behind him. Wynton Marsalis, for the first time, walked to center stage and this quartet burned hot. Now they appeared to be playing for themselves, and it seemed for all too brief a time as if they were channeling the Miles Davis group of 1967. I could have used a full second set of it.

Late in the evening, after the conclusion of a ballad, Wynton set down his trumpet. He sighed, and said: "Man; that was pleasant." With this remark, Marsalis summed up what the audience had been feeling for the entire concert.

Concert Commentary

The Dan Nimmer Trio
Milwaukee Youth Arts Center
Milwaukee, Wisconsin
January 28, 2012

OF COURSE I WAS interested in checking out a live performance by Dan Nimmer. In fact, I had been waiting for just such a date. Here is a young man from the Midwest who had gone to New York City and found a way to audition for Wynton Marsalis' open piano chair. And get the gig! I admired his ability as Wynton's accompanist, but I wanted to hear him on his own. The opportunity arose on a cold January night in Milwaukee, when Dan Nimmer graciously agreed to close the Eastside Jazzfest, a daylong teaching seminar for the youth of his hometown.

Nimmer chose a balance of originals and standards for this set. His trio began with Nimmer's own "Lu's Bounce," a 12-minute up-tempo workout that showed the pianist unafraid to take chances. As the number's head led into improvisation, Nimmer immediately went deep. A confident player, he was apparently untroubled about whether he could completely pull off each idea. He refused to take the safe path during this entire set. That's jazz! This strong beginning was followed by another fast original, "Do You Mind?".

Presenting almost 20 minutes of uninterrupted virtuosity, the trio had offered the audience what it came to hear. In fact, Nimmer sounded almost embarrassed when he told the audience that, for their third number, the group would now tone down the fireworks and play a ballad. Tad Dameron's "If You Could See Me Now" was given a beautiful interpretation, during which the pianist lovingly caressed the keys. An atmospheric performance of Antonio Carlos Jobim's "Corcovado" was next, followed by Nimmer's own composition, "Modern Day Blues."

The pianist's full-hand chord work was impressive, as were his articulate single line runs. At times, this pianist could almost have been mistaken for Oscar Peterson. But even with his technical abilities, Nimmer's emphasis on melody was a constant. Nimmer never let his considerable chops dominate a piece for the sake of show. Here is a pianist who respects the song, a fact which became increasingly clear in the non-original selections Nimmer chose to play for this recital. Keenly aware of the vast music catalog which precedes his own era, Nimmer included brief quotes of various melodic themes from jazz's past in his improvisations.

The night was very much of a family affair. Nimmer was playing for an intimate hometown audience of about 80. His parents were in the second row, and former teachers and classmates could be seen throughout the hall. The set was scheduled for an hour, and as the final selections began, Nimmer introduced an original written for his nephew "Ray." This must be one active kid, because "Ray" never stopped bouncing, and featured a lot of staccato runs. Nimmer finally seemed to be having fun, or at least relaxing a bit. Sitting at a black Steinway grand in suit and tie, his attitude was sometimes hard to gauge. He traded exuberant fours on this last trio piece with drummer Brian Ritter and bassist Jake Vinsel, both up from Chicago for this one-off gig.

After a strong and deserved ovation, Nimmer dedicated a solo piece to his parents, Ellington's "Reflections in D." His touch was so controlled that the pianist's fingers seemed to flutter above the keys more than actually play them. The Duke would have been pleased by the respect Dan Nimmer showed, both for the composer's music and for the pianist's own mother and father.

Bass and drums kicked back in for the break tune, during which the pianist acknowledged his band and the audience. I had hoped to speak with him after the set, but seeing he had family to appease, I just quickly told him how much I enjoyed his playing and then headed into the night. And as I drove home, it occurred to me that his was the first concert I had attended in a long time that I wished I had recorded from the audience. That's my concept of very high praise.

Concert Commentary

The Mike Kubicki Trio
The Jazz Estate
Milwaukee, Wisconsin
January 3, 2014

THE WISCONSIN MOOD was not good: recent high temperatures in Milwaukee had remained well below zero; sharp winds howled through the city and its people. Worse, local television coverage for the upcoming Packers playoff game was rumored to be blacked out.

Attempting an escape from this dire atmosphere, several of us braved the arctic cold and headed to The Jazz Estate, a small club that has provided live music to the faithful for many years. The room filled slowly. Ambient conversation focused on the weather. At one point I heard the owner say that he was surprised by the large turnout. There were maybe 20 people in the place. Such "large" audiences are probably the reason for another unwelcome rumor that had been circulating: The Jazz Estate may be closing soon. Say it isn't so! On this January night, at least, vibrant jazz was alive in Milwaukee.

The group scheduled to play for these winter-ravaged jazz devotees was the Mike Kubicki Trio. It was my son who had encountered Kubicki at this same venue some months earlier. He came home asking if I had ever heard of Horace Silver. I played him a few things and promised to go along the next time Kubicki was in town. It takes very little coaxing to get me to The Jazz Estate. This intimate Milwaukee setting has more of a Manhattan jazz feel than most of the actual New York City clubs I have frequented.

As if he heard why we had come, Kubicki began the night with Horace Silver's "Strollin.'" The trio then proceeded to offer an overview of important jazz pianists: compositions by Kenny Barron ("Voyage"), Cedar Walton ("Hindsight"), and a sensitive performance of Duke Ellington's "Sophisticated Lady."

Kubicki knows how to play, but he also knows how to listen. Some of the most impressive moments of the night were the pianist's effectively sparse accompaniments for his fellow musicians. The leader was generous throughout the evening, giving plenty of room to acoustic bassist Jim Paolo and to drummer Todd Howell. There were call and response segments with both players, and each was featured individually. But while the bass and drum solos were always engaging, the consistent highlight was hearing the trio's combined efforts in full flight.

Kubicki seems to enjoy playing various chord voicings more than impressing an audience with fast, single line runs. Still, when the piece called for it, Kubicki showed himself to be a versatile soloist. He is an accomplished jazz pianist who has been listening to the right records. The break tune for the first set was an up-tempo take on Herbie Hancock's "One Finger Snap," which concluded a remarkable 80 minutes of music.

After a short intermission the trio began again, picking up right where they had left off, with Hancock's "And What if I Don't?" More introspective than the first, this set included works by and about Thelonious Monk (including Barry Harris' "Off Monk"). The evening came full circle with another Horace Silver composition, "St. Vitus Dance."

On these later tunes, Kubicki willingly pushed himself onto unsteady ledges, offering the audience a chance to witness the growth of a talented pianist in a performance setting. It was exciting, and infinitely preferable to a safe and measured approach. This was experimentation—the very foundation and lifeblood of jazz!

Mike Kubicki is from the Appleton area of Wisconsin. He performs live dates with some regularity. This is lucky for the Wisconsin heartland, since his degree in chemical engineering from Purdue and his day job as a contract attorney seem to have little to do with music. Here's hoping that Kubicki will record soon, and that he continues to pursue the elusive jazz muse he seeks.

CD Review

Charlie Haden and Hank Jones
Come Sunday
Decca Records, 2012

Is there such a thing as Easter Jazz? Interpretations of Christmas tunes by jazz musicians have become commonplace, but recordings celebrating the Resurrection are rare. Let me suggest the new *Come Sunday* CD by Charlie Haden and Hank Jones as an appropriate release for the Lenten Season. This collection of sacred songs was recorded over a two-day period in early 2010, just weeks before pianist Jones made his own pilgrimage from these earthly shores. Perhaps reminded of their own mortality, Jones and Haden have chosen a set list which reflects the Savior's birth and death.

While not a Christmas collection, *Come Sunday* includes both "It Came Upon a Midnight Clear" and "God Rest Ye Merry Gentlemen" as acknowledgements of Christ's birth. The remainder of the CD contains contemplative piano/bass duets such as "Take My Hand, Precious Lord," "Deep River," and "Sweet Hour of Prayer." Calvary is an inevitable part of the Easter story, and it is told beautifully here with interpretations of "The Old Rugged Cross" and "Were You There When They Crucified My Lord?"

Little wonder that Charlie Haden and Hank Jones seem comfortable working together; this is their second studio date as a duo. The first was nearly two decades ago, when they also chose a few religious pieces for their *Steal Away* CD. But while the earlier set of "Spirituals, Hymns, and Folk Songs" provides an overview of genres, the new *Come Sunday* release is far more focused, as if the musicians had important information to convey to the listener.

Appropriately serious but not somber, this collection includes two up-tempo celebratory exchanges with "Down by the Riverside" and "Give Me That Old Time Religion." *Come Sunday* closes with Ellington's reflective title composition, itself hinting at an anticipation of what this Holy Day will bring. An Easter collection? Perhaps. But no matter how this music is interpreted, it remains an uplifting and moving set.

LP Review

Bill Evans
We Will Meet Again
Warner Brothers Records, 1980

Bill Evans doesn't need to prove anything. This might be why the pianist is content to let other performers do most of the soloing on his latest album, *We Will Meet Again*. Evans is known for his work leading trios, where the piano carries the melodic responsibilities and must introduce most of the themes. On *We Will Meet Again*, Evans has placed himself within a quintet setting.

Evans is able to embark on projects that interest him, rather than making calculated moves for the sake of his career. He has recorded albums with unexpected instrumentation, including last year's *Affinity*, featuring harmonica master Toots Thielemans. Evans has previously played on Claus Ogerman's orchestral piece, "Symbiosis," on an album of flute features with Jeremy Steig, and two albums with vocalist Tony Bennett. These were all unique side projects that Evans undertook when not engaged with trio format of piano, bass, and drums.

Instead of harmonicas or orchestras, Evans uses more traditional jazz instrumentation on *We Will Meet Again*. Drums and acoustic bass are represented by Joe LaBarbera and Marc Johnson, respectively. The other two members of the quintet are Larry Schneider on saxophone and flute, and Tom Harrell on trumpet.

Evans must be aware that some of his recordings do not conform to what people expect from him, and this seems to amuse him. While *We Will Meet Again* is dedicated to a deceased brother and contains its share of moving ballads, the album also has several moments of laughter. A tongue-in-cheek title adorns "Bill's Hit Tune," an 11-minute piece that we will not see released as a single. "Five" is a composition that has a melody line which suits a circus band. It is upbeat and nothing short of comic.

The playing by Evans' sidemen obviously pleases the leader. He gives each player more time to solo than might be expected. Evans also takes solos, of course, but he keeps a relatively low profile on most of these tunes. He does perform two solo numbers. The first is a standard, "For All We Know (we may never meet again)," the only selection on the record that Evans did not compose. It is an interesting choice, for the other unaccompanied piano number serves as a rebuttal to the notion of permanent separation: the title selection, "We Will Meet Again." In a collection of music dedicated to his recently departed brother, Evans strives to offer hope and consolation for both himself and for his listeners.

Post Script

We Will Meet Again would be the last album issued by Bill Evans during his lifetime. Evans died September 15, 1980. This review was written prior to his death.

CD Review

The Dave Brubeck Quartet
Their Last Time Out: December 26, 1967
Columbia Records, 2011

In December 1966, Dave Brubeck told his quartet that the following year would be the group's last. He wanted to retire from the rigors of touring in order to concentrate on composing. Brubeck must have also informed his record company, for two live albums from the 1967 world tour were issued: a concert recording from Mexico, *Bravo! Brubeck!*, and *The Last Time We Saw Paris*. The release of multiple performance recordings in a single year was not unusual for Brubeck. Live LPs had been a staple of his catalog since his first album for Columbia Records in 1954 (*Jazz Goes to College*) and before, with *Jazz at Oberlin* (Fantasy, 1953).

Now the final performance by The Dave Brubeck Quartet has been released. It is *Their Last Time Out*, a December 1967 concert from Philadelphia. These tapes were not in the record company's vault, but were instead retrieved from the pianist's own home closet. Brubeck doesn't recall how he acquired them. But when longtime friend and collaborator Russell Gloyd realized what they were, he took the tapes to Columbia for release. We should be glad he did.

The final night is neither sentimental nor a self-congratulatory affair. Not a hint is given from the stage that this is the last time around; it is business as usual. But by this point, business as usual for these guys was conducted at an awfully high level. Having been on the road for a full year, and together for ten, everybody's chops were sharp. Brubeck was routinely quite adventurous in front of an audience; Paul Desmond was always at the top of his game, but especially when performing on the bandstand.

"St. Louis Blues" is the oft-heard opener this night, and the mandatory "Take Five" closes the concert. Positioned between these pillars is a 90-minute history of the group. "Three to Get Ready" first appeared on the landmark *Time Out* album, and "These Foolish Things" had been in the Brubeck book since the early 1950s. "Take the 'A' Train" and "Someday My Prince Will Come" are two familiar standards of the era, made fresh by individual solos and intelligent interplay between piano and alto saxophone.

Brubeck's increasing interest in what is now called World Music is represented here by "Cielito Lindo" and "La Paloma Azul." Joe Morello is given the solo showcase "For Drummers Only," but even more impressive is his percussion work within the ensemble on the other 12 selections. Bassist Eugene Wright is solid throughout. Near the end of the program, the group plays Wright's "Set My People Free," a social theme which was to become increasingly important to Brubeck's own non-jazz compositions.

Duke Ellington was correct when he told his retiring colleague, "You'll be back." In fact, Brubeck started playing live dates with baritone saxophonist Gerry Mulligan in the spring of 1968, even returning to Mexico for another concert recording. Brubeck, Desmond, Wright, and Morello had a brief and celebrated reunion in 1976, but this Philadelphia date of December 26, 1967, was their final gig as an active band. This recording must be seen as a stopping place for the group, but it would make an excellent starting place for anyone wanting to discover The Dave Brubeck Quartet.

Post Script

Their Last Time Out comes from a mono, soundboard tape recording. Although not recorded by Columbia Records' engineers, the audio quality is excellent.

Columbia has released *The Complete Columbia Studio Album Collection*, a box set of all 19 studio albums recorded by The Dave Brubeck Quartet for this label. I hope this will be followed by a similar box of the quartet's complete live releases for Columbia. Several of these concert LPs have never been issued on CD, including *The Dave Brubeck Quartet in Europe, Brubeck in Amsterdam*, and *The Last Time We Saw Paris*, from the final 1967 tour discussed above.

Remembrance

Dave Brubeck
December 7, 2012

Dave Brubeck had been an elder statesman of jazz for decades when he died December 5, 2012, just a day shy of his 92nd birthday. He was widely respected as a jazz pianist, composer, innovator, and band leader. Brubeck was also known for his work in genres beyond jazz, most notably sacred orchestral music.

The respect Dave Brubeck inspired was well deserved. But it was not easily attained or quick in coming. On the 1960 album *Look Forward in Anger*, Mort Sahl mocks Brubeck, saying his music belongs in Disneyland. Miles Davis was quoted as saying Brubeck didn't swing. Jazz critics seemed of one mind that Brubeck's piano style was heavy handed. Many openly wondered why the quartet's great alto saxophonist Paul Desmond didn't join a better group. Oh yes, and Brubeck was white.

These pointed criticisms had to be painful; but if they were, Brubeck never let on. Certainly there were many accolades he could point to—he appeared on the cover of *Time Magazine* in 1954. And this, a full five years before his quartet would release one of the most famous and best-selling jazz albums in history, *Time Out*. The widespread popularity of Brubeck's music was undeniable when that album spawned the Top 40 radio hit "Take Five."

Record sales, jazz magazine awards, successful tours (domestic and abroad)—these were all public acknowledgements of Brubeck's talent. But even as late as 1980, when National Public Radio's Susan Stamberg interviewed Dave Brubeck for a reaction concerning the death of piano colleague Bill Evans, Stamberg appeared dismissive of Brubeck's own place in the jazz pantheon. Question after question revolved around the assumption that Brubeck was a far lesser light than Evans, unfit even to be his page turner.

Brubeck remained cool—whether the disparaging word came from an interviewer, a critic or a colleague, Brubeck remained cool.

Dave Brubeck was proud of his accomplishments, to be sure. He was happy to take credit for his innovations, most notably the unusual time signatures he introduced into jazz compositions. But there was much more. I had the opportunity to interview Mr. Brubeck in the spring of 2009. When I indicated to him that his sacred jazz writings were the first of their kind, he enthusiastically welcomed the opportunity to discuss his innovative religious compositions.

The naysayers would eventually be silenced. Sahl lost his audience, and critics busied themselves with deriding newer jazz artists. Even Miles modified his stance, telling Brubeck: "You swing. It's *your band* that doesn't swing." Ah well; it's Miles.

Brubeck would receive recognition until the very end. His quartet continued winning *Downbeat Magazine* readers' polls, and in 2009 Brubeck was honored by The Kennedy Center. But in spite of various lifetime achievement awards, Dave Brubeck never stopped exploring the vast universe of music. In my conversation with him about his sacred music, it was clear that death was not on the agenda. When I asked if he were familiar with Wynton Marsalis' religious work *In This House, On This Morning*, Brubeck quickly replied, "Not yet." I took this to mean that he would search out the work. This artist would make time to do so because he was still extremely interested in learning, and perhaps also in checking out the competition.

To say that the death of Dave Brubeck represents the end of an era in American music is not quite accurate. Brubeck was so original that he really belongs to no single era and no single place. The sound of Brubeck's recordings remains fresh and the performances inspired. Don't spend time mourning or missing Dave Brubeck. Listen to his music!

Interview
Tom Wilmeth Speaks with Dave Brubeck about his Sacred Recordings
Interview conducted May 12, 2009

Dave Brubeck left us in late 2012, but the man's music lives on through his many records. The pianist is most famous for his work with The Dave Brubeck Quartet, featuring Paul Desmond on alto saxophone. This group recorded many albums and will be remembered by even the most casual music fan for their seminal hit, "Take Five." Dave Brubeck and Paul Desmond performed and recorded together from the late 1940s until December 1967, when Brubeck amicably dissolved the quartet. Brubeck said he disbanded the group in order to give himself an opportunity to concentrate on his writings, most of which were taking the form of religious compositions.

Retirement from the concert stage was short lived. Less than a year later, Brubeck had enlisted saxophonist Gerry Mulligan to join him for some concert and studio dates. Although never as popular as the original quartet, this collaborative effort produced both fine live recordings (*Compadres*) and studio efforts (*Blues Roots*). Both of these Columbia albums are from 1968, a busy year that also saw Brubeck recording his "Oratorio for Today" entitled *The Light in The Wilderness*. This religious piece would be followed in 1969 by another orchestral work, *The Gates of Justice*.

As sacred and politically conscious orchestral compositions, these two albums fell outside the musical interests of most Brubeck fans. Although the releases went largely unnoticed, Brubeck continued his dual career as sacred music composer and jazz band leader. He would unswervingly remain on this diverse musical trek for the rest of his life.

The interview that follows focuses on the religious elements of Brubeck's career, but it should be stressed that Brubeck's social awareness was keen throughout his lifetime. In the liner notes to the 1972 album *Truth Is Fallen*, Brubeck writes, "This music is dedicated to the slain students of Kent State University and Mississippi State, and all other innocent victims caught in the crossfire between repression and rebellion." During the interview, I ask Brubeck about these liner notes and about this album's cover, an unsettling depiction of fallen, blood-stained figures by artist Elizabeth Eddy.

My opportunity to speak with Mr. Brubeck came in May 2009. The interview had been arranged so far in advance that I worried it might be cancelled because of Brubeck's busy schedule. Even at the age of 89, the pianist was still composing, performing, and recording. But true to his word, when I called at the appointed time Dave Brubeck soon joined me on the line.

When the conversation began, I was nervous; Brubeck seemed impatient. The pianist had nothing to prove and certainly did not need to be talking with me. His tone was terse, and his responses to my first questions were almost monosyllabic. But as we talked, his answers became increasingly thorough. Soon he was even thoughtful, frequently pausing before answering. The ellipses in the following interview do not indicate editing or omission; rather, they indicate Brubeck's moments of reflection.

As I began to introduce myself, I wasn't sure Mr. Brubeck was still on the line. I tried asking my first question three different ways before he finally responded. But, it got easier.

Tom Wilmeth:—Have most of the religious compositions that you perform with a jazz group started as long form pieces? Or have you written some of these works as freestanding shorter pieces for the quartet? I know that "Forty Days" and "Sermon on the Mount," for example, are taken from a longer work. Are most of your shorter religious jazz pieces excerpts from much longer works?

Dave Brubeck:—No. But some of them.

TW:—Is there a different type of mindset that you need to place yourself into when composing a religious piece—for example "Three to Get Ready" as opposed to "Forty Days"?

DB:—Well, it's usually the text. "Forty Days" is a wonderful text to set [Mark 1:12-13] and it's a wonderful tune to improvise on. So, it's the kind of thing you can do both with. "Sermon on the Mount" we've also used as a tune to improvise with the quartet. Gerry Mulligan loved that. It was a baritone solo; he loved to play it on his baritone sax.

TW:—"Sermon on the Mount" appears on the *Live in Berlin* album, which you recorded with Mulligan. I notice that at the very beginning of that selection the audience applauds, indicating their familiarity with the piece. Did you find at that time [1970] that your religious material was generally being more widely accepted with European audiences? Or was it accepted on both sides of the Atlantic?

DB:—That is very hard to know. The availability of a piece on record or CD makes it known in other countries, and sometimes a piece will become something that's played a lot, and I won't even know that that's happening until I go to that country and play a concert and people recognize it. Then I'll come to the nice conclusion that somebody has played this a lot on radio or television. We just had the *Mass* performed outside of Paris and therefore if you played that in that part of the world some of the people would have been aware of it.

TW:—Do you always keep an audience in mind? Especially for your religious pieces—Are some of those written as almost meditations or as your personal praise to God?

DB:—Well, that's a hard question to answer because, for instance, when I was asked to write something for the Pope, they gave me a sentence. And it was a situation where the Pope was processing into Candlestick Park and needed nine minutes of music and they gave me this sentence, "Upon this rock I will build my church / And the jaws of hell do not prevail against it" [Matthew 16:18]. So, you write according to what that statement means to you. And what it means to the church. And what it certainly would mean to a Pope.

TW:—Let me shift gears a little bit, if I may. I know that you are a disciple of Duke Ellington, if I may use that word. Do you consider his first major composition—"Black, Brown, and Beige"—to be a religious work of sorts? I ask because I find thematic connections between "Black, Brown, and Beige" and several of the major pieces that you have written.

DB:—Is that with "Come Sunday"?

TW:—Yes.

DB:—I thought always from the time I heard that—I thought that was wonderful.

TW:—When Ellington first performed "Black, Brown, and Beige" at Carnegie Hall in 1943, he introduced it as "a history of the Negro people." The reason I ask you about this Ellington piece is that it seems to echo some of the social concerns that you write about in your albums *The Gates of Justice* [1969] and *Light in the Wilderness* [1968], and also in the early 1970s album *Truth Has Fallen*. It seems that Ellington is combining some religious and political materials, as you do in many of your major pieces. I know that your religious work really predates Duke Ellington's—even his first sacred concert. Were you pleased that he turned to that form in the mid 1960s?

DB:—Good question. How did you know that? Nobody seems to know that.

TW:—[laughs] Well sir, I've tried to do my research. That is correct, isn't it? Your religious compositions were first?

DB:—Yeah!! I talked to Duke about it after I heard his first sacred service—I was there, and I told him I'd been writing things using improvisation and religious texts. And so I know that he wouldn't have influenced me a lot because I hadn't heard any of his sacred stuff until I heard the first one.

TW:—*The Light in the Wilderness* was released in 1968, even though you composed most of the music for the album several years before it was recorded. *The Gates of Justice* came out in 1969. So, your initial religious work predates Duke Ellington's first sacred concert, but, even so, I found the parallel themes and mindsets that you and Ellington were taking very interesting.

DB:—The first thing I wrote, in a religious sense, was after my brother's son died, at age 16. I felt so emotional about what my brother was going through. And I wanted to comfort him, so I wrote my first religious piece, which was "let not your heart be troubled" [John 14:1]. He believed in God. So…that's kind of how that evolved.

TW:—I'm sure that was comforting to him.

DB:—And you know I used that "let not your heart be troubled" passage in *The Light in the Wilderness*. But it started a few years, I would say, *before* the *The Light* composition. And I'll tell you why it happened: This Ernie Farmer, he was the president of Shawnee Press, and his wife Marjorie was maybe vice president—very high-up at Shawnee Press, and a wonderful musician—just one I trusted so much. So when Ernie saw "Let not your heart be troubled," he said, "You have a lot of…" Well, I don't know if he said 'talent,'…but "*feeling* for sacred music. Why don't you write a whole oratorio?" So *The Light in the Wilderness* came out of a whole big thing. But to me it's sacred.

One thing that I really want to stress about those works—My wife Iola has done all my texts, or most of them, if they're not taken from the Bible. She really guided me with the text on *The Light in the Wilderness* to make it be what it is. And the same is true with *The Gates of Justice* and everything else. So I've really got to tell you that she's so important in my sacred music.

TW:—This might be a minor point, but why were those two albums released by Decca Records? Did you try to interest Columbia in those works at the time?

DB:—Fortunately, Israel Horowitz of Decca was a very sympathetic person. He and The Cincinnati Symphony recorded together. And Eric Kunzel had come to my house wanting me to do his first Pops Concert, and he saw all this music on my piano and started looking through it and said, "Dave—if you finish this I want to do it with the Cincinnati Symphony." And he was recording a lot with Decca, and I think that's how it all happened.

The same thing happened almost at the same time while I was writing *The Light in the Wilderness*. And I went to… there was a concert I gave near The National Cathedral at a private school. There was a school there where we played, and after the concert the organist—a big tall man—came to me and said how much he enjoyed the improvisation. And he said, "Would you like to hear me improvise?" And I said, "Sure." I didn't know he was going to go over and open the cathedral! His name was Richard Dirksen. Fantastic composer, organist, choir director, everything.

And he sits down at the organ. So when I heard him improvise I was so thrilled because here I am alone with this giant of a man—about 6' 6"—tearing up the organ, and the organ booming! In the Cathedral! And we're alone! The place is dark except for this light near the keyboard. So he says, "You know, you should write some sacred music." So I said, "Well that's strange [laughs]; I've just started to write some." And he questioned me about it, and said, "Well, bring it by tomorrow. I'd love to see it." So I showed it to him. And he said, "Dave, you've got a long way to go, but you've got some wonderful material to work with here. And he'd gone over the themes. He said, "When you finish it, I'll do it here at the Cathedral."

That was made into a great TV show, with Dirksen and members of The National Symphony and The Cathedral Choir and this fantastic baritone soloist. Have you heard of Bill Justice? Well, when Kunzel interviewed who he wanted for soloists—out of all the guys in New York City that were considered great—he picked Bill Justice as the greatest. And I'll tell you—you can't believe how powerful he was!

TW:—Are you still actively composing and recording religious works?

DB:—Yes. I've got a lot of new things coming out. The Pacific Mozart Chorale in Berkeley, California, is doing a CD of my sacred music. Things like "The Commandments," and the credo that Mozart left out. They asked me to write that, along with three other American composers—to fill in the sections that Mozart left out! That's a scary thing.

TW:—[laughs] That's quite an opportunity, but frightening as well.

DB:—Very frightening.

TW:—I'll look forward to that. This next question jumps back a bit. As I look at your two albums from the early 1970s, *Truth has Fallen* [1972], and then *Brother, The Great Spirit Made Us All* [1974]. Based on the albums' art work, it seems that you went through a great change between the two releases. *Truth Has Fallen* has album artwork which seems very...pessimistic. And I know that era was a tough time for the country. But between the cover art for *Truth Has Fallen* and your liner notes, and the music itself—it is a pretty unsettling affair. And then within two years, *Brother, The Great Spirit Made Us All* seems far more upbeat. Am I reading too much into this?

DB:—I don't know. It's interesting what you say. [pause] What Chief Seattle says in that speech should have been taken seriously by all the most intelligent people in the United States, when he said the President in Washington sends word that we must sell him our land. If we sell you our land, will you teach your children what we have taught our children: To respect the trees, the streams, the sky, the animals." Now THAT's religion!

TW:—That's right out of The Book of Revelation: "Harm not the Earth" [7:3]. Let me read you a quote from *Truth Has Fallen*. And again, this is from some years back, but you conclude the liner notes by saying:

"Freedom of choice is narrowing so quickly that I sometimes feel that the sane heads, trying to solve real problems in a real way, have all been pushed on to a small island in a stormy sea of violence."

Those album notes are from 40 years ago, but do you think we are returning to a sea of violence? Have we ever emerged from this era?

DB:—Hm…Sea of violence. [long pause] You know I lived through World War II. In Europe. In Patton's army. And that gives a young person—I was in my twenties—a different view of the world. Most people don't realize that 60 million people were killed. Did you know that?

TW:—I did not know that number; no.

DB:—That includes the Russians; and all of Europe; and the Italians; the Europeans in general. And also in those notes [to *Truth Has Fallen*] it said something about, here are all these soldiers that basically—their religious beliefs goes with The Ten Commandments—"Thou Shall Not Kill" being one of them. And it's a completely puzzling thing. And what we're going through now is that kind of disregard for basic religion and the basic religion of Catholicism, and [long pause]… You know Abraham…in the Muslim religion—"We must obey the laws of Moses," is part of it. Can you imagine that? How strongly we are all related? Yet we're out there killing each other. So, I don't think it's any worse today.

TW:—My father flew Corsair airplanes for the Navy in the war, and he only recently has started to talk about his experiences. I purchased your recent solo piano recording, *Private Brubeck Remembers*, for him. That's a fine CD.

DB:—Thank you.

TW:—Concerning jazz with sacred themes, do you know Wynton Marsalis' extended religious piece called *In This House, On This Morning*?

DB:—Not Yet. But what I know of Wynton—he's very deep and very sacred.

TW:—A couple of nonreligious questions, if that's OK: You were and are so associated with time signature experimentation. Can I ask what you thought about The Don Ellis Orchestra, and what Ellis would do with time signatures? I'm especially thinking of Don Ellis' use of unusual time signatures on his albums *Live at the Fillmore* [1970] and *Electric Bath* [1967].

DB:—He wrote to me, thanking me for opening these possibilities.

TW:—Don Ellis was standing on your shoulders, I believe.

DB:—That's what he thought.

TW:—I was lucky enough to see him several times in the early 1970s.

DB:—He had two drummers?

TW:—Yes. And Ellis himself also would get onto drums for a while. It was a large orchestra. I grew up in Des Moines, Iowa, but that band came through a couple of times.

DB:—Yeah. Well, I thought they were great, and he was a fantastic musician.

TW:—This is out of left field, but I was listening to a very early record on the Crown label. An entire side of it is a tune called "At the Perfume Counter."

DB:—Oh yeah! [laughs] One side of an old LP.

TW:—But that tune must have had been dropped from your repertoire even by the time you started recording for Fantasy. A very early selection—am I correct about that?

DB:—That's right. I think that recording is from a date at the University of California in Berkeley. It's an old standard.

TW:—Speaking of record labels: Are you satisfied with the way that Columbia is treating your back catalog?

DB:—Currently, yes. [pause] Now, you asked why *The Light in the Wilderness* didn't go on Columbia. The president of Columbia saw me at Columbia headquarters and said, "Dave! Why are you going to Decca with your new work?" I said, "Because Columbia wouldn't take it." He said, "This is a shame. After all the money you have made for this company, and they won't sponsor something as important as what you're trying to do now." He said, "I'm really embarrassed." He was later moved from president of Columbia Records up to president of CBS.

TW:—Was that Goddard Lieberson?

DB:—Goddard. You see, that was a surprise to him. And if there was any justice in the world, Columbia should have put it out. But I'm so thankful that Decca put it out.

TW:—Yes. And it's a good recording!

DB:—It's great! Israel Horowitz—engineering…thinking…

TW:—I have nice clean pressings of both of those Decca releases. After your years with Columbia, when you went to Atlantic Records, I thought the album *All the Things You Are* was very much a high water mark. That includes the lengthy Jimmy Van Heusen medley, and there are some sax players on that record that were kind of a surprise. Isn't Anthony Braxton on there?

DB:—Braxton, who has always been a champion of me. Lee Konitz, and …

TW:—And Jack Six is still with you there.

DB:—And the percussionist Roy Hanes, who I always identify with Chick Corea. I just saw Roy; just talked to him. He said, "Thank you, Dave, for "In Your Own Sweet Way." And for a while, I opened every one of my concerts with that.

TW:—Yes; wonderful record. And that leads me back to labels: Are you pleased with the way that Fantasy is reissuing your CDs with a lot of previously unreleased bonus selections? I'm thinking of *Live at Oberlin*, especially.

DB:—Well, one of my favorite albums is that live concert at Oberlin.

TW:—I have that on red vinyl.

DB:—Yeah. And I think that was Paul Desmond at his best.

TW:—I'm so glad to hear you say that. It has been always one of my favorites. That entire album is just…smokin' from start to finish! He's just burning through chorus after chorus.

DB:—Yep. And Paul loved it.

TW:—I'll let you go here in a second, but I wanted to tell you that my son is a senior in high school, and he has performed the "Sun Up" section of your *Reminisces of the Cattle Country*. I was taking him to school today and I asked him if there was anything he wanted me to say to you. He said to tell Mr. Brubeck that in the "Sun Up" section, some of those finger stretches are really wide. And my son has large hands!

DB:—[laughs] Yeah, tell him that I have a pretty big stretch there, and I shouldn't write it like that because so many people have trouble with those 11$^{ths.}$ You tell him that I appreciate him playing that.

TW:—I saw a brief interview where President Clinton said that you gave him the original score of "Blue Rondo a la Turk." Does that sound right?

DB:—Yeah. He had it in the entrance to the Oval Office in Washington.

TW:—I've heard him interviewed since leaving office and he clearly enjoys and knows his jazz.

DB:—When I first met him he complimented me for "Blue Rondo." And then he said, "You know—I know every note of it." And he starts singing it—and when he got to the bridge [sings: bom bom bom…]. He said, "Even that part." [laughs]

TW:—[laughs] I like that. Let me ask you one last question: In Duke Ellington's autobiography *Music Is My Mistress*, the interviewer asks Duke, "Aside from God, what is the most important thing in your life?" And Duke rejects the premise, and says that "without God there is nothing." Does Duke Ellington speak for you on that one?

DB:—Well, there's another place in the Bible: "Without *Love* I am nothing." And I've set that to music.

TW:—Very good. Well, Mr. Brubeck, I want to thank you for your time and I want to thank you so much for your music.

DB:—I want to thank you for having so much great knowledge of both jazz and sacred music.

Post Script

This interview grew out of an article I had undertaken on the topic of religion in jazz. Although I did not then know the depth of Brubeck's sacred canon, I did recall that there were some tunes scattered through his jazz albums that had biblical overtones. It wasn't until my two children started to investigate my record collection that this project really took shape. As I would discuss the importance of various musicians with them, I more clearly saw the connections between Brubeck and sacred music.

It was then that I began to consider how I might contact Dave Brubeck, in hopes of speaking with him about this arguably overlooked part of his career. So I must thank my son and daughter for indirectly leading me back not only to Brubeck's many fine albums but also for instigating the interview. I also want to thank George Moore of Mr. Brubeck's organization for arranging this telephone interview.

I sent Mr. Brubeck a copy of this interview and a recording of my son performing the "Sun Up" section of his *Reminisces of the Cattle Country* (1946). Brubeck wrote back to my son, thanking him for his interest in his music. George Moore later contacted me, saying that Dave had enjoyed the phone call.

As with most interviews, there were things I later wished had been asked and areas that could have used some clarification or expansion. Still, I was satisfied that I had not wasted the man's time and was happy that he provided thoughtful responses to questions that he had not heard a thousand times before.

I close by stressing that, although the pianist is gone, his music should be heard. What follows is a list of starting places.

Selected Discography of Dave Brubeck's Sacred & Orchestral Music, and of his jazz recordings mentioned in this interview:

Jazz at Oberlin. The Dave Brubeck Quartet. Fantasy Records (1953)
Jazz Goes to College. The Dave Brubeck Quartet. Columbia Records (1954)
Time Out. The Dave Brubeck Quartet. Columbia Records (1959)
At Carnegie Hall. The Dave Brubeck Quartet. Columbia Records (1963)

Greatest Hits. The Dave Brubeck Quartet. Columbia Records (1966)

The Light in the Wilderness. Dave Brubeck. Decca Records (1968)

The Gates of Justice. Dave Brubeck. Decca Records (1969)

Truth is Fallen. Dave Brubeck. Atlantic Records (1972)

"Brother, the Great Spirit Made Us All." Two Generations of Brubeck. Atlantic (1974)

All the Things We Are. Dave Brubeck. Atlantic Records (1976; recorded 1973-74)

The Festival of the Inn: A Christmas Choral Pageant. Dave Brubeck. CBS Masterworks (1980)

Time Signatures: A Career Retrospective. Dave Brubeck. Columbia Records (1992)

To Hope! A Celebration. The Dave Brubeck Quartet. Telarc Records (1996)

Brubeck in Chattanooga. Dave Brubeck. Choral Arts Society of Chattanooga (2002)

Classical Brubeck. Dave Brubeck; London Symphony Orchestra. Telarc Records (2003)

Private Brubeck Remembers. Dave Brubeck (solo piano). Telarc Records (2004)

Brubeck Meets Bach. The Dave Brubeck Quartet. Sony Classical (2007)

I asked for this record player for my 8th birthday, in 1963. It played albums, singles, and my dad's 78s. The Beatles had not yet arrived, but I was ready!

Skip ahead a few years, and I am relaxing with part of my album collection.

Left to right: Leigh Kamman, Mitch Miller, Tom Wilmeth; St. Paul, ca. 1982

College Radio Days. Bob and me doing a late night shift.
Cedar Falls, Iowa, ca. 1976

Grafton, Wisconsin, has embraced its past involvement with the
Paramount Records label. And we have the sign to prove it.
Photo by K. Koehlinger.

I was giving a presentation in the KUNI radio station studios in about 1977. This was my concept of getting dressed-up. It is fortunate that I worked in the non-visual medium of radio.

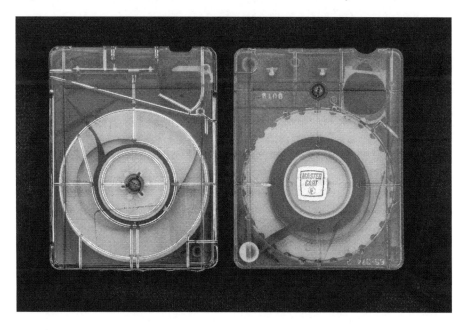

The mystery of 8-track technology—revealed!
Photo by K. Koehlinger.

My original record player from 1963 spawned interest in numerous other formats including cassettes, 8-tracks, and reel-to-reel tapes. I still embrace them all.

COUNTRY

*"You really can't sing country music unless you've spent
a good deal of time looking at the backside of a mule."*

—Hank Williams

CD Review

Eddy Arnold
The Tennessee Plowboy and His Guitar
Bear Family Records, 1998

Eddy Arnold is the most successful performer ever to appear on *Billboard Magazine*'s Top Country Singles chart. His sustained dominance included 43 Top 10 hits from 1945 to 1951. The placement of Arnold at the very top of *Billboard*'s list of chart performers surprises even most old-time country music fans, but their reaction is understandable. Prior to the release of this five-CD box from Germany's Bear Family label, it was nearly impossible to locate most of the man's numerous hits from these early, stone country days.

One forgets that Arnold had a firm grip on radio play and record sales during the seven years covered by this box. Once he switched from being the self-proclaimed "Tennessee Plowboy" to a pop chart crooner, Arnold appeared eager to put his previous pure country image (and these recordings) far behind him. Much of his RCA Victor catalog has been long out of print, at his behest.

Like his onetime manager Colonel Tom Parker, Eddy Arnold has been acknowledged as a powerful defender of his own business interests. In fact, Arnold is the only artist with enough clout to block the Bear Family label from releasing music, albeit temporarily. The singer reportedly thought that many of the recordings featured in this box set were embarrassingly weepy and maudlin.

There is plenty of emoting here, true, but this is an inseparable part of the style. When Arnold pleads, "Mommy Please Stay Home with Me," the urgency seems immediate, even after 50 years; "My Daddy Is Only a Picture" delivers the wrenching lament that the title promises. Arnold need not be embarrassed by these songs. Some say that it was exactly this type of unflinching sincerity that caused the famed record producer Fred Rose to remain permanently in Nashville.

Arnold's fine voice retains its country edge throughout these 115 recordings, heard here with sparse backing and a lone fiddle instead of the lush violin section found on his later hits. The singer says he will soon record an album called *Arnold at 80*. New material from a veteran like Eddy Arnold is something to look forward to, but the man's best release in decades comes in this straight look backwards.

CD Review

Wilf Carter (Montana Slim)
Cowboy Songs
Bear Family Records, 1999

Let us now praise consistency. Bear Family's latest collection of recordings by Wilf Carter (popularly known as Montana Slim) demonstrates how the style of this cowboy singer from Nova Scotia remained absolutely unchanged throughout his life. The eight-CD set chronicles sessions from December 1933 through late 1941, with the first song stylistically identical to the last. Part of Carter's gift was his ability to make these similar songs interesting and not seem repetitive.

Given the pervasiveness of yodels found here, the title of Carter's own song "The Yodeling Trailrider" might have proven a more accurate moniker for this performer than Montana Slim. Despite his penchant for yodeling, Wilf Carter never appeared to be influenced by Jimmie Rodgers in the same manner as Rodgers' more famous disciples from this era. The relaxed yodels of Rodgers convey the depth of life's joys and disappointments; Carter's intensive double time flourishes sound as if he is calling stray sheep on the slopes of the Appalachian Mountains.

In his own time, and today, Carter's career was diminished by the glare of brighter lights surrounding him, many of whom also began their careers with yodels. Fellow Canadian Hank Snow billed himself as The Yodeling Ranger until a friend pointed out that he had never once heard Snow yodel. Ernest Tubb featured Rodgers-styled yodels in his early appearances until a tonsillectomy literally cut these from Tubb's repertoire. Unlike Wilf Carter, Tubb and Snow spent much of the 1930s consciously emulating Rodgers. But if seemingly immune to Rodgers' style, Carter's own music would, in turn, have a limited influence upon fellow singers. In spite of an unusually long career (he died in December 1996 at age 91), Carter is the type of artist who could easily slip through the cracks of country music's collective memory.

An insular performer, Carter composed the majority of his own large catalog, consisting of valid if similar songs. Frequently criticized for this, he held to this sameness of style intentionally; the man knew who he was. He identified himself not only through his music but also in his 1961 autobiography, *The Yodeling Cowboy: Montana Slim from Nova Scotia*—the complete text of which is reproduced in this Bear Family collection. In the autobiography, as on every track of these eight CDs, Carter will tell you himself: here was a proud singer of cowboy songs, always offering the best he had. He reveled in presenting straightforward stories of the trail, especially when they were set in his beloved Canada.

Wilf Carter never tried to be anything but what he was, and he always sang from the heart. Who could find fault with that?

Book Review

Ernest Tubb: The Texas Troubadour
By Ronnie Pugh
Duke University Press, 1996

Ernest Tubb's career in country music ran from the mid-1930s until his death in 1984. In his biography of Tubb, Ronnie Pugh expresses awe over his subject's ability to hold a loyal audience for nearly fifty years. Pugh offers a detailed history of Tubb the performer—from his early patronage by the widow of Jimmie Rodgers to Tubb's own promotional crusades for unknown country performers who would become legends, including Hank Williams and Johnny Cash.

Musical changes of vast proportion constantly swirl around Tubb. Pugh shows him weathering everything from rock and roll to the Nashville Sound and the Outlaw Movement. Like the eye of a hurricane, Tubb held constant, playing his own brand of country music—no matter what was popular at a given moment or how his stylistic boundaries may have hindered him financially.

Pugh is a huge fan, but he does not try to sugarcoat Tubb's weaknesses or excuse his shortcomings, which included struggles with personal relationships and alcohol. While Tubb's life is documented here, the book centers mostly on his music. From distinctive single-string electric guitar backing to confounding vocal mannerisms, Pugh keeps a tight focus on Tubb the musician and the various incarnations of his group, The Texas Troubadours. We learn that it was Ernest Tubb who helped revive a stagnating Grand Ole Opry and suggested a name change for the form, from Hillbilly to Country. Tubb tirelessly promoted and polished the image of the genre that he simultaneously kept true to its roots.

In Pugh's biography, the reader can hear the changing voice of country music from the mid 1930s to the early 1980s. And for that half century one also hears the unique voice of Ernest Tubb. Try to think of others who have stayed in the game as long, remaining so unashamedly true to their art. It's a short list.

Book Review

The Handbook of Texas Music
By Roy Barkley
Texas State Historical Association, 2004

It's an often-asked question: How is it possible that so much great music has been created within the borders of a single state? Some reply that it's simply the state's vast size which gives Texas more than its share of important musicians. But if size alone were the determining factor, it would take most of the territory west of the Mississippi River to match what Texas alone has contributed to American music.

David Byrne once questioned Lyle Lovett about this abundance of Texas talent. Byrne was only half joking when he asked, "Something in the water down there?" While the new *Handbook of Texas Music* does not try to answer Bryne's question, it does an outstanding job of describing the varied musical landscapes of Texas that make the subject worth pondering.

This *Handbook* will appeal to all devotees of music. It is set apart from other works on similar topics by two distinctions. One is a comprehensive goal: it addresses an unexpectedly wide variety of styles, including Texas' important role in the world of classical music, with particular attention given to the San Antonio Symphony and to pianist Van Cliburn. Essays on trumpeter Harry James in the Big Band era of the 1940s, and Arnett Cobb's place within Texas' famous tenor saxophone tradition, describe the state's rich jazz heritage.

The *Handbook* is also uniquely appealing for the use it makes of well chosen photographs and reproductions of documents. An ad from the early 1970s for Austin record shop The Inner Sanctum boasts artwork rivaling posters from the days of San Francisco's famous Fillmore Auditorium. Another, sadder historical document shows an ad for the final show at Austin's Armadillo World Headquarters. Music publications and advertisements for specific records are also impressive, including an 1858 sheet music cover for "The Yellow Rose of Texas." One such artifact will be of particular interest to Milwaukee readers: a mail order ad for Blind Lemon Jefferson's 78 rpm record "Worried Blues," available from "The Popular Race Record" company, Grafton's own Paramount label.

Editor Roy Barkley has chosen to focus the *Handbook*'s coverage on deceased artists; many well-known performers from previous generations are represented, including Ernest Tubb, Buddy Holly, and Bob Wills. But with the wealth of information already available on these famous artists, such obligatory entries are not among the book's highlights. Instead, this work is especially valuable for its entries on lesser-known Texan musicians, such as Tejana singer Chelo Silva and songwriter Oscar J. Fox.

The Handbook of Texas Music is an extremely useful research tool, but general readers interested in music and musicians from Texas will also find it rewarding. Anybody appreciating the Texas tradition and its influence should read the *Handbook* from beginning to end. The individual stories told here complement one another to form a unified narrative. Together, they offer an impressive account of Texas' influence on American Music.

Book Review

Lefty Frizzell:
The Honky Tonk Life of Country Music's Greatest Singer
By Daniel Cooper
Little Brown, 1995

Influence is a tricky thing to quantify. Style is not much easier. In the first major biography of one of country music's most important figures, author Daniel Cooper does a good job of demonstrating both as he traces the lasting importance of Lefty Frizzell.

When choosing to discuss an underappreciated artist, many biographers fall into the trap of writing their book as a valentine to the subject. Cooper clearly loves Frizzell, but he avoids taking a soft-focus approach. He also avoids writing an indignant cry for recognition. Instead, this is a well-balanced account of Frizzell's amazing musical achievements and of the long, sad road to obscurity that the singer lived to witness.

Frizzell's unprecedented success paralleled Hank Williams' brief career in the early 1950s. And, as Cooper suggests, had Lefty followed Hank's lead and died young, his records might be better known today. Instead, Frizzell became a living monument: highly respected, but rarely heard by those who did not personally experience his golden era. His decline, as Cooper documents, was brought about partly by the singer's odd habits and poor career choices. By the 1960s, Frizzell routinely found himself trying to remind his dwindling audience of his phenomenal past.

As the New Traditionalist movement took hold in country music in the 1980s, numerous performers influenced by Frizzell could be heard singing his songs on the radio. These sincere acolytes included Dwight Yoakam, who had a big record with a remake of Lefty's hit "Always Late (with your kisses)." Willie Nelson had a memorable version of "If You've Got the Money, I've Got the Time," and George Strait recorded a tribute, "Lefty's Gone." These songs are all far better known by today's country radio audience than any of Frizzell's own recordings, which are rarely played. And yet, as Cooper correctly points out, it is impossible to listen to any country music station for more than ten minutes without hearing some direct Lefty Frizzell influence. This assessment is made by the biographer not as a complaint, but as a point of pride concerning his subject.

Following the death of musical prodigy Jaco Pastorius, jazz guitarist Pat Metheny stated that every electric bass player on earth owed copyright royalties to Pastorius, but there was no way to collect for an imitated style. Much the same can be said about Frizzell. Listen to Randy Travis, Strait, Dwight, and especially to Merle Haggard. They will be the first to tell you that it was Lefty who opened their ears to new possibilities, and it's Lefty's sound they've been emulating ever since. The new book by Cooper helps to show Frizzell's importance in his own day and to today's country sound. But perhaps the author's greatest achievement is the book's ability to make the reader want to search out and hear Lefty Frizzell's recordings firsthand.

Book Review

My House of Memories
By Merle Haggard with Tom Carter
Cliff Street Books, 2002

Merle's hit song insists that "Mama Tried," but her son should have tried harder on this book. Anyone reading *My House of Memories* to discover insights into Haggard's songs or specific music qualities will surely be disappointed. The first half of the book focuses on the singer's days as a juvenile delinquent, finally landing him in San Quentin State Prison. The escapades that led to this incarceration make for sometimes interesting, if repetitious reading.

Much like a false start at a recording session, this book has numerous instances of aborted tales and often pointless buildups with little or no payoff. The few individuals Haggard discusses in any depth also prove to be odd choices. He lavishly praises his longtime guitarist Roy Nichols, for example, and then details the night when Nichols got drunk and tarnished an important show for Haggard at the Hollywood Bowl.

Haggard does present a handful of music-related stories (there should be many more), one of them a vignette taking place at Milwaukee's County Stadium. Haggard was playing bass for Buck Owens at this 1964 show when Owens broke a guitar string. Buck told Merle to sing something while he fixed it. Haggard sang the current hit "He Stopped Loving Her Today." When Haggard received an ovation that bested anything the audience had given to Buck, friction erupted between the star and his sideman.

Although Haggard apparently doesn't mind, the book's halfhearted accounts of random incidents seem like a disservice to Merle, his music, and his fans. The last third of the book is especially fragmented, reading like an oral narrative untouched by an editor. Merle should have taken a cue from the comprehensive and informative autobiography of one of his favorite country performers, Hank Snow. Snow's book, like Miles Davis' autobiography, gives his life story and his music the effort that both deserve.

The subtitle of this book is "For the Record." Maybe. But it actually adds little to the existing information we have about this great artist. Haggard clearly believes it to be worthy of posterity, but fans who have genuine interest would do better to skip this written account and turn directly to the music.

At the conclusion of *My House of Memories*, Haggard talks about finding a handwritten account of his mother's life. It includes descriptions of battles against Native Americans, how she survived malaria, her travels in covered wagons, and seeing the unsettled Oklahoma territory. If Merle wants to write a compelling story, his mother's autobiography would be an excellent place to start.

Commentary
American Masters: Merle Haggard
Public Television
July 2010

I think the folks at PBS should slow down a bit on the *American Masters* series. Their work is getting sloppy. The latest entry of this Public Television program was dedicated to the great country music artist Merle Haggard. But instead of a presenting a biography, the show felt more like a hagiography. And a saint he ain't, as Haggard would be the first to tell you. The opening hour was an acceptable if not outstanding portrait of the artist as a troubled young man. But the later segments made one believe that country music will be doomed without Merle's leadership. Well shit. Haggard himself wouldn't tell you that, even at his crankiest.

Many talking heads filled the screen with praise, but curiously missing was Willie Nelson. Also absent was the great footage of Johnny Cash indicating to his television audience that Merle had served hard time in prison. These omissions smacked of the country music community's limited involvement on this project and of a hastily assembled program. Merle Haggard truly deserves the title of an "American Master," but I saw nothing in this 90-minute program that would convince the uninitiated to become familiar with the man's work. And that's a shame. Merle deserves better than the empty accolades found here.

Post Script

Merle Haggard is one of many important musicians we lost in 2016. Is it too soon to suggest that the movie industry turn its attention to making a film biography of this man? Haggard's story is compelling drama, and the movie soundtrack would be a no-brainer.

Book Review

Willie Nelson: An Epic Life
By Joe Nick Patoski
Little, Brown, 2008

In *An Epic Life*, Joe Nick Patoski sketches a portrait of Willie Nelson, drawing on the 35 years he has spent covering his subject. He does an especially good job with the early era, describing Nelson's difficulty breaking onto the music scene. Unfortunately, as the account moves to later years, the book often reads as if the journalist has merely stitched together his own newspaper articles. Repetitious information and unclear time frames frequently hinder the narrative. Patoski does offer a more thorough portrait of the artist than Nelson's own slight autobiographical account from 1988. However, in spite of its 500 pages, *An Epic Life* is not consistently successful at recounting Nelson's lengthy career with the depth it deserves.

Book Review

I Lived to Tell It All
By George Jones with Tom Carter
Villard Books, 1996

Most celebrity autobiographies today fall into one of two camps. The first consists of published therapy sessions. In these accounts, subjects strive to get in touch with their feelings while recounting past achievements and exploits. The second type is a self-congratulatory version of life, offering a heartwarming rags-to-riches story. In these tales, authors stress their entitlement to the great wealth and accolades they have achieved. George Jones' book has a little of each.

What saves *I Lived to Tell It All* from becoming yet another prose confessional is that, in addition to the sensational aspects associated with the career of Jones, the man himself occasionally peeks out from behind this official account. During these infrequent sections of candor, Jones demonstrates that he knows country music for the business it is. He also shows the enthusiasm that goes along with being one of the genre's most devoted fans and sharpest critics.

When Jones cites the blandness of today's country music songwriting, for example, he could easily start to sound like an old man lamenting the way things used to be. But Jones backs up his views with specifics. He makes a good argument concerning the lack of staying power of a lot of today's country hits by pointing out that no performers of today are bothering to record their own versions of even the biggest hits from only a few years ago. This, Jones maintains, is because so few songs of the modern country era are the least bit memorable.

Although *I Lived to Tell It All* is written for Jones' established fans, the book also connects with a wider audience when it shows glimpses of a young boy growing up on a cotton farm during the Great Depression. These sections manage to transcend the book's specific focus and country music itself. One memorable portrait drawn here is of Jones' Uncle Dub, with whom young George spent several formative summers in Texas. In tales of runaway mules and the family's well water ruined by spoiled milk, Jones captures in print what comes so naturally to him vocally—the ability to connect with his audience. His music, and the best parts of this book, convey a sense that he has been through the rough times he sings about, and he is now simply telling the audience what they already know to be true.

"Kiss and Tell" books are nothing new with celebrity autobiographies, and certainly there is more than enough of that juicy element here. Interchangeable tales of drunkenness become outright boring by the middle of the book. The blame for some of the work's redundant nature must fall to co-writer Tom Carter. Jones makes it clear from the outset that this book will contain nothing but his own memories, if even they contradict stories related by others. Still, Carter could have sharpened some of Jones' narrative without losing any real content.

A frustrated Roy Acuff supposedly once told Hank Williams: "You've got a million dollar voice and a ten cent brain." Perhaps some of Hank's natural vocal talent soaked into the awe-struck 14-year-old Jones when their paths briefly crossed during a radio broadcast. *I Lived to Tell It All* reminds the reader that, like Williams, Jones has a perfect voice for country music. Also like Hank Williams, George Jones could sometimes be the greatest detriment to his own career.

Book Review

Patsy
By Margaret Jones
HarperPerennial Books, 1995

Patsy Cline was an immensely talented singer who enjoyed her greatest success near the end of a brief career. During her life, she never found respect and admiration as great as the acclaim that followed and continues to increase, decades after her death.

In this recent biography, Margaret Jones does a good job of differentiating the legend that surrounds Cline from the often unglamorous reality of this country performer's life. And while the author occasionally falls into brief sections of psychobabble about Cline's motivations and youthful experiences, Jones is usually clear in her assessment of the singer's talents and the music arena where she competed for audiences and for quality songs.

Most refreshing here is that the book allows Cline to be human. She was not especially beautiful or ladylike, as the author lets too many sources recall. Yet while Jones does not idealize Cline, neither does she dwell on lurid or sleazy elements. Instead, *Patsy* focuses on Cline's life and career struggles in the era of country music from which she emerged. Jones does refer to her subject as a female pioneer in country music, but she wisely avoids the revisionist theory of Cline as a rejected genius solely because of her gender.

Among Jones' best sections are her descriptions of the record industry. The economics of songwriting and the battles over royalties are recounted in detail. Some biographers of popular entertainers avoid discussing the business end of the industry, but Jones shows how context and connections make a difference within the financially lucrative field of songwriting. By describing these and other elements as they affect this singer, Jones adds depth to her examination of Cline's career.

Jones also explores a geographic region that is not often studied: the nightclubs played by country music artists in Washington, D.C., during the 1950s. Cline is seen struggling in these clubs before moving to Tennessee and breaking into the Grand Ole Opry. The author also does a good job of portraying Nashville's studio scene in the late 1950s and early 1960s. Especially welcome is Jones' willingness to credit specific musicians involved with various Patsy Cline projects, in the studio and on the bandstand.

The book does contain a few slow sections. Jones could have done a better job of weeding out redundancy in the comments of her parade of sources. Many, many former colleagues tell of Patsy being "one of the guys," and how she would speak her mind without caring what anyone thought about it. While convincing, this repetition slows Jones' narrative and weakens her best prose. And while she does not dwell on Cline's death in a small plane that crashed, Jones finds weighty significance in numerous alleged premonitions and events leading to the wreck.

In spite of a few frustrating shortcomings, *Patsy* presents an interesting, well-rounded picture of this performer, now usually placed among country music's elite.

Book Review

Finding Her Voice:
The Illustrated History of Women in Country Music
By Mary A. Bufwack and Robert K. Oermann
Owl Books, 1995

Here is a stunningly comprehensive single volume on women in country music. It will please the most knowledgeable country aficionado; it may also help newly converted fans expand their tight focus on Reba and Wynona to a more well-rounded historical perspective. *Finding Her Voice* shows the debt that today's female performers owe their musical sisters of the past century.

Many music historians place the beginnings of country music at the Bristol, Tennessee, sessions of 1927. This is where Ralph Peer first recorded both Jimmie Rodgers and The Carter Family in a makeshift studio located in a hotel room during the southern summer heat. But authors Mary A. Bufwack and Robert K. Oermann pinpoint numerous important female singers of country music *before* these famous Bristol sessions, often shedding new light onto the unrecorded and underdocumented. In fact, the authors begin their chronology prior to 1900. They offer sixty fascinating pages on largely forgotten performers, all of whom helped prepare a primarily rural audience for the arrival of the hugely successful Carter Family.

Part of this volume's value is its evenhandedness in giving the same painstaking treatment to each era of country music. From Patsy Montana and Kitty Wells to Alison Krause and Pam Tillis, the work argues convincingly (and calmly) for the recognition of women. Among the numerous elements discussed here is the authors' carefully traced development of the female point of view on country records. The attitude clearly changes from that of a singer who is merely reacting to men, as in the Carter's lament "Single Girl, Married Girl," to the stance of strong will and independence, exemplified by Loretta Lynn with songs like "The Pill" and "Don't Come Home a-Drinkin' (with lovin' on your mind)." No longer do these women long only to be a "Cowboy's Sweetheart."

One can't help but feel the genuine pride of Bufwack and Oermann concerning country music as they offer an encyclopedic tour through this often-neglected subject matter. It is hard to imagine a work more extensive and specific than what they provide. In fact, there is so much information in the book that even its margins have been packed with song titles, performer lists, and statistics about various aspects of women in country music. And while meticulously researched and carefully presented, the greatest asset of *Finding Her Voice*—its completeness—also becomes its greatest hindrance to readability. This book is not so much a narrative as it is an instructional guide, fleshed out with interesting stories and wonderful photographs.

Bufwack and Oermann should be congratulated for their first-rate scholarship. The authors have been at work on the book since 1978 and, judging by the depth of material enclosed on these 594 pages, they were at their task all day every day. The country fans who buy this book will read the text thoroughly once, but they will keep it permanently in their collection for its true value—as an excellent reference volume.

Book Review

All Over the Map: True Heroes of Texas Music
By Michael Corcoran
University of Texas Press, 2005

Not another book about Texas musicians! Hell, yes! And the subject absolutely warrants it. In *All Over the Map: True Heroes of Texas Music*, Michael Corcoran writes about important (or at least interesting) musicians from the past, as he strives to rescue them from obscurity. Given this goal, it is surprising to find such names as Sly Stone and T. Bone Walker included here, and others who seem in no danger of being forgotten. Yet the author repeatedly makes the case that although T. Bone Walker's name is well known, few realize his importance to the development of the electric guitar. Corcoran finds a similar rationale for listing Ernest Tubb, Freddie King, and the genre-defying Doug Sahm. Even so, the book's main focus is on musicians who checked out years ago, such as the largely forgotten Washington Phillips and Rebert Harris.

Like other authors who aim to bring aspects of music's past back to life—Nick Tosches comes to mind, with his *Unsung Heroes of Rock*

& *Roll*—Corcoran educates while he documents his subject matter. His engaging style, perhaps developed while a newspaper columnist, enables him to present information clearly and concisely. In fact, most of the book is an assortment of Corocan's newspaper columns, drawn together into a unified whole. He has been able to omit the repetition that often mars such cobbled-together collections. The brief vignettes, usually shorter than five pages, come together for a fast and furious but sufficiently detailed journey through the musical geography of Texas. While the trip is a whirlwind of sorts, the book is not merely a windshield tour; it shows surprising depth, allowing the reader to meet these Texans on their own turf.

En route, Corcoran occasionally lets the readers stretch their legs—in the Houston section, for example, he writes a fine history of the region's late 1990s "screwed and chopped" music, only now gaining a national buzz. And during a stopover in Waco, readers will find an informative lesson on lucrative music copyrights. There, supporters of Blind Willie Johnson, a man now largely forgotten, are busy trying to ensure that publishing royalties get properly paid to Johnson's daughter. The lesson also includes information showing that Eric Clapton is "a gentleman" about paying for the old blues he has used through the years, while other famous artists must be taken to court to extract such overdue payments.

Because *All Over the Map* is organized by region, a reader interested in Austin, for example, could easily turn to the section on the Austin scene to learn about its background and a handful of its neglected founders. (The book ends with an essay lamenting many of Austin's now closed haunts and the great music once heard there.) Or one could read about Dallas and get to know Ella Mae Morse, a white singer whose black sound had an impact on the young Elvis, and who gave Capitol Records its first #1 chart hit. San Antonio is represented here, as is the huge area known as West Texas. Each area appears to be unique, producing distinctly different musicians and stories.

Commentary
Livin', Lovin', Losin': Songs of The Louvin Brothers
Various Artists Tribute CD
Universal South Records, 2003

This collection was awarded the 2003 Grammy Award for "Best Country Album of the Year" and the Grammy in the "Best Country Collaboration with Vocals" category for James Taylor and Alison Krauss' "How's the World Treating You?" In addition, the CD contains one of the final recordings made by Johnny Cash.

The music of The Louvin Brothers continues to resonate. As recently as a January 2015 broadcast of A Prairie Home Companion, *host Garrison Keillor asked his guests, The Gibson Brothers, which country brothers act was their favorite. Without hesitation, both Eric and Leigh Gibson acknowledged their love for The Everly Brothers, but they each chose The Louvin Brothers as their favorite. Keillor initially seemed surprised, but he also agreed with them.*

I have written a lot about The Louvin Brothers and had the opportunity to interview Charlie Louvin at length in the spring of 1995. The essay that accompanies the Livin', Lovin', Losin' *CD serves as a good distillation of my writings on these brothers.*

The Louvin Brothers are universally heralded as one of the greatest harmony duos in the history of country music. They wrote their own songs and performed them as well on stage as they did on record. Ira Louvin's high tenor voice would never be matched; it inspired awe in countless singers, from established stars like Bill Monroe to future stars like Emmylou Harris.

Gram Parson paid friends to search for old Louvin Brothers LPs in used record shops. It's been said that Elvis Presley had advance copies of Louvin Brothers records sent to him to give to his mother. A young Johnny Cash waited by the side of the road to catch a glimpse of Ira and Charlie Louvin drive past when he learned they were coming to his town to perform.

The Louvin Brothers were without limits. They could sing religious songs that would send you to church, then break your heart with a tale of lost love. Ira could give a recitation on topics ranging from spiritual salvation, to alcohol abuse, to a mother's love. These could make an audience weep. Ira might follow this by singing a comedy number while wearing a dress. But like other extremely versatile musicians, the brothers' wide-ranging talents proved to be a mixed blessing.

Capitol Records had The Louvin Brothers straightjacketed into a contract that allowed them to record only sacred songs. The same restrictions were imposed on them at the Grand Ole Opry. This was frustrating to Ira and Charlie, since the crowds at their live shows appreciated all their different music styles. "The audiences were loving everything we did, but the record company had no idea what to do with us," remembered Charlie Louvin. "They thought our songs were too religious for the country crowd, and too country for the gospel fans." Admirers unconcerned with labeling music knew that The Louvin Brothers were great *because* they could do it all.

One song would change everything. The Louvins had begged Capitol Records to let them record a non-sacred song, but were constantly refused. Finally, the powers at Capitol told Ira and Charlie that they could release one secular single, but if it did not become a radio hit the label would cancel their contract. Knowing what was at stake, the brothers thought hard before choosing one of Ira's originals, "When I Stop Dreaming." Holding their breath, the Louvins saw the song become a huge hit.

This opened all the doors. The brothers could now record what they pleased at Capitol, and the Grand Ole Opry no longer limited them to gospel numbers. But while the big hit freed them from stylistic restraints, the Louvins would never turn their back on sacred music, which they would intermittently record during the remainder of their career.

By the early 1960s the music world had changed. In 1963, the Louvin Brothers decided to call it quits. Charlie embarked on a successful solo career. Ira was killed in a car wreck on Father's Day, 1965. But the music the brothers created would live on, often appearing over the years in unexpected places. In 1968, The Byrds recorded the Louvin Brothers' song "The Christian Life" for their *Sweetheart of the Rodeo* album. Years later Elvis Costello would sing the Louvins' final chart hit, "Must You Throw Dirt in my Face?". Like Gram Parsons before him, Costello encourages his listeners to search out the original recordings of the Louvins' songs. All of the artists on this tribute disk would tell you the same thing.

Remembrance

Charlie Louvin
January 26, 2011

Well foot. I've been trying to break away from writing obituaries and deal with the world of the living. But here's one I can't let go by. It may sound harsh, but Charlie Louvin was the lesser half of The Louvin Brothers, a close harmony duo that you have probably never heard of unless you study country music or are at least 60 years old. And even then, it would help greatly if you were from the South.

Together, Charlie and Ira Louvin were, without question, the finest harmony singers country music has ever produced. I love the Delmores, the Stanleys, the Blue Sky Boys, the Carter Family, and many others. But for perfection of harmony, nobody can touch The Louvin Brothers. They stand toe to toe with The Everly Brothers, who influenced vocalists in the rock and pop world—most notably the harmonies of John Lennon and Paul McCartney. Unlike the Everlys, however, the impact of the Louvin Brothers stopped at the country music border.

Two main differences distinguish the Louvins from the Everlys, and help to explain the Louvins' distinctive place in American music. First, the Louvin Brothers emerged from a childhood richly influenced by the Southern Shape Note tradition. This choral style features an unmistakably rigid element in the singers' voices. Sacred Harp and Shape Note singing were unknown to Don and Phil Everly and had no impact on their approach to harmony.

The second main difference has to do with lyric content. The Everly Brothers sang songs about of teenage heartache. In contrast, many of The Louvin Brothers' greatest recordings are original gospel numbers, written primarily by Ira Louvin. These include "Just Rehearsing," "Weapon of Prayer," "Satan Lied to Me," and "The Great Atomic Power." These songs merely touch the hem of the garment of Ira's deep reservoirs of songwriting talent.

The Louvin Brothers would finally make it onto the country charts in 1955, with Ira's secular "When I Stop Dreaming." This occurred only after Capitol Records grudgingly allowed them to record one (and only one) non-gospel number. Fortunately, this test case recording proved to be a big hit, which then convinced Capitol to let them record what they pleased. This success also persuaded The Grand Ole Opry to allow the brothers to sing both sacred and secular music, a large concession. Charlie continued to perform at the Opry regularly until his death this week from cancer, at age 83. He had worked there as a solo performer once the brothers dissolved their act in 1963.

Charlie had once been the solid lead vocal line to Ira's achingly high tenor harmony. But Charlie's singing voice had been shot for decades, perhaps partially caused by the chain smoking I witnessed over three days in 1995. Charlie Louvin was not a difficult man to interview, but he seemed unhappy that people always wanted to talk about The Louvin Brothers and not his solo career. "I've sold more records by myself than The Louvin Brothers ever did," he insisted, more out of irritation than pride. He was probably right about the sales numbers; the brothers had an important but relatively short career. They hit the Top 10 of the *Billboard* "Country Music Chart" for the last time in 1958.

Brother Ira's volatile temperament never helped the group, nor did his ever increasing alcoholism. But Charlie was protective of his brother's image to the end, demonstrating joy and frustration by turns during our conversations. "Ira could do a spoken recitation in a song as good as Hank Williams," he told me. Big talk, but it was true. Of the 14 recitations Ira recorded, most are on the level of Williams' Luke the Drifter recordings—the gold standard for country recitations.

Charlie was busy copying cassettes of Louvin Brothers songs to send to various performers when I visited him at his home in Bell Buckle, Tennessee, that day in 1995. He hoped to generate fresh recording interest in the Louvins' back catalog of songs before his copyrights expired. While he worked at making cassettes, he was handing me several of the solo CDs that he had recorded over the past few years for various small labels, such as Watermelon. Charlie said he was looking forward to recording a song about tour buses called "Silver Eagle," thinking this one might get him back on the radio.

Before I left, I asked him about country peers and newcomers. "I know what goes into being a country artist," he assured me. "I know who can make it and who can't. And I know why!" He had the greatest respect for George Strait because he had a "man's haircut" and for Dwight Yoakam because Dwight had paid for an amazingly large number of roses to decorate the entire interior of the Grand Ole Opry after he heard that Minnie Pearl was ailing. When I asked him for any favorite songs by either Strait or Yoakam, an embarrassing silence followed. But he was adamant that they were both the real deal.

I thought that Mr. Louvin might be more comfortable if we discussed music of the past. He told me Jim Reeves had the best voice in country music. Charlie hated Webb Pierce and loved Ernest Tubb. "People in Nashville were just waiting for Webb Pierce to fail. But if anybody could help Ernest in any way, they'd do it!" When I asked about Hank Snow, Charlie only smiled and laughed. Finally, Louvin didn't see how anybody could consider Jimmie Rodgers to be the Father of Country Music, and he became surprisingly angry about Rodgers' reputation. "Look here, now. He had a *trumpet* on one of his records. That ain't country!"

Charlie Louvin decided he had to dissolve the Louvin Brothers partnership in the early 1960s. He was no longer able to endure his brother's drinking. Not many years afterwards, Ira would be killed in a wreck on the highway. Although well aware of Ira's talents and his troubles, Charlie never stopped missing his brother. He told me, "I get to certain parts of a song and I *still* move to one side of the microphone, like I think he's coming in to sing harmony with me. I've tried to break myself of the habit, but I can't." It's nice to know that when Charlie moves to share the microphone at tonight's performance, Ira will again be there.

Remembrance

Phil Everly
January 8, 2014

"Those boys come from Southern Iowa, you know." Actually, "those boys" were from Kentucky. But I can still hear my father telling me this 'fact' with pride each time an Everly Brothers record played on a Des Moines radio station. And in truth, Iowa *did* have a legitimate claim to the brothers. The Everlys were on a morning radio program in Shenandoah, Iowa, during the early 1950s. This was the end of an era for radio, when live performers were being supplanted by records and disc jockeys.

"We played on station KMA every morning and then we'd go to

school," Don Everly recalled some years back. "Nobody in our class had any idea that we were on the radio." In fact, the brothers themselves placed little importance on these dawn performances. At this time they were part of The Everly Family, with father Ike fronting the group. Many country performers have glowing comments about Ike Everly's ability as a guitarist, but there are few recorded examples of his work.

The same cannot be said of his sons. Don and Phil Everly sold millions of records with a sound that became the touchstone for modern brother harmony. The sound created by these two voices is still universally acknowledged as a pinnacle in American music. From The Beatles' "This Boy" to the 2013 Everly Brothers tribute CD by Billie Joe Armstrong and Norah Jones, the influence of Don and Phil remains unmistakable and inescapable.

I attended an Everly Brothers concert in October 1998. Their presence on Top 40 radio was long gone by this point; even an attempted reboot of their recording career in the mid-1980s was now a distant memory. They still sounded great, though, with Don taking the role of front man, giving a bit of background on the selections and singing the lead lines. Don's baritone and Phil's harmony tenor vocals were as distinctive as they were flawless.

If the brothers felt any fraternal attachment to one another, it became evident only when they made music together. When Garrison Keillor welcomed them as guests on his *A Prairie Home Companion* radio show in 1987, he said, "Don and Phil Everly: they taught all of us how to sing and they taught us how to fight." The brothers were standing right by Keillor at the time; they did not take issue with this assessment. It was an interesting broadcast in that many other performers on that night's show seemed awestruck by the presence of the Everlys. Bluesman Taj Mahal takes a back seat to no one. But at the conclusion of his song "Paradise," Mahal was quick to gleefully shout the names "Don and Phil" over the applause and then profusely thank the brothers for singing harmony behind him.

Country Music historians' genealogy charts for brother duos regularly cite a direct path from Rabon and Alton Delmore to Charlie and Ira Louvin to Don and Phil Everly. Various musical authorities, including *Rolling Stone*, affirm this Delmore to Louvin to Everly lineage as fact. Don Everly says otherwise. I had the opportunity to speak with Mr. Everly in 1996 when I was working on a project about the Louvin Brothers. Don was happy to talk about how much he and Phil were big fans of Charlie and Ira Louvin's tight harmonies. But Don was also quick to correct one common misconception: "Our sound was not influenced by the Louvins. We did not hear them until after we arrived in Nashville, and we already had our own style together by then."

Wondering about possible common ground with previous brother duos, I asked Don if he and brother Phil had heard much Sacred Harp or Shape Note singing within their family background. These are forms of southern music that were important in helping form the Louvins' musical heritage. Don told me that he had never heard of the term Sacred Harp music and was unfamiliar with the genre.

Concerning the Everlys' influence on other performers, I asked what he and Phil thought of Bob Dylan's 1970 version of their hit single "Take a Message to Mary." Don told me he was unaware that Dylan had recorded it. That statement, I admit, surprised me more than his unfamiliarity with Shape Note singing.

As I heard the news of Phil Everly's passing last week, another part of my conversation with his brother stuck in my mind. I had indicated how much I enjoyed the early country songs included on their 1958 LP *Songs Our Daddy Taught Us*. Don thanked me and said that he and Phil still had a much-delayed follow-up project planned. We talked a bit about older country music and some of the songs that The Everly Family performed on the radio. When Don learned that I was from Iowa, he seemed to grow nostalgic. "Oh! Then you know what a nice part of the country Shenandoah and that entire area is," he said. I asked him if he or Phil had many recordings from those early morning radio programs. He lamented that very little had survived. "Pretty much all we had came out on that [1968] album *Roots*."

A bit uncertain of how to frame the question, I tentatively asked Don about his and Phil's attempts to be known as solo artists. Fortunately, he seemed pleased that I knew that both brothers had recorded separately. He laughed as he explained how they had each tried to replace the other on their own albums by double tracking the vocals. But then he became serious and said, "See, it takes two of us to make an Everly Brothers record. And there's just no way around it."

In interviews, the brothers were candid about the arc of their career. Both acknowledged that the hits became less frequent in the

1960s after they lost access to the songwriting team of Boudleaux and Felice Bryant. Substance abuse also became an impediment. Don candidly told me, "We got deep off into pills and alcohol. When we finally woke up, The Beatles were here!"

I first became aware of the Everlys after the brothers "woke up" but found themselves unable to reignite their career. This was during the time of their final Top 40 chart hit, "Bowling Green," in 1967. Although not among their most successful singles, this record—like all of their singles—sounded to me like nothing else on the radio at that time. Even now, Everly Brothers records still sound like nothing else.

I intended to write this piece as a remembrance of Phil Everly. If this specific focus has been elusive, I think it is because one can't think of Phil without thinking of Don, or of Don without Phil. I had a professor who once taught that a person isn't able to understand the concept of *up* without simultaneously grasping the idea of *down*. And so it is with the Everlys. They and their beautiful harmonies are forever joined as one in our minds and in our ears. And maybe most strongly in our hearts.

Concert Commentary

The Everly Brothers
The Riverside Theater
Milwaukee, Wisconsin
October 30, 1998

RABON & ALTON DELMORE and Ira & Charlie Louvin have long since stopped performing as duos. But while Don & Phil Everly will always be seen as the youth of America when compared with these earlier brother harmony groups, the Everlys honored the past with grace and style, while also recounting their own important legacy during a concert stop last week in Milwaukee.

One might think that the Everly Brothers would try to make their show into a living jukebox, including as many of their numerous hits as possible. Doing so might be especially tempting just now, since a musical based on their lives is currently playing at Nashville's Ryman Auditorium. But almost the opposite occurred at this late October concert. Instead of a program comprised of their own hits, the brothers sang songs that emphasized the specific musical traditions that been influential on their music.

The 70-minute set began with two songs honoring their home state, with "Kentucky" melting into a fine rendition of "Bowling Green." The performance that followed was long on ballads, as Don and Phil knew what still best suited their voices and what their audience most wanted to hear.

Tradition aside, the reason the Riverside Theater was filled for this show was that fans wanted to experience the brothers' peerless harmony in person. Like the Louvins and the Delmores before them, the Everlys have their own distinct sound. Whether performing as a duo with only two acoustic guitars or with a full backing band, the inimitable harmonies remained intact. It's true that they no longer try for the long sustained notes of "Cathy's Clown." And they pace themselves, interspersing the upbeat numbers with less challenging, yet equally satisfying numbers. But if the brothers, now on the cusp of 60, have lost some stamina, they make up for it by their talent as mature singers. In amazement one watches Don and Phil simultaneously hit the most intricate of harmony patterns without once glancing at one another for articulation cues.

Don was the front man for the night, singing lead and giving a bit of background at various junctures. He spoke of their father Ike's ability with the guitar, and how these skills led Chet Atkins to take an interest in Don and Phil, inviting them to Nashville. In fact, the middle of the show featured a brief acoustic medley of country and folk tunes from the great *Songs Our Daddy Taught Us* LP.

Albert Lee has been playing guitar with the Everlys for some time. In Milwaukee, Lee added his instrumental lines to the harmony without stealing focus from the brothers. Buddy Emmons made an unexpected appearance as the backing group's steel guitar player; he was warmly received by this northern audience. Don and Phil briefly left the stage late in the set to let Emmons and Lee each have a featured instrumental number. And while a longer night from the brothers themselves would have been welcome, who could complain about an intermission such as this?

Everyone knows that the Everly Brothers recorded many hit singles. But the most important aspect of their legacy remains their breathtaking, uniquely influential harmonies. Charlie Louvin once remarked that he and brother Ira only saw their idols, The Delmore Brothers, perform live once, late in the Delmores' career. "And they sounded just like the records of decades before—the harmonies still fresh and pure," marveled Charlie. "Neither Ira or I were let down in the least." Charlie Louvin could just as well be describing the performance of Don and Phil Everly on their recent stop in Milwaukee. Nobody was let down.

Concert Commentary

Dwight Yoakam
Pabst Theater
Milwaukee, Wisconsin
June 14, 2006

DWIGHT YOAKAM returned to Milwaukee to offer an appreciative crowd over two hours of first-rate music. After opening with "She'll Remember" and the title track from his latest CD, "Blame the Vain," he immediately paid homage to mentor Buck Owens. Yoakam sang complete versions of Owens' hits "Act Naturally," "Crying Time," "Together Again," and (their duet) "Streets of Bakersfield."

Yoakam also sang most of his own hits, from his early success with "Honky Tonk Man" and "Guitars, Cadillacs" through a reworked "Please, Please Baby" and "It Only Hurts Me When I Cry." Intense takes of "Fast as You" and "Crazy Little Thing Called Love" were played during the generous and briskly paced set, as were moving ballads "A Thousand Miles from Nowhere" and "If There Was a Way."

Yoakam occasionally talked about the songs, noting that many album tracks rarely get heard in concert. He remedied this problem by singing "It Won't Hurt" from his first album, plus "Home for Sale," "Dreams of Clay," and a haunting version of Dave Alvin's "Long Black Cadillac." Yoakam was in strong voice and an upbeat mood throughout the night, often conducting his tight backing quartet with dance moves. He got serious, though, when thanking Wisconsin fans for 20 years of career support. Sounding almost apologetic for playing newer material, he then performed impressive renditions of "Just Passing Time" and "Three Good Reasons."

Late in the concert Yoakam honored Bonnie Owens, who was once married to Buck Owens and later to Merle Haggard. Dwight credited Owens' own role in creating the Bakersfield Sound, making sure her individual legacy was not lost in the shadows of her famous husbands. Also acknowledged was bluegrass master Jimmy Martin, who died last year.

Opening for Dwight was Robbie Fulks, who featured rollicking original material from his latest CD *Georgia Hard*. Milwaukee's own Mike Frederickson played bass for Fulks, and guitarist Grant Tye demonstrated furious single note picking and sweet steel guitar sounds. Fulks closed a strong 40-minute set of pure country with his rousing "Let's Kill Saturday Night."

Dwight Yoakam has been accused of neglecting his music, becoming distracted by Hollywood side trips. His recent Pabst Theater concert proved that Dwight remains focused on giving his fans great songs, and lots of them.

Concert Commentary

Joe Ely
Shank Hall
Milwaukee, Wisconsin
May 23, 2015

SHANK HALL found itself transported to West Texas for 90 minutes on Saturday night, thanks to a strong solo set by Joe Ely. A personal tour of his home state is what Ely promised at the outset, beginning with his first original song about Texas he thought worth keeping, "Because of the Wind." Rivers, highways, coyotes, border crossings, and the wide night sky all played a part in this Lone Star travelogue. Recurring themes included Texas truck stops, and especially the waitresses who work there.

Ely acknowledged his association with the early 1970s group The Flatlanders, but tried to defuse the mystique a bit. "We played six gigs together, and two of those were weddings." Even so, when requests came for a song by former bandmate Jimmie Dale Gilmore, Ely seemed happy to play "Tonight I Think I'm Gonna Go Downtown."

Most of the numbers were blues based, but Ely's guitar skills made each song distinctive. Ballads were particularly suited to his voice, and the night included strong performances of "Letter to Laredo," "The Highway Is My Home," and "The Road Goes on Forever." Ely has recently unearthed and released a 1985 studio recording of "Where Is My Love," which he sang with Linda Ronstadt. This Randy Banks' song has been in Ely's repertoire as a solo artist for decades, and its strength demonstrated why he wanted to have this newly discovered duet recording made available.

A trio of numbers by fellow Texas songwriters closed the evening. Ely romped through Gilmore's nighttime view of "Dallas," contemplated the unknown with Billy Joe Shaver's "Live Forever," and ended with Townes Van Zandt's song of the road, "White Freightliner Blues."

Joe Ely got his audience back from this West Texas tour in time to enjoy Memorial Day celebrations in Milwaukee. Even so, I'm ready for a return trip.

Concert Commentary

The Clark Family Experience
Rainbow Summer Stage
Milwaukee, Wisconsin
September 9, 2001

"WOULD YOU CARE to pray with us?" asks a member of the band. Stunned, the confused radio announcer suddenly tries to look busy, excusing himself from the group's pre-performance tradition. And while this backstage encounter was unexpected, the audience too would get some musical surprises from the six brothers of The Clark Family Experience.

Opening with a frenetic psychedelic arrangement of "Crossroads," the Clarks dispelled any notion that these boys were a typical country music brother act. The family tradition suggested by the group's name is certainly an element in their sound. Yet it is the well-balanced combination of traditional, gospel, bluegrass, and rock elements which lies at the heart of the Clarks' diversity and appeal. The group's eldest member (at 27) is front man and acoustic guitarist Alan Clark. He proudly stresses that the boys' father taught each son how to pick, also playing them a steady diet of Merle Haggard records.

The Clarks drew a good crowd for this noon outdoor show, in part from the recognition that comes with a pair of recent radio hits—"Meanwhile Back at the Ranch" and "Standing Still." The hour-long set included inventive, but recognizable arrangements of Merle Travis' "Nine Pound Hammer," "The Orange Blossom Special," and even a brief nod to "The Little Paper Boy."

While demonstrating their awareness of the past, the Clarks also played several selections from their forthcoming debut CD. One of these tunes was called "Always Be You," which showcased the various strengths and occasional limitations of the group. The song itself was not much, but what the brothers could put into an unexceptional composition was impressive. At several points, they transformed material that was merely adequate into interesting and even exciting music. Austin Clark's fine dobro work and Ashley's fiddle breaks were highlights throughout the set. Adam was a strong soloist on both mandolin and his Les Paul guitar.

The Clark Family Experience concluded with a hard-driving original called "I Just Wanna Play (even if the job don't pay)." The joyful attitude concerning the importance of music overpowering all other distractions came across here, summing up the siblings' attitude toward their music.

Artist Commentary
Cowboy Junkies
Fall 2012

Love is strange. Mickey & Sylvia told us this many years ago. It's still true. Otherwise, why would I have just bought a five-CD set of new material by Toronto's family group Cowboy Junkies, when the last recording of theirs that I really liked was *The Trinity Session*, which I bought more than 25 years ago? Do I love their groove that much? Did I think they would find some different musical territory to explore?

Neither. But when RCA released *The Trinity Session* in 1988, I was seriously hooked. "Hooked" may be a good word choice here for, as I told my friends, "This is heroin music." They all backed away at that statement, but it's true—*The Trinity Session* is like a narcotic. Serious, mood altering stuff. I'm talking Jamie Brockett's "Bag on the Table" type of effect on the listener. I loved every note and played their *Trinity Session* constantly.

Naturally, I explored deeper. At that point, the only other place to look for more recordings by Cowboy Junkies was their debut LP, *Whites Off Earth Now*. The odd album title caused a bit of stir, but the music was fine. This was the Timmons siblings mainly playing covers of blues songs they liked, unafraid to wear their roots on their sleeve.

I enjoyed their show at a small club in Houston, Texas, on *The Trinity Session* tour. I thought they were fine on *Saturday Night Live* and later on *Austin City Limits*. Then Cowboy Junkies seemed to hit a wall. Their follow-up record, *The Caution Horses*, lacked the sparse magic of *Trinity*. I liked their *200 More Miles* set, but this was largely a concert recreation of *The Trinity Session*, which was recorded live in the first place. Other releases, such as *Black Eyed Man* and *Pale Sun Crescent Moon*, could not recapture my interest.

So why am I buying a five-CD set of music that I'm pretty sure will disappoint me? Mickey & Sylvia are correct: love is strange.

Bonus Track

In the late 1960s, rock group Vanilla Fudge traversed similar waters as the Cowboy Junkies, singing radically slowed-down pop songs of their day. And like the Junkies, Vanilla Fudge's most successful numbers were well-chosen cover songs. They had a Top 10 hit with a drugged out version of The Supremes' "You Keep Me Hanging On." Vanilla Fudge's arrangement of Nancy Sinatra & Lee Hazelwood's "Some Velvet Morning" is quite unsettling. But then, the original hit record of that song was pretty odd to begin with. In the summer of 1967, George Harrison was a big fan of Vanilla Fudge's lethargic version of The Beatles' "Ticket to Ride." So was I.

CD Review

Junior Brown
The Austin Experience
Telarc Records, 2005

When Junior Brown has played Milwaukee, it's never been in the setting he deserved. In the mid-1990s he opened for The Mavericks; years later he played at the outdoor Rainbow Summer stage. Neither venue was conducive for a display of his talent as an amazing instrumentalist. So I was ready for Brown's new live CD to pin me to the wall. It was recorded, after all, on his home turf, The Continental Club, in Austin, Texas. However, while he performs his best-known songs, the disk never truly showcases the virtuosity of Brown's abilities as a guitarist.

For the uninitiated, Junior Brown plays a twin-neck instrument of his own design called the "guit-steel." True to its name, one neck consists of a traditional six-string guitar; the other neck is that of a steel guitar. It's a heavy instrument in many ways, needing support from a metal stand instead of a guitar strap.

Brown's effortless style shifting is at the heart of his solos. He can instantly switch from Chet Atkins' finger picking style to a Dick Dale surf sound to quoting Jimi Hendrix's "Third Stone from the Sun," all within one solo. At the end of a recent concert, an older patron was heard to say, "Son, I liked him; but I'm not sure all of that was country music."

Brown gets the song selection right on this 50-minute disk, choosing many numbers from his first albums. "My Wife Thinks You're Dead" is a song as great as the title, and "Gotta Get Up Every Morning (just to say goodnight to you)" shows Brown's fierce Ernest Tubb style preferences. But in spite of these entertaining selections, it has always been the instrumental breaks which take the live shows into the stratosphere.

Perhaps because he is playing to a familiar crowd of Austin regulars, Brown doesn't seem to be swinging for the fences. Which is too bad. There are hints of the "guit-steel" magic here, but *The Austin Experience* sounds like Junior Brown's exceptional talent was recorded on an unexceptional night.

CD Review

Béla Fleck

The Bluegrass Sessions: Tales From the Acoustic Planet, volume 2
Warner Brothers, 1999

Béla Fleck says that everything he plays is "colored by the bluegrass heartland." This would seem a self-evident statement for a banjo player to make, unless one knew much of Fleck's music. Since the early 1990s he and his group, The Flecktones, have repeatedly taken the banjo to uncharted realms, from jazz-inspired chord-change exercises to pieces performed with the Boston Symphony.

For the new *Bluegrass Sessions* release, Fleck steps away from his talented electric sidemen to assemble his bluegrass "dream band." And although subtitled *Tales from the Acoustic Planet, Volume 2*, the music here is closer in spirit and style to Fleck's fine *Drive* CD of 1987 than to volume 1 of the *Acoustic Planet* series. No matter the title, the successful collaborations found on this new *Bluegrass Sessions* include great variety, ranging from the refreshing atmosphere of an Alison Krauss CD to the excitement of Flatt & Scruggs in their prime. In fact, Earl Scruggs appears here on two numbers as a musical elder statesman, giving his approval to Fleck's new directions.

It's good to see that the impressive diversity displayed with The Flecktones has not diminished Béla's love for, or ability to perform, bluegrass music. Among the players in his dream band are veterans Vassar Clements, Tony Rice, and Sam Bush. But in spite of their high bluegrass pedigree, the ensemble does not strive to document the form as scholarly traditionalists. With a set list including "Polka on the Banjo" (sung by John Hartford) and "Major Honker," one can see that Fleck is still interested in musical cross pollination and, equally important, that his sense of humor remains intact.

Hangin' with the Stars #7

In the mid-1990s I visited Nashville quite often. Whenever possible on these trips I would attend The Grand Ole Opry. One night I needed to verify some quotes for a piece I was writing. I was invited to the backstage area during the break between the two

Saturday evening radio broadcasts. The Stage Manager pointed to a door and said, "Wait in there. I'll come and get you." I walked into the small room where an elderly man was seated in a large chair, obscured by a younger man who was hovering over him, holding a stack of albums. The walls were filled with fine, large photographs of Opry stars, probably taken by Les Leverett. I began looking at these beautiful black and white portraits, marveling at the musicians who had passed through the Opry organization.

The man with the records was talking, but I wasn't paying close attention. Then I heard him say, "Do you prefer the older recordings or your new ones?" The man in the chair said softly, "Oh, the new ones are better." I looked around to see what recordings they were discussing. Seated in the chair was the Father of Bluegrass music, Bill Monroe! He was dressed in a suit, resting between shows. He appeared weary, but he was taking the time to sign several album covers for the man. An attentive older woman stood near to Mr. Monroe; she nodded at me. The visitor continued, obviously disappointed, "Oh. I thought you would have preferred your older recordings." But Monroe had moved on, or didn't hear.

After obtaining a few more autographs, the man departed. I had nothing profound to say or to ask, and I thought that the visitor was a little too intense and had maybe worn Monroe out a bit. So I just said, "Mr. Monroe, I enjoyed your set tonight." He thanked me. I waited a bit, then asked if he would mind signing that night's Opry schedule for me. Monroe took my program and scanned it until he found his own name on the list of performers. He carefully autographed the sheet directly beside his printed name. I thanked him as the door to the room opened and the Stage Manager beckoned to me.

I have played that scene back in my head many times. What could I have asked him? What *should* I have asked him? In retrospect, I'm glad that I was completely surprised by this unexpected encounter. Because I was struck dumb, there was no chance that I could be a pest to this man who was just trying to catch a brief moment of peace.

My most vivid memory of Monroe's appearance is that he wore a dark, well-tailored suit. On his lapel there was a large broach that simply read "Jesus." It was constructed of sparkling glass, made to look like glittering diamonds. When Monroe was on the Opry stage, I believe this pin could have been easily read from the balcony.

Bill Monroe died about a year later. I'm sure that by now he has performed many shows in heaven. When I meet Jesus, I won't be a bit surprised to see him wearing a large diamond broach that says "Monroe."

Bonus Track

My short-lived backstage access at The Grand Ole Opry led to another incident where I was Hangin' with the Stars. When Hank Williams III was beginning his career, he sometimes played the Opry. Sitting in the audience, I watched Hank III perform in a white, fringed suit. When he sang, he looked and sounded a bit like his grandfather. The crowd was mesmerized. I had business backstage between the broadcasts, and as I stood in the active hallway behind the stage Hank III walked past me. I shook his hand and told him how much I enjoyed his performance. He was friendly and appreciative. There's not much to that story, but I did shake hands with Hank Williams III.

Concert Commentary

Chasin' Mason
Cedarburg Park Pavilion
Cedarburg, Wisconsin
July 23, 2010

THE COUNTRY ROCK band Chasin' Mason is a competent sextet—two electric guitars, electric bass, acoustic guitar, drums, and a vocalist. The singer could really sing and the pickers could really pick. However, somebody needs to choose material for them. They performed well, but chose to play the "sex-driven tractor" and "darned big truck" dreck from the backwater of the current country music survey. Lots of potential here, but they just haven't listened to the right records yet.

CD Review

Texas '55
Extreme Hillbilly
Planet Cowboy Records, 1999

Country group Texas 55 must be commended for their complete truth in advertising, from band name to CD title. The Milwaukee outfit's second release, *Extreme Hillbilly*, finds the band growing stronger in what seems to be a fervent mission of bringing two-step shuffles, western swing, and honky tonk music to the north country.

Group leader Rob Laplander explains, "The band's name reflects our goal of playing a mix of country styles that you could have heard on a Texas radio station in 1955." While this focus might suggest a slavish approach to a distant time and place, Texas 55 does not step into the trap of mere nostalgia and recreation. The band's freshness is due, in part, to Laplander's original numbers. Songs such as "Alcohol, Tobacco and Caffeine" and "Silent City Blues" show great respect for traditional country, but are also good songs in their own right. The influences demonstrated throughout *Extreme Hillbilly* are strong and pure. They are not derived from second or third generation material. Echoes of a young Ray Price, Johnny Cash at Sun Records, and a rockabilly Elvis echo through the entire disc.

Concert Commentary

Glen Campbell
Potawatomi Casino
Milwaukee, Wisconsin
May 31, 2001

and

Glen Campbell
With John Anderson
Washington County Fair
West Bend, Wisconsin
Summer 2007

I AM PUTTING ON my black Texas cowboy boots when I think about taking an album along for Glen Campbell to sign. I don't know why—it is something I had never done before. I dug into my stacks and pulled out one of his old Capitol LPs, *I Remember Hank Williams*. No hits on this one; they had pretty well dried up by this time. But I always thought it was a heartfelt collection, with Campbell singing Hank's tunes. It was a stormy night, so I double bagged the album cover to protect it.

My good friend and Glen Campbell fan Pete came by, and off we went. We were soon standing in the vast casino area of pinging gaming machines, when Pete pointed and said, "Hey; there he is." And sure enough, Glen Campbell was standing by an elevator, talking to a couple of fans and getting ready to go up to his room. We ran over to him. Pete said "hello" while I struggled to get my album cover out of the double plastic. Later, his two security guards laughed as they told me they came very close to decking me because they didn't know what I was trying to get out of the package. But I didn't get decked, and I did ask Glen Campbell to sign my album.

As I showed Mr. Campbell the album, the smile on his face fell and he softly said, "Uncle Boo." This particular record jacket is covered with old photographs of Glen in his youth. A large shot on the cover shows a grade-school-aged Glen and his older uncle playing guitars together on stage. He was very happy to sign the album, and we talked for a couple of minutes about Hank Williams. His manager said that Campbell had to go get ready for the show, but that he would be available later for a meet and greet.

After he left, Pete and I agreed that the album he signed for me was not one he saw every night. "Not as often as the duets album with Bobby Gentry." "No; or one of the greatest hits collections." During the concert that followed, Campbell unexpectedly played "You are My Sunshine" and "I Saw the Light." I couldn't help but wonder if the album I showed Mr. Campbell had influenced his song selection for that night's show. "Hell yes," said Pete. "He was moved by the album cover you brought. He played that old stuff because he was thinking about his Uncle Boo in that picture." I wondered. There had been an afternoon show, which the *Milwaukee Journal Sentinel* covered. So the next day I e-mailed the reviewer, asking him if Campbell had played either song at his matinee. He hadn't. Interesting.

The casino concert was very good; Campbell played some great guitar. We were able to speak with him again afterwards. I said to him, "You really liked your Stratocaster tonight," since he had played it almost exclusively for the entire set, even though an entire rack of various guitars was on stage with him. "Were you playing a Strat when you did your early session work?" I asked. "Oh no," he said. "That session stuff was all rhythm, and I played acoustic on most all of it." He mentioned the type of guitar: a Martin D-5, as I recall.

He said that the guitar kept breaking, and he would need to fix it before most of his studio work. But he admitted that he kept it in the trunk of his car, without a case. Other people were waiting to talk with him, so we retreated. A good time—almost getting decked by security and chatting up the star, who seemed pleased with the album we brought and was happy to talk.

A few years later, I saw that Campbell was going to be at the Washington County Fair, but I didn't see the need to go. Once was great. I have this notion of not messing with ideal situations. Campbell's show at the casino was so good that I didn't see the need to try to improve on that memory. Perhaps I'm odd that way. For example, I have seen Willie Nelson only once, but it was in such a perfect night that I have resisted seeing him again when he has played near me in Wisconsin. I saw Willie in a large Texas bar, playing a very long set. Can't beat that, I always thought.

But my wife pushed for going to hear Campbell at the nearby county fair. And since she had missed the other show and really wanted to go, I said OK and called Pete. He was up for it. We walked to the front for good seats and planted our lawn chairs in about the second row. Right in front of some large P.A. columns. John Anderson opened the show. Anderson plays traditional country music; he is a performer whose records I got to know when living in Texas. I wasn't listening to a lot of country radio when Anderson made his initial mark, but I do recall his brief resurgence with tunes such as "Straight Tequlia Night." Good song.

Anderson started playing, and was WAY too loud. Icepicks stabbing your ears type of sound. Too much treble, and simply too loud. We sat through it, although several folks left. But many were really loving it. One group had made a large sign encouraging John to play his early hit "Chicken Shack," which he later performed as part of a medley. Anderson, too, seemed into it and gave a very energetic performance. Still…painfully loud. I assured my wife that Campbell would have better sound, and just couldn't be this loud. I was hoping for this, anyway, and fortunately I was correct.

Campbell's set at the fair was even better than at the casino. He opened with "Try a Little Kindness" and started hitting it from there. Glen had a beautiful white 12-string guitar on a rack by him, and I was just getting ready to yell that he should play it when he grabbed it and burned through "Classical Gas." Amazing technique, and on a 12-string! Early in the show, Campbell remarked that he never tired of the following tune, and played an exceptional version of "Galveston." The ending solo just kept going, with Campbell taking several choruses of guitar leads. Smokin' and Clapton-esque. He closed with a medley of songs by The Beach Boys, on whose early records he had played, and with whom he briefly toured when Brian Wilson had tired of the road. It was a fine show. Great band and, yes, the sound was excellent.

Concert Commentary

John Hartford   and   **John Hartford**
Hancher Auditorium   *A Prairie Home*
Iowa City, Iowa   *Companion*
1976   St. Paul, Minnesota
                                      1982

I FELT HIP because I knew the name of the somber banjo player who stood behind Glen Campbell at the start of each of his *Goodtime Hour* television shows. It was John Hartford who would rise from the midst of the audience as Campbell sang "Gentle on my Mind." Hartford had written the song. One of my Des Moines friends had some John Hartford albums that were very different from the rest of the acoustic music I was hearing in the early 1970s. *Morning Bugle* and *Aereo-Plain* are the two albums I remember best. Hartford was taking his music to unexpected places, and I liked it.

Evidently, his record label was less enamored with his musical directions, for Warner Brothers dropped Hartford after *Morning Bugle*. This is a bit surprising, in retrospect, since at that time Warner Brothers had a reputation for retaining hip artists, whether they sold a lot of records or not. Working at a radio station that played huge amounts of folk music, I had the luxury of tracking artists' careers after they left the major labels. Hartford went to Flying Fish Records, where he put out a series of fine albums—by himself and with notable collaborators like members of The Dillards and Sam Bush. Hartford played with The New Grass Revival at my college in the fall of 1972, the year before I arrived. People were still raving about it; I was still regretting that I had missed it.

I did get to see Hartford perform, but as a solo act. By 1976, the stage contained simply the lone musician, his various acoustic stringed instruments, and an electrified wooden platform that he would stand on and use for percussion. It was almost a soft shoe routine, at times, with his amplified steps providing the rhythm. Hartford's latest album at that point was *Nobody Knows What You Do*. I found it an uneven affair, but liked some of it a lot. He sang a few songs from that record and a few others that I didn't know. I don't believe he played "Gentle on my Mind" that night.

I was able to get backstage and speak briefly with Hartford before his performance. He was very reserved. The only thing I recall clearly was telling him how I especially enjoyed the song "In Tall Buildings," from his new record. He seemed pleased at the specific reference, but not enough to talk about it. I let him go; he had a show to do, after all. As it was a package show of several performers, he did not play a lengthy set. He did sing "In Tall Buildings" that night, but probably not because I mentioned it.

I saw Hartford again a few years later. By 1982, the weekly *Prairie Home Companion* radio show had started to attract national attention. That Chet Atkins had been on the program legitimized it for many performers. John Hartford was one of the musicians who visited the St. Paul broadcast after Atkins had essentially given it his blessing. Hartford did a few songs at various junctures of the show, again solo.

The following afternoon I was at a used bookstore in St. Paul. Across the small shop I spotted Hartford's bowler hat. He was looking at books about the Mississippi River. This made sense, as I knew that he was a licensed steamboat pilot. I didn't want to bother him, but after he left the shop I did speak to him. I told him that I had enjoyed his songs on *A Prairie Home Companion* the previous evening. Hartford was not rude, but as he was thanking me, bowing with folded hands, he was simultaneously backing away, making his escape.

John Hartford died in 2001 from non-Hodgkin lymphoma; he was 63. He is remembered fondly by the music community—nowhere more enthusiastically than on SiriusXM's *Bluegrass Junction* station, which plays his music frequently. Or, if you don't subscribe to SiriusXM, drop by my place and we'll listen to some John Hartford records together. Loud.

Commentary
Webb Pierce: The Ty Cobb of Country Music
Fall 2013

Webb Pierce is the Ty Cobb of Country Music. By this, I mean that both men are almost without statistical peer in their respective fields. In 1955 alone, Pierce held the #1 spot on the *Billboard Magazine* "Country Music Chart" for 46 weeks! Amazing. By any measure, Webb

Pierce's chart record is stunning. Consider:

— 82 of Pierce's singles became Top 40 entries on the *Billboard* country chart
— 55 of these 82 records were Top 10 hits
— 13 of these 55 songs were #1 hits!
— and 6 of these 13 #1 hit records held that position for over 10 weeks each!

Ty Cobb's numbers also dominate his era, and far beyond:

— Cobb scored 2,245 runs
— He amassed 4,191 hits; a record that stood for 57 years
— He had 1,000 hits by the time he was 24 years old
— He stole home 35 times. Stole *home*!
— He batted over .320 for 23 straight seasons
— Three of those seasons saw his batting average exceed .400
— Today, Cobb still has the highest lifetime batting average in history, at .366

The statistics for each man are beyond enviable. Yet neither Ty Cobb nor Webb Pierce is embraced, or even really accepted into the hierarchy of their respective fields. Shunned by the formal establishment, both are now largely lost to the general baseball and country music communities.

Need more proof? On a recent episode of the game show *Jeopardy!*, a clue about the first player inducted into the National Baseball Hall of Fame, along with a photograph of the man, failed to prompt any recognition from the contestants concerning Cobb's identity.

How has this happened? In a nutshell: both Ty Cobb and Webb Pierce had such abrasive personality traits that most of their own colleagues disliked them intensely. And their respective personality reputations have impacted each man's historical reputation within his field. As much as is possible, the baseball and the country music establishments have erased each man from their histories.

If you know neither the name Webb Pierce nor his music, feel no shame. There's a reason for it. For the past several decades, Pierce's music has been played infrequently on the radio. Why? Two reasons: First, look in any standard country music reference guide or published account of Webb Pierce, whether it be the *All Music Guide* summary or an essay by Colin Escott. They all mention that Pierce was a difficult person for his colleagues to get along with. It is this nearly universal attitude of disdain that explains, in part, why Webb Pierce has become a forgotten musical figure.

One telling anecdote about Webb Pierce's manner of treating his fellow performers comes from Country Music Hall of Fame member Charlie Louvin. When I spoke with Louvin in the summer of 1995, I asked him for opinions about several of his Nashville contemporaries. For the most part, he was happy to comply. During this conversation, he brought up the name Webb Pierce. I hadn't mentioned his name; it seemed like Charlie wanted to go on the record about Pierce.

Louvin told me that Webb could make a person feel very small. Charlie and his brother Ira were doing their part of a package show one night and Webb just came out on stage between songs, interrupting their set. He put his arms around both of them and essentially told them that they were going to sing his own recent hit "In the Jailhouse Now." So they did. Webb completely took over their segment of the show. I asked Charlie if he and Ira resisted. He told me, "No, you just have to go with something like that or *you* would be the one to look bad." Once they got off stage, Webb told the Louvin Brothers: "You boys just don't know how to work the big shows." Charlie said that really stung; and it seemed to me like it was *still* stinging him!

Charlie said that the Nashville community was just waiting for Webb Pierce to fail. That it took so long for Pierce to get inducted into The Country Music Hall of Fame may speak to the lasting resentment towards him. The complaints about Pierce varied widely, from his strident personality to deceptive financial practices. Few who dealt with him professionally came away with positive reports.

If Webb Pierce's exclusion from the inner circle of Nashville favorites has impacted his legacy, his hard-edged country sound has also betrayed him. Record companies have shown little interest in making even Pierce's biggest-selling records available to today's market. This has been true for decades, even for Germany's Bear Family record label. Their four-CD Webb Pierce box set called *The Wondering Boy* is great, as far as it goes. It covers Pierce's Decca Records recordings from 1951 to 1958, his most fertile era. But after 1958, Pierce would place over three *dozen* more Top 40 country singles onto the chart, with 17 of these being Top 10 entries. None of these recordings fall within the time parameters of the Bear Family box and are now difficult to locate.

At the other end of this remarkable career, prior to 1951, Pierce recorded for his own small Pacemaker label. As with the later Decca releases, all of these Pacemaker sides are nearly impossible to find, as are his early Four Star label releases.

My question: Why doesn't Bear Family release a follow-up volume of Webb Pierce's records, from 1958 onward? Or his complete Pacemaker and Four Star label material? It's been over 20 years since the release of *The Wondering Boy*. Bear Family's 16-CD set of Jim Reeves' studio recordings is impressive, and is certainly worth having available. Six different Bear Family box sets chronicling Hank Snow's complete recorded works are in print. Like the catalogs of Gentleman Jim Reeves and Singing Ranger Snow, it seems that Webb Pierce would also be worth another box set of music to complete the portrait of this artist—material that has been out of print for many years.

As the last century came to an end, the weekly radio show *American Country Countdown* aired a special program—a survey that featured the top-ranked *Billboard Magazine* Country Music Chart performers of the 20th Century. Although virtually forgotten for decades, Webb Pierce still came in at #13 on this prestigious list! When it came time for this radio special to play a representative song by Pierce, one would have expected the huge hit "Wondering" or "There Stands the Glass."

Instead, they played a selection on which Pierce is joined on vocals by Mel Tillis, called "I Ain't Never." Why was this lesser hit from 1959 chosen over one of his much bigger songs? I think "I Ain't Never" was used so that the producers of the radio special could tone down Pierce's hard country sound. First, Pierce is sharing the vocals, so his sharp-edged singing is tempered by the second vocalist. More insidious, this is a stereo recording, with the vocals appearing on only one channel. As such, Webb's voice could purposefully be buried in the mix by covert audio augmentation. And it was. Pierce's distinctive voice is barely discernable, as if the unaltered sound of Web Pierce might be a little too intense for today's country music radio. And this, on a special dedicated to celebrating country music's past!

The sound of Webb Pierce was too pure to last beyond the man. Try to name some people who have followed him stylistically. The 2002 tribute CD called *Caught in the Web* finds various performers covering his songs, but often not in his style and certainly not with anything approaching his distinctive upper range.

Concerning Pierce's tiny amount of radio airplay, one might wonder if he had somehow alienated radio station owners and disc jockeys in the same way he did with many of his country music colleagues. The Dixie Chicks took a fast fall once they were no longer supported by country radio. But I find no evidence of Webb getting crossways with the industry, so much as with his fellow performers. Also, Pierce's career had a natural arc of a slowly decreasing number of hits over several years, as opposed to an immediate ceasing of airplay, as happened with the Dixie Chicks.

While the Chicks were abruptly shunned, modern country radio is simply uncomfortable with, if not embarrassed by, Pierce's sound. If you are a regular listener to SiriusXM Satellite Radio's fine channel dedicated to older country music, called *Willie's Roadhouse*, you will note that few of Pierce's hits get played even on that station. Or at least it's a low ratio of songs considering his historic chart record.

It is now only the visual gaudiness of Webb Pierce that may remain in the mind of the public. The Country Music Hall of Fame credits Webb Pierce's song "Wondering" for the first use of steel guitar on a country hit and even gives it a listening booth at their Nashville museum. But what does a regular patron remember about Webb Pierce when leaving the Hall of Fame? His tricked out Cadillac and maybe some of his elaborate stage outfits.

I fear that image has long ago replaced the substance of Pierce's recordings in the mind of most Country Music fans. Once in the late 1980s, Chet Atkins was the guest host for Garrison Keillor's live network radio program, *A Prairie Home Companion*. Atkins used some comedy material that Keillor had provided. At one point in the broadcast, Atkins talked to the audience about how he was remodeling his house in Nashville. He told them that for the design of his new swimming pool he had taken his cue from Webb Pierce. But instead of having the pool made in the shape of a guitar, he had his built in the shape of a guitar *amplifier*.

The line prompted big laughs from the audience, which suggests that these people were still well aware of Webb's famous guitar-shaped pool. But I would bet that most of these same people who got this joke would be hard pressed to name more than two of Pierce's 55 Top 10 country chart hits (much less own them). Go to the Country Music Hall of Fame and see his Cadillac—the interior is decorated with inlaid silver dollars; the car has a saddle for a driver's seat, a horse shoe for the brake pedal, and various guns as decor. Look at the stage outfits of Webb Pierce—they make Elvis' Las Vegas regalia look conservative. When remembered at all, Webb Pierce is recalled by most for his gaudy excess. And while that's too bad, it is not a unique situation. Rightly or wrongly, many performers become more famous than the music they create, whether it is Elton John or John Coltrane. Michael Jackson or Prince. Madonna or…Webb Pierce.

Certainly we can smile at the guitar-shaped swimming pool and marvel over the cars and clothes of Webb Pierce. But let's also take some time to focus on what gave Webb Pierce the opportunity to be gaudy and irritating—his extremely successful hit records. And lots of them.

CD Review

Hank Williams
The Unreleased Recordings
Time Life Records, 2008

When Hank Williams died at the age of 29, he had released 61 different songs. In spite of this relatively small amount of material, Williams found himself at the apex of country music.

Since Hank's death in January 1953, the Williams estate has milked revenue from the deceased star's recordings in ways that make the Jimi Hendrix vultures look like amateurs. Endless repackaging projects of Hank's songs continue to this day. Why, then, did it take over 50 years for these high quality radio recordings from the early morning *Mother's Best* radio show to see official release?

After the discovery of these programs on the dusty closet shelves at Nashville radio station WSM some decades back, various individuals have tried to take credit for their discovery and have sought economic reimbursement. Other parties have been just as adamant about keeping this material from being released to the public. It's a long and twisted tale, but the reason for the protracted bickering is, in a word: Money.

Certainly the *Mother's Best* shows are not the first worthwhile finds of previously unissued Hank Williams recordings. In the past 25 years, various glimpses into Williams' career have been legitimately released, including demo recordings, live Opry radio broadcasts, and a complete set of eight radio transcriptions called *The Health and Happiness Show*. All are remarkable. However, the newly released *Mother's Best* radio programs dig deeper.

Because these broadcasts were not purposefully created to further his career, Williams is free to sing what he pleases, often performing material that he recorded nowhere else. Here we witness Hank playing various country and religious songs that clearly moved him. For example, his affection for the maudlin can be seen in his choice of "The Blind Child." Williams' sincerity is unquestioned, and his talent as a performer so great that the listener can't help but weep with the singer over this sad tale.

These newly issued recordings are of such a high quality that they enhance Hank's already unquestioned reputation. And the Time Life label assures us that they will soon be releasing more from these radio programs. I'll be waiting.

CD Review

Hank Williams
Hank Williams Revealed: The Unreleased Recordings
Time Life Records, 2009

Absolute sincerity mixed with stunning talent. This is what Hank Williams had as a performer and as a composer of country songs. His credentials as a writer have never been in question. And now with *Hank Williams Revealed,* the latest collection of programs intended for one-time radio broadcast, Williams' abilities as a performer can be more carefully examined.

Think of these recordings as the Rosetta Stone of Southern Music. Here Williams performs pure country, ballads, hymns, and several of his own Luke the Drifter recitations. The music on this set provides an aural overview of influences reaching back to earlier centuries and to other shores. Spoken comments from Hank and his band members provide a fascinating glimpse of life in the American South at mid-century.

The Williams' estate has entrusted these much sought after recordings to Colin Escott, who has sequenced the material logically, retaining an appropriate amount of between-song conversation. Escott also provides annotations for each selection, tracing song roots and recording variants. For the completists, three unedited radio programs are included, showcasing the skills of sideman Jerry Rivers on fiddle and of Williams in the role of product pitch man.

Like an impossible gift from a parallel universe, *Revealed* includes new performances of Williams' well-known songs, plus some selections that Hank never recorded commercially. The sound is startlingly crisp. Were I not holding it in my own hands, I would not believe this collection could exist.

Commentary
Art at 78 rpm: A History of Hank Williams' Releases
October 1999

At the time of his death on December 31, 1952, country music singer Hank Williams was 29 years old. His record companies had issued 32 records under his name, most featuring Williams' backing group The Drifting Cowboys. Since each record was limited to two selections, and three titles were issued on two separate releases, Williams' entire documented career output consisted of 61 different songs. There had also been two duet singles with his wife Audrey and seven records carrying the pseudonym Luke the Drifter, which Williams used for specific types of material. Yet in spite of a professional career that lasted barely six years, producing a relatively small number of recordings, the difficulties associated with Williams' records are many.

Hank Williams was involved with 25 separate recording sessions held between December 1946 and September 1952. In addition to these professional studio sessions, producing what are called "master takes," Williams recorded material intended for radio broadcast, known as "transcription disks." He also created demonstration recordings of his compositions, or "demos," which could be played for other performers in hopes that they would decide to record a given song. Hank also made some recordings for personal use. Together, these subsets of Williams' canon are commonly known as "non-session recordings," as they were usually not produced within the formal setting of a studio, and none were intended for release to the general public.

My examination of Hank's recordings is broken into three sections. The first deals with problems that would become associated with the records first issued during Williams' lifetime. The second section discusses the complex situation surrounding what was done to Williams' work since his death, including the process of adding music onto various recordings not originally meant for commercial release. The concluding section documents the slow road to recovering the sound of the original recordings.

Recording Hit Records

Nashville songwriter and producer Fred Rose signed Hank Williams to a contract in September 1946 for the Acuff-Rose music publishers. This was Nashville's first major music publishing firm, which Rose owned jointly with country music legend Roy Acuff. Rose offered Williams a staff position, hiring him only to write songs for other artists to record. However, Rose soon realized that Hank himself should be allowed to try to record some of his own material, securing a contract for him with Sterling Records.

On December 11, 1946, Hank Williams made his first professional recordings. Although the Sterling label was located in New York City, Williams recorded his first three sessions at the studios of radio station WSM in Nashville. Like today, the music industry in the 1940s was interested in issuing recordings for the purpose of creating profit-generating hit songs. At that time, there was no such thing as album tracks; every song recorded by an artist was placed either as the featured A-side of a marketable single or as its counterpart, the B (or flip) side. In January of 1947, the Sterling label released "Calling You" as William's debut record, with "Never Again" on its B-side. In February, "Wealth Won't Save Your Soul" was issued, backed with "When God Comes and Gathers His Jewels."

Neither of these first two Sterling singles would generate enough sales or airplay to enter the *Billboard Magazine* Juke Box Folk Records chart, a weekly listing of best-selling records of this genre, whose name would later be changed to Hot C&W Sides. Even so, Rose was sufficiently encouraged by the regional sales of "Calling You" to schedule a second recording session. February 13, 1947, found Hank back at the WSM studios performing four more original numbers. Like the first session's material, these songs were released almost immediately, in March and May. And like the other records, these also failed to gain much industry recognition. But while there were no initial hit records here, some of the songs from this session would remain associated with Williams for the rest of his career, including "Honky Tonkin'" and "Pan American."

Fred Rose arranged for Williams to leave Sterling in favor of another new company, MGM Records. While the MGM name was well known in the motion picture industry, they had only recently entered the music market. Rose secured a recording contract for Williams with MGM and scheduled a session for April 12, 1947, again at radio station WSM—a date which produced four more songs. In June, "Move It On Over" was released by MGM, providing Williams and Rose with the hit record they sought. "Move It On Over" reached the #4 position on the *Billboard* country chart, insuring not only greater name recognition for Williams within the industry, but assuring him of another recording session.

In 1947 a problem was looming for Hank Williams, Fred Rose, and everyone else in the music business. The American Federation of Musicians (AFM) was unhappy with some financial aspects of the recording industry, including the amount of money being set aside by studios for union pension funds. AFM union president James C. Petrillo called for a recording ban, scheduled to go into effect on January 1, 1948. Many feared it would be a lengthy lockout, as had previously occurred in 1942. The Petrillo recording ban meant that Williams would not be able to enter the studio or make new records to further his career.

During his first two 1947 sessions for MGM, in April at WSM and in August at Nashville's newly opened Castle Studios, Hank had produced seven usable master-take recordings. With the looming AFM lockout looking more and more certain, Rose brought Williams into the studio twice more in November in an attempt to stockpile material to release during the ban. In a further effort to secure as many usable recordings as possible, the producer purchased the eight master takes from the Sterling label, immediately selling them to MGM for possible rerelease. Rose wanted to make certain that he did not run short of material.

"Move It On Over" was a fine starting place for a recording career, but a follow-up hit single was now critical. "Honky Tonkin" had been the last of the Sterling sides issued. Williams would rerecord the song for MGM, which released this new version in April of the strike-plagued 1948. And while the new release of "Honky Tonkin" would not become a huge hit, it did keep Hank's name in front of the country music public, peaking at #14 on the *Billboard* charts. Although a lesser entry by the standards of what would soon follow, this was light years beyond the reaction the same song had garnered from its Sterling release a mere 11 months earlier.

Prevented from recording new material, Hank marked time during the summer of 1948; MGM began issuing records culled from the various reserves that Rose had collected. As the label would again do after the performer's death, Williams and Rose were now scrutinizing their stockpile of holdings for suitable releases. They chose two of Hank's more recent recordings, "I'm a Long Gone Daddy" with a flip side of "The Blues Come Around." This June 1948 release nearly reproduced the success of "Move It On Over," with "I'm a Long Gone Daddy" getting to #6 on the *Billboard* chart. Later that year, MGM attempted to mine the Sterling session Rose had acquired by releasing older recordings of "I Don't Care" backed with "Pan American." Neither song would chart.

The label next tried two recordings made in the months prior to the ban. But again, neither "Mansion on the Hill" nor "I Saw the Light" would enter the charts. In retrospect, this seems extremely odd, considering that the latter song is now so closely associated with Williams and is among his most famous. In spite of several fine releases, nothing was working for Hank Williams during the last half of 1948. The AFM recording ban was rumored to be coming to an end. But if a song such as "I Saw the Light" was not enhancing Williams' reputation, the further creation of new material was arguably a moot point for his career.

With the recording ban lifted in the late 1948, Fred Rose was finally able to get Williams back into the studio. In December, Hank traveled to Cincinnati for his first session in over a year. Rose was reportedly disappointed with this session, thinking that Hank should have gathered better songs to record for his first post-strike session. He recorded two duets with his wife Audrey, one number with the studio band, and finished the date with an Irving Mills and Cliff Friend number, "The Lovesick Blues." It was an old song—one that no one seemed to remember. In fact, Hank played on this fact by initially telling Fred Rose that it was an original composition. Giving Williams the benefit of the doubt, perhaps he was taking composing credit as a ploy to get approval to record the song, since when Hank first brought "The Lovesick Blues" to Rose, the producer "wanted nothing to do with it."

But if Hank did not write "The Lovesick Blues," he certainly made it his own. In spite of Rose's hostile feelings towards it, "The Lovesick Blues" made Hank into the huge star that both men knew was possible. Perhaps it was the song's plaintive yodel, leaping back a generation and reminiscent of Jimmie Rodgers, that connected with the audience's soul. Whatever the reason, the reaction to this song was huge and immediate—Hank was big! The fact that Williams knew "The Lovesick Blues" suited his style and felt strongly enough to record it in spite of Rose's advice to the contrary is significant. It demonstrates that Williams knew precisely what he was doing when selecting material to record, just as he knew exactly what he wanted for his sound.

The Sound in His Mind

The six formal studio sessions which preceded the recording of "The Lovesick Blues" and the eighteen recording sessions which followed were all engineered using live performance techniques. This means that Hank Williams and his group The Drifting Cowboys were assembled together in the studio, performing the music for the recording machines in the same manner that a band would approach a dance hall engagement. This may seem like an obvious way to record a band, but even as Williams' first recordings were made, guitarist Les Paul was successfully experimenting with multitrack recording. With the multitrack method of production, each instrument and the voice of the singer could be recorded separately and later mixed together for a finished performance.

Les Paul's inventive influence would travel quickly and forever change the way records would be made. Webb Pierce was among the very first in Nashville to use the technique of layering various audio tracks to make a record. One of Webb's band members remembers his surprise when he attended a recording session that Pierce intentionally missed. The group's function that day was to record instrumental, or backing tracks, to which the singer would later add his vocals. Studio musicians routinely record backing tracks today, but the process of layering sound was not yet widely used during Williams' brief career. Although Hank himself never employed a multitracking or overdubbing process in any records released during his lifetime, it would be extensively used on his music after his death.

As years passed and musical styles changed, Williams' music seemed to embody an earlier era. The country sound that Hank represented was being less and less embraced by sectors of country's performers and their audiences. Country music was attempting to expand its market while simultaneously diminishing its purely agrarian image. For example, Eddy Arnold had begun his career as country as one could get, both in sound and in name. Known first as "The Tennessee Plowboy," Arnold had many big hits, including "The Cattle Call." He would leave that name, image, and style of music behind in order to court a larger audience. By the mid-1960s, Arnold could be seen in a tuxedo rather than overalls, singing pop ballads and chatting with Johnny Carson on national television.

The Nashville Sound was the local industry's answer to declining record sales; it was seen as a way to compete with the records of the much larger pop and easy listening markets. This new Nashville Sound rejected the traditional and hard-edged country sound that featured fiddle or steel guitar. Instead, The Nashville Sound was rich with lush strings, with often only the singer's voice rising above the vast aural blandness. Combining the strings of Mantovani with a country-tinged voice certainly yielded some huge chart successes. The cross pollination of styles achieved its goal of bringing large new audiences to performers like Arnold and Jim Reeves. But sadly, while the new sound would allow country music to compete with other more mainstream music genres, this supposed solution further damaged those country performers who did not choose to embrace it. Ernest Tubb, Hank Thompson, and Bill Monroe are representative of many veteran country artists who faced economic hardship, partly for staying true to their own vision of country music. These performers struggled through hard years of neglect, originally brought on by rock and roll. Now, however, the challenge to retain their fan base and attract new audiences was coming from their own musical community.

While active performers like Thompson and Tubb consciously chose the direction of their careers, the deceased Williams was now at the mercy of his record company. And record companies have one goal—to sell their product. The powers at MGM Records evidently thought that Hank's music could be made competitive within this changing market, and reach new audiences, if his sound could be augmented.

Studio musicians were brought in to add additional instrumentation to Hank Williams' original recordings—recordings that were already issued and well known. Unlike Webb Pierce's use of the multitrack overdub technique to create an original work, the process was used here to fortify Williams' already completed materials with additional accompaniment. Many of these changes seemed innocuous at first, with piano added to some of the songs, as well as percussion and newly recorded rhythm guitar tracks. Still, to those who wanted to experience Hank Williams' music in its originally recorded form, any extraneous alterations to the music were seen as pointless and distorting barriers.

Modifying the sound of a musician's work is certainly not unique to MGM's treatment of Williams' recordings, but MGM took the process to odd extremes. In 1966, the record label seemed to test the limits when it released the first of four LPs featuring extravagantly lush string backgrounds added to Williams' vocals. Entitled *The Legend Lives Anew: Hank Williams With Strings*, the record was exactly what the title indicated—the performer's master takes were adorned with lush string accompaniments. The overdubbed orchestrations obscure the sound of The Drifting Cowboys, leaving only Williams' voice to float amidst the dominating string section, in a clear attempt to recreate this deceased artist as an member of The Nashville Sound community.

These overdubbed tracks go beyond parody, placing Williams in a setting that he never intended for his music. The simplicity that Hank was striving to achieve is completely thwarted by any form of overdubbing, but nowhere more so than with the surrealistic intrusion of a string section. Yet whether it is additional drums and piano, or an entire orchestra, all of these are examples of distorted artistic intentions, as Hank Williams increasingly becomes out of place on his own records.

Examining the recordings with an ideal of original sound is by no means a universally held goal. Even some of Williams' former band members have expressed a cavalier attitude toward the overdubbed forms of Hank's music. The Drifting Cowboys' fiddler Jerry Rivers states in his book *From Life to Legend* that the overdubbed recordings are not a concern to him. Rivers speaks from an economic perspective, pointing to the extremely competitive nature of the music business. He argues that to keep Hank Williams' catalog viable, overdubs were often necessary.

At the same time, Rivers does expresses a certain amount of sorrow over the fact that these altered versions could completely replace the original recordings in the marketplace. Rivers' fears were on target, for once the overdubbed recordings had made inroads with the buying public, the unencumbered versions were increasingly difficult to find. Yet while mildly lamenting the unavailability of Hank's original recordings, Rivers still has no real criticism for the aesthetic or artistic rationale inherent in the overdubbing process. Jerry Rivers' comments are frustrating to the group that he somewhat disparagingly labels "purists." For if one adheres to Rivers' attitude, it might suggest that Williams' music should now be released with rhythmic rap or hip-hop backdrops, since these altered recordings could appeal to a new audience and generate fresh sales. This bad idea smacks of the *Hooked on Classics* series of albums from the 1980s, where various classical music pieces were recorded to a disco beat.

Some of the audio problems introduced onto Hank Williams' recordings were less obvious than the addition of an entire string section. As mentioned, all of the instruments and vocals on Williams' original recordings were performed simultaneously, created during live performances in the studio. And all of Hank's recordings were mixed to single channel, or monaural sound. This differs from the modern multitrack recording process, which is then mixed for stereo separation between the two speakers. Just as MGM recording engineers had attempted to modernize Hank's sound with newly added instruments, the process of artificial stereo enhancement was also imposed onto the Williams master recordings. The purpose of this electronic engineering was to convince consumers that the new LPs they were purchasing featured the very latest advancement in audio technology—stereo sound.

Ironically, the system used allegedly to provide sound enhancement was actually detrimental to the fidelity of the original monaural recordings. Most methods of creating false stereo from a single-channel source would merely split the audio spectrum to varying degrees, sending a lower, often muddy-sounding frequency to one speaker and a higher frequency to the other. The addition of extra instruments, coupled with the inclusion of an imitation stereo effect, forces Williams' voice to the back of the audio mix on these altered master takes, often giving the singer a hollow and somewhat distant sound.

In a different mode of enhancement, sound engineers sometimes used a method of phase inversion. This would make the music coming from stereo speakers sound as if the speakers are quite far apart from one another. This too is problematic, for it not only alters the integrity of the original recording, it also gives the music a phase shifting, or swishing sound. Furthermore, since the frequency range had been altered by the audio engineers, the original monaural sound could not be retrieved from these records even when combining the tracks by placing one's home amplifier into the mono setting to combine the tracks.

In short, all of these experimental efforts to change a monaural text into a stereo format were failures. Happily, this method has not been widely used in some years since listeners, by and large, prefer monaural recordings if this is the music's originally recorded form.

Part of the frustration arising from the record company's tampering with Williams' music reflects the fact that this artist was extremely specific about how his material should be conveyed to an audience. His strong views are evident in his song selection, his vocal mannerisms, and his performances. In Roger M. Williams' biography *Sing a Sad Song,* former members of The Drifting Cowboys are quoted as saying that Hank was insistent and stunningly blunt in his instructions to backing musicians about how a given song should sound and how an arrangement should be handled. "If one of us started jazzing it up a bit Hank would always tell us to knock it off," says Jerry Rivers.

On the bandstand, Williams knew exactly the sound he was after and would tolerate no deviation from his vision. Numerous observers agree that Williams was insistent on keeping his songs unembellished, intentionally sounding as close as possible to the relatively sparse arrangements found on his original records. Like his decision to record "The Lovesick Blues," Hank clearly knew exactly what he was doing by keeping his approach to the music free of cluttering distractions. Although the music may sometimes have seemed overly simple and repetitive for Williams' band members, many country fans would declare Hank's Drifting Cowboys to be the best country music group they ever heard.

As MGM was altering the very sound of Williams' work, other aspects of the recording industry were likewise changing. The four Sterling label releases of early 1947 were available only as 78 rpm records. This is not surprising, since this is the format that had been used exclusively for recorded music since the mid-1920s. When MGM began issuing Williams' material in June 1947, this company also made the songs available in the standard 78 rpm format of the day. But at the end of 1949, the company began issuing Hank's music both on 78s and on the new 45 rpm disk. This was a smaller, lighter record with a large center hole and purportedly superior sound quality. This new 45 rpm format had been introduced into the marketplace earlier that year by RCA Records.

While making Williams' recordings available on the new 45 rpm configuration, MGM made certain that customers could still purchase Hank Williams records on 78 rpm disks well past the performer's death, releasing music on this older format as late as 1957. MGM was certainly not the last to abandon this format, which could still be found (if searched out) into the very early 1960s. Country music fans have long had the reputation of being hesitant to embrace new technology. Although perhaps an unfair overgeneralization, there are reasons for this stereotype. After 8-track tape cartridges had been a thing of the past for most music genres, some record companies continued to make their country artists available on 8-track for a small but profitable market. Years after 8-tracks ceased to be stocked in record or retail stores, they remained available through mail order and at freeway truck stops. Although the advent of compact discs led to a somewhat shorter battle, country fans were again among the last bastion of holdouts in switching from LPs to CDs in the late 1980s.

Recording for the Radio and Himself

Besides the studio master takes, the other major category of existing Hank Williams material is comprised of non-session recordings. As indicated, these come from various sources, including recordings made especially for radio broadcast, demo recordings, and audition or home recordings. Some of these performances feature backing musicians, but most are simply Hank's voice accompanied only by his acoustic guitar.

None of the non-session recordings were meant for commercial release. But by the time of Williams' death, MGM had issued almost all of the master takes Hank had produced. Two of the four songs Williams cut at his last session in September 1952 were scheduled for an early 1953 release ("Kaw-Liga" and "Your Cheatin' Heart"). One song from this session had already been released in November, "I Could Never Be Ashamed of You." The flip side of this final single to be issued during Williams' life was the prophetic "I'll Never Get Out of This World Alive"—a song which would quickly reach #1 after the performer's death. The remaining selection from the last session would be released in April 1953, "Take These Chains from My Heart." Following these records, only two master takes remained in the MGM vaults, plus two duet numbers that prominently feature Hank's wife, Audrey. The public was clearly eager for more of Williams' music, but the problem of limited resources haunted MGM executives from the moment Hank's death was announced.

Producer Fred Rose had experienced shortages of Williams' material before, during the recording ban of 1948. Now, however, the situation was more dire, since there was no chance for subsequent recording sessions. As a result, the producer went to work with what he had. Only weeks after the singer's death, Rose assembled The Drifting Cowboys in the studio for the purpose of adding backing instrumentation to several of Hank's solo demos and home recordings. Rose's initial overdubbing sessions, in some ways, make a certain amount of sense. Williams' audience knew that a specific style was associated with his name, and these musicians had supplied Hank's accompaniment on his other recordings. Using musicians from Hank's backing group to provide accompaniment, a reasonably authentic performance could be assembled.

Two of these dubbed, non-session performances achieved the desired effect for the MGM executives by producing posthumous country radio hits for Williams. One overdubbed demo, "Weary Blues from Waiting," even reached *Billboard* magazine's Top 10, charting in the fall of 1953. These numbers had been recorded by Hank as demonstration recordings, in the hope that other artists might want them; now Rose was using them to further Williams' career.

Despite healthy sales, Rose's successful overdubbing of these non-session demos ultimately was not in the best interest of Hank's art or legacy. The altered releases did help to keep the Hank Williams name and his music in front of the public, while also supplying a demand for fresh material—a demand from both audience and record executives. However, the economic success of the first overdubbed demo releases showed the powers at MGM that his audio restructuring process could be surprisingly lucrative. The situation concerning overdubbed materials soon turned ugly as the studio quickly began to ignore the idea of how the artist would have performed a song, a line of thought purposefully pursued by Rose. Consequently, MGM did not resist placing Williams' voice within any context that would sell records, culminating with the previously discussed *Hank Williams with Strings*.

Both the master takes and the non-session recordings were considered fair game for MGM management. Solo demonstration recordings had various backgrounds added, with the song "Fool About You" making a distinctive example. This song had been recorded with just Hank and his guitar, but over the years it received two separate overdub treatments, first with a country backing, then with a rockabilly-sounding backdrop featuring a hot lead guitar and plenty of rhythm. The original, undubbed performance of "Fool About You" would not be released in the United States until 1986. Some radio performances were likewise dubbed, with the syndicated *Health and Happiness* shows of October 1949 reconfigured and issued by MGM. Featured as *On Stage*, volumes 1 and 2, these radio transcription recordings were overdubbed with extra instrumentation as well as an enhanced audience response to each number.

In addition to questionable editorial decisions concerning sound, the Hank Williams canon has even experienced the destruction or loss of original copies of several songs, leaving only the altered replicas, which serve as mocking reminders of what was actually created by the artist. Noted Hank Williams scholar Bob Pinson, principal researcher at Nashville's Country Music Hall of Fame archives, indicates that the MGM audio log books show that the company is in possession of several original, undubbed Williams demos that have never been released. These recordings, however, cannot be located in the record company vaults. It is thought that at least a few of these demos were considered to be of no further use by the company, and subsequently discarded after the overdub process was complete. As a result, no known copy exists for a few of Williams' songs in their originally recorded form.

Discarding master recordings seems like an impossible scenario. Sadly, this is consistent with MGM's cavalier attitude toward the maintenance and release of their Williams holdings. Such "carelessness," as Bob Pinson terms it, has led to situations in which songs are issued by incorrect titles, and collections are released with incomplete or inaccurate information. In one situation, however, MGM's lack of attention to their own holdings worked to the benefit of the Hank Williams collector. In 1956, MGM included "Crazy Heart" as a selection on one of its many rerelease collections of Williams' material. However, the version included on this extended play 45 rpm was not the same master take recording as had been previously available. Pinson believes that the release of this alternate version of "Crazy Heart" was a mistake made by a company that seemed to have difficulty keeping track of its own materials. Pinson is convinced that this version of "Crazy Heart" was recorded at the same session as the other version. And while not as polished as the originally released master, this alternate take of "Crazy Heart" did provide a previously unheard Hank Williams performance. As such, it was an unusually begotten, but legitimate and welcome addition to Williams' body of work.

In addition to overdubs and simulated stereo, other oddities exist. For some reason, when MGM reissued "The Blues Come Around" in one of their hits collections, the vocal chorus between two of the verses had been edited out of the recording. In another instance, when preparing the non-session recording "Ready to Go Home" for release, a guitar part was added to serve as a musical introduction, but it is sloppily attached and is at odds with the meter of the song. These situations speak to the record company's poor handling of their archival holdings, repeatedly demonstrated by a lack of care given to their cache of Williams' materials.

While the quest for accuracy has been frustratingly slow to come to Hank Williams' recordings, small victories were won as early as the mid-1970s. In May 1976 MGM issued the first collection of previously unreleased Hank Williams material in over a decade. Entitled *Hank Williams, Sr., Live at the Grand Ole Opry*, the record contained eleven performances recorded at the Opry between 1949 and 1951.

Unlike previous MGM reconfigurations of personal appearances, these recordings were issued in their original state—undubbed, and in monaural sound. Sales were good, and MGM perhaps began to realize that the music could remain in its unaltered form and find a sizable audience. There was no follow-up to the *Opry* LP, and the overdubbed releases continued to be issued by MGM. However, *Live at the Grand Ole Opry* is an important step toward releasing the artist's catalog in its original form.

Just as the *Opry* LP of 1976 arguably opened the door for future undubbed live recordings, a different collection demonstrated that Hank's original studio recordings could sell well and be accepted by a modern audience. First released in Japan in 1978, the collection *40 Greatest Hits* was superior to most previous hits collections in several ways. This two-record set contained a generous number of songs for the LP format, especially when compared to the typical United States method of packaging 24 selections on the same amount of vinyl.

The songs included on *40 Greatest Hits* were presented in chronological order, with brief annotations describing the success of each on the *Billboard* charts. Most importantly, these were Williams' original and unaltered recordings. The only exceptions were the overdubbed demos of two posthumously released songs, which had become well known as hit singles in the form presented on this collection. Although *40 Greatest Hits* was not issued in the U.S. at the time of its Japanese release, steady sales of this set in the United States as an import LP prompted Polygram Records to release it into the American market in a CD format some years later.

The *40 Greatest Hits* collection seems to have slowly influenced the American thought process about presenting Williams' material. In 1971 MGM had issued a two-LP collection of *24 of Hank Williams' Greatest Hits*. The collection included six tracks of overdubbed master takes. And while the record company chose not to substitute the superior Japanese release for their own domestic set, MGM did issue a new edition of this *24 Greatest Hits* domestic package in the late 1970s, replacing the six overdubbed selections with their undubbed counterparts. This would be considered a "silent correction," as there are no liner notes to indicate the switch, and the record number did not change. It is impossible to tell, merely by looking at the album, if it is the dubbed or undubbed pressing.

MGM Records had employed this sort of confusing methodology several times during the 1960s and 1970s. In June 1968, for example, the company released a collection of Williams' music titled *In the Beginning*. This set was first issued with 11 overdubbed master takes, and then reissued (with identical cover art and LP identification number) in a completely undubbed form. Also, when portions of the previously mentioned *Health and Happiness* radio programs were released onto LP as *On* Stage, the stereo version included overdubbed instruments and crowd noise added to the original sound. But curiously, the simultaneous release of *On Stage* in the monaural format had no such additional sounds imposed onto the audio mix.

Even after such brief if unheralded victories for original sound, however, the battle was by no means won. While Japan's *40 Greatest Hits* collection seemed to usher in a new era for releasing sonically accurate collections, MGM returned to its practice of issuing hodgepodge combinations of recordings, in various states of authenticity. As late as July 1977, the new U.S. release for Hank Williams fans was *24 Greatest Hits, Vol. 2*. This collection contained some fine lesser known performances, but seven of the included tracks were overdubbed master take recordings.

A New Generation—An Old Problem

Hank Williams, Jr., has added his own anomalies to his father's recordings. Assisted (or encouraged) by his record companies and his mother, Audrey, the younger Williams has mined the aural ghost of his famous father on several occasions. In 1971, MGM released a two-record set entitled *The Legend of Hank Williams in Song and Story*. This collection was another repackaging of the elder Williams' hits, interspersed with comments read by Hank, Jr. Featured on this set is "May You Never Be Alone," with the singing of Hank, Jr., added to his father's voice, just as instruments had previously been overdubbed onto Williams' recordings. Although the electronic studio creation of posthumous duet records has almost become fashionable, this particular pairing resulted in a recording that makes the listener as uncomfortable as the *Hank Williams with Strings* series, but with a macabre twist.

Giving the man his due, Hank Williams, Jr., has been able to create his own successful country music career, and possesses an impressive

Billboard chart history. Perhaps because by the mid-1980s he no longer leaned so heavily on his father's image, Hank, Jr., felt comfortable producing another duet. Over a decade after the overdubbed "May You Never Be Alone" was issued as an album track, a previously unknown non-session demo recording of Hank Williams was located and presented to Hank, Jr. The resulting duet of "There's a Tear in My Beer" was very well received, reaching #7 on the *Billboard* country chart. However, any excitement generated by the discovery of a recording on which Hank Williams performs a song for which there was no other known recording was blunted by the decision to overdub Hank, Jr.'s voice. The situation was made more frustrating by the fact that the original, unaltered recording of "There's a Tear in My Beer" would remain unavailable for well over a year after the duet single was issued. When it was finally released, this undubbed performance was available only as an enticing rarity on an expensive three-CD set.

Unexpected Gifts

In spite of the pervasiveness of overdubbed recordings being accepted as a part of Williams' official canon, and a seemingly cavalier attitude displayed by record executives, musical colleagues, and even family members—great changes were on the horizon. In 1985 the floodgates opened. Nashville's Country Music foundation issued the LP *Just Me and My Guitar*, consisting of twelve previously unreleased demo recordings. True to its title, the songs on the record were simply Hank accompanying himself on guitar. After the unexpectedly large sales of *Just Me and My Guitar,* the Country Music Foundation followed its success with *The First Recordings,* which contained more demos of unaccompanied songs, recorded between 1945 and 1952. These two discrete LPs have now been issued on a single CD, *Demos: From First to Last.*

Also important in 1985 was the release of the first of an impressive and ambitious undertaking of eight double-album sets on the Polydor record label (which now owned the rights to Hank's recordings). Each volume carried a "Statement of Purpose," announcing that the series would strive to present Williams' songs "in chronological order" and "in original undubbed mono." This multivolume edition offered the best collection yet of the artist's work in its original form. However, the set had its own peculiar frustrations, including the seemingly random mixture of master takes with non-session recordings. Even the producers of this project may have been somewhat dissatisfied; when later issued on CD, the tracking order of the selections was markedly different from each volume's LP counterpart.

Another problem with these Polydor releases had to do with the clarity of information provided in the liner notes, which sometimes lacked specific documentation. Colin Escott and Hank Davis alternated on composing essays for each of the two-LP sets, for which the writer would describe a few aspects of some of the included works. In spite of Escott's well established and deserved reputation for his writings on Hank Williams, the documentation in this series was not systematic and often incomplete. Escott and Davis do provide a great deal of useful information, but it is not always easy to find data on a specific song within their writings.

In contrast, during the same era as this project's release, two unrelated LPs of largely unknown Williams material were also issued, *Rare Takes and Radio Cuts* and *On the Air*. Here, Bob Pinson presents a track-by-track discussion of each song on each LP. *Rare Takes* is also noteworthy for a refreshing attitude brought to bear on Williams' fragmented recordings. Unlike the sloppy post-production work found on "The Blues Come Around" or "Ready to Go Home," discussed above, this LP contained a fine example of a damaged recording's reconstruction. "The Little Paper Boy" was a non-session, solo radio recording for which no master take existed. However, this unique performance was incomplete, as the recording lacked the guitar introduction that originally preceded the first verse. Under Pinson's direction, Country Music Foundation's audio engineer Alan Stoker copied the song's closing instrumental guitar part and carefully edited this onto the beginning of the track, where it now also serves as the song's introduction. Here, at last, was a case of technology working in favor of Hank by means of appropriately replicating a performance. The *Rare Takes* and *On the Air* releases were well-conceived showcases of Williams' non-session recordings. They demonstrated how to present both the songs and the accompanying descriptive bibliography materials in a superior manner.

The final installment of the eight-volume Polydor set was issued in 1987. Although flawed, the series held true to its original "Statement of Purpose"—these eight hours of recordings offered a fine and seemingly comprehensive examination of the art of Hank Williams. Combined with *Rare Takes, On the Air,* and the *Demos: First to Last,* these collected works (briefly) appeared to be the final word on the recordings of Hank Williams.

The Complete Works…and Beyond!

In 1990 Polydor Records released a three-CD set called *The Original Singles Collection…Plus.* Apparently taking the *40 Greatest Hits* concept as a model, the set offers an expanded overview of most of Williams' master takes and all of his hit singles. While not claiming to be comprehensive, the choice of material is interesting. An editorial decision which works to the set's advantage is the purposeful omission of the three singles recorded as duets by Hank and his wife, Audrey. As some selections on the *Health and Happiness* radio shows clearly demonstrated, Hank was more effective when not including his wife as a singing partner.

Like Japan's *40 Greatest Hits,* this longer *Singles* overview presents the recordings chronologically, allowing for a sequential view of Williams' career. Although most of these recordings are master takes, the wording on the set is a bit odd. The liner notes do boast of the fact that "the original undubbed masters have been used." The statements then muddy the waters by asserting that these master takes are "equalized as closely as possible to the MGM 78 rpm singles." This would suggest that the sonic limitations of the original pressings are preserved on these CDs, rather than utilizing the full frequency of the surviving recordings closest to the original master takes. Purposefully recreating the sound of 78 records as the sonic ideal is especially troubling, considering the poor quality of shellac used for some of Hank's earliest releases. But if the box's exterior descriptions are murky, the sound on this set is clear, presented in excellent fidelity throughout. The "*Plus*" part of this collection consists of 17 non-session recordings, several released here for the first time in their original form, including the elusive "There's a Tear in My Beer," as discussed above. These were all welcome additions to the Hank library, and more were to come.

In 1993, recordings of the complete *Health and Happiness* radio programs were issued as a two-CD set—a collection that could be seen as a very late follow-up to the *Opry* LP of 1977. Each of the eight *Health and Happiness* programs is approximately twelve minutes in length;

they present Hank and The Drifting Cowboys performing on a syndicated radio series. These radio programs, all recorded in October 1949, are fascinating both for the musical performances and for the personal presence Williams is able to transmit through the radio. MGM had previously mined these *Health and Happiness* shows for material they would issue in an overdubbed form for their two *On Stage* LPs. And the fifth entry in the eight-volume Polydor set from the mid-1980s featured a side of undubbed excerpts from these famous radio shows. Bob Pinson has also included a handful of noteworthy performances from these shows in his *Rare Takes* and *On the Air* LPs. But now all eight *Health and Happiness* programs were available in their original form—the way they were recorded and subsequently broadcast on southern radio stations in the fall of 1949.

With the release of these unedited and undubbed radio programs, the complete works of Hank Williams once again seemed available. But finality is a difficult thing to achieve. By the mid-1990s Polydor had deleted their eight-volume set of Williams' recordings. Taking this material out of print seemed to make little sense until it was learned that Mercury Records, a label operated by PolyGram (which also owns Polydor) was readying a seemingly comprehensive 10-CD package called *The Complete Hank Williams*. The release of this project was set to coincide with the month Hank would have turned 75 years old, in September 1998.

In many ways, *The Complete Hank Williams* is much like the eight deleted Polydor volumes. It purports to present a comprehensive portrait of the artist, yet it too requires other Hank Williams recordings to augment its alleged completeness. This 10-CD set contains many previously unissued recordings that shed new light onto Hank's artistry. It offers the best aural fidelity possible, while acknowledging the inherent audio limitations of these recordings. Among the newly released performances is an audio track taken from one of Hank's very few network television appearances, the short-lived *Kate Smith Family Hour*. One song from this broadcast is Anita Carter singing a duet with Williams on his "I Can't Help It If I'm Still in Love With You." This fine rendition demonstrates that Hank was successfully able to share a microphone with a female vocalist—something which rarely worked with his wife as a singing partner.

Other previously unknown or unavailable items included on the

Complete set are fascinating live performances, demos, and personal recordings that Hank had made for himself and for others. The collection boasts several recently located demos from the MGM Records vaults previously thought lost. Among the high points of the newly released materials are a Grand Ole Opry radio broadcast of a gospel number entitled "Let the Spirit Descend," a song unique to Hank's canon. Also of great interest are home recordings made in 1940, for which Williams is pretending that he and his band are hosting a radio show—something that must have seemed like a distant dream of success for the teenage performer.

However, some of the problems plaguing earlier collections are again present here, such as misleading liner notes: The *Complete* box set claims to have "Hank's debut on the Grand Ole opry." This is the fabled night in June 1949 when Hank walked to the Opry microphone as an unknown, but won over the audience so thoroughly that he played at least six encores of "The Lovesick Blues" before the crowd would allow him to leave the stage. In spite of the liner notes' claims, this sought-after recording is not included. Instead, the radio recording of the *following* week's performance of "The Lovesick Blues" is featured here. This confusion is not the fault of odd wording, as is the case of the exterior notes to *The Complete Singles...Plus* collection, but instead appears to be purposefully misleading. Furthermore, the Opry performance of "The Lovesick Blues" included on this collection is inferior to Hank's treatment of the song on a later broadcast. This superior version can be heard on the *Live at the Grand Ole Opry* LP, but is not found on the *Complete* set.

Similar to the eight-LP series on Polydor, the *Complete* set includes "a note from the producers," which defines completeness for this project. Colin Escott, co-producer Kira Florita, and executive producer Luke Lewis explain that, for them, the definition does not extend to multiple takes of songs, especially "non-essential versions which are neither special nor distinct." They conclude their list of omissions by flatly stating, "The selection of broadcast performances is not complete, but designed to reflect songs that Hank did not record elsewhere and the best 'live' performances of his most well-known songs."

Even with this rationale concerning the purposeful exclusion of known and available recordings, this set's attempt to provide the definitive Hank Williams collection is further undermined by other questionable editorial decisions. The *Health and Happiness* shows remain in print, which is probably the reason that only five of that set's 49 tracks appear on the *Complete* collection. Similarly, the fact that *First to Last* is also available is perhaps the reason that five of the solo demos from this collection are excluded here. Still, these omissions are irritating and are difficult to justify for an expensive set that boasts completeness in its title. Far more problematic, however, is the decision to ignore several once-issued recordings that have long been unavailable, such as tracks from the previously mentioned *Live at the Grand Ole Opry* LP release.

When mining audio tracks from television's *The Kate Smith Family Hour* for the duet with Anita Carter, why did the producers not also include Hank's riveting performance of "Cold Cold Heart" from this same broadcast? Any person with enough interest to purchase a 10-CD set of Hank Williams surely would find this unavailable performance both "special" and "distinct." Lastly, if a total musical portrait of the artist is desired, the collection should (but doesn't) include the handful of now deleted master takes of Audrey Williams as a featured vocalist, on which her famous husband accompanies her strictly as a solo backing guitarist. These tracks would probably not be played very often, but they should be included.

Because of extremely involved legal entanglements, some known recordings by Hank Williams are not available for release. The most famous example is the series of early morning radio shows made for Mother's Best Flour, which have never been officially issued in any form. Known now by the sponsor's name, the *Mother's Best* shows were 15-minute radio programs, broadcast weekday mornings over Nashville's WSM. Over 70 shows and 17 hours of material from these programs are known to exist, including at least 42 songs that Hank performs nowhere else. In many ways, the *Mother's Best* shows are similar to the earlier *Health and Happiness* radio broadcasts. However, the *Health and Happiness* shows were trying to establish Hank's reputation as a country artist; the *Mother's Best* broadcasts were recorded after Hank had become a huge star.

Other Hank Williams radio performances include shows sponsored by the Duck Head clothing company, but it is uncertain whether recordings of these live broadcasts exist. It can't be helped that these performances are not included on the *Complete* set. However, the fact that the set's accompanying essay does not acknowledge their existence is troubling, since it invites questions about what other elements of the Williams canon are being ignored.

The good news is that Hank Williams' music is being issued, is widely available, and is offered in its originally recorded form. His recordings are not being reconfigured for imitation stereo, and the instrumental overdubs are almost completely stripped away. In addition to the commercially available music, there are still many hours of unreleased radio recordings, most notable the *Mother's Best* programs. The possibility also exists that more unknown materials will be found. It was not until the late 1980s that the demo recording of "There's a Tear in My Beer" was located. And perhaps someone is in possession of the lost MGM undubbed demos or the elusive Duck Head radio broadcasts. The fact that these and other uncollected materials exist should not defeat the Hank Williams enthusiast. Instead, these misplaced recordings should be viewed as an encouraging situation, since one can likely look forward to the release of more material from this unique artist.

2016 Update

Since I first published this essay in 1999, much has happened with the recordings of Hank Williams:

In late 1999, Mercury Records released a two-CD set of radio broadcasts called *Hank Williams: Live at The Grand Ole Opry*. It must be stressed that this is *not* a CD reissue of the 1976 LP on the MGM label, *Hank Williams, Sr., Live at the Grand Ole Opry*. That album has never been issued on CD, which is unfortunate, as it includes a few selections that even now are found nowhere else. Two other LPs that have never been reissued on CD that also contain a few selections not collected elsewhere are *Rare Takes and Radio Cuts* (1984) and *On the Air* (1985), both on the Polydor label.

Nearly a decade after the *Opry* CD release, two separate box sets of previously unreleased recordings extracted from the *Mother's Best* radio transcriptions were issued. The first, released in 2008, is called *Hank Williams: The Unreleased Recordings*. This was followed in 2009 by *Hank Williams Revealed: The Unreleased Recordings*. Each is a three-CD set, issued by Time Life Records. Both sets have excellent track-by-track annotations and essays by Colin Escott.

A 2009 release, *Gospel Keepsakes*, is a one-CD collection of songs culled from *The Unreleased Recordings* box set (2008). Of its 15 *Mother's Best* radio performances, three of the selections are not included on *The Unreleased Recordings*. This encouraged the Hank Williams fan to purchase this *Gospel Keepsakes* release in addition to the more expensive box set.

In 2010, Time Life Records released the complete run of existing *Mother's Best* radio shows on a 16-CD set. The box includes 73 of Hank's early morning radio broadcasts, containing about 17 hours of material. This large box set includes everything found on *The Unreleased Recordings* (2008), *Revealed* (2009), and *Gospel Keepsakes*. Many fans were irritated by the sporadic manner in which Time Life Records chose to release this material.

In 2012, Time Life released a CD titled *Hank Williams: Lost Concerts*. This includes a live show recorded May 4, 1952, in Niagara Falls, New York, and another concert by Hank recorded at Sunset Park, Pennsylvania, on July 13, 1952. Neither performance had been previously released.

Lastly (for now), in 2014, Omnivore Records issued *The Garden Spot Programs, 1950*. These radio shows were virtually unknown before a transcription disk containing these recordings surfaced.

Other Hank Williams recordings do exist, or existed at one time. The label on the recently unearthed *Garden Spot* transcription disk indicates that it contains programs #4, 9, 10, and 11. This would strongly suggest that there are other Hank Williams recordings in this series that have yet to be discovered. Similarly, it was thought that Hank Snow was in possession of various radio transcriptions sponsored by Duck Head jeans, some featuring Hank Williams. Snow displays short excerpts from several of these radio programs on his 1966 LP, *This Is My Story*, on which the country star gives a spoken account of his rise to fame. Side two of this album includes a brief conversation between Williams and Snow from a 1950 Duck Head broadcast on radio station WSM, but no music. Several years before his death, Hank Snow told country music scholar Charles K. Wolfe that he intended to make copies of his Hank Williams holdings for the Country Music Foundation archives, but never did so.

Source notes at end of book.

Bonus Track

Lest we smile at the idea of tampering with existing re-cordings, believing ourselves to have gone beyond this sort of artistic sin—not so fast. The process lives on to this day. In 2015, the Elvis Presley estate released If I Can Dream: Elvis Presley with The Royal Philharmonic Orchestra. *Similar to the Hank Williams with Strings project, this new CD consists of previously released Presley recordings with a full orchestra newly added atop of Elvis' original vocals. Much like Jerry Rivers defending this process on Hank Williams records, Elvis' former wife Priscilla Presley speaks, albeit indirectly, in economic terms: "We have to keep Elvis current to keep his legacy alive." Priscilla stresses that this is an "authentic" recording, as she simultaneously praises the overdubbed vocals of Michael Bublé to Elvis' "Fever." Kory Grow of* Roll-ing Stone Magazine *calls these new additions "tasteful and smart." I call them misguided.*

BEATLES, BOB, BRUCE, AND BARRY!

"…my feelings towards Woody Guthrie… uh… cannot really be… told in… how many records of his I buy, or… or this kind of thing. It's… a lot more than that, actually."

—Bob Dylan, 1963

"Bob Dylan is not a particularly easy man to compliment."

—Elvis Costello

Commentary
In Praise of 8-track Tapes
November 2010

8-track tapes should have never existed. They were the worst idea for a music format in the history of recorded sound. In every way possible, 8-tracks present a strange and irritating anomaly. They were an abomination, a black mark on the music industry. Yet somehow they *were* manufactured, *were* marketed, and *did* catch on with the public in a big, big way. For a few years (1971-1974) 8-track tapes outsold cassette tapes and were second only to vinyl albums in total sales of prerecorded music. Their popularity did not last.

These tapes now serve as a punch line for failed music formats. For the steadily decreasing number of people who even remember them, the mention of an 8-track provides a touchstone for a distant time that brings a brief smile, if not an outright laugh; and rightly so. 8-track tapes self-destructed regularly and without warning. They were difficult to repair once damaged, and the order of the songs on these tapes varied greatly from the album version of the same release.

In sum: it is amazing that this technology was introduced into the market place. It is even more mind numbing to contemplate why it was embraced by the public, even for a short time.

But while I readily acknowledge each of these serious flaws, I love my 8-track tapes. After years of banishing them to my attic, an active 8-track player is again connected to my living room sound system. I enjoy playing 8-tracks for unwitting guests who believe they are hearing a CD. I ask them how they like the fine audio fidelity and wait with anticipation for the *klu*-clunk of every track change. Visitors humor me briefly, and then recall some reason why they must depart.

To be fair, most people in today's society appear happy with their music reproduced from narrow-spectrum ear buds and through tiny computer speakers. Most listeners don't concern themselves much with audio fidelity. And that's fine. But not for me.

Like others who came of age in the 1970s, I have memories of

8-track tapes, but mine evoke pensive reflections in addition to laughter. As I look back on my music education, I see that 8-track tapes served a unique function. Given their unyielding nature, the user of this format would be forced to listen to a tape at whatever place it happened to be in its program. Rewinding a tape was impossible with the physics of the 8-track design. Yes, there were fast-forward functions on some of the expensive players, but even these were not *that* fast. And yes, you could switch from one program (or track) to another, but this would invariably place the listener in the middle of a different song. So you listened to the tape where it happened to be in the program or removed the tape. As a friend of mine accurately said, the machine tells *you* what you are going to hear!

Because of this mechanical inflexibility, I became familiar with all of the songs on the 8-track tapes I played, not just the selections I really wanted to hear. While waiting for a specific song, I would be forced to hear the two or three tunes that preceded it on the track. And usually, as it turned out, these were not too bad. In fact, sometimes I started liking these force-fed songs more than the one I was anticipating. Bands of the era should have paid more attention to this captive audience trait of the 8-track format.

In high school, I drove around Des Moines in my mom's Chevy Impala, listening to the 8-tracks I had bought from cutout bins for 49 cents. I often purchased a title based on name recognition. The tape was usually discounted in price because there had been no radio hits on the release, so it didn't sell well. The lack of hits mattered not; by 1971 I thought I had outgrown Top 40 radio, although this delusion was only temporary. I did, however, enjoy the commercial-free element of the 8-track tape listening experience, something my XM Radio would again provide many years later.

From the bargain bins I grabbed 8-track tapes by artists I knew to one degree or another, or had at least heard of—The Byrds' *Notorious Byrd Brothers* was one, Randy Newman's *Good Old Boys* is another that jumps to mind. Both are strong records which I know well in their entirety only because of 8-track technology's forced programming.

An indisputable plus of the technology was the surprisingly high audio fidelity of an 8-track tape. This can be explained by analogue audio physics. When an 8-track tape was operating correctly, its audio spectrum would consistently outperform cassette tape recordings of its era. Why? 8-track tape played at 3 3/4 inches per second (ips). Cassette tape runs at 1 7/8 ips. Faster is better, as it allows more space on the tape to store the sound. The high end of the spectrum (the treble) is clearer, and the overall presence of the sound (or depth) is crisp and superior to sound from a cassette tape. This is why I can play 8-tracks for my unsuspecting visitors and pass the music off as digital sound. People visiting our house are not audio freaks, of course. Most are there not to see me, anyway, but to visit my wife or kids. Big shock.

But before my praise gets too lavish for this curious audio artifact, we must acknowledge the elephant in the room. And it's a biggie. The final, undeniable attribute of listening to an 8-track tape concerns an unbending physical trait, which often forced mid-song interruptions in the music. The song to be split for the track switch would suddenly fade out, the machine would switch the track with the distinctive *kla-clunk* of the playback head changing positions, and the song would fade back in. Very disruptive. A typical 40-minute album had to be split into four programs of ten minutes each. (Each program was stereo, so four stereo programs = 8 tracks.) Sometimes selections could be arranged in such an order so that no song had to be split in two to accommodate the track change. But even in this situation, the song order on the tape differs markedly from that of the original album—a song order (one would assume) that was carefully chosen by the artist.

Loosen Up Naturally, by The Sons of Champlin, is a rare example of an 8-track tape that follows the song order of its LP counterpart. This is because the album itself was a two-record set, and each of the four sides contained almost exactly 16 minutes of music. Simple solution for arranging the songs: one side of the record for each program. Here, the record company didn't even mess up the obvious by changing the running order of the songs, which often occurred. I recall seeing an 8-track of the double album *Layla* once at a party in college. The four sides of the *Layla* LP each contain 20 minutes of music. Even so, the programmers had somehow managed to split the great *title* song between two tracks. And without cause! The song you originally bought the tape to hear, diminished by an interruptive track switch.

In about 1970, I was riding home with a guy I worked with at the grocery store. He had just installed an 8-track player in his muscle car and was playing the first Crosby, Stills, and Nash album. The tape was in the middle of "Wooden Ships" when the song faded out to change audio tracks and then faded back in. I told him, "That *sucks!*" He immediately said, "No, man! That makes it *twice as good!*" I'm still not sure if he was serious or not. But for whatever reason, I soon embraced the 8-track format, and by 1973 I was so deeply involved with these tapes that I had purchased an expensive recorder and was considering transferring my LPs to tape. Fortunately, this idea had a short lifespan.

We can blame Mr. Lear (of Lear Jet fame) for 8-tracks, although his idea was never to use it as a music storage format. Lear thought they would work well for 30 or 60 *second* loops of tape for radio advertisements. And they did work great for these. The problems arose when you tried to put 15 or 20 *minutes* of tape into the cartridge. This is when the internal mechanism begins to jam. In addition, there was the fickle tape splice. This is where the end of the tape connects to itself to form a loop. It is attached by a splice that included a small piece of aluminum; it is this aluminum that signaled the machine to change the track, playing the next program. It is the most temperamental part of the system. The tape splice is definitely the weakest link, and this is what most frequently breaks.

Today I play most of my prized 8-tracks only occasionally, as I live in fear that each one will jam the next time it is used—a very real possibility. I have a few functioning tapes that I hesitate to play at all, for the reason that they could break at the next track change. My 8-track of The Beatles' *White Album* tops this list.

But this has gone on long enough. The rest of my logistics lesson on 8-track tapes must wait for another day. May your splices always hold; may your tapes never jam.

Bonus Track

The subject of 8-track tapes can take on a life of its own. Or it can for me. There were some interesting anomalies created by the introduction of the 8-track format. To fulfill time requirements of a tape, occasionally a song would be repeated, appearing twice on the tape. This occurs on Johnny Cash's Gone Girl *8-track tape and Bob Dylan's* Slow Train Coming. *More frequently, a song would be edited to fit time restrictions. On Dylan's* Bringing It All Back Home *8-track, the song "It's Alright Ma (I'm Only Bleeding)" is missing its last two verses. On his* Blonde on Blonde *tape, the organ and high hat introduction is edited from "Sad Eyes Lady of the Lowlands." On rare occasions, a selection would be lengthened to fit the 8-track format. The song "California" on John Mayall's* Turning Point *is such an instance. Saxophonist Johnny Almond takes a solo on this selection, but at the conclusion of Almond's feature, this exact solo is heard again. The makers of the 8-track elongated this number so it would better fit onto the tape.*

When RCA Records told Harry Nilsson that the running order of his songs on Aerial Pandemonium Ballet *would need to be altered to accommodate the 8-track format, he balked. Nilsson cleverly solved the problem by recording an additional track entitled "Fill" for the tape. This 30-second spoken piece does not appear on the LP, but is used because, as Nilsson explains during this whispered track, he does not want to "destroy the continuity of the album by resequencing it." He is successful—both in allowing his songs to be heard in the order he intended, and in mocking RCA Records.*

One Question With… Barry Manilow!

If I had the opportunity to ask one question of a specific individual, what would it be? Here is the penultimate entry.

Tom Wilmeth:—So, Mr. Manilow, What is up with your recording of the song "Sandra"?

Barry Manilow:—What do you mean?

TW:—Well, it's about a woman who gets married young, has several kids, and then attempts suicide by slitting her wrists with a broken glass. Not exactly "Weekend in New England" stuff.

BM:—The young woman in the song is paying tribute to her mother, in a way, by wanting to embrace her lifestyle.

TW:—Paying tribute? The story's a bit dark, isn't it? There's a suicide attempt in there.

BM:—Hey, the lyrics say that she accidentally cut her wrist. By mistake. An accident!

TW:—That slit wrist episode seems to be the centerpiece of the song. That, and how she nearly died from the "accident." And that she also suffered from postpartum depression and frequently drinks at home during the day. A pretty bleak portrait.

BM:—It doesn't exactly say all that.

TW:—Sure it does. That tune is worthy of Lou Reed's *Berlin* album.

BM:—I'm not sure if that comparison is praise or a burn. But that's a good album.

TW:—You like *Berlin*?

BM:—Very sincere. Heartfelt.

TW:—Pretty stark vignettes of extremely sad situations.

BM:—That too.

TW:—Let's get back to your recording of "Sandra."

BM:—That song is sung from the point of view of the husband.

TW:—Right, and the fact that he isn't all that troubled by his wife's actions—that is frightening in itself. This is clearly the portrait of a woman drowning, and a husband blindly in denial.

BM:—Succinct assessment. But you miss a lot by summarizing it in that way.

TW:—You mean like the daytime drinking and the depression.

BM:—Well…maybe. But the husband IS troubled by his wife's situation. He absolutely is aware—he just doesn't know what to do about it. So he writes it off to her being normal, but with a couple of occasional quirks. Easier to get through life that way. Ignore the bad stuff—it'll work out. And he was able to explain that away as well—at least to himself.

TW:—You did not write that song, did you?

BM:—I'm not finished. It's clear that the husband too is calling out for help here—or his list of unhealthy things about his wife's mental condition wouldn't be the subject matter of the song.

TW:—OK. But it still sounds like he is rationalizing a lot of stuff to himself on this. You did not write that song, did you?

BM:—I co-wrote it. I added some things to Enoch Anderson's original song. [pause] I only performed that tune in concert for a short time, very early in my career.

TW:—It wasn't all that early—it was in your set when you played Carnegie Hall in about 1972. Or was Carnegie Hall an early, forgettable gig?

BM:—You have long since passed the one-question mark, so just back off a bit. But concerning playing that song live—you need to remember the time and the audience.

TW:—Meaning?

BM:—The time was the early 1970s, so there was a bit of "women empowerment" theme in that song. Or maybe instead of the woman empowerment thing, you can see it as a wife who is also a real person, with real problems—in a very different type of love song.

TW:—She doesn't seem very "empowered" to me. She knows she missed something, but isn't sure what.

BM:—Well, you are right about criticizing the husband. He should be throwing his wife a lifeline, but he is pretending that there is no problem. Or he doesn't really see one.

TW:—So it's an anti-man song?

BM:—Once again, it's not that simple. "Sandra" is not an "anti-man" song; it's an "anti-not-caring" song. An "anti-not-being-in-touch with your human surroundings" song. It's not an us-versus-them song for gender studies. I'll say it again—it's a love song, but not one that fits with flat character situations.

TW:—OK, but you had to search out that tune. You clearly really wanted it in your live set. Even the original songwriter had never heard "Sandra" performed until your recording came out.

BM:—I like that song and I liked performing it.

TW:—You mentioned the time. What about the audience?

BM:—Very New York; and most of my fans were very New York in the beginning even if they did not physically live in New York.

TW:—Large gay audience?

BM:—Some, but not as prominent as you might think. I never really courted that. I had seen that world from the inside, working with Bette. And I knew that it would be a limiting thing for me to specifically target such a niche audience.

TW:—OK. So why did "Sandra" stay in your set list for such a short time?

BM:—It sort of creeped people out—especially once I started to get non-New York City fans.

TW:—It "creeped people out." Go figure.

BM:—Perhaps even more important—it is a depressing tune. It would take me a couple of really "up" songs to get the audience back from the doldrums that the song induced.

TW:—Powerful stuff. So, "Sandra" was a song that would shatter the mood of your live show. Yet you intentionally performed it, knowing the work it would take you to get the audience back. That's quite a risk for a performer. Even now, for good or for bad, the song really distinguishes itself amidst any collection of your material. Any second thoughts over recording that song, or about including it in your show, even briefly?

BM:—Not at all. Listen—that would have been a very easy tune to bury. It only appears on my second studio album, *Manilow II*, which has long ago been supplanted by various hits collections. I think it's even out of print now. "Sandra" appears on none of my hits collections, as you might guess, so the only place to get the song now is on the expensive box set in the form of the live Carnegie Hall recording you mentioned.

TW:—Oh. You mean your 4-CD, 1-DVD box set that contains very few of your best-known songs?

BM:—Guilty.

TW:—But you did beat me to the punch on that box set topic—the place where you buried this intriguing oddity.

BM:—I knew you were about to ask. The reason I put it on there is because I do like the song and I wanted to have some tangible evidence that it had been in my set. Sort of my take on *Another Side of Barry Manilow*.

TW:—In a one-song form.

BM:—Right.

TW:—Your specific parallel to the title *Another Side of* is a reference to Bob Dylan's fourth album.

BM:—Correct. The one where he deals with unexpected topics.

TW:—Yeah; I've heard it. Is it true that Bob Dylan once hugged you in a hotel hallway, told you that everybody really admired what you were doing, and then walked on down the hall?

BM:—Yes; that is a true story. I used to wonder if he was mocking me, but I don't think he was. I think he is a fan of strong melodies. And love songs.

TW:—Like "Sandra."

BM:—*Just* like "Sandra."

Important *Nota Bene*: This exchange is complete and absolute fiction.

Concert Commentary

Bob Dylan with The Band

Chicago Auditorium

Chicago, Illinois

January 4, 1974

WHEN I FIRST ENCOUNTERED Bob Dylan's music I became so mesmerized that I had to tell the whole world—often to the irritation of my immediate audience. I had done this in a major way with The Beatles a few years earlier, then with Dylan and later with Bruce Springsteen.

My first memory of hearing Bob Dylan sing one of his own songs was in the spring of 1966 at my grandparents' farm in Greenfield, Iowa. Having my ever-present AM radio with me, I listened to Des Moines' KIOA until the sun set, when I could pick up WLS out of Chicago, WHB from Kansas City, and many others. In the west Iowa farmlands, the nighttime AM radio waves were clear and uninterrupted.

That weekend, KIOA had started to air a very odd song. It sounded as if it had been recorded at a party. Horns were blatting and barely playing together; there was a marching band feel to it, with the drummer rat-a-tat-tatting at the start of the record. It sounded strident and unpolished, like nothing else on the air. Worst of all, the singer was occasionally cracking up, laughing during his vocals! I found this really irritating and very unprofessional. How could a record company put out such a single, and why was KIOA playing it?

I now laugh to think about how angry the record made me. But it sure did. Music was to be taken seriously, after all; we couldn't have this sort of thing polluting the air waves! It wasn't the song itself that I objected to, but rather the singer's cavalier attitude. By this time I had made up my mind to become a professional disc jockey; my love of music and of records themselves went increasingly deep.

The record that irritated me, of course, was Bob Dylan's "Rainy Day Women #12 & 35," which includes the tag line about getting "stoned." I had no clue what that meant, but other Iowans must have, for the record was not on KIOA's playlist the following Monday. Maybe the weekend jock had a promo copy and played it. Station management probably pulled the song when people complained. Or maybe the owners just got nervous. KIOA, after all, was a radio station that would not play Peter and Gordon's Top 10 hit "Lady Godiva" in 1966 because the lyrics humorously alluded to a naked woman on a horse. The following year, the station pulled a record by The Hombres because parents complained of a line that repeatedly urged listeners to allow unspecified things to "hang out." Like now, the broadcast industry did not want to run the risk of alienating advertisers. I didn't think much more about the short-lived radio anomaly that had irritated me until years later, when I realized what I had been hearing.

Some of my friends were into Dylan earlier than I. Part of this was due to my myopic devotion to The Beatles. I listened to Top 40 radio and to The Beatles, and that was about it for several years. In 1967, my brother wanted to get me a record for Christmas. I gave him a list of Beatles records I had yet to obtain. He complained that he wanted to get me something besides The Beatles. I couldn't think of anything. He decided on the first LP by Peter, Paul & Mary, a very good album that I listened to a lot. Peter, Paul & Mary would become popular interpreters of Dylan's songs, but there were none by him on their first release.

I was still largely unaware of Dylan when the "Lay Lady Lay" single was released in the summer of 1969. A disc jockey on KIOA played it and then said, "That's Bobby Dylan, believe it or not. Quite a change of voice for him!" I believed the announcer, but wasn't really sure what he meant since I had no basis for comparison. I had no idea that this smooth song of seduction was by the same performer who had irritated me so thoroughly a few years before. I liked "Lay Lady Lay," but for me it was just another good song on the radio. I did not seek out the single or try to learn more about the singer.

Around this time I first heard Bill Drake's *History of Rock & Roll* radio marathon, a life-changing experience for me. In this "rockumentary" was a lengthy section on Bob Dylan. The program praised him highly. I asked one of my high school teachers what he knew about

Dylan. He loaned me four albums, and my music education was forever altered. The albums were *Freewheelin'*, *Bringing It All Back Home*, *Highway 61 Revisited*, and *Blonde on Blonde*.

I nearly wore those records out. I listened to them repeatedly, absorbing them like nothing since my Beatles records. Those four albums were a true epiphany for me, and even now I prefer *Freewheelin'* to any of his other acoustic albums of the time. Nothing can compete with it. And the triad of electric jewels: *Bringing It All Back Home*, *Highway 61 Revisited*, and *Blonde on Blonde*. Stunning.

For the rest of high school and into college I would obsess over Dylan. He was then at a low tide in his career. Bob's most recent LP at the time was *New Morning*—pleasant enough, but certainly not on the level of his best work. Dylan had not toured since 1966, and it looked as if he had stepped off the concert stage for the last time. With the fast pace of changes in popular music, Bob was being forgotten by all but his true fans. By now, I was one.

The first new Dylan release that I recall after my conversion was not really a Dylan album at all; it was Bob's live set from the *Bangladesh* benefit concert LP. A friend and I were approaching the Music Factory record store in Des Moines' Drake University area when we heard the music spilling onto the sidewalk. We stood by the cash register as the clerk played the entire Dylan side for us.

The five-song *Bangladesh* set was the only officially released concert material by Dylan that we had for quite a long time. Even today, it stands as an above average live performance by the man. That sounds like a put down, but Bob can be erratic in concert. The *Bangladesh* set is well played, enjoyable, and Bob seems to be working at it. This set was also important since it demonstrated Bob's ability to play live, if he so chose. A tour would not be impossible for him. Several years would pass before he would undertake a traditional concert tour, but such a highly anticipated event was given new hope by his appearance at this August 1971 benefit.

Then, in October 1973, an unexpected thunderbolt. Our campus radio station announced that Dylan was to tour the U.S. starting in January. I rushed down the three flights of stairs to my girlfriend's dorm room, confidently announcing, "We're going to see Dylan!" I explained that he was about to play some concert dates. Always the supporting optimist, she laughed at me and said, "You'll never get tickets for that."

Irritated by this negative attitude, I assured her that I would. Jumping through requisite hoops, I did acquire tickets to the second night of the tour, in Chicago. I always felt it poetic justice that she did not accompany me on that trip. I went, instead, with a far more appropriate and appreciative Dylan fan.

After we arrived in Chicago and searched out the arena where the concert was to be held, we walked around the area to find something to eat and to get a newspaper. This was to be the second of Bob's two nights in Chicago, and we wanted to see a review of the previous evening's concert. I didn't really notice anything about the area, but we were soon approached by one of Chicago's finest, a large and friendly police officer who asked us if we were from the area. No, we explained, and excitedly told him about the impending Dylan concert. He smiled, and urged us to sit in our car until the concert began. Rough neighborhood, it seems. We were oblivious.

Arriving early, we had parked close to the hall, which showed absolutely no indication that a major concert was to be held there that night. A small sports arena marquee above one side door read, "Tonight: The Hawks." We thought the sign might have been a sort of code since The Hawks was the original name of Bob's backing group, The Band. Probably Bob's sense of humor, if he had a hand in such things.

My recollection of getting to the seats is dim. It seems that we were herded through a series of dark hallways to get to our upper-level seats. People would later ask me what the name of the tour was and what sort of souvenir merchandise was for sale. The tour did not have a name and there was nothing for sale. This was before tours were identified by titles of the artist's latest album. Asylum Records would issue the new *Planet Waves* album half way through the tour. But this was not the *Planet Waves* tour. It was simply Bob Dylan back on the road after almost eight long years—a major event in itself. Some would later call it the "comeback" tour.

As to merchandise, no T-shirts were being sold and no souvenir programs. Nobody thought about or wanted them, as far as I could tell. Everybody was there for the concert, and the trappings were unimportant. I later wondered if promoter Bill Graham missed the boat on that profit stream of merchandise; not long after this, hawkers would regularly fill amphitheater vestibules before concerts selling many forms of memorabilia related to the evening's music.

By all subsequent accounts, we witnessed one of the best performances of the entire tour. The opening night had seen Dylan remain on stage during The Band's numbers, with Bob and his backing group alternating songs. The second night, which we attended, had the more logical approach of alternating *sets*, with Bob playing about six songs, leaving the stage for The Band's set, and then returning to conclude the first half of the concert.

I had not been able to sleep much the night before because of excitement, and I was so tired that I was worried I wouldn't enjoy the show. No such problem. Once the lights dimmed and Bob took the stage, all was well. I remember thinking that I would be happy if he would play either "Just Like Tom Thumb's Blues" or "It's Alright Ma (I'm Only Bleeding)," but I expected neither because they were not famous enough tunes. However, early in the first set, Bob burned though "Tom Thumb's Blues" with The Band at his heels, and he later concluded his solo acoustic set with "It's Alright Ma." Beyond expectations.

I like The Band, but I was there to see Bob Dylan. Others must have held stronger feelings, for a small amount of heckling took place when Bob was not on stage. For the most part, though, the audience was quiet and attentive. I did enjoy each song The Band played during its own set, and was especially pleased when they sang "The Long Black Veil." I already knew Joan Baez's recording of this haunting song, and would later encounter Lefty Frizzell's version.

I loved the concert. Exactly what I had hoped for, and more. I was disappointed, then, when the live LP *Before the Flood* came out the following summer. The recording seemed very different from the performance I had witnessed. I later discovered why: I attended the second concert of the tour; the live album was recorded on its final nights, six weeks later in Los Angeles. I thought that all the takes on the record were rushed, and that Bob seemed to be shouting his way through the songs. When I saw him in Chicago, he was singing.

Also, at only three songs, the album's acoustic set was frustratingly brief. This was to make room on the record for material by The Band, I guess. Dylan played six or seven solo acoustic songs in Chicago. I have learned to enjoy this live album, and even think an expanded version of *Before the Flood* would be a good idea for one of Columbia's bootleg series releases. Still, that record does not represent what I experienced in Chicago.

As much as I was into Dylan in 1974, my knowledge of his full repertoire was by no means complete. I deeply loved *Freewheelin'* but did not pretend to know all of his early acoustic work. This is a round-about way of saying that when Bob played "The Lonesome Death of Hattie Carroll" during the acoustic set, I did not know the song. I recall thinking at the time that if Bob could still write tunes of this quality, things were OK. And even though "Hattie Carroll" was by no means a new song, things were in fact better than OK.

When finally released midway through the tour, *Planet Waves* proved to be quite a good album; it remains one of Dylan's underrated works. Interestingly enough, Bob performed a song during his acoustic set when I saw him that was recorded for, but not included on, *Planet Waves*, called "Nobody 'Cept You." The unissued studio recording with The Band would later surface in 1991 on the first collection of Columbia's official bootleg releases. As Dylan followers have determined (based on audience recordings), Dylan's final live performance of "Nobody 'Cept You" took place during his concert held the night before *Planet Waves* was released. This suggests to me, perhaps contrary to popular opinion, that Bob is very aware of his album contents and their release dates.

The excitement created by that January 1974 concert stayed with me a long time. But if this tour reawakened some fans to Bob, I think that being in front of audiences may have reawakened the artist as well. In the fall of that year Dylan released an album of new songs. It was called *Blood on the Tracks*.

Book Review

Bob Dylan: The Recording Sessions, 1960-1994
By Clinton Heylin
St. Martin's Press, 1995

Clinton Heylin's credentials as a Dylanologist are firmly in place. He wrote the biography *Behind the Shades* (1991) and he deals extensively with Dylan recordings in his book *Bootleg* (1996). In his latest book, *The Recording Sessions, 1960-1994*, Heylin guides the reader through the maze of Dylan's time spent in the studio. The book acts as a logical and welcome companion to the ongoing *Performing Artist* series of Paul Williams, which documents Dylan's concert career.

Dylan is unique, in part, because of the large number of songs he has written. Undaunted, Heylin discusses not only each officially issued recording, but also the vast amount of unreleased material that has been left in the record company's vaults. Heylin's scrutiny of Columbia Records' ledgers, and other relevant studio materials is impressive. He is able to piece together what must be have taken place at sessions which are now decades old. Dylan's outtakes and his discarded songs are all discussed at length, as is the official canon.

The logic here is sound, the analysis reflective, and the documentation meticulous. *The Recording Sessions* contains insights into Dylan's studio work that are thought provoking and will certainly excite any devotee. And yet, Heylin as author and historian is betrayed by his own demons. Not content to praise and blame only his subject's studio methodology, Heylin insists on dragging in unrelated criticism concerning the studio practices of The Beatles.

What is especially exasperating is Heylin's repeated mocking of other Dylan scholars, most notably Jeff Rosen. It was Rosen's job to assemble some of the multitude of unreleased studio material for Columbia's *Biograph* and *Bootleg Series* box sets. By taking repeated cheap shots at Rosen, Heylin appears to be a spoiled child, angry and jealous at not being chosen to oversee these projects. Similarly, the author lambasts guitarist Robbie Robertson for his handling of the 1975 album *The Basement Tapes*, the first authorized release of this well-publicized cache of informal Dylan recordings from 1967. These constant attacks are unacceptable. Heylin's comments do not merely show one researcher questioning the work of a colleague. Instead, he invokes slander, undermining his goal of serious scholarship.

Heylin also falls into the trap of elitism as he regularly includes Dylan quotes into his commentary that are needlessly obscure and often irrelevant. Although the book's introductory essay states that a certain amount of previous knowledge is expected when approaching this material, the author seems determined to brag repeatedly about the superiority of his mental data base on Dylan. It grows tiresome, for just as Heylin shows immature leanings toward his peers, he at times demonstrates condescension toward his readers.

If one can look past the carping and the arrogance, there is a storehouse of useful and interesting information in *The Recording Sessions*. When Heylin sticks to his subject, his scholarship is first rate if not always clearly presented. But the author is too easily distracted, repeatedly throwing tantrums over a topic that he believes should be his domain alone.

Bonus Track

> *A few years ago I presented a paper on Mark Twain at a conference in Elmira, New York—Twain's residence in his later life. At the reception, the college's interim president was working the room, thanking each speaker individually for his or her involvement. He asked about my other interests. I told him that I was working on an article about Bob Dylan. My interlocutor frowned and finally said, "Is there really enough material for that sort of thing?" I politely indicated that the length of Dylan's career in music had, at that time, exceeded Twain's writing career by a decade. The interim president suddenly remembered that he needed to go speak with someone else.*

Book Review

Just Like Bob Zimmerman's Blues: Dylan in Minnesota
By Dave Engel
River City Memoirs / Amherst Press, 1997

Reading this book is like looking through a multisided, narrowly cut glass prism. It explores various aspects of Dylan in depth, but all within the strict focus of Hibbing, Minnesota. Perhaps the words "historical context" should be emblazoned on its spine, for Dave Engel strives throughout *Dylan in Minnesota* to give the reader a sense of location within a specific era. The author goes far beyond merely presenting the hometown background of his subject. Engel strives to place the reader into Bob Dylan's boyhood milieu through total immersion.

The main audience for this book will be fans of Minnesota's famed native son, but Engel says he wrote his book also as a valuable document for those interested in a key mining town of the Upper Midwest. Like the iron ore dug from the soil of this region, Engel is relentless in his excavation of materials, offering an interesting portrait of Hibbing at midcentury. In fact, the book's historical documentation sometimes threatens to overwhelm the focal point of Dylan.

In addition to volumes of newspaper accounts on everything from local politics to race relations to the area's geographical landscape, Engel has sifted through interviews, lyrics, and miscellaneous writings by Dylan himself. Some of these passages are well known; others are Engel's excavations, culled from the very edges of the Dylan universe. All pertain to Hibbing.

When I spoke with Engel about his book, I asked if he had considered including a section on other Midwestern touchstones, such as Dylan's early performances at the University of Minnesota's coffee house, the Ten O' Clock Scholar, or Bob's time spent in Madison on his way to New York. Engle dismissed the idea. "That stuff is way outside my realm," he explains. And true enough, the tight focus presented here does allow the author to dive deeply in to a single, yet multifaceted topic. If the author sometimes causes the reader to wonder what a given topic has to do with Bob, at least the book always stays within the framework of Hibbing during Dylan's youth.

Engel explains that part of his motivation in writing *Just Like Bob Zimmerman's Blues* was to correct wrongs he saw in most other publications when they dealt with Dylan's Midwestern influences. While not dismissing the work of Dylan biographers Antony Scaduto, Robert Shelton, or Clinton Heylin, Engel maintains that "those guys are just flat-out wrong on a lot of stuff when it comes to Hibbing." He continues, "They were writing from a coastal mindset and, as such, simply couldn't believe that Dylan emerged from the upper Midwest. Lots of writers get lazy and won't check the facts when it comes to the important Minnesota part of Dylan's story." Engel has some difficulty with all of the major Dylan biographies' sections on Hibbing, but he is especially incensed by Bob Spitz's treatment, saying his writing is "very derogatory. It's condescending, and every bit a put down" of the Midwest.

Interestingly, the author has high praise for a largely forgotten

1972 book on Dylan by Toby Thompson, called *Positively Main Street*. With chapters accurately called "Gushes," the book was seen by many as a young fan's star-struck view of Dylan, written in fanzine style. But Engel points to Thompson's book as being superior to the more traditional biographies when dealing with Hibbing, even calling *Positively Main Street* an "enduring testament." Says Engel, "That book is the first to really take the reader to Minnesota and let him walk the streets of Hibbing. None of the others, before or after, did that."

Engel is intent on clarifying the real story from both the romanticized and the derogatory fiction surrounding Bob Dylan's Hibbing. It was often Dylan himself who would intentionally distort his own background, especially in early interviews. By remaining with reliable prose accounts and truth-telling photographs of the region, *Just Like Bob Zimmerman's Blues* successfully sheds light on an overlooked and occasionally maligned portion of the Dylan legacy.

Asked what he felt was the most surprising item he came across during his three years of research on the project, Engel corrects my question. "It wasn't so much of a surprise, because I knew that there had to be a lot of genuine materials out there which had been overlooked" about Dylan's youth. But one of the "happiest days," he admits, was "when I found a newspaper photo from the *Hibbing Tribune* with Bob Zimmerman lined up as a member of the 1955-56 Teen Age Bowling League Champions." Like many of the photos in Dave Engel's book, this shot of Dylan as a part of the Gutter Boys bowling team had never been republished after its initial newspaper run. Perhaps Texas musician Emily Kaitz is more on target than anybody knew when she sings of "Bob Dylan's 300 Game."

Commentary
Jazz in the Key of Bob
May 23, 2011

Bob Dylan turned 70 last week. That statement alone is a mind-bender. That he is still on the road more than 100 nights of the year is amazing. Yet it's true. I noted with interest *Rolling Stone* magazine's latest issue, which celebrates Bob's 70th birthday with a list of his best 70 songs, as chosen by their editors. The issue also contains lists of Bob's most inscrutable lyrics ("Gates of Eden") and songs they think are unfairly overlooked ("Dark Eyes"). These lists put me in mind of a tape I compiled ten years ago, for Bob's 60th birthday. Inspired by the famous bootleg *Elvis Presley's Greatest Sh*t*, my idea was to create a set list of Dylan recordings that would make a hilariously bad collection.

It sounded like a fun plan, an inverted exercise in fan devotion. I set to work, drawing first, of course, from the notorious 1970 double album *Self Portrait* and then from various backroads of the Dylan canon. My final list included such original songs as "Wigwam," "Billy 4," "Handy Dandy," and "New Pony." The tape also featured Bob's versions of other composer's songs, like "Let It Be Me," "Froggy Went a-Courting," "You Belong to Me," and "This Old Man." All officially released tracks.

But to my consternation, once the tape was completed, it was not the humorous artifact I had intended. Instead, I discovered what perhaps I had known from the start: even a set spotlighting Bob Dylan's strangest odds and ends held interest. The very selections I had intended to mock actually held up well to repeated listening.

One of the songs I included came from the 1970 album *New Morning*. This was the album that Bob supposedly recorded quickly to shore up his sagging reputation after the poorly received *Self Portrait* project. The song I used from *New Morning* was "If Dogs Run Free." It was included on my tape not because I thought it was bad, but because it was like no other recording in Dylan's canon. "If Dogs Run Free" is as close as Bob has come to recording a jazz tune. The number is a spoken work of hipster monologue, a la Kenneth Rexroth. Scatting in the background behind Bob's narrative is Maeretha Stewart, along with the single-note improvisations of Al Kooper's tinkling piano accompaniment.

I am not arguing here for Dylan to be viewed as a jazz artist, of course, in spite of this one-song genre exercise. "If Dogs Run Free" stood out for me because the concepts of jazz and Bob Dylan are not often linked. While not obvious matches, they are also not mutually exclusive. Dylan has certainly recorded songs that do not adhere to traditional folk, blues, or rock chord changes. His "Too Much of Nothing" is interesting for its ascending chromatic chords, while other songs from this same era, such as "Yea! Heavy and a Bottle of Bread," and "Tiny Montgomery," each use only two chords.

Yet no matter the simplicity or complexity of the songs' structure, few musicians seemed to have taken interest in arranging Dylan melodies for a jazz setting in the 1960s. This, even as Beatles' melodies were making occasional inroads into jazz with albums like Count Basie's *Beatle Bag* (1966) and George Benson's *The Other Side of Abbey Road* (1970). However, there were a few.

Among the first jazz renditions of Dylan's material is Bud Shank's 1963 release *Folk & Flute*, which included three songs written by Dylan: "Quit Your Lowdown Ways," "Blowin' in the Wind," and "Don't Think Twice, It's Alright." Although a jazz player, Shank was apparently riding the expanding folk music scene, as he had previously done with his jazz arrangements of Brazilian, bossa nova, and Broadway music. And even though the album's title contains the word *Folk*, a quartet including Joe Pass on guitar, Charlie Haden's bass, and session leader Shank on alto sax and flute, must be seen as an outing for jazz musicians. Surprisingly, baritone sax man and cool jazz pioneer Gerry Mulligan was another established jazz musician to record Dylan early on. In his tellingly titled 1965 album *If You Can't Beat 'Em, Join 'Em*, Mulligan included an unusual version of "Mr. Tambourine Man" as a piano feature.

The first full album of jazz arrangements for Dylan's songs appears to be *Dylan Jazz*, from 1966. One can argue about whether these are truly jazz charts, but with high-caliber session cats like the then-unknown Glen Campbell on guitar, Jim Horn on reeds, and Hal Blaine on drums, it makes for some interesting interpretations. Also of note, this album was co-produced by Leon Russell. Like Shank's inclusion of "Quit Your Lowdown Ways," which Dylan wrote but had not himself released, *Dylan Jazz* also included an unissued original, "Walkin' Down the Line." This strikes me as an indication that these jazz musicians were making some of their song selections from published sheet music, not from listening to Dylan's albums.

At his 1968 Carnegie Hall concert, vibraphone virtuoso Gary Burton plays Dylan's "I Want You." After the melody is introduced by Burton and guitarist Larry Coryell, this brief number becomes a solo feature for acoustic bassist Steve Swallow. Dylan's melodies apparently lend themselves well to jazz bass solos. The same year that Burton played "I Want You" with his quartet, Keith Jarrett's 1968 trio recording of Dylan's "My Back Pages" also featured a bass solo, this time by

Charlie Haden. This performance is the opening track of Jarrett's live album *Somewhere Before,* on Vortex Records. The number was also used as the B-side of a Keith Jarrett single. Its A-side was the pianist's arrangement of Dylan's "Lay Lady Lay." This jazz single did not chart, and Jarrett's version of "Lay Lady Lay" appears on none of his albums.

It's hard to know whether Jarrett himself had any input on the release of these selections, but what is unmistakable is the pianist's appreciation of Dylan's music and lyrics. In a 1987 interview for National Public Radio's *Sidran on Record,* Jarrett tries to explain to host Ben Sidran some indefinable aspects of music by quoting the song "Shelter from the Storm." He recites a passage where Dylan personifies the concept of Beauty—describing her journey as she traverses a sharp and fragile precipice. Jarrett repeats Dylan's lyric twice, telling Sidran that it is this type of elusive beauty he is trying to capture at each performance and on every recording.

In the late 1960s, Gary Burton and Keith Jarrett were among the young lions of jazz. They were trying to look at music in a different way than their respected elder statesmen, most of whom had little interest in Bob Dylan. Bassist Rob Stoner encountered this situation head-on when he accompanied Dylan to Chicago in December 1975, to play on the PBS television special *The World of John Hammond.* The program was to bring together many of the music legends Hammond had signed to Columbia Records. Among those performing on this two-part tribute were some giants from the jazz community—Benny Goodman, Red Norvo, Teddy Wilson, Benny Carter, and Milt Hinton. While Stoner does not get specific with names, he says that none of the jazz performers would even talk to him because he was associated with Bob's band. These had been his musical heroes, laments Stoner, who was crushed by their collective snub.

Known as a superlative wordsmith, it is clear that Dylan has also worked hard on his melodies and song structures. In the first volume of his *Chronicles* autobiography, a somewhat defensive Dylan asks, "If my songs were just about words, then what was Duane Eddy, the great rock and roll guitarist, doing recording an album full of instrumental melodies of my songs?" Perhaps unaware of Duane Eddy, some jazz musicians would nonetheless soon follow his lead.

If most jazz musicians were slow to hear Dylan, he had certainly been listening to them. Also in *Chronicles,* Dylan remembers his early days in New York. "I'd listen to a lot of jazz and bebop records," and to the arrangements of Gil Evans. "There were a lot of similarities between some kinds of jazz and folk music." Dylan then lists several Ellington compositions, including "Tattoo Bride" and "Tourist Point of View," concluding that, to him, "They sounded like sophisticated folk music." It is also in this section where Dylan talks of the influence of jazz records by Roland Kirk, Dizzy Gillespie, and Charlie Christian's sides with Benny Goodman. Living and working in an early1960s New York City, Dylan attended various jazz clubs, being especially taken with pianist Thelonious Monk. When Dylan introduced himself to Monk as a folk music performer, Monk told the young man from the Midwest, "We *all* play folk music."

I don't pretend that these remarks provide anything approaching a comprehensive examination. Many jazz artists not discussed here have recorded Dylan tunes, from Duke Ellington's version of "Blowin' in the Wind" to guitarist Michael Hedges' "All Along the Watchtower." The trend continues—early in 2016, saxophonist Charles Lloyd issued his new album *I Long to See You*, which opens with an eight-minute version of Bob's "Masters of War." Surprisingly few jazz vocalists have waded into these Dylan waters, although Janet Planet has recently released an entire CD of Dylan's work. We should be surprised by none of these jazz interpretations. As Bob himself explains, "Musicians have always known that my songs were about more than just words, but most people are not musicians."

Bonus Track

I have always found it interesting that Gary Burton chose to arrange Dylan's "I Want You" for his jazz group. Years ago, I spoke with Texas guitarist Jimmy Raycraft between sets. His band, The Thin Men, had just performed a rocking instrumental medley of Bob's "I Want You" coupled with The Beatles' "I Want You (She's So Heavy)." I mentioned to Raycraft that Dylan's "I Want You" was a good choice for his quartet because the song is so melodic. He immediately countered, "No, man! 'I Want You' has NO melody. That's what makes it so great! Dylan sings all of those lyrics on one note!"

Bonus Track

Dylan's work also interested other American musicians. Johnny Cash publicly embraced Dylan's songs and his artistry. Cash was adamant that Dylan's fans should allow Bob to choose his own direction—acoustic, electric, protest, or new categories. Another less vocal but equally surprising champion of Dylan's music was Earl Scruggs. I maintain that Flatt & Scruggs—the most famous of all bluegrass duos—broke up their act because of Earl Scruggs' fascination with Dylan's songs. This may sound like an overstatement, but if Dylan's music was not the cause for the split, it certainly represented the different paths the two men wanted to take. On their later albums, Flatt & Scruggs recorded enough Bob Dylan songs to fill a 60-minute tape. I know; I compiled one. Earl loved the new directions of the late 1960s; Lester couldn't relate. They parted.

The great country guitarist Chet Atkins was never one to reject a melody because of its genre. Atkins recorded instrumental versions of several Dylan compositions and even performed a medley of three Dylan tunes on a 1970 episode of Porter Waggoner's syndicated television show. Atkins always seemed to have his ears wide open. I saw him play in St. Paul in the early 1980s, during one of his first visits to the Prairie Home Companion *radio show. Seated alone on stage, he finished tuning and then said to the audience, "Well folks, you take a good song where you find it." And with that, he played a beautiful version of the recent #1 pop hit by Blondie, "Heart of Glass." When I later spoke with Atkins, he voiced dismay over those among his audience who refused to listen to new music. Atkins had obviously held an unbiased view of melody for some time, as he recorded an instrumental version of Dylan's "Blowin' in the Wind" as early as 1965.*

Commentary
Last Thoughts on Bob Dylan's 'Last Thoughts'
23 January 2011

I have not written much about Bob Dylan in a long time. It got to the point where I figured, what's the use? There was such a glut of writings about the man. It was the birth of the Internet that started to make me question whether I was really a Dylan fan any longer or not, a question which always makes my two grown children howl with laughter. True, I have all of Dylan's officially released materials. Over the past decades I have faithfully purchased the spate of soundtrack and CDs by various artists to get Bob's individual tracks, going so far as to buy a three-CD Joan Baez box set to acquire the elusive "Troubled and I Don't Know Why" duet. I still go to see him when he comes to town, as I have since the 1974 tour, and I chose XM Radio over Sirius because XM carried the *Theme Time Radio with Bob Dylan* program.

On the Internet, however, the Dylan world had become an ever expanding universe, and what was once a lot of fun quickly seemed to turn into an often mean-spirited and territorial competition. And so I walked away for a while—not from the music, but from the community of Dylan commentators. I write the following because a question floats to my frontal lobes with surprising regularity, and (although I could have easily have missed it) I have not seen this specific topic discussed by others.

There was a high-quality Dylan bootleg LP that many of us prized in the mid-1970s, when these underground concert releases really came into their own. Known by the title *Are You Now or Have You Ever Been?*, this black-market album included excerpts from a New York City concert at Town Hall from April 1963. These were the days when Bob was the brightest beacon of the folk community. For the concert's encore, Dylan recites his recently completed poem, "Last Thoughts on Woody Guthrie." Already a veteran of high-profile New York gigs, he nevertheless seems quite nervous as he introduces what he knows will be a lengthy spoken piece. Sans guitar, it will be outside of Dylan's regular style—almost an *a cappella* performance. In his introduction, Dylan speaks of Guthrie's personal importance to him. He then begins a unique recitation of adulation.

Dylan performed this spoken work only once. The 1963 recording would be legitimately released on the first of *The Bootleg Series* sets, issued by Columbia Records in 1991. What I found interesting is that Dylan's prefatory remarks to the piece have been edited. This becomes immediately clear when comparing the unedited bootleg recording to the sanctioned Columbia release. The deletions made to Bob's introduction jolted and irritated me the first time I played the official recording. I always felt that within this introduction was a brief glimpse into Bob Dylan as fan. It provided a seemingly unguarded moment, with Dylan acknowledging deep devotion to his predecessor Woody Guthrie.

The careful editing of these introductory remarks was not made for the purpose of saving time, I'm convinced, but primarily for content. True, Dylan's halting delivery is cleaned up, making the speaker's words appear to flow smoothly in places where they had sometimes been choppy and uncertain. Yet it is the halting nature of this spoken introduction that helps the audience recognize the heartfelt and unrehearsed elements at play. The unedited tape certainly does not make the speaker sound inarticulate, if that was a concern.

Much more important than speech fluidity, however, is the content edited from this already brief introduction. Excised from Columbia's official release is Dylan's sincere attempt to explain to that night's audience the depth of Woody Guthrie's pull on him. In a deleted section of the tape, Dylan says that Guthrie's appeal "cannot really be told in how many records of his I buy, or this kind of thing. It's, uh…a lot more than that, actually." I assume it was Dylan himself who ordered the lines removed before the recording's official release, but this decision could also have been made by individuals at Columbia Records. Either way, I'm thinking that the cuts must have had Dylan's approval.

But *why* was this content removed for the 1991 release? In these comments about the intangible attachment of fan to artist, Dylan twice stresses how Guthrie is "more than a folk singer." These lines are also cut. When Dylan then explains that his feelings about Guthrie could not be measured by "how many records of his I buy," did Bob think that this stated rejection of equating album purchases to one's devotion toward an artist might hurt his own future record sales? I think not. I believe lines were edited from this introductory segment because they cut too close to the bone.

That is, I think these lines must have touched on something that the artist did not want revealed. Was it his youthful attempt to express unchecked devotion to Guthrie that Dylan later decided to bury? Did he want to downplay this element of devotion in himself, having been the recipient of such unsettling fan worship for most of his own career? Whatever the reason, this seems to be a window that, by 1991, Bob wanted closed. Dylan's younger self concludes his grasp at articulating his inexpressible feelings toward Guthrie with, "It's a lot more than that, actually." His thoughtful and nearly distracted tone here is telling, almost as if that 1963 audience has melted away, and Dylan is speaking to himself.

Interesting too is how Dylan categorizes his work here by saying what it is not. Earlier in this piece I refer to "Last Thoughts on Woody Guthrie" as a poem. Most observers would agree with this assessment. Not Bob, at least not in 1963. At the very beginning of the unedited bootleg recording Dylan says to the audience with urgent sincerity, "I have a po--. I have—it's not a poem here, but uh…it's something, uh…" He then quickly shifts topics, telling how this is his first solo concert in New York. It is interesting that he almost calls the work a poem and then stops himself abruptly—specifically indicating that this is "*not* a poem." But even though Dylan may have rejected the term *poem* for this work, and couldn't place it within a more suitable genre, he was certainly right when he said—"It's something." There is nothing else like "Last Thoughts on Woody Guthrie" in the rest of Dylan's recorded work.

I said earlier that I had purposefully stayed away from writing about Bob Dylan for quite some time. After all, it seems that short of reviewing new releases, it's all been covered. And maybe the topic I address here has already been discussed by others. Even so, this is my take on Dylan's spoken introduction to "Last Thoughts on Woody Guthrie." In the 20 years since Columbia Records officially released the track, my feelings about the edited introduction have gone from great irritation to great interest. This essay, then, is speculation initially born of anger toward the record company, fed by my unending fascination with the artist. And truncated introductory comments or not—I'm just glad Columbia had tape rolling that evening.

See the Appendix for collated transcriptions of this performance.

Bonus Track

There is only one other time in the pre-electric canon where I believe Dylan gets this close to unconsciously confiding to an audience his private thoughts about music. Near the end of the 1964 Halloween concert (also in New York City) Dylan is about to close the main part of the evening's set with one of his strongest songs. As he begins the chords to "The Lonesome Death of Hattie Carroll," he uses the same joke for the second time that night: "This is a true story, right out of the newspapers again." Perhaps this line is a comment about the press of the day often calling him a topical songwriter.

He again tells the audience: "Just the words have been changed around," a line Bob finds funny but which generates only a small amount of polite laughter from the audience. There is then a very brief pause, as if the performer really is considering the subject before continuing, "It's like conversation, really." Although clearly exuberant here and throughout this 1964 concert, Dylan speaks the line thoughtfully, as if this connection had just occurred to him. Then he is off into the beautiful waltz cadence that becomes "Hattie Carroll." I find this comment, like that concerning his feelings toward Guthrie the year before, most revealing—this one addressing his approach to composing lyrics.

CD Review

Bob Dylan
The Bootleg Series, Volume 6—Concert at Philharmonic Hall
New York City; October 31, 1964
Columbia Records, 2004

The Halloween 1964 concert has always been among my favorite Bob Dylan recordings. I obtained a bootleg LP of this concert in the mid-1970s, and it has been an important touchstone of my Dylan collection ever since. I am glad that Columbia has made it commercially available, for it features stellar renditions of some of his most interesting material. I wrote the following piece some years before Columbia officially issued the recording.

October 1964 appeared to be a tough time for Bob Dylan. The previous August saw the release of his fourth LP, *Another Side of Bob Dylan*, an album which stridently marked new thematic directions for New York City's folk idol. Although hating the record's accurate title, Dylan was purposefully shedding the mantle of political lightning rod and protest singer. Instead of commenting on social injustices, here was a collection of odd love songs and brooding introspections. These solo performances are, typical for Bob during this era, engaging and inspired. But the songs! An eight-minute diatribe about his ex-girl-friend's sister, a parody of Alfred Hitchcock's *Psycho*, lusty musical longings, and advice directed toward former lovers and would-be friends. Including more than a few strange moments, the album was met with furrowed brows by Dylan aficionados expecting songs of political protest.

Another Side of Bob Dylan remains an oddity. Although it contains two of his most recognizable tunes ("All I Really Want to Do" and "It Ain't Me, Babe"), the unusual nature of the album extends to its very sound—a brittle tone that seemed "to cry out for electricity," to quote a good line from a critic whose name I have long since forgotten. The new record did not seem to present a logical extension of his previous album, *The Times They Are A-Changin',*" released just six months before. Here the listener must retune expectations or get off the train. And the Dylan trip was really just getting under way.

Perhaps Dylan was affected by the negative press and hard feelings over the new LP. He rarely sang most of these songs live. This Halloween concert of 1964 is the only documented concert performance of the album's "Spanish Harlem Incident." Even with the inclusion of this number, Dylan played less than half of his new record's selections that night, even ignoring "My Back Pages" and "Chimes of Freedom." Happy or not with his recent past, on this night Bob was looking toward the future. Although his next album, *Bringing It All Back Home*, would not come out for five months after this concert, Dylan performs three major centerpiece numbers from that forthcoming work: "Mr.

Tambourine Man," "The Gates of Eden," and "It's Alright Ma (I'm only bleeding)."

Yet even while offering a sometimes challenging program for his audience, Dylan courts the crowd beautifully. Switching between concert favorites and songs unknown, he also offers the audience several unreleased older jewels that would have been highlights on any other artist's album of the time, including "If You Gotta Go, Go Now" and "Momma, You Been on My Mind." The former he places between the two new heavy numbers of the night ("Gates of Eden" and "It's Alright, Ma"), to allow the audience to breathe, no doubt. He also performs two of the protest songs that had been withheld from official release at the time of this concert: "Who Killed Davey Moore" and "Talkin' John Birch Society Blues."

While mixing older material with some newly completed songs, Dylan's instincts never fail him concerning pace and balance. Listen closely to the opening of "A Hard Rain's A-Gonna Fall." He begins the guitar line for "The Ballad of Hollis Brown," but stops and mutters, "Nah…I can't… I'll do this instead," and proceeds with a fine version of "Hard Rain." Hollis Brown's individual plight no longer spoke to him; it was confining. "Hard Rain" contains lyrics which refuse to focus on one man or a specific incident, instead suggesting a number of strikingly complex, yet more universal interpretations. This rich, apocalyptic selection is the prototype from which the evening's three new songs evolve, and offers the most important early example of his "chains of flashing images," as Dylan himself described his lyrics to the late *San Francisco Chronicle* music critic Ralph J. Gleason.

Dylan gives strong readings to the few songs he does sing from *Another Side Of*. "To Ramona" sounds like a true plea for the woman to help herself, and he uses the opening of "I Don't Believe You" to lighten the serious mood which "It's Alright, Ma" has created. (I maintain that Dylan's alleged forgetfulness at the start of "I Don't Believe You" is the clever manipulative ruse of an experienced performer.) And given the strong rendition of "Spanish Harlem Incident," one can only wonder why this number immediately fell out of Dylan's active repertoire. Still, Bob did not totally ignore the new LP. Both "It Ain't Me, Babe" and "All I Really Want to Do" were deemed strong enough selections, even at the time, to close the concert and to use as an encore, respectively.

I have often said that the young Dylan had talent dripping from his fingertips. This Halloween 1964 recording is not a performance by that young man. Instead, it reveals a maturing Dylan in a creative growth spurt, and during this show we hear him evolving right before our ears. In hindsight, it is perhaps ironic that on his most recent release, Bob tries to explain his situation to his fans as straightforwardly as any artist can be expected to. To those who want him to be their eternal folk champion, he says it all with the song's title: "It Ain't Me, Babe." And to those who won't forgive him for a lack of overtly political songs on the new record, he anticipates their heated disappointment. In "My Back Pages," Dylan explains (in his own way) that he can no longer be expected to champion social causes; he is no longer that person.

Yes, perhaps these were tough months for Bob Dylan. His most recent LP had longtime fans worried, and the artist himself would rarely acknowledge many of these songs at concerts for decades to come. Yet the attitude Dylan displays at this show is positively buoyant. He is writing some of the best songs of his career, and immediately showing them to his audience. In fact, the inclusion of such a large number of these unfamiliar selections was a gutsy move. He could have easily relied on a pure oldies show, which he refused and still refuses to perform. Notice, for example, the intentional omission of his most recognizable anthem, "Blowin' in the Wind."

In the summer following this concert, Dylan released a partially electric album (*Bringing It All Back Home*) and fronted a rock band at the Newport Folk Festival. The October 1964 performance from New York City heard here is an important link between Bobby Dylan, the folk darling of Greenwich Village, and Dylan the electric traitor of Newport. Neither label was ever accurate, of course. But this concert demonstrates that with such a talented individual as Bob Dylan, not even his own devoted audience could possibly know what to expect from him; they would struggle with their own reaction to his changing art. What is indisputably clear from this recording is the fact that a young man—armed with only a guitar, a harmonica, and his own original songs—was able to hold an audience rapt for over 90 minutes; I still find this wildly impressive. As the respectful audience in the hall that night demonstrates, the wisest and most rewarding thing one can do is to listen to this concert with a focus and intensity that matches Dylan's breathtaking performance.

CD Review

Bob Dylan
The Bootleg Series, vol. 10—Another Self Portrait
Columbia Records, 2013

I—As with most things Dylan, the news slipped onto the "Bob-o-Sphere" in unconfirmed drabs: the next volume of The Bootleg Series was to consist of outtakes from the album *Self Portrait*. What?! This had to be either a joke or madness on the part of Columbia Records. An expanded set from Dylan's most universally reviled record? Why?

With confirmation that *Self Portrait* would indeed be the focus for Volume 10 of this ongoing archival series, questions did not abate. It seemed like a strikingly odd choice for a project, especially frustrating for fans aware of what could instead have been released from Columbia's vaults: an expanded edition of *The Basement Tapes*, live recordings from any number of tours, such as shows with The Band, or even a concert from the unique religion tours. Any of these potential releases made more sense than to place the spotlight back onto the rightfully forgotten *Self Portrait* album, made up primarily of unflattering interpretations of songs that Bob did not write. As sideman Al Kooper said of the original project, "Strange, strange, strange."

This week's appearance of the *Another Self Portrait* box set made me recall what was happening in my life when the original album was first released…

As usual, I was listening closely to music broadcast from our "Oasis in the Cornfield," KFMG (FM), a remarkably progressive radio station, especially so considering the time and place: 1970 in Des Moines, Iowa. The station had made me aware of many new artists during my high school years, from the obscure (Spooky Tooth) to the gods (Led Zeppelin). On their "Millard Fillmore Memorial Record Hour," KFMG would play three new LPs all the way through without interruption. Tape recorders were poised and ready all over mid-Iowa for this weekly gift, which can now be seen as an early form of streaming.

Hip radio announcer Ron Sorenson seemed excited on this particular morning in June, which is to say less mellow than usual by underground FM Radio standards of the day. The station had just received its promotional copy of a new Bob Dylan album, and Soren-son immediately started playing it. After about four songs, he cut in and talked about how Dylan was known to do a variety of unexpected things, and the new album seemed to fit this category. Sorenson was upbeat and respectful, but I don't recall hearing any more music from Bob's latest release that morning.

The album, of course, was *Self Portrait*. I admit to knowing little about Dylan at that time. But then, thanks to Bill Drake's seminal *History of Rock and Roll* radio marathon and an influential high school teacher, I began to realize that Dylan's talent called to me. Although I strove to get Bob's entire catalog, I swore that I would never need to buy his irritatingly expensive double album *Self Portrait*. I had been convinced by a hostile press and abusive word of mouth that the album was without merit.

But, being the completest and Bob fan that I was, I did at last buy a copy in 1973 when I reached college, first playing the record alone in my dorm room while expecting the worst. But darned if there weren't a few gems in there as early as side one: the country waltz "I've Forgotten More Than You'll Ever Know" and Gordon Lightfoot's "Early Morning Rain" were standouts. The album is definitely uneven. And that's being kind. However, as I recently said to a colleague, there *is* a good albeit brief batch of fine songs in there. But it's almost as if Bob doesn't want you to find them. Handful of strong tunes or not, I soon shelved the LP. It was too much trouble to pick through the sides to hear "Livin' the Blues," "Alberta," "It Hurts Me Too," and a few others. Plus, when deciding to play something by Bob, it was impossible for *Self Portrait* to compete with Dylan's far superior albums.

Unbeknownst to me when I bought the album that fall, we were only months away from the upcoming 1974 concerts by Dylan with The Band, his first tour since 1966. The media frenzy touting Bob's return would be followed by *Planet Waves* and then *Blood on the Tracks*. At this point, there was little need to revisit *Self Portrait*; the record was relegated to the category of a curiosity in the Dylan collection.

It has remained so until last spring. In fact, finding a CD copy of *Self Portrait* was not easy. It eventually became available, but Columbia was slow to reissue it on CD. Seeing an actual copy in a store (or even in somebody's collection) was nothing short of unusual. It was in the backwater of the catalog, held dear only by the same type of true believers who archly defend the Rolling Stones' *Satanic Majesties Request* or Miles Davis' *On the Corner*.

The release of the box set has made many fans return to their vinyl copies of the record. And how has the original *Self Portrait* aged over the course of 43 years? It is no better or worse than it ever was. The album's opening "All the Tired Horses" track is unexpected, hypnotic, and relaxing. It holds the listener in suspense and builds anticipation for remarkable things to come. They never do. Not really. Songs that you want to be good are often derailed by slovenly performances, such as "Belle Isle." Curiosity follows curiosity, with very few numbers distinguishing themselves.

Four live tracks taken from the 1969 Isle of Wight performance made one glad to have a recording of Bob performing his otherwise unavailable "Quinn the Eskimo," a radio hit for Manfred Mann. The listener could also appreciate the unpolished street choir harmony of "Minstrel Boy," and marvel at Dylan's inclusion of the festival's inferior rendition of "Like a Rolling Stone," a ragtag performance during which he frequently forgets the words. So very, very odd.

II—Bob Dylan is currently enjoying a dual recording career. Columbia Records issues Dylan's new material as well as the ongoing series culled from his unique legacy, titled *The Bootleg Series*. One assumes that Dylan is involved with his current albums, such as last fall's *Tempest* (2012), but I have been told that Bob has no interest in, or input into, his own ongoing *Bootleg Series* releases. Does Dylan even want his record company to issue these sets? Hard to know. When Capitol Records began repackaging The Beatles' catalog in the mid-1970s, Paul McCartney lamented the problematic nature of competing with one's own past. To give credit where warranted, Columbia Records has done a good job of keeping Dylan's new albums far apart from the release dates of his archival releases, making certain that Bob's new material is not competing with *his* past.

The Bootleg Series has consisted of well chosen, focused collections of sought-after Dylan recordings. The music in each set is previously unreleased, which is why they are of such great interest to fans. This is also why the new Volume 10, *Another Self Portrait*, seems to be an unlikely entry for the series. Drawing attention to this much maligned record from 1970 is also vexing, especially when the *Self Portrait* title could have been easily circumvented. In fact, calling the new set *Another Self Portrait* is a bit misleading. This really is a very different album, with only passing similarity to the box's namesake release. It might just as easily have been titled *A "New" New Morning*, since nearly a third of the songs come from unused material recorded for that release. One wonders why Columbia (or maybe Bob) is playing on the *Self Portrait* title.

Of the 35 tracks included, only about half are really associated with the original *Self Portrait* album. The rest are from sessions for the previously mentioned *New Morning* (1970), plus unissued takes from material that was newly recorded for *Greatest Hits, Volume II* (1971), one song from *The Basement Tapes* (1967), and another from *Nashville Skyline* (1969). Even so, I doubt if many will complain about producer Jeff Rosen straying from a strict *Self Portrait* focus to include these related recordings.

The two disks of previously unreleased studio material range from good to great. To give a proper description and assessment to this collection of songs would require a separate review. But to sum up, the music holds one's interest much better than the original *Self Portrait*. Dylan followers are aware of most of these previously unreleased songs. A few selections unknown even to most collectors are found here, but these are not the pinnacle of either disk.

But how is the box's much anticipated third disk—of the concert recorded at the Isle of Wight in August 1969? Well, it's historic, that's for sure. Consider: This is the only full length concert performed by Dylan between May 1966 and January 1974. It is the only concert Dylan ever gave using his *Nashville Skyline*, "Lay Lady Lay," voice. It presents one song unique to the Dylan canon, "Wild Mountain Thyme," plus several songs that Bob has rarely played live, most notably those from the *John Wesley Harding* LP. He is backed by The Band, and he also performs a brief solo set. Some of the songs' arrangements are strikingly different from their studio album counterparts. Revision has always been a part of Dylan's approach to his own work in concert, but these versions seem purposefully altered to suit the "Nashville" voice he uses here.

Procurement of a soundboard tape for this Isle of Wight concert has stymied bootleggers for decades. Until now, the only available copy of the concert was an audience tape, pressed onto vinyl by the underground Trade Mark of Quality label. It was the complete concert and, although the audio was listenable, its sound was the very definition of a low-fidelity field recording. It was known that Columbia had professionally recorded this concert, because of the four songs that were included on the original *Self Portrait*, but the rest of the program remained unissued until now. This live set is very much worth hearing, but it is still not convenient to obtain, as it appears only on the expensive edition of this *Another Self Portrait* release.

Concerning the performance: if one is expecting the dominating power of the 1966 concerts with The Band or the gleaming polish of their 1974 shows, this concert might disappoint. For the most part, this is a laid-back, off-the-cuff affair—as if the group were playing on your back porch or at a county fair in the Midwest. Bob seems genuinely pleased to be in front of an audience, where he presents a very good, if occasionally unsteady, one-hour set.

III—One final oddity worth mentioning appeared even before *Another Self Portrait* was announced for release. Excitement was generated by rumors that Columbia was about to issue an expanded edition of *Blood on the Tracks*. The record company clumsily confirmed this fact. But a *Blood on the Tracks* box did not materialize. Instead, *Another Self Portrait* was unexpectedly released. So, is this new entry in *The Bootleg Series* merely a place holder for die-hard fans while Columbia readies a *Blood on the Tracks* collection?

Perhaps the record company is finding it difficult to keep track of its numerous Dylan projects. Columbia is already promoting their late fall 2013 release of a 42-CD box of *The Complete Bob Dylan Album Collection*. The expanded *Blood on the Tracks* box is clearly being readied. It is unknown when Bob will record his next collection of new material. Speculating on reasons for the appearance of *Another Self Portrait* at this time, similar to the bemusement over the original release, the questions remain unchanged and unanswered:

Why this material? Is this box set Dylan's last laugh on his audience over an album he felt was unfairly maligned? Or does Bob even care that this set is released?

Why now? Is this volume merely meant to serve as a stopgap for other, more desirable collections of Dylan material that Columbia is preparing?

Why so expensive? Just as *Self Portrait* was a lavish album with a textured cover, the customer paid a bit more for the packaging. The expanded *Another Self Portrait* release takes that paradigm to stratospheric dimensions.

And yet, these questions all become irrelevant. One of the unexpected studio tracks included on the new box is an unreleased take of the traditional number "Spanish is the Loving Tongue." Bob must like this song, as he has recorded it several times. There were two previously released renditions, each with a distinctly different arrangement. One was issued as the B-side of the single "Watching the River Flow" (1971). The other was placed onto the 1973 conglomeration album entitled simply *Dylan*. The newly released recording of "Spanish is the Loving Tongue" features just Bob's voice and piano. After hearing it, I stopped the CD and wrote to several friends, insisting that this performance alone was worth the price of even the expanded edition. And I meant it.

Bonus Track

In the above review, I refer to the six-CD edition of The Basement Tapes *as a "lavish" release. Little did we know what lavish meant! Only two years later, Columbia would release an 18-CD box set in its ongoing Bootleg Series, documenting Dylan's time in the studio, 1965-66.*

Commentary
By the Time We Got to Mole Lake...
April 21, 2011

An article was recently published by a recording engineer who worked on Dylan's 1974 masterwork, *Blood on the Tracks*. As a former radio board operator, I read this piece with great interest. It brought back both fond and frightful memories of laboring in radio studios over professional recording consoles. I have never worked with or close to Bob Dylan, but a couple of people asked me to write up these memories, believing they might offer some tangential insights into the one true Bob. They don't, but as I thought about the weekend described below I realized that maybe I did have something worth recounting.

I was 22 years old in the summer of 1977, about to start my senior year at the University of Northern Iowa at Cedar Falls. I had been working at the school's FM radio station KUNI for over three years, longer than a lot of the full-time staff. I pulled 30-hour weeks, primarily doing DJ work. This was no low wattage, house current college station going out to dorm rooms; we were 100,000 watts of clean FM power, covering a large chunk of eastern Iowa. It was fairly early in the National Public Radio era. The station was still absolutely commercial free and the announcers could largely play whatever we pleased, as long as it fit the format of the specific show. There were some program underwriters who we had to acknowledge, but nothing obtrusive.

At KUNI we had classical music mornings but were known for specializing in folk music. Why? Because our station manager liked folk music. In fact, each weekday afternoon we had over three hours of it! From 2 to 4 P.M. we aired a record show called *Folkways*. Later in the day, after *All Things Considered* and the evening local news, we did another 90-minute show featuring bluegrass. Then students from the school's African American community played two hours of soul and funk on *Nationtime*. The night concluded with several hours of current rock and whatnot on a program called *Progression*.

I was lucky to be involved with Public Radio at an extremely fertile time. As I say, the music for each show was selected by the announcer, a fact that stuns current radio broadcasters into stupors of envy. I still occasionally come across an errant playlist of mine stuck away in some music book: titles of songs that I aired during one of my lengthy late-night shows. These weekend shifts did little to help my social life in college, but I didn't care. I now find these unearthed lists simultaneously humorous and embarrassing, but usually on target for their time. I got into radio for one reason: music. I was able to play my fill on KUNI from the spring of 1974 to the late fall of 1978.

By 1977 the station began receiving some grants for special projects. There was a folk festival to be held in northern Wisconsin, and the boss wanted it recorded. My recording partner and I loaded up the car with a high quality Nagra reel-to-reel tape machine, some microphones, and lots of blank tape. Off we went, not dreaming that an August weekend in Wisconsin might require something more than shorts and a T-shirt. As it turned out, weather would not be our biggest surprise.

We arrived the day before the festival started and felt major culture shock. Never before had I seen such dire poverty. The roads within the Mole Lake Indian Reservation were mere dirt ruts; the houses were tin or cardboard shacks; everything looked abused and broken. In the midst of this community was a large field with a raised stage at one end. There were designated areas in the surrounding woods for trailer parking and tent camping. I was glad that we would be staying at a hotel off the reservation, some 20 miles away. We needed a getaway from the long and pretty intense days. Although I had been an active camper during my Boy Scout era, this was not the same. Even before we left the festival grounds each night, things were getting loud in the camping areas—the sounds of alcohol-fueled fun and fights.

But the thing I remember most vividly was that, in the midst of this destitute situation, the government was putting in concrete sidewalks. SIDEWALKS! When there was no real street for miles around, only glorified cow paths used as roads. With just a cursory look, I could have named a dozen things that this reservation needed before sidewalks.

Despite a location set deep in the northern Wisconsin woods, the festival featured some known names, both country and folk. Doc Watson was there, Lester Flatt's band performed, and several other lesser local groups I can't recall right now. Most of the big-name acts were from the South, and I could tell right away that I was not the only one somewhat irritated by the surprisingly cold nights. Doc Watson played fairly late on the first evening and seemed very aware of the time remaining in his set. He was undoubtedly eager to return to the relative warmth of his tour bus. Still, he put on a solid show, and the crowd loved it. I remember late in the set he said, "Well, it's pretty cold for him tonight, but let's saddle up that 'Tennessee Stud,'" and he proceeded to play the song in stellar fashion.

Doc's son Merle was with him, as usual. I interviewed Merle briefly, but he was more interested in chatting up the local girls who were inviting him to a party. Still, he answered my questions about record labels and album obligations without haste or hesitation. For example, I remember him telling me that their contract called for one album a year. The one time I tried to speak to Doc Watson, he told me to go find Merle. That's fine; Doc needed Merle's eyes. Merle Watson was killed a few years after this festival, when a tractor ran over him. Doc would later say how he could never have been able to tour had Merle not been there to help with all aspects of the road.

Lester Flatt's band was the headlining act the second evening. The steel guitar player noted how holding his instrument's silver bar "was just like hanging onto a piece of ice all night." I'm afraid that I didn't appreciate Lester Flatt's set as much at that time as I should have. First, I was behind the stage, recording—not able to see the performance— and second, the scales had not yet truly fallen from my eyes about the brilliance of some country music. The next day I was told by several observers that this had been an exceptionally good night for the veteran performer.

"Why?" I asked.

"Because," I was told, "Lester didn't once need to leave the stage during the entire set."

At first I thought they were joking, but they weren't. These were devotees who had already seen the man perform several times that summer. I later learned that during Flatt's final days on the road, health problems were sidelining him *during shows* with some regularity. He would often need to go into the wings and rest for a bit as his band played on. I recall seeing Mrs. Flatt standing in the makeshift backstage area, dressed as if she were to perform in the Opry spotlight: aging elegance incarnate. But I felt badly for her, as she looked very concerned the entire time her husband was on stage. When I learned of Lester's declining health, I understood. At the other end of the age spectrum on stage that night was teenage Marty Stuart, a talented sideman for Flatt in the 1970s.

By the time of this Mole Lake gathering, folk and bluegrass festivals had been big business for well over a decade. Even so, I was still enthralled with the whole idea of being at a festival! And being there to record the music made me feel like a useful part of the scene. Woodstock was a full eight years in the past, but its shadow remained a long one. The title of this piece bears witness: "By the time we got to Mole Lake"—our intentional variation of Joni Mitchell's musical tribute to the original Woodstock festival. We must have said that line every three minutes.

I don't recall much about the other bands except for one local group opening with a hot, bluegrass take on The Beatles' "I've Just Seen a Face." There were the typical show business elements that are not especially fond memories—self-important organizers chief among them. Also, we had trouble getting a few of the performers to sign our release forms, which would allow for radio broadcast of the recordings we were making. Doc Watson consented without hesitation, but some of the lesser names wanted to hear the sound mix on the tapes before signing; they really gave us ego trip troubles. We had finally endured enough arrogance from one performer. We said to him, "Hey! Doc Watson trusts our mix. Are you a bigger name than Doc Watson?" This shamed the guy into signing.

Eric Weissberg also performed, still getting bookings from his huge 1973 Top 40 instrumental hit, "Dueling Banjos." The number was featured during an unforgettable scene early in the movie *Deliverance*. In fact, Weissberg named his backing band Deliverance, although he seemed a bit embarrassed by the whole thing. Prior to his unexpected success with "Dueling Banjos," Weissberg had largely been (and remained) a first-call studio musician, recording with performers from Barbra Streisand to Billy Joel. He also occasionally did film soundtrack work. But I didn't search out Eric Weissberg to talk about Billy or Barbra or "Dueling Banjos" or soundtracks. I wanted to ask about his time backing Bob Dylan on the *Blood on the Tracks* album. Weissberg was tolerant, but not enthusiastic about our conversation.

The afternoon had warmed the festival grounds considerably. As we began to talk, a couple of his band members looked on, bored. I began to ask my questions when Weissberg interrupted: "I have sort of a thing I say to interviewers, and if this doesn't cover what you want, then we can speak in specifics." I agreed, of course, and he then recounted his work as a studio musician. He told me that after *Deliverance* was released he got a phone call from his agent, telling him that "Dueling Banjos" was racing up the chart. Weissberg couldn't believe it and, having no idea that the number was being released as a single, thought his agent was joking. He acknowledged the hit as a fluke, but he was now making the most of it while he could.

That biographical nutshell was interesting, but what about Dylan? I asked why Bob called him to play on the *Blood on the Tracks* album, and about his connection to Dylan. Weissburg told me, "I met Bob in the very early 1960s, when I was at school in Madison and he was en route to New York City for what I think must have been his first trip there. I didn't think he even remembered me, so I was surprised when I got a call to play on a session for him. It was odd from the start. I didn't know if he wanted just me or if he wanted me to bring my band. So I brought the group along."

Weissberg's responses became slower and more thoughtful; I was now entering into nonstandard interview territory. I asked him if it was a pleasant, relaxed session or if there had been a lot of tension in the room: "I'll tell you, it was the strangest recording session I have ever worked on. Bob barely ran down the tune to us and then we were off recording it. Then the engineer immediately rewound the tape so Dylan could hear it. And while the song we had just recorded was playing back in the studio—*loud!* —Bob was showing us the chord changes for the next tune. At the same time! I had never seen anything like it. Completely unorthodox studio method. I didn't really enjoy the session, and I can't imagine that Bob enjoyed it."

Eric Weissberg and his band Deliverance appear on the *Blood on the Tracks* album for one song, "Meet Me in the Morning." So when Weissberg mentioned learning chord changes for a second tune, I immediately asked about it. "As I recall, we did two songs—the one that appears on the album and one other." He thought for a moment and said, "Seems like it was a blues, but I can't be sure." Although the recording was unreleased at the time of our interview, Weissberg's memory was accurate. The other tune recorded at the session was "Call Letter Blues," which would finally be issued by Columbia in 1991 on the first of *The Bootleg Series* CDs. I asked if multiple takes of either or both songs had been recorded: "I think we did each tune once," he said. "That was it. Then we packed up and it was over."

I thanked Mr. Weissberg for his time, and he departed to another part of the grounds. But then, after their boss was well out of earshot range, members of the Deliverance band chimed in with force: "That session was an absolute joke. Weissberg was being nice about it. Dylan got so drunk that night that Eric had to restring his guitar for him when Dylan broke a string. And it wasn't even good stuff; he was getting smashed on his ass on Ripple or some cheap-o crap."

These guys had been there, and they were clearly not impressed. Not fans. Anger in their voices. No one among them was the least bit in awe of Dylan; they sounded disgusted. I don't know who was making most of the proclamations, but all were in agreement: it was a bizarre night. I tried to question them more about the date, but they had said their piece. Everybody hated the experience.

After hearing these sidemen recount their Dylan studio encounter with such intense derision, it struck me that Weissberg had taken the high road during our conversation. Clearly frustrated when recalling the oddness of the Dylan session, Weissberg expressed astonishment, not anger. He said that he had never seen any recording process run in such a manner. And this assessment coming from a professional studio musician who had played on hundreds of studio dates!

And that was pretty much it. The other recording engineer and I began our long drive back to Iowa late that night, with some festival glamour and mystique having been drained from our consciousness. It had been a good time, often a fun time, but nothing to romanticize. And people hating on Bob! Go figure.

As we drove through the Wisconsin night we saw what appeared to be a major forest fire. It was spread over several distant hilltops, raging some miles away from us but very clear against the dark sky. I wanted to drive toward it for a closer look but was told that was a stupid idea. True, of course. But I couldn't stop thinking about the fire, even years later, and how beautiful it had appeared that night. Like the dangerous flames which had attracted me, I also escaped largely unscathed from my experience with a music festival. I saw some unpleasant business elements, social problems, and personality quirks up close. But I returned to Iowa undaunted, still unsinged and an optimist concerning the regenerative powers of live performances and of music itself.

Post Script

So what happened to those reels of music and the interview tapes? Most of them were broadcast at least once on KUNI (FM) in Cedar Falls, but after that they seemed to drift away. This is odd, in retrospect, because I made myself safety copies of just about everything at that time. But not these. Because they were played over the air in a well-publicized special, copies from the broadcast could be sitting in somebody's basement in eastern Iowa on cassette tapes. But where the master reels went, I don't know. Over the years, I have asked former and current employees of the station to keep an eye out for these tapes, but they are not to be found. That's OK—they would be nice to have, but...perhaps anticipating their eventual return is even better.

Commentary
Bob Dylan's Sacred Song
September 2013

Prior to the encore at an April 1980 concert at Toronto's Massey Hall, Bob Dylan urges members of the audience to send him their prayer requests. This unprecedented offer comes in the midst of one of Dylan's most controversial periods—known as his Gospel Era, when Dylan was performing only his recently composed, overtly Christian songs.

The idea of getting a personal note to Bob Dylan, or even thinking that he would care to read a fan's prayer request, would have been ludicrous shortly before this unique offer, as it would be again soon afterwards. But the performer appears sincere here, even if it is doubtful whether any fans' missives actually made their way into Dylan's hands that night.

By April 1980, Dylan had already been on the road for several months with his Christian tour, performing concerts made up exclusively of his newly written sacred material. He had first publicly performed three of these songs the previous fall on *Saturday Night Live*, an appearance designed to promote the release of his new LP, *Slow Train Coming*. This album was highly anticipated at the time of its August 1979 release. The entertainment media had been dumbfounded by rumors of Dylan's religious conversion.

Although the singer's overtly religious attitude was accepted by some longtime fans and tolerated by others, the audiences at Dylan's gospel era concerts had been problematic from the start. Fans that rejected his sacred material were not hesitant in expressing this opinion. One infamous evening came early in the tour. On an audience recording made at the concert in Tempe, Arizona, on November 26, 1979, Dylan sounds angry and disgusted as he chastises the audience. He tells them that they are a "real rude bunch," rebuffing their hostile shouts by telling them they can "rock and roll all the way down to The Pit!"

Some audiences, however, were enthusiastic about the new songs. Dylan was met with a receptive crowd in Denver, Colorado, in January 1980. A partial soundboard recording survives from this concert. Dylan's set of religious numbers is well received; the crowd seems to know the songs and is happy to hear them. There are no indications of frustration from audience or performer. But nights of such positive rapport between artist and audience on this tour were rare.

Dylan's final performance of purely religious material was held in Dayton, Ohio, on May 21, 1980. Two concerts had been scheduled, but ticket sales were so sluggish that the audiences were combined. In the fall of 1980, after a brief break from touring, Dylan returned to the tour circuit and began incorporating some of his older songs into his concerts. Including a few well-known numbers could be seen as a form of compromise. And while the addition of familiar songs into the set list was met with relief and enthusiastic approval, the repertoire was still too heavily weighted toward gospel songs for some fans. Dylan seemed extremely aware of the expectations that audiences brought to the concert hall. He would often say at the conclusion of these shows, "I sincerely hope that you heard something that you came to hear tonight." Dylan continued to tour with a set list that combined his sacred and his secular works. At the end of the 1981, he would take an extended break from playing live dates.

Dylan returned to the concert stage in May 1984. With overtly religious numbers having almost completely evaporated from his set lists, he appeared to be picking up where he had left off in 1978, prior to his Christian conversion. By the time the 1984 tour began, the religion era seemed like only a strange dream which most of his fans were willing to forget. The following year, Dylan gave a lengthy interview to Cameron Crowe. In it, Dylan reflected on his audience's attitude during the Gospel Era: "I was suffering from that so-called religious backlash at the time, and that had a lot to do with affecting people's opinions." Dylan continued: many people think that if something "comes from the Bible it can be cast off as being too, quote, 'religious.' Make something religious and people don't want to deal with it; they can say it's irrelevant. I think people were prejudiced against" those songs.

In the fall of 2012 Dylan released his 35th studio album, *Tempest*, featuring songs often punctuated by violent lyrics. It is difficult to reconcile some of the stark imagery present in these songs with Dylan's comments about the album, made to journalist Mikal Gilmore. Dylan said that he had originally intended the album to be a cycle of twelve religious songs, but his concentration level was not up to the task. Dylan was also uncharacteristic in musing aloud about whether he made the correct decision concerning the songs he decided to release on *Tempest*.

When Dylan returned to stage performances following the release of *Tempest*, it was assumed that he would be playing some of the album's ten new songs in concert. But when the tour resumed in October 2012, Dylan performed 33 concerts during which he confounded fans by rarely acknowledging that *Tempest* had been released. Ignoring these new songs was an unexpected move, even by Dylan standards. Was this hesitancy to perform the *Tempest* material in concert the result of the second thoughts about the songs, as he expressed in the interview?

When Gilmore asked Dylan if the religious songs he originally intended for the *Tempest* album had been similar to the material found on *Slow Train Coming*, the singer immediately rejected the comparison. Dylan said that he wanted to compose works which were more in line with "Just a Closer Walk with Thee." This is a song of praise and an acknowledgement of faith more than a theological challenge to the listener, as found with the accusatory "When You Gonna Wake Up" or "Watered-Down Love." From what he says to Gilmore, it sounds like the songs Dylan wanted to write were much closer in spirit to the material on his *Christmas in the Heart* holiday release than most of the songs from the Gospel Era.

As with all conversations with Bob Dylan, the reporter (and the reader) must remain aware of Dylan's penchant for evasiveness. In 2004, CBS television reporter Ed Bradley was having difficulty getting Dylan to say very much. Bradley finally asked Dylan why he had regularly given opaque responses to interviewers for most of his career. To this, Dylan gave one of his longest comments of the exchange: "I realized… that the press, the media…[are] not the judge. God's the judge. And the only person you have to think twice about lying to is yourself or to God. The press isn't either one of them. I just figured they're irrelevant."

Long before *Saved, Infidels, or Tempest,* observers have been simultaneously aware of, and skeptical about Dylan's commitment to religion and the Bible. In a 1968 interview at his New York City apartment, Dylan surprises John Cohen with allusions to biblical parables.

When Cohen asks how he knows these references, Dylan asserts, "I have always read the Bible."

Cohen is not convinced: "I don't think you're the kind of guy who goes to the hotel, where the Gideons leave a Bible, and you pick it up." Unperturbed, the songwriter shrugs off the interviewer's preconception of him.

"Well," replies Dylan, "You never know."

Bonus Track

In 1986, an upbeat Dylan spoke with Minneapolis music critic Jon Bream, who reminded Bob that he had not played a concert in his home state since 1978. Bream asked why he didn't perform in Minnesota on one of his religion tours from a few years earlier. A smiling Dylan tells the reporter, "They're all religion tours."

This response reminds me of an exchange that music writer Ben Fong-Torres once had with Dylan. Bob's 1974 tour had ended, and Fong-Torres briefly encountered Dylan later that year at a Crosby, Stills, Nash and Young reunion show. Fong-Torres complimented Bob on his recent Before the Flood *album and asked Dylan a couple of seemingly benign questions, like how he liked the CSNY concert so far. Normal conversation stuff. Dylan replied with a few non sequiturs, including comments about Frank Sinatra in Australia and the weather in San Francisco. The author paused a moment and then told Dylan: "Your next record ought to be a comedy record," to which Bob replied: "All my records are comedy records!"*

Book Review

Bob Dylan—A Life in Stolen Moments; Day by Day: 1941-1995
By Clinton Heylin
Schirmer Books, 1996

A book purporting to be a day-by-day assessment of an artist's lengthy career can't help but become an extremely linear biography. And although author Clinton Heylin has previously written two exhaustive books on Dylan, his new *A Life in Stolen Moments* is not mere rehash or a milking of his topic. In fact, in some ways this recent addition updates the best of Heylin's previous work and is among the most useful volumes in the expanding Dylan book market.

A Life in Stolen Moments strives to be comprehensive. Heylin lists the dates of all known live performances and their locations. He also discusses Dylan's major (and minor) set list changes between and within specific tours. This alone makes interesting reading, since Bob has been known to alter his song list with great regularity. Heylin also summarizes all major print interviews with Dylan, emphasizing notable exchanges.

Calendar accounts of popular entertainment figures often smack of fanzine journalism. Heylin avoids that sort of superficiality. He provides a solid examination of his subject, with careful attention to accuracy. In addition, he has outgrown a tendency to attack his fellow Dylanologists, a weakness of Heylin's earlier work. He no longer appears to believe that he alone should be allowed to write about Bob Dylan. This change may owe something to the format of *Stolen Moments*. There are fewer places here for the author to engage in the cheap shots that punctuated much of his previous writing on Dylan. Instead of an attitude of competitiveness, Heylin here provides brief and helpful notes to explain the relationship of various tangential figures to the primary subject. When Dave Van Ronk or Hurricane Carter is mentioned, Heylin offers a summary indicating the person's place in Dylan's career.

A Life in Stolen Moments provides a well-researched, readable complement to Paul Williams' ongoing *Performing Artist* trilogy on Dylan in concert and to Heylin's own *Recording Sessions* book. While there is no single best book about this complex musician, readers looking primarily for a factual account of Dylan's career should turn to Heylin's *Stolen Moments*.

Indirect Questions

In the mid-1990s, a respected magazine for record collectors called *Goldmine* ran a feature article on guitarist Mick Ronson. In it, the guitarist's girlfriend talked about Ronson's time spent with Bob Dylan's Rolling Thunder Review tour of the mid-1970s. She said that Ronson complained to her that he found it frustrating to be on the road with Dylan in part, because Bob would call up tunes in different keys each night. That is, he would not play the same song in the same key at each show.

I found this odd and unlikely, and I believed that audience recordings from this tour would disprove this claim. I wrote a letter to *Goldmine*, which ran my brief missive under the heading "Songs in the Key of Bob." In the letter I took issue with the claim about key changes related by Ronson's girlfriend, even though I certainly had never been in a band with Dylan. I stressed that Bob was a supremely talented musician and performer, but that he was not a Marian McPartland type of artist, able to play a song in all twelve different keys. *Goldmine* published no response or rebuttal.

Sometime later I had the opportunity to speak with recording artist Marshall Crenshaw. He had once auditioned to be Dylan's bass player, but it didn't work out. I posed the question to Crenshaw: when he was rehearsing with Bob for three days, did Dylan call up the same tune in different keys? Crenshaw paused for a moment and then told me: "I can't really answer that. Bob never had us run the same tune more than once." This makes sense, as Crenshaw was participating in tryouts and not true band rehearsals.

I remain unconvinced that Dylan regularly changes the keys of the songs he performs in concerts. It seems like something he would do, though, just to mess with his side men, but I hear no aural evidence of this on the tapes of his shows.

As always: Informed rebuttals welcome.

Post Script

I wrote the above piece some 20 years ago, expecting it to be a moribund issue. Interestingly enough, in *The Bootleg Series* release of *The Basement Tapes*, Dylan himself inadvertently seems to offer a convincing rebuttal to my thoughts about his use of different key signatures. At several points during these 1967 recordings, Dylan and The Band will start to play a song. Then the musicians stop, and they begin the song again, but in a different key—one more suited to Dylan's vocal range. The group, including Bob, appears able to switch keys with little effort. At one point, late in these lengthy sessions, Dylan even asks aloud: "What key haven't we played in yet?" He does not appear to be joking.

Concert Commentary

Bob Dylan
BMO Harris Bradley Center
Milwaukee, Wisconsin
November 8, 2012

NO SONGS FROM *Tempest* were played in Milwaukee. Bob played no guitar during this show. Neither fact made the least difference. The concert was as good as any I've seen Dylan perform in my nearly 40 years of following this strange and compelling musician.

Before attending this concert, I was concerned. Bob Dylan had scheduled himself with more tour dates for the fall of 2012 than any recent concert season. It was reported by some that his voice was shot (but people had been saying that for decades). More troubling, friends in other cities were reporting numerous walk outs in mid-concert, sometimes including the friends themselves!

I was also surprised because, for the first time in my experience with Dylan concerts, this one was being advertised on television. Short commercials aired during local news and on late-night TV. I figured this meant ticket sales must be sluggish. If true, this added fuel to my premise about the potential problems for Bob caused by being on the road for so many dates. He had lately been covering the Midwest like a blanket. Fine for the obsessive fans, but this smacked of the heavy touring schedule Dylan employed during the early 1990s, prior to the revitalization brought on by the release of *Time Out of Mind*. At the time, Texas friend Tony Davidson and I feared that "Dylan was using up his audience."

I had low expectations. How much longer could Dylan keep delivering? And if this was the beginning of the end of Dylan as a touring artist, how much effort would he be putting forth? Set lists for the current tour indicated that he had barely touched the songs from his new *Tempest* CD in concert. Was this a sign that it was too much trouble to work up new tunes for a stage he soon planned to abandon? Many questions. And as with all things Dylan, conjecture is pointless.

My concerns were misplaced. The concert left me elated. Of the many times I have seen Bob Dylan since January 1974, this concert was perhaps the most completely satisfying. I had bought tickets on the first day of availability. They seemed to be good seats, but it's always tough to tell. After all, this show was to be held in the Bradley Center, where the Milwaukee Bucks play basketball. In other words, a very large room, and not one designed for music.

My son and I arrived at the hall and found that our seats were great! In the second row off the floor, not the second row of a distant balcony. As 7:30 approached and opening act Mark Knopfler prepared to play, my son asked me if I thought a lot of people were waiting until Bob hit the stage to sit down. After all, the place was not at all full. The entire upper level of the sports arena had been curtained off, and the lower levels were very thinly populated. About the time I was forming my response, Knopfler's band began their first tune. I was surprised and happy: surprised about the very low attendance (this was less than sparse) and happy that the concert was beginning on time—a few minutes early, in fact.

I knew not to expect Dire Straits tunes, but I was not impressed by the hourlong performance by Knopfler and his eight-piece band. Talented multi-instrumentalists, to be sure, but I was not connecting with much of it. Surrounded by talkers and drinkers, we headed to the lobby to wait out the set—something I rarely do. When we returned to the hall, I instructed my son to just follow me with confidence. I didn't think the ushers would care if people shifted positions on a night such as this, and they didn't. We moved over two sections and spread out in one of the unpopulated areas. This vast stretch of open seats gave us slightly better sight lines.

Dylan came on stage with no fanfare. He had recently dropped the practice of having an announcer provide a spoken overview of his career before his entrance. The band kicked into "Watching the River Flow," and we were off and running for the 100-minute evening of music. The "River" rolled along pleasantly, but what surprised me most was how good the sound was, for a Bob Dylan concert in general and for a sports arena in particular.

Bob then seated himself at the grand piano and began a beautiful version of "Girl from the North Country." The song is a favorite of mine, but once again the biggest surprise was the sound: the lyrics were clear *and* every piano note was audible. I have attended some shows when none of Bob's piano playing could be heard, which may have been intentional. Before the concert, I indicated how I believed that Dylan sometimes *liked* muddy sound—a contention bolstered by critics and by Bob himself.

Mark Knopfler joined Bob's backing quintet for this second tune. Knopfler came on stage with no announcement or fanfare, departing after three songs in similar fashion. With Knopfler adding a third guitar to those of Charlie Sexton and Stu Kimball, the group played "Things Have Changed" and "Tangled Up in Blue." One interesting aspect of "Things Have Changed" was the guitar interplay between Knopfler and Sexton, who dueled it out at the song's conclusion. Usually when two instrumentalists are musically sparring, they face each other. But as these guitarists traded licks, they both kept their eyes riveted on Bob, still seated at the grand piano. Knopfler actually had his back to Sexton as their guitar leads entwined.

The concert continued with two rarely-heard tunes from very different eras of Bob's past work: "Million Miles" and "Chimes of Freedom." After this last song my son said to me, "They seem to have a little trouble with a few of their endings." I said, "Yeah. They don't play some of these a whole lot. And even on the oft-performed ones, Dylan may change things in mid-song." That's why all band members' eyes remain fixed on Bob, no matter what.

The stage was adorned with a number of old-style lights on high, black tripods such as those that would illuminate Hollywood movie lots. These lights were functional, also offering a bit of interesting ambience. Although dwarfed by its surroundings, Dylan's Oscar for his song "Things Have Changed" was clearly visible on the piano. Draped around this golden statuette, as my sharp-eyed son pointed out, was what seemed to be Bob's Presidential Medal of Freedom, awarded the previous spring by Barack Obama.

The night continued with some expected numbers, such as "Rollin' and Tumblin'" and "Highway 61 Revisited." But nestled between the frequently-heard songs were an additional two infrequently-played numbers. While "Love Sick" was a big song for Bob as his resurgence began in 1997, it is no longer a concert standard. Even more welcome was the closing track from 2006's *Modern Times* CD, "Ain't Talkin'." Beautiful versions of all these songs were played with conviction by a road-tested band. After the moody "Ain't Talkin'," the tight ensemble launched into "Thunder on the Mountain," and I knew we were on the evening's downhill slope. What I expected, and what followed, were "Ballad of a Thin Man," "Like a Rolling Stone," "All Along the Watchtower," and (as an encore) "Blowin' in the Wind."

During "Ballad of a Thin Man," I was again struck by the quality of the sound. Bob came center stage and sang the song clearly, line for line. This was an intentionally crisp vocal performance by Dylan because the sound had been set to echo the singer's voice for a single repeat. The initial vocal was distinct, and the echo also was effectively clear and haunting. At most Dylan shows I have attended, this type of echo nuance would be completely lost in the overall muddled sound.

As the concert ended and the house lights came up, I thought of several people I wished had experienced the evening with us. I also noted again how poorly attended the concert had been. It brought to mind the words of my friend Mike Toft of Minneapolis, who gave Dylan a lot of credit for not jumping on the 50th Anniversary wagon. That struck a chord with me. It would have been easy for Bob to stay off the road for a while to create demand, followed by a huge and highly touted payday tour. With Keith Richards defending $800 face value ticket prices for an upcoming Rolling Stones show in Chicago, one wonders who is interested in making music and who wants to make money. But that topic is fodder for another time.

As for the state of Bob Dylan, my fears were allayed. This concert showed no signs that Bob was at all tired or cruising on autopilot. True to form, he did exactly as he pleased. I, too, was pleased, just to be sitting there with my son, watching and listening. I have been told by the statisticians that on this night in Milwaukee Dylan played "Like a Rolling Stone" for the 2,000th time. Let's hope that Bob is thinking in baseball terms, perhaps aiming for that elusive 3,000 mark.

Concert Commentary

Bob Dylan
Riverside Theater
Milwaukee, Wisconsin
May 13, 2015

WEDNESDAY NIGHT'S Bob Dylan concert was as meticulously crafted as a classical music program by the Milwaukee Symphony. Long known for altering his set list from night to night, Dylan now presents an unchanging program of songs, no matter the location.

A Texas friend saw this tour when Bob played Houston last week. He felt certain that Bob would acknowledge his surroundings by performing "If You Ever Go to Houston." Nope. Even when in his old stomping grounds of Minneapolis/St. Paul, Dylan gives no special nods to location. The set lists for the three nights he played in Minnesota were identical to each other and to the rest of this tour.

What does this tell us? That this artist wants his audience to hear these songs in this order, the great majority culled from his newer releases. "Things Have Changed" opens the evening, clearly announcing that listeners should abandon all expectations of a greatest hits review. There will be no "Lay, Lady, Lay," "All Along the Watchtower," or "Like a Rolling Stone" tonight.

To my surprise, the sold-out Riverside Theater audience seemed fine with this. An occasional shout would come from the crowd, but the most discernable yell was not for an old song, but to offer an early Happy Birthday greeting. In his most recent interview, Dylan talked about how his younger audience is far more accepting of his current concerts, stating that many of his early fans are now locked in a music "time warp." Based on the enthusiasm shown by this tour's audiences, Bob is an accurate judge of his fan base.

A few old songs did surface. "Tangled Up in Blue" and "Simple Twist of Fate" came near the end of the first set and the start of the second, respectively. And when the audience recognized these numbers, certainly they were pleased. But there was absolutely no sense of: "At last; this is what we came for!" In fact, reactions nearly as strong greeted the start of "Pay in Blood," "Forgetful Heart," and "Duquesne Whistle."

Dylan seemed especially intent on having the audience absorb his lyrics. Gone was the muddy sound that has sometimes diminished his shows. I am convinced that the improved fidelity was not simply a happy accident of this specific evening. To insure sound clarity, bassist Tony Garnier played guitar as often as he played either his acoustic or electric bass. The crisp sound was also helped by drummer George Recile's light use of brushes on several numbers. Any rhythm that might have been needed to accentuate the understated bass and drums instrumentation was always present in Stu Kimball's solid guitar work.

As for Bob, he no longer plays guitar at all. Piano has become his primary instrument. Dylan split his time between a baby grand and center stage, where both a modern and an old time ribbon microphone stood. Unlike concerts of a decade ago, the piano is now clearly present in the sound mix, and there is no secondary keyboard in the band. Dylan occasionally played rudimentary piano on his early albums, but now he seems very comfortable with the instrument.

Donnie Herron is Bob's utility man. Herron rapidly switches between a wide variety of string instruments, strategically located on a raised platform near Dylan. It was interesting to observe Herron as he intently watched Bob's hands on the piano keys, making sure that his string part would fit exactly with what Dylan was playing.

In addition to piano, Dylan still plays harmonica. These harp interludes invariably drew enthusiastic responses. Bob selected his harmonica for a given song from a wooden box near the piano. Lined with emerald green fabric, it was placed below a bust that appeared to be of Mozart. While this perhaps sounds pretentious, it actually fit well with the comfortable stage ambience. Some lovely, subdued lighting elements occasionally adorned the dark curtain that draped the entire rear of the stage. These were usually vertical shafts of golden light—static forms, as opposed to disruptive light shows or recognizable images.

As the evening's program unfolded, only once did I think Bob might be calling up a tune that the band was not expecting. Late in the second set, Dylan said something to lead guitarist Charlie Sexton.

Sexton immediately removed the electric guitar he had just put on and quickly strapped on an acoustic. The song list remained unaltered—it was Sexton's instrument Bob wanted changed. Even within a rigid set list, Bob is still experimenting with musical variables.

Dylan had been moving between the piano and center stage all night, often strolling the length of the performance space as the band played. But during the chords that linked the beautiful "Long and Wasted Years" with the final song of the main set, Dylan stopped by the drum platform and stretched repeatedly. He then walked to the microphone and sang "Autumn Leaves." His graveled voice was a perfect match for this song of longing and remembrance.

The two numbers performed for the encore, like the entire program, were carefully selected. The first was a beautiful version of "Blowin' in the Wind." More than a closing crowd pleaser or a reminder of Bob's origins, it demonstrated the continued relevance of the song. Like Hal Holbrook's recent Milwaukee performance that channeled the frighteningly timely political views of Mark Twain, Dylan's words still illuminate and challenge his audience.

The final selection presented each night of this tour is "Stay With Me." Perhaps Bob is using its theme as a thank you to his audience for remaining loyal to him during his lengthy career. It could also express a hope that they continue to listen. Maybe those stretching exercises he did before "Autumn Leaves" suggest that Dylan is only now getting warmed up.

Artist Commentary
Bruce Springsteen
Like a Rocker Out of My Dreams

Prior to 1975, I had listened to Bruce Springsteen about as much as most enthusiasts of new rock music. That is, not a lot. I knew who he was, but I received few requests for his music when I ran the campus radio station. I had seen ads for the first album, praising the dense imagery in Springsteen's songs. Even as an English major, I was not motivated to investigate this wordy tunesmith. I wasn't truly aware of the man until his *Born to Run* album. The album's title song was great, of course, and I had heard "Jungleland," but I still wasn't knocked out.

Then with the promotional debacle of Bruce's picture appearing on covers of both *Time* and *Newsweek* during the same week, I thought his days were probably numbered. I bought *Darkness on the Edge of Town* when it was released in 1978 and liked it well enough. But the album seemed a comedown from *Born to Run*, particularly since it had taken him such a long time between records.

A friend called me in the fall of 1980 to tell me that Bruce was on tour and would be playing in St. Paul. Could I get us tickets? He would be driving up from Iowa and was excited. I somewhat grudgingly said I would try. At this point, I didn't really care about Springsteen. I equated Bruce with Bob Dylan's electric tour 1966. And if I wanted that, why not just listen to the real thing? But I did get us tickets for the show. I imagined Bruce would do a normal-length show, encore with "Born to Run," and that would be it. As it turned out, there was nothing normal about it.

Springsteen was on the road to promote his new double album, *The River*. It was early in the tour. In fact, the album had not yet been released. The band came on stage, Bruce greeted the crowd, and they kicked into a full tilt version of "Born to Run." I leapt to my feet. Was this possible? Who begins a show with his best-known tune? This unexpected opener led immediately into "Prove It All Night," the one chart hit that the *Darkness* album had produced. At that song's conclusion, Springsteen yelled, "Can you stand some more?" and the band drove into "Tenth Avenue Freeze-Out," a standout track from the *Born to Run* album. I looked at my friend and shouted, "He's opening with the encore!"

And from that moment, Bruce Springsteen had me. I was forever a fan and eternally grateful that the man had dedicated his life to music. Bruce understood. It was a calling. Dedication to music was a deep passion over which both performer and audience had no choice. But that was not a bad thing; music gave hope. It provided a reason to live, to get out of bed, to go to work. Bruce grasped all of this; he must have in order to perform in such a manner. The music was life-or-death to him, as it was for his fans.

Bruce and his E Street Band played quite a few new songs from *The River*, which were of course unfamiliar to the audience. Even so, all were well received. Near the end of a lengthy set, Springsteen played the double shot of favorites, "Badlands" and "Thunder Road." I thought these numbers were signaling the end of the concert, to be followed by a brief encore. What a great experience! I was hooked. This was beyond anything I could have expected.

Bruce took the microphone and said, "We're gonna take a 15-minute intermission; see you in a little bit." An intermission! That was the *first set?* My admiration went to new levels. E Street Band guitarist Steve Van Zandt later said that even he was surprised by the length of the shows during that tour: "I thought we'd go out and make 'em crazy for 90 minutes and call it a night." Bruce had other plans.

The second set was also remarkable. Springsteen was able to sustain his energy, the quality of his songs, and my interest. Bruce saved a few gems for the end of the concert: "Backstreets," "Rosalita," "Jungleland," the "Detroit Medley." The show went beyond the three-hour mark, but my devotion has lasted a lifetime. I have attended several Springsteen concerts since that night, and each one has been great. Even so, there is nothing quite like the first concert experience. This might have been especially true for me, as I had been indifferent about even attending the show.

My Iowa friend later told me that I made up for lost time. I got to know all of Bruce's albums quite well. Then came another milestone: Minneapolis FM station KQRS rebroadcast their tape of the 1978 Springsteen concert from Detroit's Agora Ballroom. I recorded this show and was again stunned by the power of the performance. I nearly wore out my reel deck playing the tape, which contained tangible proof of Springsteen's concert abilities. My enthusiasm was not always catching; some friends even told me to back it down a little. I couldn't; this Bruce guy had shown me new potential for what old-school rock could be. And more.

Years passed, a wedding took place, children arrived, children grew, records and music books that had been on shelves were again being read and played. My daughter sat at the piano one morning. She was working through the chord changes to "Backstreets," part of the *Born to Run* folio that had recently been unearthed. After a while she looked up and said, "Dad, do you have a copy of this album?" "Um… yes I do."

Shortly after this, I began to show my daughter some of my Springsteen holdings. These included the normal albums, but I had also purchased all of the singles as they were released. "See," I showed her, "Each of these 45s has a song on its flip side that is *not on the album*! And they're good songs! It's like getting another album side of Bruce!" She looked thoughtfully at the picture sleeves and at the records.

"I used to be a fan," I enthused.

"Yeah," she said. "I'm starting to get that."

To this day, both of my children laugh mightily as they recount how Dad *used to be a fan*! And not just of Bruce, but he was also a "former fan" of Bob Dylan, The Beatles, Elvis...

A few years ago there was a contest on Sirius/XM Radio—part of a promotional campaign for the box set reissue of *Darkness on the Edge of Town*. The handful of winners would go to New York City and meet Bruce Springsteen. They would participate in a roundtable forum and then talk with Bruce individually for a minute or so. You could also have him autograph an item of your choosing. I'm not big on such things, but this was Bruce! I entered the contest with enthusiasm and high hopes; I did not win. I had already picked out what I was going to have him sign: my reel-to-reel tape of his *Nebraska* album, which I doubt if he sees every day.

I knew that entering this contest placed me in the realm of a starstruck adolescent. I didn't care. I wanted to meet Bruce. Not chosen, and somewhat resigned, I said to my daughter, "It's OK. All I have to say to him is how much I love his music and how important it has been to me. He's already heard that from about a million people."

She looked at me and said, "Yeah. But he's never heard it from you."

I recently read that *The River* tour of 1980-81 is the least-known of Bruce's post-*Born to Run* outings. It is overshadowed both by the now famous 1978 *Darkness* tour, which has so much excellent audio documentation from FM broadcasts, and the subsequent high-profile 1984-85 tour for *Born in the U.S.A.* I'm sure all of that is true, but it was early in *The River* tour that Bruce Springsteen first spoke to me in what he often calls a "conversation with his fans." I am so glad we could talk.

Post Script

After I wrote this piece, Bruce Springsteen released an expanded box set of *The River*. It contains all of the music on the original double album, an earlier version of the record that Springsteen almost released, called *The Ties That Bind*, and various studio outtakes from *The River* recording sessions. The package also includes live video footage of a concert from early in this tour. As such, Springsteen's *River* tour from 1980-81 is increasingly well documented. In January 2016, Bruce began a string of U.S. dates where he performed the entire *River* album in concert.

Book Review

A Day in the Life: The Music and Artistry of The Beatles
By Mark Hertsgaard
Delacourt Press, 1995

If someone had no other books about The Beatles, this Mark Hertsgaard work might provide a solid, one-volume overview. It offers a valid summary of other sources, some interesting commentary, and intelligent analysis of the music and the musicians. However, most fans of the Fabs will already know the bulk of the material Hertsgaard provides here.

Quick to berate other books that focus on The Beatles, Hertsgaard's *A Day in the Life* has a few shortcomings of its own. The work is fragmented and choppy, with the group's career not presented sequentially. The end of The Beatles' touring days in 1966 is discussed; then the chronology jumps backwards to 1965, describing recording sessions for *Help!* and *Rubber Soul*.

Hertsgaard contends that his book is unique in the ongoing cascade of Beatles books because he is the first to realize that source materials should be documented. And true—he has researched his topic well, letting the reader know (for 89 pages) where he has taken his quotes. Oddly enough, though, these authoritative quotes are often taken from the very works that he derides.

The author's insights on the sound of the recordings are, at times, thought provoking. Still, for all his supposed access to unheard Beatles tapes, he sheds little new light on this topic. At times, his descriptions of alternate takes and working versions of individual songs are tantalizing, tracing a song's development during the recording process.

More often, his descriptions offer little more than giddiness over the fact that these unheard tapes exist.

For his analysis of the music, the author promises that he will make no leaps of faith and will offer no unsupported conjecture. Contrary to these claims, Hertsgarrd does climb onto various unsupported limbs. One curious omission has to do with the absence of any discussion on the haunting *backmasking* recording effects that spawned the "Paul Is Dead" hoax. Certainly these studio tricks merit discussion here as innovations, or at least oddities.

Were I given access to the tape vaults at Abbey Road studio and had listened to unreleased Beatles music with producer George Martin, I too would likely wear this fact on my sleeve. However, I hope that I would avoid portraying all other writings on the group as mere gossip. This air of exclusivity quickly wears thin, diminishing Hertsgaard's serious and appropriately researched discussion of the music.

A Day in the Life makes a fine coffee table book. A guest could pick it up, casually turn to any page, and become engrossed for several minutes. But as an uninterrupted narrative purporting completeness in its treatment of The Beatles' music, this work is less than successful.

Book Review

Memories of John Lennon
Edited by Yoko Ono
Harper Entertainment, 2006

Now that her Broadway play about John has flopped, Yoko must feel a renewed urgency to remind the world of his importance. She does a bad job of this in her new and completely superfluous book, inviting famous names to wax nostalgic about her late husband. The results are mixed, at best. Beatle insider Klaus Voormann does provide some insight as to what a relaxed John Lennon must have been like while chatting with an old friend in his New York apartment. More often, the celebrity speakers seem self-conscious as they acknowledge that they have nothing to say. Instead, each offers unremarkable accounts of how they heard about John's death. At the low end of this misguided valentine is author Jim Henke, who claims a lifelong total oneness with

Lennon (whom he never met), and Donovan Leitch's massive ego trip concerning how John begged Leitch to teach him fingerpicking guitar style. As John might say, "Absolute rubbish."

Book Review

McCartney
By Christopher Sandford
Carol & Graf Press, 2006

McCartney is the latest Beatle biography. Christopher Sandford stresses from the outset that his goal is to praise and quantify his subject's great talent, but he takes an odd route to reach his destination. The book opens with an account of McCartney's largely forgotten drug bust in Japan and his subsequent week of prison time. The author seems somewhat fixated on this 1980 episode, returning to it at regular intervals. Sandford's praise also has an uncomfortable ring to it. Championing McCartney as the truly creative Beatle, the author sometimes hurts his own case by crediting Paul with everything short of discovering Elvis and curing cancer. It is true that since Lennon's murder, revisionist history has dealt McCartney an unfair blow concerning his importance to The Beatles. But Sandford's defensive tone wears thin, with Paul McCartney miscast in the role of underappreciated victim.

Concert Commentary

Paul McCartney
Tom Sees a Beatle
Miller Park
Milwaukee, Wisconsin
July 16, 2013

I WANTED TO GET to this show early enough to watch the people, and was not disappointed. There seemed to be an unspoken contest going on for who had the coolest T-shirt related to Paul or The Beatles. There were many beautiful examples, and I was not hesitant to indicate this opinion aloud if I thought a design was unusually good. To a person, they were pleased for the recognition. I didn't get punched, anyway.

My only Beatles garb was a thick, hooded sweatshirt; this was just not happening on an outing where it was 90 degrees in the shade. I have told my kids that I would bleed for Paul, but there seemed little point in getting heat stroke for him prior to the show. Instead, a portrait of Elvis Presley adorned my relatively subdued blue and black T-shirt, a recent acquisition from Graceland. I was given glances of suspicion all night long. But Paul would have dug it; a security official had told me he heard Paul singing The King's "Burning Love" during the prolonged sound check.

It was an excited but well behaved gathering of fans. I approached a police sergeant on a Harley and smiled, "Expecting trouble from this crowd tonight?" I thought he might laugh, but he was terse, "I just wish they would get these doors open." He knew of what he spoke, for less than 10 minutes later I saw this same officer assisting a woman who had evidently fainted from the heat. Or maybe it was the thought of soon seeing Paul McCartney; I didn't ask.

As we waited, overheard conversations (and our own) never strayed far from the topic of Paul. We challenged each other: name another current act who could sell out Miller Park today. The Rolling Stones and…we agreed it was a short list. 43,000 tickets sold. And even then, some fans couldn't get in. When The Beatles played Shea Stadium in 1965, they performed to 56,000 people. This was an unheard of audience at the time. Now, nearly 50 years later, a member of that group can regularly fill stadiums. Remarkable. And deserving!

How good was the show? Just getting there was quite inconvenient (even by rock standards), the heat was oppressive, my seat could not have been farther from the stage (binoculars did not help). And, because of cumbersome scaffolding, we had an obstructed view. Tickets, parking, memorabilia, and beer—all were overpriced. But when Paul came out and kicked into "Eight Days a Week," none of this mattered. The sound was excellent. The people around us were seated, attentive, and quiet throughout the concert. Large screens showed the action on the stage, focusing of course on Paul. All was well.

Immediately following "Eight Days a Week" came "Junior's Farm." This largely-forgotten 1974 hit must be a favorite for Paul to rock-out on, as he has included it in most of his recent tours. "All My Loving" followed, a nod to America's initial awareness of The Beatles, and the first song they performed on *Ed Sullivan*. "Listen to What the Man Said" came next; it was played, shouted Paul, "for the Wings fans!"

I won't attempt to critique all 38 songs and the nearly three hours of continuous music. Let me instead reflect on a few high points and surprises in a concert filled with pinnacles.

With the deep song catalog that McCartney possesses, one of the joys came from unexpected selections. Dropping a beautiful "And I Love Her" into the set reminded me of just how many great—not good, but great—songs Paul McCartney has written. At the other end of the spectrum from this gentle ballad came a molten take on "Helter Skelter," which set the ballpark a-rockin' late in the evening.

One poignant moment came with Paul at the piano. After performing "The Long and Winding Road" he quietly said, "This one's for Linda," and began an outstanding version of "Maybe I'm Amazed." I found this choice doubly interesting. Just as it professes a lasting love for his departed wife, "Maybe I'm Amazed" was the first solo record to announce that, for Paul McCartney, there would be life after The Beatles.

There were no cover versions of songs written by others. The closest Paul came to including non-originals was when he performed George's "Something" and John's "Being for the Benefit of Mr. Kite." The first was an acknowledged tribute, with Paul playing Harrison's own ukulele. The latter was introduced only as a song that Paul had never performed before in Milwaukee. Paul instead saved the tribute to his fallen band mate for a heartfelt introduction to "Here Today," an acoustic ballad lamenting missed opportunities for communication. A rapt audience felt privy to intimate secrets as Paul revealed how he wished he had taken time to talk with John about their friendship. Both before and after the song McCartney stressed that people should tell others how they feel while they have the chance.

Purposefully breaking this somber mood of regret, Paul jumped into the barrelhouse feel of "Your Mother Should Know," followed by "Lady Madonna," "All Together Now," and "Lovely Rita." Let me stress here that these were all full-length versions of each song. This was no stripped down, get-it-over-with approach. There were no medleys.

Prior to "All Together Now," Paul again indicated that this was a song new to his Milwaukee concerts. It was impressive to me that he was well aware of his surroundings. At one point he asked, "How many here from Chicago?" Big cheers. "How many here from Milwaukee?" Big cheers. "How many people here tonight from neither place?" Overwhelming majority cheers. Paul laughed.

Just as McCartney knows his location, he knows his fans. When explaining that he would be performing "Paperback Writer" on the very guitar he used when making the record, the crowd was ecstatic. Speaking of guitars, McCartney played a lot of acoustic during the set, including a 12-string for "I've Just Seen a Face." He played various electric 6-string guitars, and I was happy to see his famous Hofner 500/1 "violin bass" make an appearance at numerous points.

As Paul launched into a powerhouse of hits, it was clear that we were approaching the conclusion of this generous set. And what a cluster: "Band on the Run," "Back in the U.S.S.R.," "Let It Be," "Live and Let Die," and "Hey Jude." The band left the stage, but everybody knew that an encore would be coming. Two, in fact. And while these encores featured more stellar songs, including "Day Tripper" and "Get Back," it was another song that spoke to me most distinctly.

As Paul came out for the second encore, he entered the spotlight alone with an acoustic guitar. He then played an unaccompanied version of "Yesterday." To hear the man who wrote this song play it live… it seemed like a gift. I am well aware that this composition is mocked by some and reviled by others. It matters not; "Yesterday" is probably Paul McCartney's most perfect song.

Paul began to leave the stage, acoustic guitar in hand. His band entered, jokingly attempting to convince him to strap on the electric and rock out one more time. They smoked through the end of Side 2 of *Abbey Road*: "Golden Slumbers," "Carry That Weight," and "The End." Paul thanked us again for coming and said that he would see us the next time he was in town. Good attitude!

I was euphoric; we had just seen Beatle Paul! This had not been a recital by regal Sir James Paul McCartney; nor was it a pop show from the "Cute One." This was a hard rockin' concert by one of the most important (and melodic) bassists in recorded music. The evening's set list was composed of McCartney's own brilliantly diverse songs, as if the performer were auditioning for God Himself. I believe Paul would have passed that audition.

We waited for the next bus and kept talking about the show. Just as arrival to the concert was a bit rocky, departure was worse. But nobody cared. I think if somebody had told me I needed to walk back to my house, I would have been OK with it.

One Question With... Paul McCartney!

After listening to a Milwaukee radio announcer completely waste his opportunity to speak with Paul, I decided to return to one of my favorite exercises: If I had the opportunity to ask one question of a specific individual, what would it be? Here is the final entry.

Tom Wilmeth:—Paul, the B-side of your 1973 single "My Love" contains a recording of a song you wrote called "The Mess." For many years, the song appeared nowhere but on this single. "The Mess" is a live recording, and it sounds as if you are playing to a modest-sized audience. I assume this song comes from a solo concert during your series of unannounced college dates in England in the very early 1970s, immediately after The Beatles broke up. Do you plan to release any more live recordings from these early post-Beatles concerts?

Paul McCartney:—You know, it's a pleasure to meet someone who is obsessive about my solo catalog as well as The Beatles' career.

[This one isn't trying to be funny.
It's just a dream that Paul would actually enjoy talking with me.]

Nota Bene: As with all other entries in this series, the above conversation is complete fiction.

Bonus Track

Ellie Wilmeth to Tom, commenting on this book:—
"You need to identify some of these people more clearly."
Tom:—"Everybody knows who I mean when I say 'John and Paul'."
Ellie:—"Maybe, but you talk about them like they are our neighbors!"

Remembrance

George Harrison—Ten Years Gone
March 27, 2011

Poor George. Not only did he live his professional life in the deep shadows of John and Paul, his own albums were usually dismissed as the backwater of the Beatles' solo catalog. George had neither the artistic excuses of tortured genius John Lennon nor the straight-to-the-chart pop sensibilities of Paul McCartney. Even Ringo had greater consistency on Top 40 radio after the split than George.

I was initially guilty of overlooking George once I became a Beatle devotee on that Sunday night in February 1964. This shortcoming was later legitimized, I thought, when I read a quote by Beatles' record producer, George Martin, who admitted to not fostering Harrison's talent as much as he might have. Martin said something like, "When you have John Lennon and Paul McCartney in the studio, you don't really need to go looking for additional talent." But that's a paraphrase. And if Martin did not foster George's songwriting abilities, Harrison himself must admit to not always helping his own cause once his solo career got under way.

Many critics, however, were inconsolable in their grief over George's death. There was, of course, an international outcry of sorrow over the death of a Beatle. But this was really the society mourning its own youth, as many observers pointed out at the time. Still, I recall that much of the press spoke of George as if he were an active musician, and as if his career had been cut short.

I am not proud of being a bit harsh in reacting to these ill-informed musicologists at the time of George's passing. Perhaps because of this collective assessment by the numerous Beatle experts who emerged at the time, I countered with a backlash that included a mean-spirited challenge. I said to my college classes, "Many are lamenting the loss of George Harrison today, but I defy these people to sit through any two of his solo albums in a single stretch." Cruel? Yes. Accurate? You bet.

Sadly, even Harrison's best solo release suffers from the dreaded "double album syndrome." George took it to a new level, though, by making *All Things Must Pass* into a three-record set. It's an obvious statement, often made: *All Things Must Pass* would have been a great single LP. (For you youngsters, that's about 40 minutes of music.) If judiciously trimmed, the record would easily rank among the strongest in the entire solo Beatles canon. As it stands, with two versions of "Isn't It a Pity" and an entire LP of guitar jams, it is a deeply flawed gem. This extraneous material would have made great fodder for bootlegs. Or, it would have made for some excellent bonus tracks in the CD age.

Paul McCartney might defend his bandmate's record in the same way he has defended The Beatles' *White Album*. During one of the *Anthology* interviews, McCartney says, "People talk about how there is too much stuff on it, or it should have been a single album, or this or that. I don't like to play those games. It came out; it sold well. It's The Beatles' *White Album*. Shut up!" OK Paul. It's George's *All Things Must Pass* album; and I will shut up.

The music world mourned George's death and celebrated his life. As did I! Two interesting things came out of these public reminiscences that I found telling. In 1988, Harrison appeared as a guest on the call-in show *Rockline*, hosted by Bob Coburn. The week following George's November 2001 death, this radio interview was rebroadcast. One of the callers asked George if he had any unreleased music that the public had not yet heard. Harrison laughed and said that his personal vault of unreleased tapes would make Jim Reeves look like a novice. I don't think the listener or the program's host understood this reference. But I thought this comparison to Reeves showed that George remained a country music enthusiast.

Jim Reeves had one of the smoothest voices ever recorded. His records "He'll Have to Go" and "Four Walls" were hits on both the country and the pop charts. Reeves died in a plane crash in the fall of

1964. But because of the huge amount of material that he had record-ed, which remained unreleased at the time of his death, Reeves would have 27 posthumous hits on *Billboard Magazine*'s Country Music Top 40 chart. Five of these releases went to #1. *After* the singer's death. Un-precedented! But the fact that Harrison was aware of Reeves' penchant for stockpiling his own unreleased recordings says worlds to me about this Beatle's connection to music. He was a fan.

The other Harrison story is also radio related. The week after George died, Casey Kasem did a brief feature on the departed Beatle during the "Long Distance Dedication" segment of his *American Top 40* radio program. This was a regular feature of each weekly broadcast where Casey would read a letter that a fan had sent him. The letter would include some sort of personal story and a request that Casey dedicate a song to a specific person. The dedications usually involved the writer trying to reconnect with a lost love, or a parent reaching out to a child. The stories ranged from upbeat to maudlin.

The week after Harrison's death, Kasem told his listeners that in 1964, while he was working as a disc jockey in Los Angeles, he had received a letter from a young girl named Elaina. In it, she described how she had briefly met and even hugged George after a concert at San Francisco's Cow Palace. Kasey read the letter on his show. The passion that Elaina's letter expressed toward her favorite Beatle and the re-sourcefulness she used to contact him gave Kasem the idea to include a segment on his radio program. Casey initially called this segment "The Sweetheart Tree." During these segments he would read a love letter sent from a listener, followed by an appropriate song. And with that, the "Long Distance Dedication" feature was born, which Casey credits to Elaina's letter about meeting George Harrison.

I do not play my solo George Harrison albums very often. I think that if I were striving to convince a stranger of Harrison's talent, I would select a few of his guitar solos. Then I would play his song "Don't Bother Me," from *Meet the Beatles*. I would play *Abbey Road*—but not for George's compositions, rather for his guitar work. I have always felt that *Abbey Road* is Harrison's finest moment as a musician. Start to finish, his playing on that album is sublime. But having said that, I don't recall any Beatle recording where he falters or gets in the way of a song.

Poor George. He was the guitarist in the world's biggest band. As he himself remarked in the *Beatles Anthology* video, "I'd like some of these bands like U2 to take a look at film from the Beatlemania days. Then they'd know what it's like to be in a *popular* band." Wow. But true; footage of their fame is nearly unbelievable. And yet, for all the success and accolades, I don't get the sense that George really enjoyed the Beatles ride all that much, at least after the initial rush. In that same video Harrison also said, "The fans gave their money and their cheers. But we gave our central nervous systems." It's hard to envy a lifestyle that is described in those terms by one who has lived it. Here's hoping that George has now regained the parts of himself that he felt were stolen by fame and by (what he himself referred to as) this material world.

Commentary
What I Learned from Elvis Presley

I never met Elvis Presley. I never saw him perform. In fact, the one time I had an opportunity to attend a concert by the man, I passed. But that's a tale of regret best saved for another time. I have been thinking about Elvis fairly often lately. Not so much because of his music, although that is, of course, the key to why he permanently resides in my head. These days The King comes to mind because of the way he carried himself during his uniquely troubled life.

Elvis' recordings changed everything in popular music. "Before Elvis there was nothing," John Lennon famously proclaimed. Various circumstances soon interfered with Elvis' ability to demonstrate his talent to its fullest degree: the isolation dictated by his unprecedented popularity, the Army, Hollywood, and finally—and perhaps most devastating—a lack of quality songs to record. As the 1960s began, the Elvis Presley story had begun its sad downward spiral. His best recordings had already been released.

It is not surprising, then, that while growing up in the 1960s, my indifference toward Elvis was indicative of my generation's attitude. The Elvis Presley records I heard on the radio during my late grade school and junior high days were restricted to the two oldies played per hour on KIOA in Des Moines, or on WHB in Kansas City and Chicago's WLS. I knew they were great songs and I liked them, but I did not understand the historical importance of these records nor did I search out more by this artist. That would all come later.

My stronger connection to Elvis' music came not through the occasional hit I would hear on the radio, but from the back bedroom of my aunt and uncle's house in Marshalltown, Iowa. It was there that I unearthed a stack of 45 rpm singles and a small record player. When my family visited these relatives, I would repeatedly play these records. Most of the singles were unimpressive, but the few Elvis records were transcendent. I wore out the double-sided hit "Hound Dog"/"Don't Be Cruel" and "All Shook Up." There were a couple of Elvis purchases in the stack that seem surprising to me now—my uncle had both "Don't" and "One Night." I marveled at the sound of these records. I studied them.

Then, in February 1964, The Beatles sang a few songs on *The Ed Sullivan Show*, and my life was never the same. It has been said that the 1960s really began in earnest only when The Beatles arrived. Without question, they changed America's musical landscape in a single Sunday night. One change that came for me after I watched The Beatles was the simultaneous widening and narrowing of my musical interests. My focus narrowed from the music of my father's big band and movie soundtrack records to a fixation on The Beatles. But, unbeknownst to me at this time, my sphere was also widening to include the many influences that The Beatles were providing through their cover songs. These were artists that American radio had stopped playing—Chuck Berry, Little Richard, The Miracles, and Carl Perkins. Beatles on the record player and Top 40 on a radio was my musical diet.

I had not forgotten about Elvis, but neither did I follow his career. I'm sure that all of his Hollywood movies of the 1960s played Des Moines when they were released—they must have—but I don't even recall seeing newspaper ads for them. They were never on my cultural radar, nor on anyone else's I knew. I have memories of watching Elvis' *Comeback Special* on NBC, but I only had a passing interest in it at the time. When this Elvis television special aired in December 1968, The Beatles' *White Album* had been released the previous month. Musically, little else mattered.

The Wilson sisters from Heart have talked about how Elvis did not have a powerful influence on them, describing him as a huge but unapproachable figure from the past. Bruce Springsteen acknowledged

Presley as "a small fire," but one whose influence had diminished by the early 1960s. I think this feeling was widespread. Elvis' hits were massive but, even by 1963, they seemed to have come from a very long time ago. In 1966, records produced only one decade earlier may as well have been recorded in 1929. The ensuing ten years had already turned the decade of the 1950s into a dim, distant era. Blame The Beatles. Blame television. But it was true.

More years passed. I was ahead of the curve among my college group in a personal reawakening to Elvis. In 1973, I bought *Elvis' Golden Records*, "the greatest hits album by which all other greatest hits records must be measured," to quote an accurate assessment in *The All Music Guide*. My college girlfriend laughed at me when I bought it, but I didn't care. It's a surprisingly generous collection of 14 songs, and each one is great. Many of these hits reminded me of the back room in Marshalltown, and soon I also loved the ones previously unfamiliar to me. I wondered: If these had all been big hits (and they had), why did radio only play three or four of them as oldies during my junior high years? I began to ponder the narrow-minded choices of radio programmers.

To demonstrate the lack of interest among young people of my generation: When Elvis died on that August day in 1977, I was in my last year of college. Walter Cronkite's news bulletin interrupted an afternoon rerun of *All in the Family*. I was stunned, but I could not think of even one person to call who would not mock his passing. When the news became widespread, tasteless jokes were everywhere. The worst were told by my musician friends. Maybe that's understandable, since Elvis had transformed himself into a punch line long before his death. But it still unsettled me to hear mean-spirited disrespect gleefully heaped onto someone so important to popular music.

The 1970s ended; 1980 began. John Lennon was murdered in December. More cruel remarks about death, but these seemed to stick in the throats of even the most cynical speakers. Overnight, John became everybody's lifelong favorite Beatle. Paul was suddenly unhip for being extremely popular as a solo performer. Prior to Lennon's murder, some of McCartney's younger fans had been unaware of Lennon's existence; many marveled that Paul had been in a band before Wings. John's death suddenly validated Lennon's uneven solo career in a way that never happened for Elvis. The recordings that Presley made from the early 1960s until his death were routinely written off as dreck. It is only recently that Elvis' post-army canon has been examined with a serious eye, a crusade led by Roy Carr, Mick Farren, Ernst Jorgensen, and Peter Guralnick.

The legacy of Presley's recordings was sometimes hindered by The King himself. During a rare 1971 press conference, Elvis was asked about his first records, made for Memphis' Sun Records label. Elvis chuckled and said that those singles now "sound kinda funny" to him. In spite of Presley's own casual dismissal of his early work, these were the records prized by his most devoted fans—that "kinda funny" sound found only in the Sun Records studio of Memphis. If Presley could be so cavalier about some of his greatest recordings, maybe the artist had truly lost his sense of musical direction.

When John Lennon met Elvis, Lennon suggested that Presley make some records like those from his days at the Sun label. This was probably not the best topic for a first meeting. But had Elvis countered, asking John why he didn't still record songs like "She Loves You," Lennon would probably have been livid. This was, after all, late summer 1965. The Beatles were already into their acoustic, Dylan-influenced *Rubber Soul* era. Speaking of Bob Dylan, during the rehearsals for the Bangladesh charity concert of 1971, George Harrison asked Dylan if he planned to sing "Blowin' in the Wind" during the concert. Dylan supposedly replied to Harrison, "Are you going to sing 'I Want to Hold Your Hand'?" Maybe Colonel Parker was right when he said: "You don't sell your past."

OK. So what have I learned from Elvis Presley? How he treated everyone with respect—Elvis Presley was nice to the people he met. I have no doubt that exceptions can be found. But when one reads the many tales of people's personal encounters with the man, what comes through time and again is how Presley actually talked to each individual fan as if that fan were the most important person in the room, if not on the entire planet. If you could get to him, Elvis didn't try to rush away. He was engaged; he would listen.

Chet Atkins tells how he was almost "sir-ed" to death by Elvis in the early days of their studio work together, but Atkins also stresses that Elvis always seemed to be sincere during these exchanges. One biography describes an episode where Presley chastised his entourage for not being nice enough to the media and to his fans. Elvis reprimanded them: "If I can do it, you can do it." He probably only had to say this once. I find these episodes as impressive as they are inspirational. In fact, when somebody is talking to me about a topic I have no interest in—I try to be nice. I am thinking about how Elvis would handle it. Probably with patience.

What else have I learned? I fear that as early as 1960, The King of Rock and Roll had stopped listening to music. Peter Guralnick's *Last Train to Memphis* documents how Elvis' session musicians were forbidden to discuss music with Presley. Colonel Parker insisted on complete control over what Elvis recorded—any input from outsiders was taboo. Guralnick recounts how a session musician was once threatened for suggesting an appropriate song to Elvis.

Dolly Parton talks about how excited she was to learn that Elvis was planning to record her song, "I Will Always Love You." However, shortly before the session she received a phone call from Colonel Parker. He told the songwriter that Elvis required publishing rights to all of the material he recorded. Parton said "no" to the Colonel. She had regrets that Elvis would not sing her song, but she had better economic sense than to trade away the rights to one of her compositions. I am guessing that this is not an isolated incident, just a high profile one.

I do not need to keep my ears tuned for potential songs to record, but I do strive to expose myself to new music. I wonder again if Elvis simply stopped listening. I don't recall any biographies discussing Elvis tuning-in to late night radio. Multiple television screens were reportedly his constant companion at Graceland, not radio. I also don't remember reading of any instance when Elvis sought out record shops. The King would lead treks to jewelry stores in the middle of the night, when he was assured of privacy, and it seems that the Memphis movie theater was permanently on call for his nocturnal screenings. But nothing is said about covert trips to Memphis record stores. Had The King purchased (and listened to) new records in the way he bought new Cadillacs; had he encountered songs on the radio he liked enough to insist on recording; if trusted friends had recommended appropriate material—his later recording career could have been very different. I think Elvis became distracted and cut himself off from his own life blood: Music.

I do not make records; I listen to records. But parallels emerge. The few regretful music memories I have are clustered around various opportunities I was given, but did not embrace. Either I thought that I had no interest a certain style of music or (worse), I thought I was above it. This attitude has caused me to miss some fine performers. Still, as I look over the table of contents of this book, it's hard for me to get despondent about shows I didn't attend. I have been very fortunate to have seen many impressive concerts and to have listened to a lot of great music. Even so, I wish the scales had fallen from my ears a bit earlier. I now strive to keep my mind musically alert and my ears open to new sounds. It's a full-time job.

What did I learn from Elvis Presley? Try to be nice to everybody and stay open to all forms of music. I can handle that.

APPENDIX A

Recommended Recordings

These entries primarily consist of releases that I discuss in this book. Also included are personal favorites. This list is not meant to be a definitive guide. For most artists, I have limited my entries to three or fewer. Not every artist mentioned in the book is listed below. Three of the subjects (Frank Zappa, Jaco Pastorius, and Dave Brubeck) have their Recommended Recordings list incorporated into the book's essay.

Part One—Popular (and unpopular) music: Pop and Rock

The Allman Brothers Band
Live at Fillmore East
Idlewild South
The Association
Hits Collection
Live
Joan Baez
In Concert, part 2
One Day at a Time
Noel
The Beach Boys
Greatest Hits
Pet Sounds
In Concert (1972)

Captain Beefheart
>   Trout Mask Replica
>   Shiny Beast (Bat Chain Puller)

Broadcast (with Trish Keenan)
>   Haha Sound

Chuck Berry
>   Hits Collection

Bobby "Blue" Bland
>   Hits Collection

James Brown
>   Gold
>   Live at the Apollo

Jackson Browne
>   Saturate Before Using
>   Running on Empty

Buffalo Springfield
>   Buffalo Springfield (1st album)
>   Again

Chicago
>   Chicago Transit Authority
>   Chicago (II)

Eric Clapton
>   Layla and Other Assorted Love Songs
>   Derek & The Dominoes: In Concert
>   24 Nights
>   One More Car, One More Rider

The Clash
>   London Calling
>   Live at Shea Stadium

Todd Clouser's A Love Electric
>   Man with No Country

Bruce Cockburn
>   Life Short, Call Now
>   Small Source of Comfort

Joe Cocker
> Joe Cocker (1st LP)
> Mad Dogs & Englishmen

Elvis Costello
> My Aim is True
> Imperial Bedroom

Cream
> Disraeli Gears
> Live Cream, vol. 2

Crosby, Stills, Nash & Young
> Crosby, Stills & Nash (1st album)
> Déjà vu
> 4 Way Street

Neil Diamond
> The Bang Collection
> Hits Collection

The Doobie Brothers
> Hits Collection

Eagles
> Hits Collection

Girls
> Broken Dreams Club

Grand Funk Railroad
> Closer to Home
> The '71 Tour

The Guess Who
> Greatest Hits
> Canned Wheat

Arlo Guthrie
> Alice's Restaurant
> Any of the concert LPs with Pete Seeger

Richie Havens
> In Concert
> The End of the Beginning

Heart

The Essential

James Hunter

People Gonna Talk

Elton John

Madman Across the Water

11-17-70

Greatest Hits, vols. 1, 2, and 3

Janis Joplin

In Concert

Cheap Thrills

Pearl

Carole King

Tapestry

Really Rosie

The Kinks

Lola vs. Powerman and the Money-Go-Round

The Kink Kronicles

Hits collection

Motorhead

No Sleep 'til Hammersmith

All the Aces

Poco

Deliverin'

Gold

Prince

Purple Rain

Sign of the Times

The Hits/The B-Sides

Lou Reed

Berlin

New York

R.E.M.

Murmur (expanded)

Dead Letter Office

The Rolling Stones
    Beggars Banquet
    Let It Bleed
    Sticky Fingers
    Some Girls
    Hot Rocks
Santana
    Abraxas
    Lotus
Paul Simon
    There Goes Rhymin' Simon
    Graceland
Simon and Garfunkel
    Bookends
    Greatest Hits
Gil Scott-Heron
    The Revolution Will Not Be Televised
The Sons of Champlin
    The Sons of Champlin (1st LP)
Squeeze
    Singles 45's & Under
    East Side Story
James Taylor
    James Taylor (1st LP)
    JT
    Greatest Hits, vols. 1 and 2
Vanilla Fudge
    Vanilla Fudge (1st LP)
Tom Waits
    Closing Time
    Small Change
    Mule Variations

The Who
> Meaty Beaty Big and Bouncy
> Tommy
> Who's Next
> Live at Leeds

Stevie Wonder
> Innervisions
> Fulfillingness' First Finale
> Songs in the Key of Life
> Looking Back

Yes
> The Yes Album
> Tales from Topographic Oceans
> Progeny: Highlights from Seventy-Two

Neil Young
> Everybody Knows this is Nowhere
> After the Gold Rush
> Sleeps with Angels

Part Two—Jazz

Louis Armstrong
> The Chicago Concert (1956)
> Portrait of the Artist as a Young Man (box set)

Kenny Burrell
> Blue
> Live at the Village Vanguard
> Have Yourself a Soulful Little Christmas

Gary Burton
> The New Quartet
> Duster
> Live at Carnegie Hall

Ron Carter
> Telephone (with Jim Hall)
> Etudes

John Coltrane
> Blue Train
> Giant Steps
> A Love Supreme

Chick Corea
> An Evening with Chick Corea & Herbie Hancock: In Concert
> In Concert: Zurich (with Gary Burton)
> The Enchantment (with Béla Fleck)

Miles Davis
> Kind of Blue
> The Complete Concert: 1964
> Bitches Brew
> Jack Johnson

Duke Ellington
> The OKey Ellington
> At Newport (1956)
> Unknown Session
> Live at The Whitney

Don Ellis
> At Fillmore
> Tears of Joy

Herb Ellis
> Seven Come Eleven (with Joe Pass)
> Texas Swings

Bill Evans
> Sunday at The Village Vanguard
> We Will Meet Again
> Paris Concert, editions one and two

Ella Fitzgerald
> Live in Berlin
> Ella Fitzgerald (Ken Burns *Jazz* series)

Stan Getz
> Big Band Bossa Nova
> Getz/Gilberto (with Joao Gilberto)

Dexter Gordon
>Homecoming
>Blue Note and Prestige label compilations

Alex de Grassi
>A Windham Hill Retrospective

Charlie Haden
>Liberation Music Orchestra
>Folk Songs
>Beyond the Missouri Sky (with Pat Metheny)

Jim Hall
>Live
>Alone Together (with Ron Carter)

Herbie Hancock
>Best of (Blue Note)
>Headhunters

Eddie Harris
>Swiss Movement (with Les McCann)
>Live at Newport
>E.H. in the U.K.

Keith Jarrett
>Shades
>Solo Concerts (Bremen and Lausanne)

Hank Jones
>Come Sunday (with Charlie Haden)

Grace Kelly
>Man with the Hat (with Phil Woods)

Stan Kenton
>National Anthems of the World
>Hits collection

Cleo Laine
>At Carnegie Hall
>Shakespeare and All That Jazz
>Porgy & Bess (with Ray Charles)

Charles Lloyd
>Dream Weaver
>Love-In

The Manhattan Transfer
    Anthology: Down in Birdland
Wynton Marsalis
    Live at Blues Alley
    Live at The Village Vanguard
    Live at The House of Tribes
Pat Metheny
    Bright Size Life
    Travels
Gerry Niewood
    Gerry Niewood and Timepiece
Oscar Peterson
    Trio Live in Chicago
    Trio at The Stratford Shakespeare Festival
Jean-Luc Ponty
    King Kong
    A Taste for Passion
Return to Forever
    Light as a Feather
    Hymn of the 7th Galaxy
Howard Roberts
    Howard Roberts is a Dirty Guitar Player
    Equinox Express Elevator
Sonny Rollins
    Blue Note, Milestone, and RCA label anthologies
Woody Shaw
    Stepping Stones
Stanley Turrentine
    Blue Note label anthology
Eberhard Weber
    The Colours of Chloe
    Yellow Fields
Weather Report
    Weather Report (1st LP)
    Sweetnighter
    Live and Unreleased

Part Three—Country

Eddy Arnold
   The Essential Eddy Arnold
Junior Brown
   Twelve Shades of Brown
Glen Campbell
   Greatest Hits
Patsy Cline
   Greatest Hits
Cowboy Junkies
   The Trinity Session
Joe Ely
   Greatest Hits
   Live at Liberty Lunch
The Everly Brothers
   Hits Collection (Cadence)
   Hits Collection (Warner Brothers)
   Songs Our Daddy Taught Us
Béla Fleck
   The Bluegrass Sessions, vol. 2
   Live Art (with The Flecktones)
   Pretty much any recording he is on.
Lefty Frizzell
   Hits Collection
Merle Haggard
   Hits Collection
   Same Train—A Different Time
George Jones
   Hits Collection (Smash)
   Hits Collection (Columbia)
   Cup of Loneliness (Mercury)

The Louvin Brothers
> Satan is Real
> Tragic Songs of Life
> Radio Favorites

Bill Monroe
> The Essential Bill Monroe & The Bluegrass Boys

Willie Nelson
> The Early Years (Liberty)
> Greatest Hits (Columbia)
> Red Headed Stranger

Webb Pierce
> Hits Collection

Ernest Tubb
> Country Music Hall of Fame Series
> The Complete Live 1965 Show

Hank Williams
> 40 Greatest Hits
> Health and Happiness Shows

Dwight Yoakam
> Guitars, Cadillacs, etc., etc.
> This Time
> Three Pears

Part Four—Beatles, Bob, Bruce, and Barry!

The Beatles
> The Beatles: 1962-1966
> The Beatles: 1967-1970
> Live at The Hollywood Bowl

John Lennon
> Plastic Ono Band

Paul McCartney
> Wings Over America

George Harrison
   All Things Must Pass
Ringo Starr
   Ringo
Bob Dylan
   The Freewheelin' Bob Dylan
   Bringing It All Back Home
   Highway 61 Revisited
   Blonde on Blonde
   John Wesley Harding
   Bob Dylan's Greatest Hits, vols. 1, 2, and 3
Bruce Springsteen
   The Wild, The Innocent and The E Street Shuffle
   Born to Run
   Tunnel of Love
   High Hopes
   Live: 1975-1985
Barry Manilow
   Barry Manilow II (includes "Sandra")
Elvis Presley
   Sunrise
   30 #1 Hits
   2nd to None
   Amazing Grace

APPENDIX B

Transcripts of Bob Dylan's (a) full, (b) edited, and (c) collated spoken introductions to "Last Thoughts on Woody Guthrie," given April 12, 1963, at New York City's Town Hall. Materials transcribed by Tom Wilmeth.

FULL TRANSCRIPT (from the *Are You Now or Have You Ever Been* LP bootleg):

"I have a po--. I have -- it's not a poem here, but uh, … it's something, uh, … This is the first concert I ever played alone, really, in New York, and uh, … uh, uh. There's a fella out in Brooklyn State Hospital; his name is Woody Guthrie and uh, … [applause] … uh, … but, uh, … Woody is really sort of more than a folk singer. Uh, he's … he's really something else more than a folk singer, and uh, … There's this book coming out that's doing a … dedicating it to him, and they asked me to write, uh, something about Woody … uh. Sort of like, 'What does Woody Guthrie mean to you?' – in 25 words. And uh, … and I couldn't do it. I wrote out five pages, and uh, … I have it here. It's a … have it here by accident, actually. [Dylan—very slight laugh] But, but I, I, I'd like to say this out loud. So, uh, … th', my feelings towards Woody Guthrie. Uh, … cannot really be, uh, … told in, uh, … how many records of his I buy, or … or this kind of thing. It's … uh, … a lot more than that, actually. … So, uh, … if you can sort of roll along with this thing here; this is called 'Last Thoughts on Woody Guthrie' … um. 'When your head gets twisted and your mind grows numb …'" -- [beginning of poem]

EDITED TRANSCRIPT (officially released in 1991 by Columbia Records on

The Bootleg Series, Vol. 1)

"There's this book coming out and ... they asked me to write, uh, something about Woody. ... uh. Sort of like, 'What does Woody Guthrie mean to you?' – in 25 words. And uh, ... and I couldn't do it. I wrote out five pages, and uh, ... I have it here. It's a ... have it here by accident, actually. [Dylan -- very slight laugh] But, but I, I, I'd like to say this out loud.

So, uh, ... if you can sort of roll along with this thing here; this is called 'Last Thoughts on Woody Guthrie' ... um. 'When your head gets twisted and your mind grows numb ...'"

COLLATED TRANSCRIPT (***bold/underlined/CAPITALIZED*** material used by Columbia in the official release):

"I have a po--. I have -- it's not a poem here, but uh, ... it's something, uh, ... This is the first concert I ever played alone, really, in New York, and uh, ... uh, uh. There's a fella out in Brooklyn State Hospital; his name is Woody Guthrie and uh, ... [applause] ... uh, ... but, uh, ... Woody is really sort of more than a folk singer. Uh, he's ... he's really something else more than a folk singer, and uh, ... ***THERE'S THIS BOOK COMING OUT*** that's doing a ... dedicating it to him, ***AND THEY ASKED ME TO WRITE, UH, SOMETHING ABOUT WOODY ... UH. SORT OF LIKE, 'WHAT DOES WOODY GUTHRIE MEAN TO YOU?' IN 25 WORDS. AND UH, ... AND I COULDN'T DO IT. I WROTE OUT FIVE PAGES, AND UH, ... I HAVE IT HERE. IT'S A ... HAVE IT HERE BY ACCIDENT, ACTUALLY. [DYLAN -- VERY SLIGHT LAUGH] BUT, BUT I, I, I'D LIKE TO SAY THIS OUT LOUD.*** So, uh, ... th', my feelings towards Woody Guthrie. Uh, ... cannot really be, uh ... told in, uh, ... how many records of his I buy, or ... or this kind of thing. It's ... uh, ... a lot more than that, actually. ... ***SO, UH, ... IF YOU CAN SORT OF ROLL ALONG WITH THIS THING HERE; THIS IS CALLED 'LAST THOUGHTS ON WOODY GUTHRIE' ... UM.*** 'When your head gets twisted and your mind grows numb ...'"

APPENDIX C

Works Cited and Sources Consulted

Introduction: "The Green Door"
Joel Whitburn. *The Billboard Book of Top 40 Hits*, 7th ed. New York: Billboard Books, 2000.

Part One—Popular (and unpopular) Music: Pop / Rock / Blues

Title page : David Byrne
David Byrne. *Stop Making Sense* LP, inner sleeve (Sire Records, 1984)

Concert Commentary: Grand Funk Railroad
Grand Funk Railroad, Live: The '71 Tour. Booklet essay by David K. Tedds. Capitol Records, 2002.
Jerry Silver (pseudonym). Interview with the author. Des Moines, Iowa. Spring 1971.

Concert Commentary and Bonus Track : The Association
Fred Bronson. *The Billboard Book of Number One Hits*. New York: Billboard Pub., 1985.
Steve Miller. *The Monterey International Pop Festival*. Accompanying booklet. Rhino, 1992.
Stephen K. Peeples and Sandy Gibson. *The Monterey International Pop Festival*. Accompanying booklet. Rhino Records, 1992.

Concert Commentary: Chuck Berry
Joel Whitburn. *The Billboard Book of Top 40 Hits*. 7th ed. New York: Billboard Books, 2000.

Bonus Track : The Guitars of Layla
Randy Poe. *Skydog: The Duane Allman Story*. San Francisco:
Backbeat Books, 2006.

Concert Commentary and Bonus Track: Frank Zappa
Frank Zappa interview with Jamie Gangel. *Today Show*. NBC
television, 1993

Remembrance: Captain Beefheart
Tom Waits. Interview with the author. Minneapolis, Minnesota.
October 29, 1977.
Captain Beefheart. *Safe as Milk*. reissue. Accompanying booklet.
Buddha Records, 1999.

Artist Commentary and Bonus Tracks : Tom Waits
Tom Waits. Interview with the author. Iowa City, Iowa.
November 22, 1976.
---. Interview with the author. Minneapolis, Minnesota. October
29, 1977.

Second Hand News: The Guess Who
Denise Bachman. E-mail correspondence with the author.
September and December 2010.

Bonus Track : Harry Nilsson
Harry Nilsson. *Aerial Pandemonium Ballet*. LP, back cover. RCA
Records, 1971.

Remembrance: Joe Cocker
Joe Cocker. *The Long Voyage Home*. Booklet essay by Paul Grein.
A&M Records, 1995.

Hangin' with the Stars #2: Joan Baez
Garrison Keillor. Conversation with the author. St. Paul,
Minnesota. February 22, 1982.

Concert Postscript: James Taylor
Piet Levy. *Milwaukee Journal Sentinel*. November 6, 2014.

CD Review: Neil Young
Jimmy McDonough. *Shakey: Neil Young's Biography*. New York:
Anchor Books, 2002.

One Question with: Neil Young!
It is worth stressing here that this exchange is complete fiction.
Andy Greene. *Rolling Stone*. November 11, 2008.

Second Hand News: Buffalo Springfield
Gerald E. Bloomquist, KRNT Theater booker, conversation with
the author. Des Moines, 1971.

Bonus Track : Pete Townshend
A Whole Scene Going . BBC television. January 1966.

Concert Commentary: The Rolling Stones
Get Your Ya-Yas Out. Spoken introduction. London Records,
1970.
An Interview With Mick Jagger By Tom Donahue: April 1971.
Rolling Stones Records, promotional LP.

One Question with : Keith Richards!
It is worth stressing here that this exchange is complete fiction.
Sara Gay Forden. "Keith Richards: The New Face of Louis
Vuitton Luggage." *New York Times*. March 5, 2008.

Concert Commentary: The Beach Boys
Keith Badman. *The Beach Boys—The Definitive Diary of
America's Greatest Band: On Stage and In the Studio*.
Backbeat Books, 2004.
Rock & Roll. Episode 2: "In the Groove." PBS television, 1995.

Concert Commentary: The Kinks with Cheap Trick
Rob Jovanovic. *God Save The Kinks: A Biography*. London:
Aurum Press, 2014.

One Question with : Neil Diamond!
It is worth stressing here that this exchange is complete fiction.
Joel Whitburn. *The Billboard Book of Top 40 Hits*. 7th ed. New
York: Billboard Books, 2000.

Remembrance: Lou Reed
Aidan Levy. *Dirty Blvd.: The Life and Music of Lou Reed*.
Chicago: Chicago Review Press, 2015.

Concert Commentary: Motorhead with Clutch and Valient Thorr
Tim Grierson. *Wilco: Sunken Treasure*. London: Omnibus Press,
2013.

Bonus Track : A Heavily Sampled Artist
R. J. Smith. *The One: The Life and Music of James Brown*. Garden City, NY: Avery Press, 2012.

Concert Commentary: Stevie Wonder
Mark Ribowsky. *Signed, Sealed, and Delivered: The Soulful Journey of Stevie Wonder*. Hoboken: Wiley, 2010.

Bonus Track : Peter Buck and R.E.M.
Brett Milano. *Vinyl Junkies: Adventures in Record Collecting*. New York: St. Martin's Press, 2003.

Part Two—Jazz

Title page: Ray Marklund
Ray Marklund. Conversation with the author. St. Paul, Minnesota. 1981.

Book Review: *Louis Armstrong: What a Wonderful World*
Michael Erlewine, ed. *All Music Guide to Jazz*. 2nd ed. San Francisco: Miller Freeman, 1996.

Interview: Eddie Harris
Conversation with the author. Minneapolis, Minnesota; December 1979.

Remembrance: "Mitch Miller Memories"
Mitch Miller. Conversation with the author. Milwaukee, Wisconsin. December 1999.

Remembrance: Gerry Niewood
Conversation with the author. Cedar Falls, Iowa; 1977.

Concert Commentary: Ella Fitzgerald and Cleo Laine
Paul Smith, pianist. Conversation with the author. Minneapolis, Minnesota; March 1980.

Concert Commentary: The Manhattan Transfer
Alan Paul. Conversation with the author. St. Paul, Minnesota; August 1980.

Interview: Gary Burton
Gary Burton. Conversation with the author. Minneapolis, Minnesota; 1976.

Ralph Towner. Conversation with the author. Minneapolis, Minnesota; 1976.

Commentary: *"The Tennessee Firebird*: Gary Burton in Nashville"
Rick Bieber, film director. *Crazy*. Screen Media Ventures, 2008.
Gary Burton. E-mail correspondence with the author. August 2012 – January 2014.
---. *Learning to Listen: The Jazz Journey of Gary Burton*. Berklee Press, 2013.
Richard Cook and Brian Morton. *The Penguin Guide to Jazz on CD*. 7th ed. Penguin, 2004.
Richard Kienzle. E-mail correspondence with the author, June 2013.
Marc Myers. "Interview: Gary Burton." *Jazz Wax Magazine*, July 26, 2010.
Joel Whitburn. *Joel Whitburn's Top Country Singles, 1944-1993*. Record Research, 1994.

Concert Commentary: Kenny Burrell Trio
Kenny Burrell. Conversation with the author. Bloomington, Minnesota; December 12 1981.

Concert Commentary: Jean-Luc Ponty and Eberhard Weber
Eberhard Weber. Conversation with the author. Minneapolis, Minnesota; October 7, 1979

Interview: Bobby Lyle
Bobby Lyle. Conversation with the author. St. Paul, Minnesota; April 1980

Interview: Leroy Jenkins
Leroy Jenkins. Conversation with the author. Minneapolis, Minnesota; February 28, 1980.

Interview: Oscar Peterson
Oscar Peterson. Conversation with the author. Minneapolis, Minnesota; March 23, 1980

Remembrance: Dave Brubeck
Susan Stamberg interview. National Public Radio; September 1980.

Interview: Dave Brubeck
Telephone conversation with the author. May 12, 2009.

Part Three—Country

Title Page : Hank Williams
Roger M. Williams. *Sing a Sad Song: The Life of Hank Williams.* 2nd ed. U of Illinois P, 1980.

Book Review: *The Handbook of Texas Music*
David Byrne interviews Lyle Lovett. *Sessions at West 54th Street.* PBS Television; Sept. 1998.

Commentary: *Livin', Lovin', Losin': Songs of The Louvin Brothers*

Remembrance: Charlie Louvin
[The following are Works Consulted for the above two Louvin Brothers pieces.]
Charlie Louvin. Interview with the author. Bell Buckle, Tennessee; March 1995.
---. Written correspondence with the author. October 1994 – April 1998.
Kathy Louvin. Telephone interview with the author. February 1997.
Bill C. Malone. Conversation with the author. June 1997.
John Morthland. *The Best of Country Music.* New York: Doubleday, 1984.
Gordon Stoker. Telephone interview with the author. April 1996.
Joel Whitburn. *Top Country Singles: 1944-1993.* Record Research, 1994.
Charles Wolfe. *In Close Harmony: The Story of The Louvin Brothers.* Univ. of Mississippi P, 1996.
---. *The Louvin Brothers: Close Harmony.* Bear Family Records (booklet). Bear Family Records, 1992.

Remembrance: Phil Everly
Don Everly. Telephone conversation with the author. June 5, 1996.

Bonus Track: Vanilla Fudge
Joel Whitburn. *The Billboard Book of Top 40 Hits.* 7th ed. New York: Billboard Books, 2000.
Graeme Thomson. *George Harrison: Behind That Locked Door.* New York: Overlook, 2015.

Hangin' with the Stars #6: Bill Monroe
> Bill Monroe. Conversation with the author. Nashville, Tennessee, 1995.

Concert Commentary: Glen Campbell
> Glen Campbell. Conversation with the author. Milwaukee, Wisconsin; May 31, 2001.

Commentary: "Webb Pierce: The Ty Cobb of Country Music"
> Chet Atkins, guest host. *A Prairie Home Companion.* National Public Radio. Fall 1984.
>
> Eric Blabac. *Encyclopedia of Baseball Statistics.* I-universe Books, 2010.
>
> Bob Kingsley, host. *American Country Countdown.* Syndicated radio program; spring 2001.
>
> Otto Kitsinger, essay. *Webb Pierce: The Wondering "Boy," 1951-1958.* Accompanying booklet. Bear Family Records, 1990.
>
> Charlie Louvin. Interview with the author. Bell Buckle, Tennessee; March 1995.
>
> Joel Whitburn. *Top Country Singles: 1944-1993.* Record Research, 1994.

CD Review: Hank Williams: *The Unreleased Recordings*

CD Review: *Hank Williams Revealed: The Unreleased Recordings*

Commentary: "Art at 78 rpm: A History of Hank Williams' Releases"
> [The following are Works Consulted for the above three Hank Williams pieces.]
>
> Richard Carlin. *The Big Book of Country Music: A Biographical Encyclopedia.* Penguin, 1994.
>
> Hank Davis. Liner Notes. *Early Les Paul.* Capitol Records, 1982.
>
> ---. Liner Notes. *Hank Williams: I'm So Lonesome I Could Cry: March 1949—August 1949.* Polydor Records, 1986.
>
> ---. Liner Notes. *Hank Williams: I Won't Be Home No More: June 1952—September 1952.* Polydor Records, 1987.
>
> Michael Erlewine, ed. *All Music Guide to Country.* Miller Freeman Press, 1997.
>
> Colin Escott. "Notes on the Music." *The Complete Hank Williams.* Mercury Records, 1998.
>
> ---. Notes. *The Original Singles Collection...Plus.* Polydor Records, 1990.

Colin Escott and Hank Davis. Liner Notes. *Hank Williams: I Ain't Got Nothin' But Time. December 1946—August 1947.* Polydor Records, 1985.

Colin Escott, Kira Florita, and Luke Lewis. "A Note from the Producers." *The Complete Hank Williams.* Mercury Records, 1998.

Colin Escott, George Merritt and William MacEwen. *Hank Williams: The Biography.*
Boston: Little Brown, 1994.

Otto Kitsinger. Essay. *Webb Pierce: The Wondering Boy.* Bear Family Records, 1990.

Bob Pinson. Interviews with the author. Nashville, Tennessee. January 1995, October 1997, and February 1999.

---. Liner Notes. *Hank Williams: On the Air.* Polydor Records, 1985.

---. Liner Notes. *Hank Williams: Rare Takes and Radio Cuts.* Polydor Records, 1984.

Jerry Rivers. *Hank Williams: From Life to Legend.* Denver: Heather Enterprises, 1967.

Arnold Rogers and Bruce Gidoll. *The Life and Times of Hank Williams.* Butler Press, 1993.

Joel Whitburn. *Joel Whitburn's Top Country Singles, 1944-1993.* Record Research, 1994.

Roger M. Williams. *Sing a Sad Song: The Life of Hank Williams.* U of Illinois P, 1980.

Part Four—Beatles, Bob, Bruce, and Barry!

Title Page: Elvis Costello and Bob Dylan
Elvis Costello. *Unfaithful Music & Disappearing Ink.* New York: Blue Rider Press, 2015. P. 552
Bob Dylan. Spoken introduction to "Last Thoughts on Woody Guthrie." *Are You Now or Have You Ever Been (His Gotham Ingress).* TARKL Records. [bootleg release]

One Question with : Barry Manilow!
It is worth stressing here that this exchange is complete fiction.

Book Review: *Just Like Bob Zimmerman's Blues: Dylan in Minnesota*
Dave Engles. Telephone conversation with the author. Fall 1997

Commentary: "Jazz in the Key of Bob"
Bob Dylan. *Chronicles. Volume One.* New York: Simon and
Schuster, 2004.
Sidran on Record. Guest, Keith Jarrett. National Public Radio,
1987.
Bob Spitz. *Dylan: A Biography.* New York: McGraw Hill, 1989.
"The World of John Hammond." *Soundstage.* PBS television
broadcast. September 1975.

Commentary: "Last Thoughts on Bob Dylan's 'Last Thoughts'"
Bob Dylan. Spoken introduction to "Last Thoughts on Woody
Guthrie." *The Bootleg Series*, vols. 1-3. Columbia Records,
1991.
---. Spoken introduction to "Last Thoughts on Woody Guthrie."
Are You Now or Have You Ever Been (His Gotham Ingress).
TAKRL Records.
[bootleg release; see Appendix B for full transcripts.]

Bonus Track: "The Lonesome Death of Hattie Carroll"
Bob Dylan. *Concert at Philharmonic Hall: Live 1964. The Bootleg
Series*, vol. 6 Columbia Records, 2004.

CD Review: Bob Dylan: *Another Self Portrait*
Al Kooper. *Another Self Portrait.* Accompanying booklet . *The
Bootleg Series,* vol. 10.
Joel Whitburn. *The Billboard Book of Top 40 Hits.* 7th ed.
New York: Billboard Books, 2000.
Peter Ames Carlin. *Paul McCartney: A Life.* Old Saybrook, CT:
Tantor, 2009.

Commentary: "By the Time We Got to Mole Lake…"
Marty Stuart. Conversation with the author. Hartford,
Wisconsin; February 4, 2012.
Merle Watson. Conversation with the author. Mole Lake,
Wisconsin; August 1977.
Eric Weissberg. Conversation with the author. Mole Lake,
Wisconsin; August 1977.
Members of Eric Weissberg's band, Deliverance. Conversation
with the author. Mole Lake, Wisconsin; August 1977.

Commentary: "Bob Dylan's Sacred Song"
> Bob Dylan. Stage comments. Toronto concert. April 20, 1980.
> Unreleased video tape.
> ---. Stage comments. Tempe, Arizona, concert. November 26,
> 1979. Unreleased audio tape.
> ---. Stage comments. Various 1980 U.S. concert dates. Unreleased
> audio tapes.
> Michael Gilmore, interviewer. *Rolling Stone*. December 27, 2012.
> Ed Bradley, interviewer. *60 Minutes*. CBS television, 2004.
> John Cohen and Happy Traum, interviewers. June-July, 1968. In
> *Bob Dylan: A Retrospective*. Ed. by Craig McGregor,
> New York: Morrow, 1972.

Bonus Track : Religion Tours and Comedy Albums
> Jon Bream. *Dylan: Disc by Disc*. Minneapolis: Voyageur Press,
> 2015.
> Ben Fong-Torres. *Not Fade Away: A Backstage Pass to 20 Years of
> Rock & Roll*. San Francisco: Miller Freeman Books, 1999.

Indirect Questions: Mick Ronson
> *Goldmine Magazine*. Mick Ronson feature and author's letter.
> July 9, 1995 and August 1995.
> Marshall Crenshaw. Telephone conversation with the author.
> June 4, 1996
> Bob Dylan. *Complete Basement Tapes*. Columbia Records, 2014.

Concert Commentary: Bob Dylan (2012)
> Keith Richards interview. BBC Radio. October 2012.

Concert Commentary: Bob Dylan (2015)
> Michael Gilmore, interviewer. *Rolling Stone*. December 27, 2012.

Commentary: Bruce Springsteen: "Like a Rocker Out of My Dreams"
> *Little Steven's Underground Garage*. Syndicated radio program.
> Fall 2015.

Book Review: *Memories of John Lennon*
> Ben Brantley. *New York Times*. Review of *Lennon* (musical).
> August 15, 2005.

One Question with: Paul McCartney!
> It is worth stressing here that this exchange is complete fiction.

Remembrance: George Harrison: "Ten Years Gone"
    George Harrison. *The Beatles: Anthology*. Chronicle Books, 2000.
    ---. *Rockline* interview. Bob Coburn, host. Syndicated radio
        broadcast, February 1988.
    Casey Kasem. *American Top 40*. Syndicated weekly radio
        broadcast, December 8, 2001.
    Paul McCartney. *The Beatles: Anthology*. Chronicle Books, 2000.

Commentary: "What I Learned from Elvis Presley"
    Chet Atkins. Telephone interview with the author. August 1996.
    Michael Erlewine, ed. *All Music Guide to Rock*. 2nd ed. San
        Francisco: Miller Freeman, 1997.
    Albert Goldman. *The Lives of John Lennon*. Chicago: Chicago
        Review Press, 1988.
    Peter Guralnick. *Last Train to Memphis: The Rise of Elvis Presley*.
        Boston: Little Brown, 1994.
    ---. Careless Love: The Unmaking of Elvis Presley. Boston: Little
        Brown, 1999.
    Alanna Nash, et al. *Elvis Aaron Presley: Revelations from the
        Memphis Mafia*. New York: HarperCollins, 1995.
    ---. *The Colonel: The Extraordinary Story of Colonel Tom Parker
        and Elvis Presley*. Chicago: Chicago Review Press, 2004.
    Philip Norman. *John Lennon: The Life*. New York: Ecco/
        HarperCollins, 2008.
    Dolly Parton. *Dolly: My Life and Other Unfinished Business*.
        New York: HarperCollins, 1994.
    Bruce Springsteen. SiriusXM Radio. *E Street Radio*. "The Bruce &
        Stevie Show." August 2015.
    Graeme Thomson. *George Harrison: Behind That Locked Door*.
        New York: Overlook, 2015.
    Ann Wilson and Nancy Wilson. *Rockline* interview. Bob Coburn,
        host. Syndicated radio broadcast, 1988.

A WORD ABOUT THE AUTHOR

Tom Wilmeth was born and raised in Des Moines, Iowa. He later lived in St. Paul, Minnesota, and in College Station, Texas, where he earned a Ph.D. from Texas A&M University. Since 1991, he has been a Professor of English at Concordia University Wisconsin in Mequon. He and his wife live in Grafton, Wisconsin—former home of the Paramount Records label. Tom remains a collector of popular (and unpopular) music.

Photo by K. Koehlinger

A WORD ABOUT THE WRITINGS

Some parts of this book have been previously published in various locations. Several jazz reviews come from my time spent in St. Paul during the late 1970s and early 1980s. The Minneapolis newspapers *Sweet Potato,* *The Twin Cities Reader,* and *Trax* were all kind enough to accept my work. More recently, I have written music reviews for Milwaukee's weekly arts magazine, *The Shepherd Express,* and two of the concert reviews included here were first published in *The Milwaukee Journal Sentinel.* On the national front, I have placed items in the online edition of *JazzTimes Magazine.* "A History of Hank Williams' Releases" was first published in the September 1999 issue of *The Papers of the Bibliographic Society of America.* A handful of the country music reviews first appeared in the print edition of *No Depression.* Most of the pieces in this book are published here for the first time.

May 31, 2016

INDEX

A

Abercrombie, John, 216.
Acuff, Roy, 333, 369.
Adderley, Cannonball, 252.
Adler, David R., 181.
Air, 261, 286.
Akioshi, Toshiko, xiii, 194.
Alexander, Monty, 211.
Alias, Don, 289.
Allen, Rick, 236.
Allison, Mose, 25.
Allman Brothers Band, The, ix, 13-15, 135, 469.
Allman. Duane, 14-15, 88, 484.
Almond, Johnny, 399.
Alpert, Herb, 7, 243.
Alvin, Dave, 347.
Anderson, Bill, 186.
Anderson, Enoch, 400.
Anderson, John, 357-358.
Anderson, Jon, 80.
Anita Kerr Singers, The. 226.
Anthrax, xii, 125-126, 129-131.
Arber, Alan, 250.
Armstrong, Billie Joe, 343.
Armstrong, Louis, xii, 143, 163-169, 176, 286, 294, 474, 486.
Armstrong, Ralphe, 247.

Arnold, Eddy, xv, 323-324, 373, 478.
Art Ensemble of Chicago, The, 262.
Asch, Albert, 76.
Ashby, Dorothy, 150.
Association, The, ix, 5-6, 62, 469, 483.
Atkins, Chet, xvii, 54, 81, 223-226, 235, 346, 352, 361, 365, 417, 466, 489, 493.

B

Bach, Johann Sebastian, 76, 262.
Bacharach, Burt, 104.
Bachman, Randy, 36-37, 39.
Bachman & Turner, x, 40.
Bachman-Turner Overdrive, 39-40.
Baez, Joan, x, 47-49, 407, 418, 469, 484.
Bag of Balls, 116.
Baja Marimba Band, The, ix, 7.
Baker, Chet, 252.
Baker, Ginger, 90-91, 93.
Band, The, xvi, 403, 406-408, 425-426, 428-429, 443.
Banks, Brenton, 228.
Banks, Randy, 349.
Barkley, Roy, 326-327.
Barraco, Rob, 112.

Barrett, Syd, 102.

Barron, Kenny, 198, 297.

Barry, Jeff, 72.

Barylick, John, 103-104.

Basie, Count, 294, 414.

Beach Boys, The, xi, 67-69, 104, 359, 469, 485.

Beatles, The, x, xvi, xvii, xxi, 8, 21, 36, 42, 44-45, 50, 60, 63, 67-68, 71-72, 86-88, 102, 130, 163, 172, 185, 240, 282, 285-286, 316, 343, 345, 351, 393, 398, 403-405, 409, 414, 416, 427, 433, 452-457, 459-466, 479, 490, 493.

Beck, Jeff, 286.

Beiderbecke, Bix, 170.

Belushi, John, 46.

Benjamin, Joe, 228.

Bennett, Tony, 163, 173, 299.

Benny, Jack, xi, 74-75.

Benson, George, 96, 233, 414.

Bernhardt, Warren, 222.

Berns, Bert, xi, 71-73.

Berry, Chuck, ix, 8-9, 464, 470, 483.

Betts, Dickey, 13.

Big Brother and the Holding Company, ix, 13.

Billy, Chuck, 127-128.

Black Sabbath, 115, 125, 130.

Blaine, Hal, 414.

Blakey, Art, 194.

Blanchford, Terrence, 279.

Bland, Bobby "Blue," xii, 132, 470

Blind Faith, 87, 93.

Blondie, 417.

Blood, Sweat & Tears, 12, 185.

Blue Cheer, 132.

Blue Sky Boys, The, 340.

Blues Project, The, 102.

Bolden, Buddy, 286.

Braxton, Anthony, 259, 262-263, 312.

Brecker, Michael, 289.

Bridges, Ben, 144.

Bonoff, Karla, 32.

Bradley, Ed, 439, 492.

Bradley, Harold, 228.

Bradley, Owen, 223.

Bream, Jon, 440, 492.

Brewer, Shirley, 146-147.

Broadcast, xii, 156, 158.

Brockett, Jamie, 351.

Brodsky String Quartet, The, 104.

Brothers Johnson, The, 119.

Brothers, Thomas, 165, 167-168.

Brown, Charles, 224.

Brown, Michael, 152.

Brown, James, xii, 134-137, 143, 240, 470, 486.

Brown, Junior, xvi, 352, 478.

Brown, Ray, ix, 32-33, 470.

Brown, Ruth, 72.

Browne, Jackson, ix, 32-33, 470.

Brubeck, Dave, xv, 176, 182, 231, 236, 252, 300-305, 314-315, 469, 487.

Brubeck, Iola, 308.

Bruce, Jack, xi, 90, 93-95.

Bruford, Bill, 82.

Bryant, Boudleaux, 345.

Bryant, Felice, 345.

Bryars, Gavin, 30.

Bublé, Michael, 391.

Buck, Peter, xii, 155, 486.

Buffalo Springfield, x, 59, 61-62, 470, 485.
Bufwack, Mary A., 335,
Burke, Solomon, 72.
Burns, Ken, 169, 292, 475.
Burrell, Kenny, xiv, 118, 236, 241-246, 286, 474, 487.
Burton, Gary, xiii, 215-217, 220, 222-230, 233, 263, 414-416, 474-475, 486-487.
Bush, Sam, 353, 360.
Byrds, The, 56, 172, 339, 396.
Byrne, David, 1, 326, 483, 488.

C

Cahn, Sammy, 293.
Cale, J. J., 29.
Campbell, Glen, xvi, 357, 360, 414, 478, 489.
Campbell, Phil, 121.
Captain Beefheart, ix, 21, 23, 25, 470, 484.
Carnes, Kim, 32.
Caro, Robert, 167.
Carr, Roy, 466.
Carroll, Will, 127.
Carson, Johnny, 74, 163, 373.
Carter, Anita, 386, 388.
Carter, Benny, 176, 415.
Carter, Carlene, 32.
Carter, Ed, 68.
Carter, Hurricane, 441.
Carter, Ron, xiii, 197, 199, 205, 279-280, 474, 476.
Carter, Tom, 329, 332-333.
Carter, Wilf (Montana Slim), xv, 324-325.
Carter Family, The, 240, 335, 340.

Cash, Johnny, xvii, 286, 325, 331, 338, 356, 398, 417.
Cavett, Dick, 242.
Cetera, Peter, 13.
Chambers, Martin, 85.
Chambers, Paul, 203.
Champlin, Bill, 11-13.
Champs, The, 182.
Chapin, Harry, 44.
Charles, Ray, 45, 72, 135, 224, 476.
Chasin' Mason, xvi, 355.
Cheap Trick, xi, 69-70, 148, 485.
Chicago (Transit Authority), 11-13, 102, 181, 470.
Chief Seattle, 310.
Chopin, Frédéric, 76.
Christe, Ian, 114.
Christian, Charlie, 233, 286, 416.
Clapton, Eric, xi, 14, 86-87, 89, 92-93, 286, 337, 470.
Clare, Kenny, 209.
Clark, Dick, 72.
Clarke, Stanley, xiii, 95, 194-196, 198, 232.
Clark Family Experience, The, xvi, 349-350.
Clash, The, xii, 124, 127, 130, 470.
Clements, Vassar, 353.
Cliburn, Van, 327.
Cline, Patsy, 333-334, 478.
Clinton, Bill, 313.
Clinton, George, 151.
Clinton, Hillary, 55.
Clooney, Rosemary, 172, 286.
Clouser, Todd, xi, 94-96, 470.

Clutch, xii, 114, 118-122, 125, 485.
Cobb, Arnett, 327.
Cobb, Ty, xvi, 361-362, 489.
Cobham, Billy, 200.
Coburn, Bob, 461, 493.
Cochran, Eddie, 132.
Cockburn, Bruce, xii, 107-110, 470.
Cocker, Joe, x, 45-46, 91, 471, 484.
Cohen, John, 439, 492.
Cohen, Leonard, 105.
Coleman, Ornette, 24, 260.
Coltrane, John, xiii, 69, 180, 202-203, 225, 257, 286, 366, 475.
Connors, Bill, 196.
Conrad, Thomas, 274.
Conte, Luis, 50.
Cooder, Ry, 25-26.
Cooke, Sam, 134.
Cooper, Alice, 23, 106.
Cooper, Daniel, 328.
Cooper, Jerome, 204.
Corcoran, Michael, 336.
Corea, Chick, xiii, 169, 195-196, 229-232, 249, 251, 253, 265-266, 279, 281, 312, 475.
Coryell, Larry, 225, 230, 414.
Costello, Elvis, xi, 62, 79, 104, 155, 339, 393, 471, 490.
Cowboy, 10.
Cowboy Junkies, xvi, 106, 350-351, 478.
Cowell, Stanley, 243.
Cox, Anthony, xiv, 238.
Craig, Gary, 108.
Cramer, Floyd, 223, 226, 229.

Cray, Robert, 134.
Cream, xi, 86-94, 96, 471.
Crenshaw, Marshall, 442, 492.
Cronkite, Walter, 465.
Crosby, Bing, xiii, 169-170.
Crosby, David, x, 56.
Crosby, Stills & Nash, 471.
Crosby, Stills, Nash & Young, x, 27, 55, 61, 471.
Crowe, Cameron, 438.
Cruz, Aaron, 95.
Cult, The, 129.
Cummings, Burton, 37, 39.
Cyrille, Andrew, 260.

D

Daffan, Ted, 224.
Dale, Dick, 352.
Dameron, Tad, 295.
Danielsson, Palle, 272.
Dankworth, John, 208.
Darin, Bobby, 72, 158.
Dark Star Orchestra, The, xii, 110-113.
David, Benoit, 80-83.
Davies, Ray, 70.
Davis, Anthony, 260.
Davis, Hank, 384, 489-490.
Davis, Miles, xiv, 192, 196, 199, 203, 252-253, 267, 273, 277, 280, 283, 291, 294, 302, 330, 427, 475.
Dean, Roger, 78, 80.
Death Angel, xii, 125-127
Dee, Mikkey, 121.
De Grassi, Alex, xiv, 240-241, 476.
De Johnette, Jack, 216.

Delaney & Bonnie, 87.

Delmore Brothers, The, 347.

Derek & the Dominoes, 88, 91.

De Rogatis, Jim, 102-103.

De Rosier, Mike, 83.

Desmond, Paul, 175, 206, 301-302, 304, 312.

Diamond, Neil, xi, 72-73, 471, 485.

Difford, Chris, 84.

Dillards, The, 360.

Dire Straits, 444.

Dirksen, Richard, 308.

Dixie Chicks, The, 365.

Donahue, Tom, 65, 485.

Doobie Brothers, The, x, 34-35, 118, 471.

Dorsey, Jimmy, 170.

Dorsey, Tommy, 170, 175.

Dowd, Tom, 72.

Drake, Bill, 404, 426.

Draper, Jason, 138.

Drifters, The, 72.

Duke, George, 20.

Dunbar, Ansley, 21.

Durham, Bobby, 209.

Dylan, Bob, xvi, xvii, 5, 44-45, 48, 53-54, 61, 67, 111, 115, 124, 171, 203, 344, 393, 398, 402-404, 406-408, 410, 412-413, 415, 417-422, 424-427, 429-430, 434, 437, 439, 441-447, 450, 452, 466, 480-481, 490-492.

E

Eagles, ix, 10-11, 13, 25-27, 56, 101, 243, 471.

Eals, Clay, 55.

Earth, Wind & Fire, 119.

Eaton, Rob, 110.

Eckstine, Billy, 203.

Eddy, Duane, 415.

Eddy, Elizabeth, 305.

Edwards, Bob, xxi.

Efimove, Kostia, 250.

Eicher, Manfred, 215, 263.

Ellington, Duke, 76, 175, 177, 185, 204, 207, 242, 256-257, 262, 266, 270, 282, 286, 291, 293, 297, 301, 306-307, 313, 416, 475.

Elliot, Mike, 215.

Elliot, Ramblin' Jack, xxi.

Ellis, Don, xiii, 182-185, 248, 311, 475.

Ellis, Herb, xiv, 235-237, 286, 475.

Ely, Joe, xv, 348-349, 478.

Emerson, Lake & Palmer, 74.

Emmons, Buddy, 224, 346.

Emory, Ralph, 58.

Emotions, The, 119.

Engel, Dave, 410, 412.

English, Dino, 112.

Entwistle, John, 94.

Erskine, Peter, 284, 289.

Ertegun, Ahmet, 72.

Escott, Colin, 363, 368, 384, 387, 389, 489-490.

Evans, Bill, xv, 76, 242, 275, 299-300, 303, 475.

Evans, Gil, 269, 416.

Everly, Ike, 343.

Everly Brothers, The, xv, 338, 340, 342-346, 478.

F

Fallon, Neil, 40.

Family, 16.

Farmer, Ernie, 308.

Farndon, Pete, 85.

Farner, Mark, 3, 5.

Farrell, Joe, 194.

Farren, Mick, 466.

Ferguson, Maynard, 183, 200.

Ferguson, Sherman, 242, 245.

Fitzgerald, Ella, xiii, 207-208, 475, 486.

Flatlanders, The, 348.

Flatt, Lester, 432-433.

Flatt & Scruggs, xvii, 353, 417.

Fleck, Béla, xiii, xvi, 75, 115, 169, 231-232, 353, 475, 478.

Fleet Foxes, 56.

Fleetwood Mac, 35.

Flo & Eddy, 21.

Flock of Seagulls, A, xi, 84-85.

Florita, Kira, 387, 490.

Fong-Torres, Ben, 440, 492.

Foote, Shelby, 292.

Ford, Gerald, 134-135.

Fortune, Sonny, 286.

Foster, Al, 204.

Fowler, Walt, 50.

Fox, Oscar J., 327.

Franklin, Aretha, 72, 91, 172.

Frederickson, Mike, 348.

Freed, Alan, 72.

Freeman, Scott, 14.

Frehley, Ace, 126, 130.

Friend, Cliff, 371.

Friend & Lover, 7.

Frizzell, Lefty, xv, 286, 328-329, 407, 478.

Fugs, The, 23.

Fulks, Robbie, 348.

G

Gadd, Steve, 50.

Gale, Eric, 200.

Gales, Larry, 242.

Gallup, Cliff, 286.

Garbarek, Jan, 272.

Garcia, Jerry, 110.

Garland, Hank, 223-224, 226-228.

Garland, Judy, 293.

Garnier, Tony, 448.

Garrett, Mike, 98.

Garrison, Jimmy, 203.

Gaye, Marvin, 51, 139-140.

Genesis, 249-250.

Gentry, Bobby, 357.

George, Lowell, 103.

Gershwin, George, 265, 278.

Getz, Stan, xiii, 214-215, 224, 475.

Gibson Brothers, The, 338.

Gibson, Don, 58.

Giddins, Gary, 169.

Gillespie, Dizzy, 270, 416.

Gilmore, Jimmie Dale, 348.

Gilmore, Marcus, 232.

Gilmore, Mikal, 439.

Girls, xii, 155-156.

Glass, Philip, 263.

Gleason, Ralph J., 423.

Gloyd, Russell, 301.

Godchaux, Donna, 110.

Godchaux, Keith, 110.

Goffin, Gerry, 52, 72.

Goldings, Larry, 50.

Gomez, Eddie, 222.

Goodman, Benny, 175, 415-416.

Goodman, Steve, x, 54-55.

Goodrick, Michael, 230.

Goodwin, Bill, 211.

Gordon, Dexter, xiii, 200-202, 476.

Gordon, Max, 241.

Gorelick, Kenny, 282.

Gottlieb, Danny, 221.

Gould, Glenn, 274, 276.

Graham, Bill, 289. 406.

Grand Funk Railroad, ix, 3, 5, 118, 471, 483.

Granz, Norman, 202-204, 270-271.

Grappélli, Stephane, 229.

Grateful Dead, The, 32, 96, 110-113, 130.

Gravatt, Eric , 290.

Great White, 103.

Greenwich, Ellie, 72.

Gregor, Evan, 211.

Grow, Kory, 391.

Guess Who, The, x, 36-40, 213, 471, 484.

Guralnick, Peter, 169, 466-467, 493.

Guthrie, Arlo, x, 53, 471.

Guthrie, Woody, xvii, 53, 393, 418-420, 481-482, 490-491.

H

Haden, Charlie, xv, 298, 414-415, 476.

Haggard, Merle, xv, 286, 329-331, 348, 350, 478.

Hall, Jim, xiv, 233, 236, 474, 476.

Haggerty, Terry, 12.

Hammerstein, Oscar, 208.

Hammond, John, 178, 415, 491.

Hancock, Herbie, 229, 253, 265-266, 278-281, 297, 475-476.

Hanes, Roy, 230, 312.

Hardin, Tim, xiii, 222.

Harrell, Tom, 299.

Harris, Barry, 297.

Harris, Eddie, xiii, 186-187, 194, 213, 476, 486.

Harris, Emmylou, 338.

Harris, Richard, 6.

Harrison, Al, 195.

Harrison, George, xvii, 49, 87, 264, 285, 351, 460-462, 466, 480, 488, 493.

Hart, Lorenzo, 207.

Hartford, John, xvi, 353, 360-361.

Hathaway, Donny, 144.

Hauser, Tim, 214.

Havens, Richie, x, 42-45, 471.

Hawks, The, 406.

Haynes, Roy, 225.

Hazelwood, Lee, 351.

Heart, xi, 83-84, 493.

Heath Brothers, The, xiv, 241-243.

Heath, Jimmy, 243.

Heath, Percy, 242.

The Heavy, 80.

Hecht, Hernan, 95

Hedges, Michael, 240, 416.

Hell, Richard, 125.

Henderson, Joe, 199.

Hendricks, Jon, 178.

Hendrix, Jimi, 15, 17, 97, 135, 143, 240, 289, 352, 366.

Henke, Jim, 454.
Henriquez, Carlos, 293.
Hertsgaard, Mark, 453.
Hervey, Eric, 250.
Heylin, Clinton, 408, 411, 441.
Hicks, Bill, 103.
Hines, Earl 'Fatha,' 176.
Hinton, Milt, 415.
Hitchcock, Alfred, 210, 422.
Hodges, Johnny, 174.
Holbrook, Hal, 449.
Holiday, Billie, 177, 192.
Holly, Buddy, 49, 115, 327.
Hombres, The, 404.
Honeyman-Scott, James, 85.
Hooters, The, 44.
Hope, Bob, 7.
Horn, Jim, 414.
Horowitz, Israel, 308, 312.
Horowitz, Vladimir, 253.
House, Son, 153.
Howe, Steve, 80-82.
Howell, Todd, 297.
Hubbard, Freddie, 286.
Hughes, Marvin H., 228.
Humphrey, Hubert, 136.
Hunter, James, xii, 134, 172.
Hutto, J. B., 98.

I

Ian, Janis, xi, 102.
India.Arie, 143, 149.
Iron Maiden, 130.
Isaak, Chris, 155.
Isley Brothers, The, 72.

J

Jackson, Ali, 294.
Jackson, Michael, 67, 101, 150, 366.
Jagger, Mick, 65, 75, 485.
James, Harry, 175, 327.
James, Skip, 153.
Jarrett, Keith, xiv, 234, 255-256, 266, 271-272, 273-277, 414-415, 476.
Jefferson, Blind Lemon, 153, 327.
Jenkins, Leroy, xiv, 258-263, 264-266, 269-270.
Jobim, Antonio Carlos, 295.
Joel, Billy, 91, 434.
John, Elton, ix, xiv, 15-18, 275-277, 366, 472.
John, Keith, 146.
John, Little Willie, 146.
Johnson, Alphonzo, 288.
Johnson, Blind Willie, 337.
Johnson, Jimmy, 50.
Johnson, Lyndon, 167.
Johnson, Marc, 299.
Johnson, Robert, 92, 286.
Johnston, Tom, 35.
Jones, Elvin, 203.
Jones, George, xv, 11, 106, 276, 332-333, 478.
Jones, Hank, xv, 268, 298, 476.
Jones, Margaret, 333.
Jones, Norah, 213, 343.
Johnstone, Davey, 16.
Joplin, Janis, 13, 472.
Jorgensen, Ernst, 466.
Journey, 101.
Judd, Wynona, 335.
Justice, Bill, 309.

K

Kaitz, Emily, 412.

Kamman, Leigh, xiii, 171-172, 174, 176, 179, 317.

Kasem, Casey, 156, 462, 493.

Kath, Terry, 13.

Kaylan, Howard, 21.

Keane, Helen, 242.

Keillor, Garrison, 48, 64, 338, 343, 365, 484.

Kelly, Grace, xiii, 210-213, 476.

Keenan, Trish, xii, 156, 158-159, 470.

Kelley, Norman, 73.

Kenton, Stan, xiii, 169-175, 184-185, 476.

Kienzle, Rich, 224-225.

Kilgore, Ryan, 149.

Kimball, Stu, 445, 448.

King, B. B., 92.

King, Carole, x, 51-52, 72, 472.

King, Freddie, 336.

King, Martin Luther, Jr., 136.

King, Stephen, 106.

Kingsley, Bob, 157, 489.

Kinks, The, xi, 69-71, 472, 485.

Kirk, Roland, 416.

Kiss, 126, 130.

KJLH Radio Free Gospel Choir, The, 143-144, 151.

Knight, Terry, 4.

Knopfler, Mark, 444-445.

Kooper, Al, 413, 425, 491.

Konitz, Lee, 312.

Krause, Alison, 213, 335.

Kubicki, Mike, xv, 296-298.

Kunzel, Eric, 308.

L

LaBarbera, Joe, 299.

Laine, Cleo, xiii, 207-208, 476, 486.

LaLanne, Jack, 171.

Lambert, Hendricks & Ross, 27.

Landau, Michael, 50.

Lane, Don, 27.

Laplander, Rob, 356.

Lawrence, Rahn, xi, 99-100.

Leadon, Bernie, 11.

Lear, William Powell, 398.

Led Zeppelin, 115, 130, 425.

Lee, Albert, 346.

Lee, Alvin, 45.

Lee, Peggy, 146.

Left Banke, The, 18.

Leiber, Jerry, 72.

Leitch, Donovan, 455.

Lemmy, 115, 119-122, 124.

Lennon, John, xvii, 41, 71, 340, 454, 460, 463, 465-466, 479, 492-493.

Lesh, Phil, 111.

Leverett, Les, 354.

Levy, Morris, 72.

Lewis, George, 260.

Lewis, Jerry Lee, 18.

Lewis, Luke, 387, 490.

Liberace, 272.

Lieberson, Goddard, 312.

Lightfoot, Gordon, 426.

Lil' Ed & The Blues Imperials, xi, 97.

Lindley, David, 33.

Lievano, Joaquin, 247.

Little Feat, 103.

Little Richard, 464.

Little River Band, The, xi, 83-84.
Littleton, Kelly, 99.
Lloyd, Charles, 69, 273, 416, 476.
Loggins, Kenny, 10.
Lorber, Jeff, xiv, 281-282.
Louvin Brothers, The, xv, 158, 338-342, 344, 363, 479, 488.
Louvin, Charlie, xv, 338-342, 345, 347, 363, 488-489.
Lovett, Lyle, 30, 326, 488.
Lowe, Jim, xix.
Luke the Drifter, 341, 367-368.
Lunceford, Jimmy, 176.
Lundvall, Bruce, 279.
Lyle, Bobby, xiv, 251-252, 257-258, 268, 272, 487.
Lynn, Loretta, 335.

M

Madonna, 275, 366, 457.
Mahal, Taj, 343.
Mahavishnu Orchestra, The, 195, 247, 287.
Mainieri, Mike, 222.
Manfred Mann, 427.
Mangione, Chuck, 183, 206, 243.
Manhattan Transfer, The, xiii, 213-214, 477, 486.
Manilow, Barry, xvi, 399, 402, 480, 490.
Mankowski, Woody, 251.
Mantovani, 373.
Marini, Lou, 50.
Marklund, Ray, 161, 176, 486.
Markowitz, Kate, 50.
Marsalis, Wynton, xiv, 169, 178, 212, 215, 291-292, 294-295, 303, 311, 477.

Martin, George, 454, 460.
Martin, Steve, 54-55.
Martino, Pat, 211.
Mason Profit, 10.
Mathis, Johnny, 172.
Mattson, Jeff, 110.
Mavericks, The, 352.
Mayall, John, 86, 399.
Mays, Lyle, 234, 289.
McAuliffe, Leon, 224.
McBride, Christian, xiii, 196.
McCann, Denise, 36, 39.
McCann, Les, 187, 476.
McCartney, Linda, 457.
McCartney, Paul, xvii, 49, 88, 94, 340, 427, 455-461, 479, 491-493.
McCoy, Charlie, 224.
McCuller, Arnold, 50.
McDonald, Michael, x, 34-35.
McEntire, Reba, 335.
McLaughlin, John, 94, 286-287.
McPartland, Marian, 442.
Mehldau, Brad, 180.
Meisner, Randy, 11.
Mendelssohn, Felix, 74.
Menuhin, Yehudi, 287.
Messina, Jim, 11.
Metallica, 107, 127, 130.
Metheny, Pat, xiv, 220-221, 233, 289, 329, 476-477.
Mickey & Sylvia, 350-351.
Middler, Bette, 286.
Milano, Brett, 155, 486.
Miller, Glenn, 115, 175.
Miller, Marcus, 279.
Miller, Mitch, xiii, 171-173, 317, 486.

Miller, Steve, 6, 483.
Mills, Irving, 371.
Mingus, Charles, 195.
Miracles, The, 464.
Mitchell, Joni, 289, 291, 433.
Monk, Thelonious, 198, 252, 292, 297, 416.
Monkees, The, 52.
Monroe, Bill, xvi, 338, 354-355, 373, 479, 489.
Montana, Patsy, 335.
Montgomery, Wes, 135.
Moody Blues, The, 81.
Moore, Bob, 228.
Moore, George, 314.
Morello, Joe, 228, 301.
Morris, Alisha, 148.
Morrison, Van, 72.
Morse, Ella Mae, 337.
Motorhead, xii, 114-116, 118-121, 123, 126-127, 130, 472, 485.
Mozart, 208, 263, 309, 448.
Mull, Martin, 213.
Mulligan, Gerry, 176, 301, 304, 306, 414.
Murray, Dee, 16.

N
Nash, Graham, 44, 56.
Nash, Ted, 293.
Natural Life, 178.
Neil, Fred, 40.
Nelson, Ricky, 12.
Nelson, Willie, xv, 164, 169, 236, 243, 286, 328, 331, 358, 479.
New Grass Revival, The, 360.
Newman, Randy, 46, 396.

Nichols, Roy, 329.
Niewood, Gerry, xiii, 206, 477, 486.
Nilsson, Harry, xvi, 40-41, 46, 399, 484.
Nimmer, Dan, xv, 293-296.
Nirvana, 130.
Nixon, Richard, 109, 135.
Nordine, Ken, 96.
Norvo, Red, 415.
Nugent, Ted, 100.

O
Oakley, Berry, 13.
Obama, Barack, 446.
Oermann, Robert K., 335.
Ogerman, Claus, 299.
Olson, Nigel, 16.
O'Neill, Eugene, 207.
Oregon, 216.
Osborne Brothers, The, 224.
Osegueda, Mark, 126.
Osibisa, xi, 79.
Otter, Anne Sofie von, 104.
Owens, Bonnie, 348.
Owens, Buck, 224, 286, 329, 347-348.
Owens, Christopher, 155.
Ozawa, Seiji, 75.

P
Page, Jimmy, 45.
Palmer, Bruce, 62.
Palmer, Jason, 212.
Parker, Charlie, 177, 189, 192, 195, 203, 270, 286, 292.
Parliament/Funkadelic, 151.
Palmer, Robert, 260.
Paolo, Jim, 297.

Parker, Colonel Tom, 323, 493.
Parks, Van Dyke, 105.
Parsons, Gram, 339.
Parton, Dolly, 467, 493.
Pass, Joe, 235, 242, 268, 414, 475.
Pastorius, Jaco, xiv, 196, 212, 283, 285-286, 288, 290-291, 329, 469.
Patoski, Joe Nick, 331.
Patton, Charley, 153.
Patton, George, 310.
Paul, Alan, 214, 486.
Paul, Les, 81, 118-119, 121, 350, 372, 489.
Paul Winter Consort, The, 216.
Pavarotti, 201.
Peacock, Gary, 275.
Pearl Jam, 130.
Pearl, Minnie, 342.
Peer, Ralph, 335.
Perkins, Carl, 464.
Perrone, Tony, 243.
Peter and Gordon, 404.
Peter, Paul & Mary, 404.
Peterson, Oscar, xiv, 235, 253, 266-272, 295, 477, 487.
Petrillo, James C., 370.
Petrusich, Amanda, 154.
Pettiford, Oscar, 177.
Phillinganes, Greg, 144.
Phish, 62, 286.
Pinson, Bob, 379-380, 384, 386, 490.
Poco, ix, 10-11, 13, 472.
Phillips, Sam, 158.
Phillips, Shawn, 10.
Phillips, Washington, 336.
Phoenix, Joaquin, 285.

Pierce, Webb, xvi, 286, 342, 361-366, 372, 374, 479, 489-490.
Pink Floyd, 102.
Plant, Robert, 115.
Planet, Janet, 416.
Poe, Edgar Allen, 107.
Ponty, Jean-Luc, xiv, 20, 148, 247-249, 260, 477, 487.
Porter, Cole, 239, 256, 292.
Post, Jim, 7.
Powell, Bud, 192.
Presley, Elvis, xvii, 124, 169, 338, 391, 413, 456, 463, 466, 468, 480, 493.
Priscilla, Presley, 391.
Pretenders, The, xi, 84-85.
Price, Ray, 356.
Prince, xii, 46, 132, 138, 158, 243, 257, 266, 275, 301, 366, 472.
Prine, John, 47.
Proust, Marcel, xxi.
Pugh, Ronnie, 325.

Q
Quicksilver Messenger Service, The, 32.

R
Rainey, Ma, 153.
Ramones, The, 125.
Randolph, Boots, 223, 228.
Raycraft, Jimmy, 416.
Reagan, Ronald, 47.
Recile, George, 448.
Reed, Lou, xi, 105-107, 127, 400, 472, 485.
Reeves, Jim, 115, 223, 228, 274, 342, 364, 373, 461.
R.E.M., xii, 155, 472, 486.

Return to Forever, 195-196, 200, 229, 249, 477.
Revolutionary Ensemble, The, 259.
Rexroth, Kenneth, 413.
Riccardi, Ricky, 163-165.
Rice, Tony, 353.
Rich, Charlie, 158.
Richards, Keith, 66, 446, 485, 492.
Riley, Ben, 198.
Ritter, Brian, 296.
Ritter, Tex, xiii, 169, 186.
Rivers, Jerry, 368, 375-376, 391, 490.
Roberts, Howard, xiv, 95, 178, 237-238, 477.
Robertson, Robbie, 409.
Rodgers, Jimmie, xii, 169, 276, 286, 324-325, 335, 342, 372.
Rodgers, Richard, 207-208, 257.
Rolling Stones, The, x, 64-65, 115, 277, 282, 286, 337, 427, 446, 456, 473, 485.
Rollins, Sonny, xiii, 204-205, 477.
Ronson, Mick, xvii, 18, 442, 492.
Ronstadt, Linda, 349.
Rose, Fred, 323, 369-372, 378.
Rosen, Jeff, 409, 428.
Rosen, Kevin, 111.
Roth, Ed, xiii, 181-182.
Rotten, Johnny, 125.
Rubin, Rick, 285.
Runaways, The, 83.
Rundgren, Todd, 5, 158.
Runswick, Daryl, 209.
Russell, Leon, 46, 414.
Ruth, Babe, 166.

S

Sahl, Mort, 302.
Sahm, Doug, 158, 336.
Salvant, Cecile McLorin, 293.
Sample, Joe, 135.
Sam the Sham, 102.
Sanborn, David, 52.
Sanders, Pharoah, 251.
Sandford, Christopher, 455.
Santana, 88-89, 473.
Sauter-Finnegan Orchestra, The, 176.
Scaduto, Antony, 411.
Schacher, Mel, 5.
Scheinman, Jenny, 180.
Scheuerell, Casey, 247.
Schmidt, Timothy B., 11.
Schneider, Larry, 299.
Scott-Heron, Gil, xii, 134, 473.
Scruggs, Earl, 353, 417.
Seeger, Pete, xxi, 230, 471.
Selvin, Joel, 71-73.
Seraphine Danny, 181.
Setzer, Brian, 65.
Sex Pistols, The, 125.
Sexton, Charlie, 445, 448.
Shady, Slim, 157.
Shaffer, Paul, 202.
Shakti, 287-288.
Shank, Bud, 414.
Shankar, Ravi, 264, 287.
Shaver, Billy Joe, 349.
Shaw, Woody, xiii, 201-202, 477.
Shelton, Robert, 411.
Shepherd, Kenny Wayne, 115.
Sherwood, Billy, 83.
Shorter, Wayne, 239, 279-280, 283, 288.

Sidran, Ben, 415.

Siegel, Corky, xi, 75-76.

Siegel, Janis, 213.

Siegel-Schwall Band, The, 75.

Silva, Chelo, 327.

Silver, Horace, 297.

Simmonds, Jeremy, 103.

Simmons, Patrick, 34.

Simon, Paul, x, 50, 66-67, 140, 473.

Simon and Garfunkel, 66-67, 473.

Sinatra, Frank, 103, 172, 440.

Sinatra, Nancy, 351.

Singer, Matthew, 155.

Six, Jack, 312.

Stone, Sly, 251, 336.

Smallwood, Richard, 144.

Smith, Jimmy, 135.

Smith, Kate, 386, 388.

Smith, Paul, 209, 486.

Smith, R. J., 135, 486.

Snow, Hank, 120, 227, 286, 324, 330, 342, 364, 390.

Sons of Champlin, The, ix, 12, 397, 473.

Sorenson, Ron, 425.

Soskin, Mark, 204.

Spector, Phil, 72.

Spicher, Buddy, 224.

Spitz, Bob, 411, 491.

Spitzer, Nick, 157.

Spooky Tooth, 425.

Springsteen, Bruce, xvii, 27, 44, 124, 148, 243, 403, 449-450, 452, 464, 480, 492-493.

Squeeze, xi, 84-85, 473.

Squire, Chris, 81-83.

Stamberg, Susan, 303, 487.

Stanley Brothers, The, 340.

Stanley, Ralph, 117.

Starr, Ringo, 196, 460, 480.

Steely Dan, 11, 50, 79, 81.

Steig, Jeremy, 299.

Stevens, Matt, 211.

Stewart, Maeretha, 413.

Sting, 289.

Stoker, Alan, 384.

Stoller, Mike, 72.

Stoner, Rob, 415.

Strait, George, 328, 341.

Stray Cats, The, x, 64-65.

Strayhorn, Billy, 239, 293.

Streisand, Barbra, 434.

Stuart, Marty, 433, 491.

Stuermer, Daryl, xiv, 249, 251.

Sult, Tim, 118, 121.

Swallow, Steve, 219, 221, 225, 230, 414.

T

Tabakin, Lew, xiii, 194.

Tana, Akira, 242.

Taste of Honey, A, 83.

Tatum, Art, 253, 266, 270-271.

Taupin, Bernie, 17.

Taylor, Cecil, 269.

Taylor, James, x, 23, 44, 49-51, 338, 473, 484.

Tchaikovsky, Pyotr Illyich, 293.

Teagarden, Jack, 176.

Tempesta, John , 129.

Ten Years After, 45.

Testament, xii, 125-130.

Texas '55, xvi, 356.

Thielemans, Toots, 299.

Thigpen, Ed, 268.
Thomas, Robert, Jr., 284.
Thompson, Hank, 285, 373.
Thompson, Toby, 412.
Tilbrook, Glenn, 84.
Tillis, Mel, 364.
Tillis, Pam, 335.
Titcomb, Gordon, 53.
Titelbaum, Richard, 259-260.
Tosches, Nick, 336.
Toto, 83.
Toussaint, Alan, 46.
Townshend, Pete, x, 63, 115, 485.
Towner, Ralph, xiii, 216, 222, 230, 487.
Traugott, Jeff, 241.
Travis, Merle, 350.
Travis, Randy, 329.
Trucks, Derek, 92.
Tubb, Ernest, xv, 276, 324-327, 336, 342, 352, 373, 479.
Turner, Big Joe, 72.
Turrentine, Stanley, xiii, 205, 477.
Turtles, The, 21, 61.
Tuuk, Alex van der, 153-154.
Twain, Mark, xvi, 153, 410, 449.
Tweedy, Jeff, 117.
Tyner, McCoy, 203, 205, 253.

U

Uncle Tupelo, 117.
Underwood, Ian, 20.
Underwood, Ruth, 20.

V

Valient Thorr, xii, 114, 116-120, 485.
Van Heusen, Jimmy, 312.
Vanilla Fudge, xvi, 351, 473, 488.

Van Ronk, Dave, 441.
Van Zandt, Townes, 349.
Vaughn, Sarah, 253.
Vaughn, Stevie Ray, 33.
Vinsel, Jake, 296.
Vixen, 83.
Voegeli, Tom, 275.
Volman, Mark, 21.
Voorman, Klaus, 454.

W

Waggoner, Mark, xiv, 238-239.
Waggoner, Porter, 417.
Waits, Tom, ix, 13, 24-25, 28-29, 31-32, 96, 104, 212, 473, 484.
Wakeman, Oliver, 82-83.
Wakeman, Rick, 77, 82.
Walker, T. Bone, 336.
Wallace, Mike, xxi.
Waller, Fats, 286.
Walsh, Joe, 11.
Walton, Cedar, 297.
War, 182.
Warnes, Jennifer, 46.
Washburn, Abigail, 232.
Watson, Doc, 432, 434.
Watson, Merle, 432, 491.
Watts, Charlie, 286.
Watts, Nathan, 144.
Weather Report, xiv, 197, 282-283, 287-291, 477.
Weather Update, 290.
Webb, Jimmy, 6, 46.
Weber, Eberhard, xiv, 197, 216, 248, 477, 487.
Weir, Bob, 111.
Weissberg, Eric, 434-435, 491.
Wells, Kitty, 335.

West, Bruce & Laing, 94.
Wexler, Jerry, 72.
Whitburn, Joel, 177, 483, 485, 487-491.
White, Alan, 80, 82.
White, Chet Jr., 156.
White Lightning, 4.
Whiteman, Paul, 170.
Who, The, x, 62-63, 71, 77, 115, 131-132, 182, 185, 286, 474.
Wilco, 117, 485.
Williams, Aaron, xi, 96, 99.
Williams, Andy, xiv, 246.
Williams, Audrey, 388.
Williams, Buster, 198.
Williams, Denise, 145, 147.
Williams, Hank, xvi, 54-55, 173, 224, 227, 321, 325, 328, 333, 341, 355, 357, 366-372, 374-375, 377, 379-391, 479, 488-490, 495.
Williams, Hank, Jr., 382.
Williams, Hank, III, xvi, 355.
Williams, Paul, 409, 441.
Williams, Roger M., 376, 488, 490.
Williams, Tony, 94, 200.
Wills, Bob, 224, 286, 327.
Wilson, Ann, 493.
Wilson, Brian, 68, 359.
Wilson, Carl, 68.
Wilson, Nancy, 83, 493.
Wilson, Teddy, 415.
Winter, Paul, 216.
Winwood, Stevie, 45.
Wolf, Julie, 108.
Wolfe, Thomas, 167.

Wonder, Stevie, xii, 92, 139-143, 145, 147-148, 151-152, 182, 204, 232, 474, 486.
Woods, Phil, 178, 210-211, 476.
Wooten, Victor, 100.
Word of Mouth, 291.
Wright, Eugene, 301.

Y

Yardbirds, The, 86.
Yes, 77-78, 79-83.
Yoakam, Dwight, xv, 286, 328, 341, 347-348, 479.
Yonnet, Frederic, 149.
Young, Lester, 268.
Young, Neil, x, 57, 60, 62, 222, 276, 474, 484-485.

Z

Zappa, Dweezil, 22.
Zappa, Frank, ix, 5, 19-20, 21-25, 70, 469, 484.
Zavod, Allan, 247.
Zawinul, Josef, 283-285, 288-290.
Zonn, Andrea, 50.

59273436R10293

Made in the USA
Charleston, SC
01 August 2016